Gettysburg's Other Battle

Gettysburg's Other Battle

The Ordeal of an American Shrine during the First World War

MARK A. SNELL

The Kent State University Press ◼ Kent, Ohio

Library of Congress Catalog Card Number 2017038349
ISBN 978-1-60635-331-8
Manufactured in the United States of America

LIBRARY OF CONGRESS CATALOGING-IN-PUBLICATION DATA
Names: Snell, Mark A., author.
Title: Gettysburg's other battle : the ordeal of an American shrine during the First World War / Mark A. Snell.
Description: Kent, Ohio : The Kent State University Press, 2018. | Includes bibliographical references and index.
Identifiers: LCCN 2017038349 (print) | LCCN 2017039086 (ebook) | ISBN 9781631013065 (epub) | ISBN 9781631013072 (ePDF) | ISBN 9781606353318 (hardcover)
Subjects: LCSH: Gettysburg (Pa.)--History, Military--20th century. | World War, 1914-1918--Pennsylvania--Gettysburg. | Gettysburg National Military Park (Pa.)--History--20th century.
Classification: LCC F159.G5 (ebook) | LCC F159.G5 S64 2018 (print) | DDC 355.009748--dc23
LC record available at https://lccn.loc.gov/2017038349

22 21 20 19 18 5 4 3 2 1

For my sons

Mark Henry Snell,

Gettysburg High School, Class of 2001 and The Citadel, x2005

and

Matthew Alan Snell,

Gettysburg High School, Class of 2004 and

Indiana University of Pennsylvania, 2010

On the green they watched their sons
Playing till too dark to see,
As their fathers watched them once,
As my father once watched me

—Edmund Blunden, 1920,

veteran of the Great War

Contents

Preface

During a field trip to Gettysburg National Military Park by the U.S. Military Academy Class of 1909, Cadet George S. Patton Jr. took the time to reflect on the momentous battle that had occurred in and around this small, yet historic town in southcentral Pennsylvania. Writing to his future wife on May 11, 1909, from the Eagle Hotel, which sat on the corner of Chambersburg and Washington Streets, Patton painted a mystical portrait of the battlefield. "There is to me strange fascination in looking at the scenes of the awful struggles which raged over this country," he penned. "A fascination and a regret. I would like to have been there too." He continued:

> This evening after supper I walked down to the scene of the last and greatest struggle on Cemetery Hill. To get in a proper frame of mind I wandered through the cemetery and let the spirits of the dead thousands laid there in ordered rows, sink deep into me. Then just as the son [*sic*] sank behind the South Mountains I walked down to the scene of Pickett's great charge and seated on a rock just where . . . two of my great uncles died I watched the wonder of the day go out. The sunset painted a dull red the fields over which the terrible advance was made and I could almost see them coming growing fewer and fewer while around and behind me stood calmly the very cannon that had so punished them. There were some quail calling in the trees nearby and it seemed strange that they could do it where man had known his greatest and last emotions. It was very wonderful and no one came to bother me. I drank it in until I was quite happy. A strange

> pleasure yet a very real one. I think that it takes an evening like that to make one understand what men will do in battle. It was a wonderful yet foolish battle.[1]

Six years later, in the midst of what Americans at the time called "the Great European War," Cadet Edwin Kelton, USMA Class of 1915, likewise on a senior class trip, shared his own impression of the battlefield:

> We had a glorious time at Gettysburg. The weather most of the time was ideal. Only when on top of the steel tower on Big Round Top did the mist get so thick that we could not see the battlefield. Monday morning we spent in driving over the field, reading tablets and trying to get an idea of how the fighting did take place. I can't say that we learned much in the way of tactics and how to lead troops, but at least we gained a wholesome respect for those boys and men who advanced in solid lines upon an infantry line that was hurling death at them, besides artillery sending out a steady stream of shrapnel. . . . No, I have not much desire to see this country go to war again, but if the Germans don't wake up pretty soon I shall be forced to become an Ally.[2]

The Germans, however, did not "wake up," and many of these young West Pointers, including Patton and Kelton, would be called on to apply the lessons they learned—at the Academy and during their Gettysburg tours—on European battlefields after America's entry into the Great War, after Congress declared war on Imperial Germany the first week of April 1917. (In the following chapters, the terms "Great War" and "World War" are used interchangeably.) However, one graduate from the Class of 1915—the so-called Class the Stars Fell On—a young man from Abilene, Kansas, by the name of Dwight David Eisenhower, would spend part of the conflict back in Gettysburg instead of France, where he yearned to serve.[3]

Unknown to most Americans today, the site of the famous 1863 battle would become the location of two large U.S. Army camps in 1917 and 1918, temporary homes to thousands of young soldiers destined for the battlefields of France and Belgium. The soldiers would have a deleterious environmental impact on Gettysburg National Military Park, they would bring vice and crime to the famous little town, and they would unwittingly infect the citizens with a deadly disease that killed far more civilians than had the great battle fifty-five years earlier. But they also trained for, and some of them died in, America's first great overseas conflict. Too, some were inspired by their short stay on the Civil War's bloodiest battlefield.

This book merges two of my intellectual interests—the American Civil War and World War I—under one cover in an effort to understand how the influx of tens of thousands of American soldiers, not wearing blue or butternut and gray, but olive drab and khaki, changed the town of Gettysburg, the environment and the people who lived there. Some of the areas of inquiry include the temporary environmental effects created by those soldiers—and their lodging, training, feeding, sanitary, and storage facilities, along with the tread of hundreds of horses, mules, and vehicles—on an area that had become an American shrine. Also examined is the social and cultural interaction between those soldiers and the civilians (as well as their government—local, state, and federal) who lived and worked in Gettysburg and the surrounding area. In addition, the impact of the Great War on Gettysburg and its environs—aside from the influence of the two camps—is assessed: the county's newspaper reporting on the war before and after the United States' entry; the reaction of the citizenry and their efforts to support the war effort; and the county's human contribution to the armed forces and civilian relief agencies. Finally, the biological effects of the flood of thousands of uniformed outsiders descending on Gettysburg will be explored, especially when some of those soldiers—for the most part young and healthy—brought an invisible killer to town: the Spanish influenza.

Before the end of 1917, soldiers from six regiments—the 4th, 7th, 58th, 59th, 60th, and 61st U.S. Infantry—had been trained and quartered on the battlefield along the Emmitsburg Road in what was officially given the nondescript name of "Camp, U.S. Troops." After their departure, the fledgling U.S. Army Tank Corps replaced them in 1918, and the area was redubbed "Camp Colt," in memory of the Connecticut revolver manufacturer. By the time the camp was formally closed in early 1919, nearly 300 soldiers and civilians had died from the Spanish influenza, a pandemic that killed more people worldwide than the war itself. This book is an effort to tell the forgotten story of Gettysburg's citizens and their temporary guests during the Great War, a drama that took place on one of the most significant stages in American historical memory. But it is more than that. I have borrowed an idea from David Kennedy, the Donald J. McLachman Professor of History Emeritus at Stanford University, who wrote the landmark study *Over Here: The First World War and American Society.*[4] In the preface, he writes: "I have used the occasion of the war as a window through which to view early twentieth-century society." And so, I too am using the Great War as a "window" to examine a unique American community, one in the throes of modernization while at the same time trying to capitalize on, yet preserve a part of, the nation's past. That struggle continues even today. Perhaps the best analogy is that Gettysburg—despite its historical significance—serves more as a magnifying glass, rather than a window, that allows us to both view and illuminate a rural American community during the Progressive Era and World War I.

The prologue sets the stage for the following chapters, using the occasion of the Fiftieth Anniversary of the Battle of Gettysburg, and specifically the U.S. Army's role in administering the commemoration, for a glimpse of the famous southcentral Pennsylvania town, the nation, and even the world on the eve of the World War. I also introduce and profile several young Americans from 1913 who had been or would be associated with the town and battlefield of Gettysburg. The first chapter provides the reader with a capsule history of Gettysburg from the end of the battle through 1914. I try to show how national and world events, technological change, commerce, federal and state legislation, and court decisions affected the citizens of Adams County and influenced demographics, the economy, social and cultural trends, and the residents' politics and political views. Just as important is the increasing role of the federal government in the lives of the county's citizens when an 1895 Act of Congress created Gettysburg National Military Park, Progressive Era legislation wrought economic and social change, and a landmark Supreme Court decision changed forever the role of the federal government in the preservation of America's heritage.

The next chapter focuses on the outbreak of war in Europe and the reactions of Americans in general—and Adams County residents in particular—to the growing crises in the Old World and the New. The remaining chapters comprise the crux of the book and focus on American entry into the war and the changes it brought to the people of Adams County, as well as the increasing role of the federal government in their lives, something to which they had become more and more accustomed since the founding of Gettysburg National Military Park two decades earlier. Of special importance was the War Department's decision to locate two military training camps on the battlefield, one in 1917 and another in 1918. Moreover, the people of the county, just like Americans elsewhere, experienced wartime measures such as military mobilization, conscription, bond drives, propaganda, material and food conservation, and censorship. They also experienced war-related personal loss and bereavement. After the 1863 battle, Gettysburg buried one civilian who had lost her life during the fight. In 1918, Gettysburg and Adams County would bury more than a hundred noncombatants as a result of a disease another generation of American soldiers unwittingly brought to the town. But the county also lost many of its own young men in uniform, some who still lie overseas in places like Aisne-Marne, Oise-Aisne, and Meuse-Argonne American cemeteries, or whose names are inscribed on their Walls of the Missing.

As the nation tried to apply the lessons of the federal government's Progressive reforms to the war effort, the people of Gettysburg and its surrounding communities followed suit. Yet, unlike most other American towns and cities, Gettysburg was hallowed ground. An earlier generation of its residents already had felt the ravages of war as had few other American communities outside of Sharpsburg, Maryland; Richmond, Fredericksburg, Winchester, and Petersburg, Virginia; Vicksburg, Mississippi; Chattanooga, Tennessee; and Atlanta, Georgia. Of these, only Petersburg, Chattanooga, and Gettysburg would experience the Great War up close and personal, not from battle but from military occupation. However, neither Petersburg nor Chattanooga had achieved Gettysburg's status of an American shrine, as manifested by the fiftieth anniversary celebration/commemoration in the summer of 1913. To many Americans in 1917, Gettysburg *was* the turning point of the Civil War, and that conflict heretofore had been *the* turning point in American history. Gettysburg also was known across the world as the place where, on November 19, 1863, an American president had summarized the war's meaning and thus elevated and cemented Gettysburg's salient place in that cataclysmic struggle. In 1917 and '18, however, that same sacred ground was desecrated. It would take years for Gettysburg National Military Park to recover. Unlike the battlefields of the Ypres Salient, Gallipoli, the Somme, and the Argonne Forest, which all bear many visible signs of warfare, few vestiges of the Civil War remain at Gettysburg. Monuments and a national cemetery adorned Gettysburg during the Great War, and even more memorials are present today, just as monuments, memorials, and cemeteries now mark the Great War battlefields of France, Belgium, Italy, Slovenia, and Turkey. Trenches and shell craters still scar the earth at some places, like Verdun, Beaumont Hamel, Vimy Ridge, Blanc Mont, and other sites, but much of the Western Front is now pastoral or built over, as is Gettysburg. Yet the only reminder of Gettysburg's Great War heritage is a tiny marker, a memorial tree, and a wayside exhibit astride the Emmitsburg Road to commemorate Camp Colt, along with a small exhibit in the park museum. Had a future president of the United States not commanded that camp in 1918, it doubtless would not have been remembered at all.

When the world conflict abruptly ended on November 11, 1918, Gettysburg slowly returned to normal, but since 1863, "normal" in Gettysburg meant moving forward while clinging to the past. The final chapter and epilogue examine how Gettysburg, and all of Adams County, remembered its contributions to the war effort and the concurrent human loss, something made more difficult by the place's standing as a national shrine, famous for an earlier epoch in American history, not for a war that did not, after all, end all wars.

While researching and writing this book, I was astonished to find so many historical figures who had been connected to Gettysburg and were intimately involved with or participated in the era's major events, from local soldiers, sailors, and marines who were present during the U.S. intervention in Mexico; to a radical suffragist who also was a nationally recognized nursing expert; to the most decorated American soldier of the war who trained at Gettysburg in 1917, among many others. But the most famous was the commander of the 1918 camp who would advance in rank in the next forty years to become the Supreme Commander of the Allied Expeditionary Forces in World War II and then the thirty-fourth president of the United States. These were just some of the tens of thousands of men and women who shared a connection to an American community made illustrious not by the war in which they were involved during the second decade of the twentieth century, but one that had been forged in fire a half century earlier, made even more famous when the sixteenth president gave what at the time seemed a lackluster speech to dedicate a national cemetery but later became one of the most revered public addresses in American, and even world, history. This is their overlooked, but not quite forgotten, story.

Acknowledgments

As I researched and wrote this monograph, many people provided advice, research assistance, input, constructive criticism, guidance, and motivation. At Gettysburg National Military Park (GNMP), John Heiser, archivist and librarian, made available the few primary sources concerning Camp Colt. Greg Goodell, collections curator of GNMP, and his assistant, Andrew Newman, made accessible rarely seen maps, photographs, and correspondence. At the Adams County Historical Society, historian and licensed battlefield guide Timothy Smith, Executive Director Ben Neeley, volunteer docents Bonnie Richardson and Roger Rex, and photographic historian Bill Frasanito assisted me with my research in the society's collections. At the U.S. Army Heritage and Education Center, Col. (ret.) James "Scud" Scudieri, U.S. Army, an old friend from our West Point history department days, assisted with my research. Mitchell Yockelson of the National Archives, an expert on the Great War and an old friend, provided valuable insight concerning the various record groups that held documents relative to Gettysburg's two army camps. Also at the National Archives, Marcus Martin in the Still Pictures Unit was especially helpful. Megan Harris at the Library of Congress was polite, accommodating, and professional. At the Shippensburg University Library, Kirk Moll, Christy Fic, and Denise Wietry expedited the scanning and electronic transmission of a master's thesis on Camp Colt written by one of their alumni, David Weaver, a licensed battlefield guide at GNMP. Dean Shultz, president of Gettysburg Engineering Co., an engineer by profession but a historian by avocation, and his wife, Judy, determined the approximate acreage of Camp of the U.S. Troops/Camp Colt from blueprints of the cantonment's layout.

Among those who read and commented on the manuscript, led me to sources and photographs, loaned their professional expertise, or assisted with research, I must acknowledge Anne and Dale Gallon of Gallon Historical Art; Susan Bouvier of Shiremanstown, Pennsylvania; Jim Ankrum of York, Pennsylvania; Jennifer Murray of the University of Virginia at Wise; Jennifer Keane of Chapman University; Bradley Keefer of Kent State University at Ashtabula; Cynthia D. Miller of Frederick, Maryland; Peter Miele at the Seminary Ridge Museum of the Gettysburg Lutheran Seminary; Maj. William Mecum, U.S. Army, ret.; Linda S. Sherman, RN; Jamie Lille, RN, NP; Walter Powell, past president of the Gettysburg Battlefield Preservation Association and former historic preservation officer for the Borough of Gettysburg; Tina Beals of Hanover, Pennsylvania; my brother-in-law, Richard Wojewodzi; and local historians Debra Sandoe McCauslin and John B. Horner. Gettysburg Licensed Battlefield Guide Sue Boardman, Eric L. Dorr and his assistant, Cheryl Reichling, of the Gettysburg Museum of History and J. Karl Anderson of the Gettysburg Soldier Factory opened their private collections to me; and Gary Maring shared family memories about his father and uncle, who were orphaned by the Spanish flu. Frederic "Freddy" Castier, of St. Quentin, France, an old friend who stomped much of the Argonne Forest with me, assisted with the translation of a handwritten document from 1918, penned in Freddy's native language. Steven A. Floyd of Gettysburg told me about photographs of the 1917 Camp of the U.S. Troops that were in the GNMP collection and then was gracious enough to provide me with digitized copies of the images.

At the Pennsylvania Archives, Jonathan Stayer and Heather Heckman were more than helpful. At the Kent State University Press, former acquiring editor Joyce Harrison and current acquiring editor Will Underwood, as well as Mary Young and Christine Brooks, were supportive and pleasures with whom to work, and my copyeditor, Erin Holman (or as I call her, "St. Erin"), ensured that my grammar, spelling, punctuation, syntax, and documentation conformed to Kent State's guidelines and continues to make me look like a much better writer than I can take credit for. Finally, Susan Songy and Peter Fitzgerald of Baltimore, Maryland, were instrumental in helping me construct the statistical graphs concerning the Spanish influenza.

PROLOGUE

1913

Reunion Summer

The Fiftieth Anniversary of the Battle of Gettysburg, in midsummer 1913, was indeed the commemoration to end all commemorations. It marked Gettysburg as a great meeting place of American history and patriotism, and it was a grand success largely because of the efforts of the officers and enlisted soldiers of the U.S. Army. On July 1, 1913, the Gettysburg National Park Commission's annual report to the War Department predicted: "This great project . . . has awakened great interest and enthusiasm throughout the land, and indicates that this celebration will be one of the grandest events in the history of the country."[1] (The report's mandated due date just happened to coincide with the first day of the event.)

The patriotic affair—also called the Peace Jubilee—was held on the actual battlefield, which an 1895 Act of Congress had established as Gettysburg National Military Park, and for the next several decades administered by the U.S. War Department.[2] As early as January 1912, War Department officials had met with representatives of the Pennsylvania Commission, Fiftieth Anniversary of the Battle of Gettysburg, and the Joint Special Committee of the Congress to make provisions for the anniversary event. Congress authorized $150,000 to the War Department on August 26, 1912, matched by an equal amount from the Commonwealth. Soon after, the army set up a "joint headquarters" in Gettysburg with the Pennsylvania Commission.[3]

The bulk of administrative and logistical matters concerning the anniversary became the responsibility of the army's Quartermaster Department, which possessed expertise in transportation, supply, lodging, and food service for large numbers of men. The task would be monumental, with requirements to feed, shelter, and transport 53,000 elderly northern and southern veterans whose

Veterans arriving at Gettysburg for the Peace Jubilee (Library of Congress)

average age topped seventy years. The army sent nearly 1,500 soldiers to the "Great Camp," as the cantonment of the reunion would be called. The War Department deemed the soldiers "necessary for . . . proper administration of its many . . . details, and to police and protect the camp . . . [and] the avenues throughout the battlefield." When the reporters (155—invited as guests of the government) and the contracted cooks, bakers, and kitchen police (2,170) were added to the list, the total number of "campers" exceeded 57,000.[4]

To command the Great Camp, the army detailed Brig. Gen. Hunter Liggett, who would become well-known during the World War as commanding general of the American Expeditionary Force's First Corps and by conflict's end would command the First Army. Liggett was remembered many years later when a post in California was named after him, but two junior officers who served at Gettysburg were destined to surpass him in the annals of American military history: lieutenants in 1913 were Simon Bolivar Buckner Jr. and George S. Patton Jr. The son of the Confederate general who surrendered Fort Donelson to U. S. Grant in 1862, Buckner rose to the rank of lieutenant general and became the ranking American soldier to die from enemy action during World War II, when he was killed while commanding the Tenth U.S. Army on Okinawa in 1945.[5] In the summer of 1913, however, he served as Liggett's military assistant. George Patton—

whose great uncle was mortally wounded at Gettysburg while commanding the 7th Virginia Infantry—accompanied the 1st Squadron, 15th Cavalry Regiment. This unit, along with two battalions of the 5th Infantry; Battery D, 3d Artillery; Company C, 1st Engineers; 288 officers and enlisted men of the Medical Department, and, of course, the Signal Corps and Quartermaster Corps, comprised the bulk of the Regulars at Gettysburg that year.[6] Remarkably, the usually garrulous Patton had little to note on this trip to Gettysburg, his first since he was a West Point senior in 1909. From his letters, the future general obviously was not enamored with his role as a "park policeman," as he called it. Of the elderly veterans, Lieutenant Patton wrote: "They are a disgusting bunch, dirty and old, and of the people who 'God Loves.' One old hound has been beating a drum ever since he got here. Two others have a cannon which they fire as often as possible."[7]

From June 29 until July 6, the Union and Confederate veterans took part in the pageant honoring their deeds from a half century earlier. Many of the addresses and official functions of the reunion took place in a venue known as the

A Union veteran playing his drum (Library of Congress)

Great Tent—which could seat in excess of thirteen thousand people—that troops from the Quartermaster Corps erected just east of the Emmitsburg Road, near the historic Codori Farm buildings, where George Pickett directed and watched his division of Virginians in their heroic yet fruitless assault on Cemetery Ridge five decades before. But in 1913, the young soldiers, north and south, east and west, all served the same master, and all wore the same standard, greenish-brown uniform and round campaign hats. To truly appreciate the magnitude of the U.S. Army's responsibilities during the reunion, consider the following statistics: camp dimensions: 247 acres; tents erected: 6,592; mess kits issued: 54,000; meat consumed: 156,410 pounds; telephone wire laid: 90 miles; medical cases treated: 9,986. There also was the necessity to supply fresh, cool water and sanitation facilities, some 90 latrines which could serve more than three thousand

Some of the many field kitchens at the 1913 Reunion (Library of Congress)

Left: Two young soldiers, most likely assigned to the 5th U.S. Infantry, on guard in the veterans' camp (Library of Congress); *right:* Two water reservoirs built for the camp (Library of Congress)

Part of the veterans' camp sprawled across the fields where Pickett's Charge occurred (Library of Congress)

people. Complicating matters was the heat, exceeding 100 degrees on July 2. (The Medical Department also would be a significant part of the army contingent. By far, the majority of admissions to the army's medical facility were because of heat prostration and physical exhaustion.) Then, there was the confusion created by thousands of wandering tourists. And, of course, the frailty of the honored guests: nine veterans (eight old Yanks and one aged Reb) died during the event or on their way to or from their distant homes.[8] (One Union veteran survived both the battle and the reunion but fell from his train and was killed near Canton, Pennsylvania, on his way home to Wellsville, New York.[9])

Despite the congestion, the oppressive heat and the median age of the ex-combatants, the commemoration went off with nary a hitch. The camp's chief surgeon, Lt. Col. Alfred E. Bradley of the Medical Corps, proudly reported later: "The camp was unique; surely never before in the world's history have so great a number of men so advanced in years been assembled under field conditions." The U.S. Army even got to show off its modern equipment and tactics when, on July 2, "under the direction of the Chief of Staff of the United States Army [Maj. Gen. Leonard Wood], special detachments of each arm of the Regular Service [are] to participate as directed," stated the after-action report. This special, daylong event was known simply as "Military Day." (July 1 was called "Veterans Day, the 3rd was set aside as "Civic Day," and the Fourth of July, appropriately, was dubbed "National Day."[10]) Andrew Cowan, a Union veteran whose New York artillery battery defended Cemetery Ridge near the so-called Bloody Angle on July 3, 1863, ominously declared on Military Day, "Our regular army is an honor to the nation. It ought to be twice as large. . . . Let

Left: Major General Hunter Liggett, Secretary of War Lindley M. Garrison and Major General Leonard Wood at the Gettysburg Peace Jubilee (Library of Congress); *right:* Senator Boies Penrose, R-PA (Library of Congress)

us be prepared to command peace."[11] President Woodrow Wilson, Virginia-born, who as a child witnessed Confederate and Federal troops march in front of his home in Staunton during the Shenandoah Valley campaigns of 1862 and 1864, was the keynote speaker and guest of honor on July 4, 1913. Yet, through a bureaucratic foul-up, Wilson almost spent the anniversary relaxing in New England. The *Gettysburg Compiler*, a local newspaper aligned with the Democratic Party, explained what happened, but the editors put their own spin on the situation, blaming Pennsylvania's Republican senator, Boies Penrose, for not inviting the new commander in chief:

> It is most gratifying to the hosts of Blue and Gray that Commander-in-Chief President Wilson will be at Gettysburg on Friday. . . . It is dollars to doughnuts that if Senator Penrose's candidate for president, had been in the White House, that Senator Penrose's Governor of Pennsylvania [John K. Tener, also a Republican] would have seen to it that Senator Penrose's President would have been officially invited months ago. . . .
>
> It was [Democratic] Congressman A. Mitchell Palmer of Pennsylvania, who . . . had a conference with the President on last Saturday and pointed out the importance of the Gettysburg celebration, that did not appear in the late invitation; its nation-wide significance and particularly the spirit of sectional sympathy that would result from a speech by a Southern-born President at the reunion of the North and South.[12]

The Republican-aligned *Star and Sentinel,* however, was not as enthusiastic about Wilson's participation.[13] So the new president, in office for only four months, made the trip to Gettysburg after all, and in his speech to the veterans and spectators he reflected on the actions of soldiers who had fought five decades earlier. Four years later, during his second term, the chief executive who would make as his 1916 campaign slogan "He Kept Us Out of War," had his own bloody conflict with which to contend.

The next day, July 5, 1913, the commemoration came to an end and the veterans and onlookers began heading for home, but the modern-day soldiers remained. Now it was time for the clean-up and repair of any damage caused to Gettysburg National Military Park. Again, the U.S. Army was responsible for the lion's share of the massive effort. Some of the arduous tasks that the quartermasters, signalers, engineers, and their civilian contractors performed included tearing down the tents, filling in ninety pit latrines, disassembling the plumbing for the water fountains, collecting and re-spooling miles of temporary telephone and electrical wire, disposing of trash and kitchen waste, ripping out the impermanent roads that crisscrossed the Great Camp and generally doing whatever else was necessary to return the battlefield to its pre-anniversary appearance. In a July 9 column, a reporter for the *Star and Sentinel* reflected, "The big camp was a grand success from any point of view. The Quartermaster Department in charge of camp construction and equipment left nothing undone and everything was carried out just as it had originally been planned. Seldom if ever has this department of the United States Army been put to a greater task . . . and never has such a task been handled with greater precision or satisfaction." The newspaper even included a large photographic image of the Quartermaster Department's officer in charge at the semi-centennial commemoration, Maj. James E. Normoyle, who, according to the caption, "Directed Preparations for the Great Peace Camp."[14]

The Gettysburg National Park Commission reported that "by July 8 the veterans had left the camp to return to their homes, and the work of restoring the field was begun by the park commission and carried rapidly forward. A few of the tents were left on the ground for the use of the regular troops in charge of the material, and some for the use of a school of instruction in military training for students detailed from various colleges." The commissioners concluded that "the officers of the Quartermaster's Department, United States Army, in charge of the work in connection with the encampment, completed their duties and gave up their headquarters on Baltimore Street and left Gettysburg August 13."[15] Thus ended the Fiftieth Anniversary of the Battle of Gettysburg and the U.S. Army's role in its administration. The college encampment that followed the Peace Jubilee was one of two in the country, the other in Monterey, California. They were the first of many camps in what came to be called the "preparedness movement," a program of instruction that would supply the grist for the U.S. Army's officer corps during the Great War.

On March 4 of the same year, the United States had inaugurated its twenty-eighth president, the first southern-born chief executive since the Civil War. Promising a "New Freedom" during his 1912 campaign against incumbent Republican William Howard Taft and former president Teddy Roosevelt of the upstart Progressive, or "Bull Moose," Party, Woodrow Wilson targeted three major reforms: busting the trusts, regulating the banking industry, and lowering the tariff. In his first year in office he would sign legislation affecting all three: the Clayton Anti-Trust Act, the Federal Reserve Act, and the Underwood-Simmons Tariff Act. The voters of Adams County, Pennsylvania, with Gettysburg as its seat, supported Wilson, but with just 51 percent of the vote.[16] Four months after his inauguration, the president delivered the keynote speech of the Fiftieth Anniversary Commemoration. His words echoed the conciliatory spirit of the nation that hot Fourth of July, 1913, the essence of which he had striven hard to emphasize throughout the 1912 campaign: "We have found one another again as brothers and comrades in arms, enemies no longer, generous friends rather, our battles long past, the quarrel forgotten—except that we shall not forget the splendid valor, the manly devotion of the men then arrayed against one another, now grasping hands and smiling into each other's eyes." Perhaps it was in that same spirit of reunion—for white southerners and northerners, white conservatives and progressives, white farmers and industrialists—that he avoided the divisive issue of race, the ultimate cause of the Civil War. He alluded to the matter only when in response to the question of which people he was elected to lead, he answered, "the people themselves, the great and the small, without class or difference of kind or race or origin; and undivided in interest."[17] The policies of his two administrations, however, would prove otherwise, at least as they related to the civil rights of his black citizens.[18]

Toward the end of his own Gettysburg address, Wilson reflected on the martial aspects of the commemoration to contrast the battle of five decades yore with the challenges that lie ahead:

> The orders of the day are the laws upon our statute books. What we strive for is their freedom, their right to lift themselves from day to day and behold the things they have hoped for, and so make way for still better days for those whom they love who are to come after them. The recruits are the little children crowding in. The quartermaster's stores are in the mines and forests and fields, in the shops and factories. Every day something must be done to

push the campaign forward; and it must be done by plan and with an eye to some great destiny.

The images conjured by his concluding sentence would not reflect his presidency: "Come, let us be comrades and soldiers yet to serve our fellow-men in quiet counsel, where the blare of trumpets is neither heard nor heeded and where the things are done which make blessed the nations of the world in peace and righteousness and love."[19] A. Scott Berg, a recent Wilson biographer, wryly and unflatteringly compared the president's rather bland speech to Lincoln's famous address. Berg wrote of Wilson's presentation: "The world will little note what he said there."[20] In reality, the world had little more than a year remaining before it plunged into conflagration, rendering the president's words meaningless.

Trouble already was simmering in Europe. At the exact time that Union and Confederate veterans were arriving in Gettysburg, Bulgaria was preparing to attack Serbia and Greece over the results of the First Balkan War, which had begun nine months earlier, in October 1912, when the Balkan League—Bulgaria, Greece, Serbia and Montenegro (all under the watchful eye of Tsarist Russia)—declared war on the Ottoman Empire, in an effort to wrestle Macedonia from

President Wilson, tipping his top hat, departing the Great Tent (Library of Congress)

Turkey. A Gettysburg confectioner and owner of a local sweet shop, Gus Varela, returned to his native Greece, according to Gettysburg's *Star and Sentinel* newspaper, "to join the Greek Army when war was declared against Turkey . . . [and] was one of the first American Greeks to offer his service to his country on the opening of hostilities with Turkey."[21] The conflict was brief, the Turks were thrashed, and the Ottomans lost Albania and Macedonia, thus ending Turkish domination over the Balkan countries. The war officially ended on May 30, 1913, with a peace treaty, but several members of the Balkan League were dissatisfied with Bulgaria's share of its Macedonian spoils of war. Albania, at the insistence of the European powers, was granted nationhood, further complicating postwar diplomacy. On June 1, Serbia and Greece formed another alliance, and the Second Balkan War began four weeks later. The Bulgarians were quickly defeated, and another peace accord was signed, this one on August 10. Serbia gained the Kosovo region as well as northern Macedonia, while Greece acquired Crete and southern Macedonia. The Bulgarians kept only a small portion of Macedonia. Aggravated by the outcome, Bulgaria moved closer diplomatically to the Austro-Hungarian Empire. Serbia lost its holdings in Albania because of Austro-Hungarian pressure, causing Serbian nationalists to become even more belligerent toward the Hapsburgs than they had been before the wars. Stories of that war even showed up in the *Gettysburg Times* a few months later, when the newspaper ran a story titled, "Many Died in Balkan War: Census of Bulgaria Shows Astounding Decrease in Male Population." The Balkans cauldron boiled over when a Serbian nationalist assassinated the Austrian crown prince and his wife in Sarajevo, on June 28, 1914.[22] Only one year after Wilson delivered his Gettysburg speech, what began in the Balkans as a kitchen fire was about to engulf most of Europe and spread to other parts of the world. Wilson and his fellow Americans could bask in "peace and righteousness" for only thirty-four more months before they, too, were caught in the flames.

July 1913 was the midpoint of the major league–baseball season. Three months earlier, on April 20, while only a month in office, President Wilson had thrown out the first pitch for the opening game, the Washington Senators versus the New York Yankees—the first year that the latter organization went by its now-famous name (the team previously was called the New York Highlanders). Gettysburg's hometown hero, Edward Stewart Plank—nicknamed "Gettysburg Eddie"—was having yet another banner season as a left-handed pitcher with the American League's Philadelphia Athletics, the thirteenth of his fourteen years with the A's. Eddie finished with a record of eighteen wins and ten losses, and the Athletics would capture the American League Pennant and go on to defeat the National League champion New York Giants four games to one in

Left: Eddie Plank in his Gettysburg College baseball uniform, circa 1900. (Adams County Historical Society); *below:* Connie Mack, rear (closest to camera), seated next to Eddie Plank on Little Round Top, November 1913. Note the World Series Champions pennant draped on the car. (Adams County Historical Society)

the World Series. Plank suffered a tough tenth-inning loss for the A's during game two against the great Christy Mathewson but would recover and out-duel Mathewson in game five, giving up only two hits in the Giants' Upper Manhattan park, the Polo Grounds, thus winning the world championship. Several weeks later, Plank gave the Athletics' renowned manager and part-owner Connie Mack a tour of the Gettysburg Battlefield.

Born in 1875, just twelve years after the battle, Eddie was nearing the end of his playing career in 1913, having turned thirty-eight years old only a few weeks before the World Series. Nonetheless, he would play four more seasons, finishing his career with the St. Louis Browns in 1917.[23] His major-league days over, Plank returned to Gettysburg and opened a service station and Buick dealership on the northeast corner of Stratton and York Streets, the latter thoroughfare also known as the Lincoln Highway. He thus capitalized on the tourist traffic made possible during the post–World War era by the automobile age and the modern highways and motels that accompanied it.[24] (He also took advantage of the increased tourism when he became a battlefield guide after the war.) Gettysburg Eddie died of a stroke in 1926. In 1946, he was elected to the Baseball Hall of Fame in Cooperstown, New York.[25] He is buried in Evergreen Cemetery, made famous by the namesake hill on which it is situated, a landmark so doggedly defended by the Army of the Potomac some sixty-three years before the famous lefty was laid to rest.

The summer of 1913 was not so momentous for everyone who someday would make the national headlines. From May through August, the young men at West Point who had just finished their second year of studies were given a much-needed leave of absence from the Academy. Cadet Dwight David Eisenhower was an excellent baseball player when not sidelined by injuries, and two years earlier, on June 14, 1911, he had become part of the Long Gray Line. In his memoirs, Eisenhower recalled the summer of 1913: "[We] were given a furlough—about two and a half months. This aroused as much enthusiasm in us

Cadet Dwight David Eisenhower, U.S. Military Academy Class of 1915 (Eisenhower National Historic Site)

as the prospect of graduation. I looked forward to it and when the time arrived went back to Abilene to see my family and renew friendships in the little town to which I still felt very close." He returned to West Point at the end of the summer. In May two years later, when he was a "Firstie" (what cadets were—and still are—called during their senior year), Ike traveled to Gettysburg with his classmates to study the battlefield. A few weeks after the sojourn to southcentral Pennsylvania, he was commissioned a second lieutenant of infantry. Many years later, he reflected, "From my first day at West Point, and any number of times thereafter, I often asked myself: What am I doing here? Like the other young men, I sometimes wondered—where did I come from, by what route and why; by what chance arrangement of fate did I come by this uniform?"[26] Little did Second Lieutenant Eisenhower realize that his first command as a young infantry officer would be on the same fields where Longstreet's Grand Assault had unfolded on July 3, 1863, spearheaded by twelve thousand Confederate infantrymen led by young officers his own age.

Another young man with command aspirations, this one already well familiar with the town of Gettysburg, was Keller E. Rockey, a 1909 graduate of Pennsylvania College. Rockey was born in Columbia City, Indiana, but had studied at Mercersburg Academy in neighboring Franklin County—while his father served as a Lutheran minister in Waynesboro (likewise in Franklin County)—before attending college in Gettysburg. He then went to graduate school at Yale before joining the Marine Corps in 1913, undergoing officer's training in Norfolk, Virginia. Upon gaining a second lieutenant's commission, he was assigned to sea duty aboard the USS *Nebraska* and then reassigned to the new battleship USS *Nevada*, the U.S. Navy's first super dreadnought. Unlike Eisenhower, Rockey would fight in the upcoming war and would serve in the Pacific during America's next great conflict.[27]

A soldier assigned to assist with the Fiftieth Anniversary of the Battle of Gettysburg was about to shed his army uniform and don the clothing of a college student. Sgt. Adolph Weidenbach was a German immigrant who had attended the University of Heidelberg and the Sorbonne in Paris before coming to the United States. He then enlisted in the 5th U.S. Infantry in 1910. While assisting with the anniversary events, apparently, he decided to attend Pennsylvania College, which by 1913 was being unofficially called Gettysburg College. (The school would officially change its name in 1921.) Because of his previous studies, Weidenbach entered classes that autumn as a senior. Upon graduation, he accepted a commission as a second lieutenant in the U.S. Army Officers' Volunteer Reserve Corps. When trouble brewed on the Mexican border in 1916, he would take a commission in the Regular Army and then made the service a career, eventually changing his name to Charles Andrew Willoughby. During the Great War, he served in France as an intelligence officer and would rise steadily in rank to serve in the Pacific theater during the Second World War and later in Korea.[28]

As Weidenbach was enrolling in Pennsylvania College, growing up in an upper-middle-class family in West Farmington, Ohio, was an eight-year-old boy who had ancestors who fought in the Civil War. The lad was big for his age, and four years later, in 1917, he looked much older than his physical age and passed for an eighteen-year-old. Ernest L. Wrentmore loved fishing and the outdoors. When he was old enough, he joined the Boy Scouts. And, at the grand old age of thirteen, he became the youngest soldier to fight in the American Expeditionary Forces in 1918. Wrentmore came to Gettysburg in the summer of 1917 to begin the process of becoming a soldier.[29]

Elsewhere in the United States in 1913, the Sixteenth and Seventeenth Amendments to the Constitution were ratified, the former paving the way for the first permanent federal income tax and the latter establishing the direct election of senators by popular vote; suffragist Ida B. Wells and her followers (including Adams County resident Lavinia Dock) demonstrated in Washington, D.C., for women's political rights in a struggle that would lead to the ratification of the Nineteenth Amendment in 1920; on the West Coast, the port of Los Angeles was improved and deepened in anticipation of increased vessel traffic from the scheduled opening of the Panama Canal in 1914; in New York City, the tallest inhabited structure in the world, the Woolworth Building, opened; British actor Charlie Chaplin began his Hollywood career when he signed with the Keystone Film Company; on Manhattan's East Side, a traveling exhibition of more than a thousand works of modern art was viewed by a hundred thousand New Yorkers before moving on to Boston and Chicago; and the greatest American art collector of the era, as well as the most important and powerful financial giant on the planet, J. P. Morgan—died of natural causes just before his seventy-seventh birthday. A recent historian has reflected on what Morgan's passing meant to America and the world:

> The death of J. P. Morgan represented the end of a particular era of capitalism—born of nineteenth-century precepts of unfettered free markets—which had given rise to the trusts and the tycoons, the tremendous enrichment of the elite, and the cultural afflictions of New York's aristocracy of wealth. Now in its place, there began to emerge an era where the state would play a more directive role in the national economy and where mass production and mass consumption would become America's hallmarks, rather than the prosperity of its elites. In 1913 America jolted decisively, from the age of Morgan to the age of Ford.[30]

Indeed. That year, Henry Ford, who was born four weeks after the Battle of Gettysburg and whose company already had been in business for a decade in 1913, unveiled the continuous moving assembly line for his Model-T, thus out-producing his competitors, lowering the price of his automobiles and raising the wages of his factory workers (who also were potential customers).[31] American industry and the American lifestyle, which depended more and more on cars and trucks than on horses and mules, undeniably had been "jolted decisively . . . to the age of Ford." Although Eddie Plank later sold Buicks, the entire auto industry owed its remarkable success to the engineer from Dearborn. (Plank's brother Ira, however, owned a Ford dealership in Gettysburg about a block away from Eddie's business.[32])

Another community halfway across the globe also was hosting a celebration of sorts in the summer of 1913. The Exposition Universelle et Internationale (also known as the World's Fair), was held in Ghent, Belgium, where the peace treaty between the United States and Great Britain had been signed in December 1814, a diplomatic agreement that ended hostilities between the two nations but not soon enough to stop the bloody Battle of New Orleans in January 1815. The exposition, which began in April 1913 and lasted through the end of October, showcased the progress and modernity of the world's industrialized nations. In autumn 1914, just a year after the exposition's closure, Ghent was in the path of German invaders, who continuously occupied it until November 10, 1918. Germany's was the most modern exhibit at the Exposition Universelle et Internationale, even though it had been funded not by that nation's government but by Friedrich Krupp AG, a steel and armaments producer.[33] In 1914, Krupp-manufactured siege artillery, including the heavy mortars called "Big Berthas" (firing 42-centimeter shells—about sixteen and a half inches in diameter at their base) would help to bring down the massive Belgian fortifications at Liege, Namur, and Antwerp. Then, in May 1915, after the contending forces had settled into trench warfare, on the other side of the German lines in Flanders Lt. Col. John McCrae, Royal Canadian Medical Corps, penned the most famous English-language poem of the Great War, "In Flanders Fields."

Some 180 miles south of Ghent in the City of Light, Igor Stravinsky's ballet, *Le Sacre du Printemps* (The Rite of Spring), choreographed by Sergei Diaghilev, premiered on May 29, 1913, to a raucous, largely unaccepting Parisian audience. Stravinsky and Diaghilev ushered in a new era of music and dance that symbolized the trend toward "modernism" in the arts.[34] A recent cultural historian has postulated that the so-called modernists of the era viewed their movement as "an avant-garde claim to originality, autonomy and rupture [that] dominated debates about art, literature and music. Violent experiment was one radical desire that made the prospect of war seem thrilling, a fulfillment of the theory that to build a new world the old one had to be demolished. War would be cleansing, purifying the corruption of bourgeois taste."[35] For middle-aged and elderly Gettysburg residents—the *bourgeoisie*—who in 1913 still could recall the terrible events of fifty years before, certainly few remembered their experience as thrilling, purifying, or cleansing. Dreadful, tense, nerve-wracking, frightening, gruesome, and depressing were more appropriate descriptions of the battle and its aftermath. Yet no one in the town of Gettysburg, except perhaps for the music professors at Pennsylvania College and the Gettysburg Lutheran Seminary—who might have read about the ballet's premier months later in their professional journals—would have even heard of the uproarious first-night performance in Paris of *Le Sacre du Printemps* or the modernism it heralded.

Back in the western hemisphere, events of a less-than-artistic kind were happening in Mexico. Seventy-seven years earlier, in 1836, the United States' southern neighbor had lost Texas in a bloody revolution that resulted in Texan independence. Then, in 1845, when the Republic of Texas became the twenty-eighth state, a diplomatic dispute over the country's southern border—the Mexicans claimed it was the Nueces River, the Americans insisted it was the Rio Grande—escalated into war in 1846. The fighting was short but decisive, and the Mexicans lost even more territory with the signing of the Treaty of Guadalupe Hidalgo in 1848: this time, a vast expanse that would become California; Utah; Nevada; most of Arizona; and parts of Colorado, Wyoming, and New Mexico. Some of the generals who battled against each other at Gettysburg fought as junior officers on the same side in Mexico: Lee, Meade, Longstreet, Hancock, Armistead, Pickett, Ewell.

Mexico fought its own civil war, which began in 1858 and concluded in 1861 just as the American Civil War exploded. With his economy in shambles, the new Mexican president, Benito Juarez, suspended his country's debt payments to foreign governments. The United States obviously was preoccupied with internal problems and thus unable to enforce its self-proclaimed Monroe Doctrine, so France, Great Britain, and Spain invaded Mexico to safeguard their own economic interests. The British and Spanish soon withdrew, but the French stayed; sent a large occupying force; and installed an Austrian archduke, Maximillian, as Mexico's emperor. The Mexicans defeated a French army at the Battle of Puebla on May 5, 1863 (Cinco de Mayo), but the French remained in power. When the American Civil War ended in the spring of 1865, the French were pressured to pull out; a Mexican army under Gen. Porfirio Diáz occupied Mexico City in 1867; and Maximillian was captured, tried, and executed.[36] Juarez died in 1872 and was replaced by Diáz, who ruled as a dictator until 1911.

Diáz encouraged foreign investment in his country, but it was the upper class of Mexican society that benefited, setting the stage for unrest and, eventually, revolution. Diáz was overthrown in May 1911 and replaced by Francisco Madero, a liberal. Madero's military commander was Victoriano Huerta, but the general turned on his president and had him arrested and murdered. Woodrow Wilson's ambassador to Mexico, Henry Lane Wilson, officially recognized Huerta as the new president, despite that he ascended to power through a bloody coup.[37] The stage was set for further Mexican unrest and, then, U.S. intervention in 1914 and again in 1916. The daily *Gettysburg Times,* one of several county newspapers, kept constant vigil of the turmoil.

Gettysburg's celebratory year had come to a close. Adams County had welcomed tens of thousands of veterans, soldiers, spectators, journalists, and politicians, their trip made possible by improved road networks; railroads; automobiles; and the hotels, restaurants, gas stations, and other visitor-related businesses that already had been profiting from heritage tourism. Gettysburg commerce had benefitted from the throngs of participants and the publicity that the Fiftieth Anniversary Commemoration had received, including an appearance by the president of the United States. On January 1, 1914, the *Gettysburg Times* reported,

> Gettysburg gave its noisiest greeting for many years as 1914 made its appearance at midnight Wednesday and for fifteen minutes the town let loose every known instrument of noise on which it could lay its hands. . . . The year which has just closed will go down in history, so far as Gettysburg is concerned, second only to 1863. The celebration here in July centered the eyes of the entire civilized world on this little town and for generations to come the remarkable anniversary will be related. That it will never be duplicated is undisputed and Gettysburg's celebration last July makes 1913 unique.[38]

Gettysburg, Adams County, the Commonwealth of Pennsylvania, the United States of America, and the rest of the world, particularly Europe, soon would feel the catastrophic tremors that ushered in a new era of human history. The grim reaper's toll for the Battle of Gettysburg totaled approximately fifty-one thousand casualties on both sides, with at least seventy-five hundred killed outright and many more of wounds later. One civilian—twenty-year old Virginia "Jennie" Wade—was slain during the battle. (She, like Eddie Plank, lies in Evergreen Cemetery.) Historical events, however, are better understood when placed in perspective. Exactly fifty-three years later, on July 1, 1916, the first day of the Battle of the Somme, soldiers of the British Empire would suffer their worst day in history, sustaining almost sixty thousand casualties, with more than nineteen thousand killed in action in one day alone.[39] And the battle would last until the third week in November—concluding about the same time as the fifty-third anniversary of the Gettysburg Address—with a total casualty count of almost 1.5 million soldiers (from the British Empire, France and its African colonies, and Germany). In a new age of industrialization and the kind of war it spawned, much had changed in those two-and-a-half score and three years since 1863, both on the battlefield and off. But an even bigger killer was lurking somewhere in the respiratory tract of an unsuspecting host, a pathogen far more lethal to Gettysburg's citizens than the errant bullet that had lodged in the back of a young woman more than a half-century in the past, and even more deadly to the world than the Great War itself.[40]

CHAPTER ONE

Between Two Wars

Gettysburg, 1865–1914

Most American community histories begin with the prehistory of the area and a description of the region's natural features, including a sketch of its aboriginal inhabitants. This is followed by a discussion of European colonization and habitation (and, depending on the region, forced African relocation and settlement), the basis of the colonial economy (such as subsistence farming or tobacco growing), the social and cultural backgrounds of the colonists and their interactions with the native peoples, settlement patterns based on the availability of land and geography, and the framing of the colonial government, followed by political struggles eventually leading to the War for Independence. Then, these studies examine their communities' places of within the structure of laws created by newly adopted state and federal constitutions. (Gettysburg and the southcentral Pennsylvania region also would undergo a short stint of military occupation during the Whiskey Rebellion, and the town became the seat of local government in 1800, when Adams County was carved out of existing York County.) Next, the evolving social and economic growth of the area usually is discussed, key personalities (normally defined by a person's socioeconomic or political standing) are highlighted, and then the "inevitable" events leading up to the Civil War are laid out before the reader. Finally, the community's response and sacrifices in the Great Rebellion (if it is a history of a northern town or county) or the Late Unpleasantness (if the community was part of the Confederate States of America) are described, usually in prodigious detail.

Historical minutiae and background of this sort are absolutely imperative for a comprehensive county or community history, but for the microcosmic study found within the covers of the current volume, this level of detail is a bit superfluous.[1] Until the shattering events of the Civil War, and most especially the momentous battle of 1863, Gettysburg was not much different than the new Republic's other rural-Pennsylvania county seats, such as York, Scranton, Chambersburg, Lancaster, Bedford, Carlisle, and Lewistown, or, for that matter, nearby Maryland seats of government, like Westminster, Frederick or Hagerstown, and even towns farther to the south and north, like Staunton, Virginia, or Morristown, New Jersey. (The *major* exception to the similarity of communities in the antebellum northern and southern states was the continuing existence of slavery in the South.) But momentous historical events tend to overshadow just about everything else in a town's history, especially those communities that witnessed decisive or especially bloody battles. Just as the 1781 siege defined Yorktown, Virginia, and the 1916 slaughter defined Verdun, France, the clash between the Army of the Potomac and the Army of Northern Virginia defined Gettysburg and set it apart from the other American communities and, for that matter, the rest of the world. And when, on November 19, 1863, Abraham Lincoln paid tribute to the fallen Union soldiers, he *redefined* not only the battle but the war in general, thus bequeathing to Gettysburg lasting international fame.[2] Though he was unaware of the significance of his words in 1863, the sixteenth president was placing Gettysburg on history's pedestal along with other villages, towns, or cities like Agincourt and Waterloo; or future battlefield communities such as Stalingrad, Sainte-Mère-Église, and Bastogne.

The great battle had forever changed Gettysburg and Adams County. Its two institutions of higher education, the Gettysburg Lutheran Seminary and Pennsylvania College, had suffered battle damage, and their buildings had been used as field hospitals. The town's churches had also served as hospitals. Citizens whose property had been damaged by Union soldiers could seek restitution from the federal government, but each property owner had to prove that northern soldiers had caused the destruction or had confiscated livestock, grain, fence rails (for firewood), or other personal property. Property owners could file claims with the Commonwealth of Pennsylvania for damages sustained from Confederate activity (minus the loss of livestock and poultry). Few residents, however, were successful in recouping their losses from either level of government. Battle damage to the surrounding area was widespread, and the detritus of combat, including human and horse remains, could be seen for many years afterward. Trees were so badly damaged from small arms and artillery fire that in some areas of the battlefield, such as Culp's Hill, few would survive, stripped of their life-sustaining bark.

Effect of musketry on trees at Culp's Hill, July 1863 (Library of Congress)

On July 2 and 3, Federals intentionally set ablaze the Bliss Farm—situated between Union and Confederate lines on Cemetery and Seminary Ridges—to prevent Rebel sharpshooters from using it to snipe at blue-clad officers. These farm buildings, along with the Sherfy Barn about a half mile to the south, which caught fire from battle action, were the only structures totally destroyed, but any that stood in the way of the opposing forces sustained damage. Bullet-riddled fences and trees, discarded or abandoned equipment, and soldiers' graves remained—even after the majority of Union dead were moved to the Gettysburg National Cemetery.[3]

A year after the battle, the county's populace was reminded that the war had not ended just because the contending forces had departed in July 1863. Confederate general Jubal Early staged a raid into Maryland in the summer of 1864, culminating with the Battle of Monocacy on July 9, followed by an attack three days later on Fort Stevens in the District of Columbia. On July 30, Early's cavalry force, under the command of Brig. Gen. John McCausland, burned nearby Chambersburg to the ground, partly for its citizens' inability to pay a ransom but primarily in retribution for Union army depredations in the Shenandoah Valley.[4]

When the war finally came to an end in the spring of 1865, Adams County's returning soldiers, many from Companies F and I, 87th Pennsylvania Infantry; Companies B and G, 138th Pennsylvania Infantry; Company K, 1st Pennsylvania Reserves and Company C, Cole's Maryland Cavalry (whose veterans, along with Company K, 1st Reserves, actually had fought at Gettysburg) came home to tend to their shops, farms, and families. Years later, these men and others—some three thousand county residents served in the Union forces—would organize a veteran's society, Post 9, Pennsylvania Department, Grand Army of the Republic (GAR). The society named it the Corporal Daniel Skelly Post in memory of a Gettysburg resident and soldier in the 87th Pennsylvania who had been mortally wounded during the 2d Battle of Winchester in the opening phase of the Gettysburg campaign. The unfortunate soldier, who went by the nickname Jack, had been a friend of John Wesley "Wes" Culp—a Gettysburg youth who had moved south before the war and enlisted in the 2d Virginia Infantry in 1861. Too, Jack was romantically involved with Jennie Wade, the town's only battle fatality. Culp found a mortally wounded Skelly in a Confederate hospital after the Winchester battle. He then marched to Gettysburg with the rest of his command but once engaged in battle he was shot in the head and killed outright, near the hill that bore his family name. Thus, all three of these young Gettysburgians failed to survive the campaign. Culp and Wade were killed on July 3, and Skelly passed on July 12, one of the 178 Adams County Federal soldiers who did not survive the war.[5]

The region's postwar economy remained primarily agricultural, as it had been in the century leading up to the sectional conflict, but tourism eventually competed with farming and fruit growing. In the immediate decades following the war, fruit production and processing leapt to center stage, especially north and west of Gettysburg. In the immediate postwar decades, the manufacturing industry was not as important to the local economy as agriculture and tourism and was limited primarily to garment-sewing, furniture production, and brickmaking. By the turn of the century, cigar manufacturing became the most swiftly growing business in Adams County. In 1912 alone, some fifteen new cigar manufactories began operations in McSherrystown, a mostly Catholic enclave in the southeast corner of the county. Additional rail spurs were built and county and municipal roads were upgraded in the early twentieth century to withstand heavier loads caused by automotive traffic, and electric streetcars plied Gettysburg's streets and hauled visitors to battlefield sites.[6] Thus, improved transportation not only benefitted Adams County commerce, and especially its orchard owners and canning-plant operators, but it also conveyed an increasing number of tourists to the town and catered to their needs.

Some of the earliest visitors—bereaved loved ones of the fallen, journalists, curious onlookers, and relic seekers—came before the war even had concluded, but in the postbellum decades they were followed by countless throngs of sightseers. Residents and outsiders quickly grasped the historic significance—and economic benefits—of the battleground and began their efforts to preserve the most significant pieces of terrain soon after the armies departed. David McConaughy, Pennsylvania College graduate, local attorney, and entrepreneur, was the driving force behind the movement to memorialize the fields of mortal strife. He started buying parcels of the battlefield almost as soon as the smoke cleared, and on April 30, 1864, he succeeded in having the Pennsylvania Assembly legally incorporate his Gettysburg Battlefield Memorial Association (GBMA). The association purchased additional land as funds became available both from the legislature and private concerns. The GBMA erected wooden observation towers, improved the existing remains of defensive works, and even attempted to historically interpret the battlefield by marking and describing important locations, such as Cemetery Hill, Little Round Top, and the so-called Bloody Angle. By 1880, the national GAR took over controlling interests in the GBMA, but it continued McConaughy's vision of constructing tour roads and placing regimental memorials on the field.[7]

Another Pennsylvanian, although not a Gettysburg resident at the time of the battle, likewise played a critical role in preserving and interpreting the battlefield, especially the area where Pickett's Charge was thwarted during the afternoon of July 3. John Bachelder did not serve in the Union army, but he did accompany the Army of the Potomac as an artist during the 1862 Peninsula campaign. He returned to Pennsylvania at the unsuccessful conclusion of that campaign, but when Lee's army was defeated at Gettysburg, he packed his bags and traveled to Adams County within days of the battle's end. He would spend his remaining years chronicling and interpreting the terrible trials of July 1863, as well as preserving the land where those momentous events had transpired. Bachelder became a board member of the GBMA and in 1883 was appointed the association's official "superintendent of tablets and legends," a position that allowed him to control a balanced historical interpretation of the battle for the growing number of northern *and* southern pilgrims, veterans, and tourists coming to the battlefield.[8]

Hotels, restaurants, guest houses, private museums, livery stables, souvenir and relic dealers, photographic studios, and battlefield guides became important parts of Gettysburg's economy, and eventually automobile service stations and garages were built and benefitted from the increased tourist flow, too. An alleged medicinal spring was discovered near McPherson's Woods, site of hand-to-hand combat during the battle's first day, and in 1869 the Gettysburg Katalysine Springs Hotel was built just west of Willoughby's Run, serving as a spa and resort and taking advantage of health-conscious visitors and battlefield pilgrims as well. The Springs Hotel stayed in business until the turn of the century, when vacationers began spending their summers at Atlantic and Chesapeake resorts instead.[9]

While the Springs Hotel and the battlefield were attracting tourists to Gettysburg in the postwar decades, but before automobile transportation, railroads brought visitors and manufactured goods to the area, not just to Gettysburg but to other Adams County towns like Fairfield, Biglerville, New Oxford, Littlestown, and East Berlin. By 1890, three main railroads were servicing the county: the Western Maryland; the Pennsylvania Railroad; and the Gettysburg & Harrisburg (a spur of the Philadelphia & Reading Railroad). In addition, the East Berlin Branch of the Western Maryland stretched from a point about a mile east of New Oxford, skirting the York County border for about ten miles northward to East Berlin. A separate trolley line connected Littlestown, in southeastern Adams County, to Hanover, in southwestern York County.[10] In 1884, a spur of the Gettysburg & Harrisburg, a new line just completed from the state capital, was laid from its Gettysburg terminal across the fields of Pickett's Charge, crossing the Emmitsburg Road, to its terminus near the Taneytown Road just east of Little Round Top, to service the growing tourist trade. Farmers also took advantage of this spur to ship their products to distant markets.[11]

The year that brought the fiftieth anniversary commemoration to Gettysburg carried news that a Lincoln Memorial Highway would be built, eventually stretching from New York City to San Francisco. From the York County border at Abbottstown, through the town square in New Oxford to Gettysburg's traffic circle and westward across Seminary Ridge, traversing the battlefield of July 1, making its way past Cashtown and then across the South Mountains to the Franklin County line and points west, the Adams County section of the concrete highway was completed in 1922. What came to be called "America's Main Street" spanned Adams County from its eastern to western border for thirty-one miles, thus officially ushering Gettysburg into the modern automotive era. Eventually, the Adams County section of the highway would be part of U.S. Route 30.[12]

After the Civil War, the majority of Adams County voters tended to cast their ballots for the Democratic presidential candidate. Even the war hero Ulysses S. Grant, who had toured the Gettysburg Battlefield and National Cemetery in 1867 as the 1868 Republican candidate, did not receive the majority of Adams County's votes in that year's election. Then, as the incumbent running against Horace Greeley in 1872, Grant garnered only 51.4 percent of the county's vote. (Grant probably got the majority of the popular vote in Adams County that year because Greeley, the Democratic candidate, also was the candidate of the Liberal Republicans, a minor third party.) In fact, in only three of twelve presidential elections between 1868 and 1912 did Adams County voters cast their majority for the Republican candidate: Grant in 1872, William McKinley in 1896, and Teddy Roosevelt in 1904. In 1912, Teddy and the new, short-lived Progressive Party hurt Republican incumbent William Howard Taft in the national election, ensuring a victory for Woodrow Wilson. In Adams County, Taft received only 11 percent of the votes. Historian Robert Bloom concluded that the 1912 election "was the nadir of Republican strength in any Adams County election." Nonetheless, because of Roosevelt and his Bull Moose followers, Wilson received only a 51 percent majority in the county. Between the Civil War and the Great War, Democratic gubernatorial candidates normally could count on Adams County's support as well—except for in 1894, when a terrible recession that had begun in the previous year hurt the Democrats nationwide. In local elections during the same period, Democrats carried 70 percent of the voters; most of these contests, however, were won before 1890. The next year, Republicans began to make steady progress at the local level of government. By 1906, eleven county towns had become boroughs and exercised their own self-government of local affairs.[13]

Despite these political changes, by the time of the Great War, Gettysburg remained the only town in the county of appreciable size. By 1860, gas streetlights illuminated its thoroughfares. When a power plant was built in the borough in 1893, electric streetlights began replacing other forms of public illumination, yet it would be another two decades before electric lighting appeared in people's homes, unless they owned their own electrical generators. Gettysburg had boasted a public water system since 1823; sixty years later a reservoir was constructed on East Cemetery Hill to deliver improved water pressure, but private wells still provided some of the residents' water supply, although this water was not always potable. Sewage was another issue that local government attempted to solve. Outhouses and cesspools were numerous within the town's borders at the turn of the century, and the problem would not be remedied until just before the Great War. By 1913, Gettysburg and eleven other Adams

County communities had volunteer fire companies, but none were yet in possession of automotive fire engines. Using a horse-drawn steam engine, Gettysburg's volunteer firemen could pump water from forty fire hydrants that had been installed at strategic locations on borough streets. For fires higher than one story, the department also owned a hook and ladder.[14] Adams County had a sheriff's department, with an elected sheriff; it provided the only local law enforcement in the county until Gettysburg's police department began operations in 1909, with a chief and two officers.[15] Although the Pennsylvania State Police had been organized in 1905, its geographical areas of responsibility were situated primarily in the coal- and steel-producing regions, but during the 1913 reunion it had a large presence—150 troopers—both for ceremonial duties and law enforcement. (In fact, three of the state troopers detailed to the semicentennial event were Gettysburg natives, and all three were veterans of the Regular Army.[16]) Lawbreakers sentenced to jail time were incarcerated in the Adams County Jail on East High Street, which had been in service since 1851. Indigent citizens were housed at the Adams County Almshouse and its farm complex just north of town on the Harrisburg Road.[17]

The county could also boast its fair share of lawyers, educators, dentists, and physicians. Most of the lawyers' offices were in Gettysburg, where the courthouse was located, but medical practices were spread across the county—by 1880 there were fifty-nine physicians countywide and three Gettysburg dentists. No hospital existed in Adams County before the World War, however. Patients requiring surgery or other serious treatment were forced to travel to hospitals in Harrisburg (opened in 1873); York (1880); Chambersburg (1895); or Frederick, Maryland (1902). A majority of the county's towns and hamlets also had their own post offices, and in 1900 the Rural Free Delivery (RFD) began operations; by 1907 Adams County had nine RFD routes. with 3,139 names receiving mail in this fashion. By 1911, forty-one post offices, including two RFD stations, were in operation in Adams County. Also in 1911, Congress funded a new federal building to house the Gettysburg post office and other federal agencies, with hopes that it would be operational by the 1913 reunion. Construction delays, however, postponed its grand opening until February 26, 1914. About the same time, two telephone companies were competing for customers in Gettysburg borough.[18] For residents wishing to get their news by means other than gossip, they could read one of three weekly Gettysburg newspapers, the *Star and Sentinel, Adams County News,* and *Gettysburg Compiler,* or the *Gettysburg Times,* a daily paper; in the outlying communities citizens had available the *New Oxford Item, East Berlin Record,* and *York Springs Comet,* all published once a week.[19]

Although the county infrastructure was modernizing, it was not due to increased population. The largest growth came between 1870 and 1880, with the number of citizens increasing from about 30,000 to approximately 34,000. For the next several decades, there was only a slight change in demographics: the black population actually decreased, from 565 in 1870 to 471 in 1880, dropping dramatically to 319 in 1890, then slightly increasing to 338 in 1900, and decreasing again to 325 in 1910.[20] These statistics foreshadowed the Great Migration of American blacks to the large northern urban centers that began in 1915 and continued for the next five and a half decades.

Primary and secondary education in Adams County after the Civil War was characterized by the traditional one-room schoolhouses that remained in use through the first decades of the twentieth century. Although Progressive education brought great changes across the United States, especially in more populated areas, Adams County was slow to adapt. Nonetheless, teacher professional development had improved in the decades between the Civil War and the Great War, as had teacher salaries. Still, the great majority of teachers were not college graduates. African American students were segregated into their own primary school in Gettysburg that survived through the first decades of the twentieth century. It provided students with up to sixth-grade educations, as did public schools for white students. The Commonwealth's School Law of 1895 brought change to Pennsylvania and Adams County, especially regarding secondary schooling for white students. Gettysburg High School was a little ahead of the Pennsylvania mandate, however, graduating its first class in 1887, with a total of ten students. By the time of the United States' entry into the World War, eight high schools—for white students—were in existence in the county, Gettysburg High School having the largest student population. In agrarian northern Adams County, citizens pushed for a high school that stressed vocational training along with the normal academic curriculum; this came to fruition in 1917. Thus, Adams County youth who served in the military or its support agencies during the Great War were better educated than those who had fought some fifty years earlier.[21]

Gettysburg was unique among most rural Pennsylvania communities on the eve of the Great War in that it was the home to two institutions of higher education, the Lutheran Theological Seminary and Pennsylvania College. The Lutheran Seminary, founded in 1826, was the oldest of its kind in the United States. Pennsylvania College was created six years later, initially as a preparatory school for young men who wanted to enter the seminary but were found wanting in basic academic subjects. Both schools remained open during the Civil War, and their buildings served as temporary hospitals during the 1863 battle. By the 1890s, the Lutheran Seminary was the largest of its kind in the

Valentine Hall, Gettysburg Lutheran Seminary in 1903 (Library of Congress)

United States, and on the eve of the Great War Pennsylvania College had an enrollment of several hundred students. (Women had been admitted to the school as early as 1888.) Then, in 1911, the college's curriculum was broadened from its liberal arts roots to include a general engineering department. The presence of these two institutions undoubtedly helped to shape the collective character of the community but, as Robert Bloom noted, "Adams Countians may have taken for granted the cultural distinction brought the community by the presence of the Seminary and College."[22]

The presence of the Lutheran Seminary likewise symbolized the strong hold that German Protestant faiths had on Gettysburg and Adams County. By the time of the Great War, some 60 percent of the county's congregations were Lutheran or Reformed. The Roman Catholic Church, however, grew in strength after the Civil War. By the end of the next conflict, about 25 percent of the churchgoing population in Adams County was Catholic, while the remaining 15 percent of the faithful attended other Protestant services. Those of Eastern Orthodox and Jewish faiths did not have the strength in numbers for their own churches or synagogues.[23] In direct consequence of the Battle of Gettysburg, one church structure is unlike any other in the county. The Memorial Church of the Prince of Peace in Gettysburg was the brainchild of Union and Confederate veterans attending the twenty-fifth anniversary commemoration, in 1888. The *Official Program of the Army of the Potomac and the Army of Northern Virginia* called for a structure "to be named the National Memorial Church of the Prince of Peace . . . [on] whose loving unity the terrible events of the Civil War made no mark, is surely the one above all others to embrace the memorials of both sides in rearing a lasting Temple to the Prince of Peace." Situated on the corner of Baltimore and West High streets, in July 1900 the Episcopal church opened its doors for its first worship services.[24]

Two of the most significant pieces of federal legislation to affect Gettysburg and its nearby communities were the passage of bills that together led to the creation of Gettysburg National Military Park (GNMP). The first of these, signed into law on May 25, 1893, appropriated federal dollars for marking the battlefield with permanent tablets and upgrading existing tour roads. The law also specified that both Union and Confederate positions would be marked. Finally, it created a three-man commission to oversee the work. The law did not, however, make the battlefield a national park. The commission included John Bachelder of the GBMA; Lt. Col. John B. Nicolson, a Union veteran of the

Prince of Peace Episcopal Church, image circa 1900–1906 (Library of Congress)

battle and also a member of the GBMA; and former Confederate brigadier general William H. Forney, who had been wounded and captured at Gettysburg. (Forney passed away in 1894 and was replaced by Maj. William P. Robbins, a Gettysburg veteran of the 4th Alabama Infantry.) Secretary of War Daniel Lamont, to whom they reported, directed the commissioners to stay within their $25,000 budget, permanently mark the lines of battle, buy only small tracts of land where the fighting actually occurred, and elect a chairman. Nicholson was made chairman, and staff and laborers were hired to carry out the mission. The most significant of the initial employees were Emmor B. Cope and his assistant, S. A. Hammond, whose major task was to survey the battlefield. (Cope was a Union veteran who had been given the mission—soon after the battle by none other than George Meade himself—to map the field of conflict.) The commission set aside funds to rent a room in Gettysburg where Cope and Hammond could conduct their work.[25]

The commission's major problem in its first year was the threat posed to the historic landscape by the trolley—the Gettysburg Electric Railway Company, which began construction of its line the same year the commission was created. The commission's powers, however, were limited, and it would be up to Congress and the attorney general of the United States to take the necessary measures to begin condemnation of the railway in the name of historic preservation. Predictably, the case soon became tied up in the courts.[26]

The legal proceedings did not deter the Gettysburg Commission or the work of Emmor Cope and his assistant, who within months of their employment had drawn an accurate map (indicating troop positions) and determined the best routes for access roads. Several tracts of battlefield land also were purchased, and the GBMA's board voted to donate its holdings to the U.S. government. Meanwhile, Secretary Lamont pressed Congress to pass legislation that would make the battlefield a national park, just as Chickamauga and Chattanooga and Shiloh had been given National Military Park status in 1890 and 1894. To the rescue came one of the Army of Potomac's corps commanders, Maj. Gen. Daniel Sickles. Commanding the Third Corps at the Battle of Gettysburg, Sickles had moved his troops without authorization on July 2 and nearly caused a disaster of epic proportions. He lost his leg during the fight, and only prompt reinforcement by elements of the Second and Fifth Corps saved the day. In 1892, Sickles, then serving as chairman of the New York State Monuments Commission, ran for election in New York's Tenth Congressional District. But unlike his July 2 performance so many years earlier, Sickles was successful, and soon after taking office he championed the idea of making Gettysburg a national park, in late 1894 introducing legislation to do just that. His bill passed both houses in early 1895,

Congressman Daniel Sickles, D-NY, circa 1902 (Library of Congress)

and President Grover Cleveland signed it into law on February 11, thus making the Gettysburg battlefield the third National Military Park.[27]

The new law served as the authority to acquire the land already in the possession of the GBMA (in exchange for paying the organization's debts) as well as other important tracts related to the battle. Non-GBMA land would be either purchased from willing sellers or condemned. The law also authorized the formation of the GNMP Commission under the auspices of the War Department, to oversee and manage the park's operations. (The members of the previous commission filled the positions of the GNMP Commission.) Penalties also were specified for persons committing acts of vandalism, taking relics, disturbing natural resources (such as hunting, fishing, and cutting down trees), and defacing or removing breastworks and monuments. Likewise, the law directed the commission to continue marking and interpreting the battlefield and building roads in the park. With a $75,000 initial appropriation to accomplish these tasks, the commission was given the additional responsibility of erecting a monument to commemorate the Gettysburg Address.[28]

Meanwhile the courts continued to adjudicate the case against the Gettysburg Electric Railway Company, which by the time of the park's creation was on the desk of the U.S. District Court. That court eventually ruled in favor of the railway company. U.S attorneys appealed to the Supreme Court, which heard the case on January 8 and 9, 1896. On January 27 of the same year, in *United States v. Gettysburg Electric Railway Co.*, the justices reversed the lower court's verdict and ruled in favor of the government, a landmark decision for historic preservation that set a precedent for public condemnation of private property by right of eminent domain—specifically historically significant land—that was deemed to be in the public interest. Most importantly, Justice Rufus Wheeler Peckham opined:

> Can it be that the government is without power to preserve the land, and properly mark out the various sites upon which this struggle took place? Can it not erect the monuments provided for by these acts of Congress or even take possession of the field of battle, in the name and for the benefit of all the citizens of the country, for the present and for the future? Such a use seems necessarily not only a public use, but one so closely connected with the welfare of the republic itself as to be within the powers granted Congress by the constitution for the purpose of protecting and preserving the whole country.[29]

Despite the unanimous ruling, the Gettysburg Electric Railway continued trolley operations on the battlefield until the advent of the automobile made the business economically unfeasible. The company folded in November 1916, twenty years after the Supreme Court decision.[30]

In 1896 Congress passed another law that would affect the new military parks, especially Chickamauga and Gettysburg. The legislation provided for the military parks' use for training by the Regular Army and the National Guard.[31] Two years after this law's passage, Congress declared war on Spain, ostensibly because of Spanish treatment of Cuban revolutionaries but also because of the alleged Spanish involvement in the sinking of the battleship USS *Maine* in Havana Harbor. To prepare its regulars and national guardsmen for combat, acclimate them to the heat of a Caribbean summer, and locate them relatively close to the port of embarkation (Tampa, Florida), the War Department established Camp Thomas on Chickamauga National Military Park in the northwest corner of Georgia.

Named for the Union hero of that battle, Maj. Gen. George H. Thomas, who had earned the nickname "The Rock of Chickamauga" for his corps' stand on Snodgrass Hill on September 20, 1863, the camp became a major cantonment for troops destined for the war zone. Camp Thomas was only in existence for a few months—the peace treaty was signed in December—but it set a precedent for the use of military parks as transient army training grounds during times of national emergency. The camp also caused a severe short-term environmental impact on the historic site and its associated cultural resources from the presence of nearly seventy-one thousand soldiers and more than fifteen thousand horses and mules. In addition, the proximity of so many men and animals in a relatively small area led to the onset of disease, particularly typhoid fever. Before the war came to an end, 761 soldiers had perished at Camp Thomas from typhoid, more than the total of U.S. combat fatalities during the war itself, and 48 percent of all U.S. military deaths from that particular disease during the conflict.[32]

The chairman of the Chickamauga and Chattanooga National Military Park Commission, Henry V. Boynton, reported that "the park was left in a most filthy and deplorable condition by the outgoing troops so far as unfilled sinks in many camps and unburned refuse of various kinds could defile it."[33] The park eventually was restored to its prewar condition, but at a cost of more than $14,000. After the conflict, troops remained in the area, in 1904 establishing Fort Oglethorpe, which provided maneuver, training, and cantonment space for National Guard and Regular Army units from the time of its creation through the end of the Great War. Approximately sixty thousand doughboys trained at Fort Oglethorpe and its sub-posts during that conflict, once again causing significant temporary damage to the cultural resources and park infrastructure.[34]

Long before the Chickamauga Battlefield was used as a training area, the fields surrounding the town of Gettysburg were employed for the same purposes. The first time a large body of troops "invaded" Gettysburg after the war was when the Pennsylvania National Guard went into division camp at Gettysburg for seven days in 1884. Camped on the battlefield, the part-time soldiers were reviewed by Gen. Phil Sheridan, a Civil War legend in his own right, in 1884 the commanding general of the U.S. Army.[35]

The Pennsylvania National Guard, and sometimes Regular Army units assisting with the commemoration of various monument commemorations, camped or trained at Gettysburg on several more occasions during the rest of the nineteenth century and into the early years of the twentieth. Once in a while, the presence of guard units had little to do with training. In 1889 a Guard regiment from the Johnstown area went to Gettysburg to support the veterans' encampment of the Grand Army of the Republic. Because they had lost most of their arms and equipment in the great Johnstown Flood, these guardsmen could not attend regular summer maneuvers with the rest of the state forces.[36]

The first appearance of a large force of Regulars at Gettysburg was not until 1894, the same year Congress began the legislative process of creating a park, when elements of the active Army went into camp with the Pennsylvania National Guard. According to an early historian of the Guard, "The Cavalry and artillery were encamped with Regular Army artillery on the east side of the

Taneytown Road. General Headquarters and the rest of the troops were on Seminary Ridge on the same ground occupied by General Lee's forces during the Battle of Gettysburg."[37] Regulars, guardsmen from several states, and even U.S. Marine Corps officers used GNMP and surrounding private farmland for training and "outdoor classrooms" into the early years of the twentieth century.[38] Unlike, Chickamauga, however, Gettysburg National Military Park would not become a training area during the War with Spain in 1898.

Around the turn of the century, cadets from the U.S. Military Academy began making the five-hundred-mile round trip to Gettysburg during the spring of their senior year. This staff ride, made by the entire First Class of the Corps of Cadets, became an annual occurrence and lasted through 1916. During these excursions, cadets studied the lay of the land, analyzed the strategy of commanders, and evaluated unit tactics through the use of terrain walks and guided tours. For a bird's-eye view of the field, they could ascend one of five steel observation towers that had been constructed under War Department contract, with the original intent that senior officers visiting from the National War College in Washington could study the battle in greater detail during their own field trips.[39]

Cadets who visited the park during these early years of the twentieth century included many future commanders of World Wars I and II and the Korean War, such as "Vinegar Joe" Stillwell, Henry "Hap" Arnold, James Van Fleet, Omar Bradley and of course Patton and Eisenhower. Some officers from these classes would pay the ultimate price of patriotism, just as their predecessors had done at Gettysburg only a few decades earlier. In 1905 one cadet wrote: "The [trips] have taught us many things which are not in the books and which some of us never would have learned otherwise."[40] The last staff ride of that era was in May 1916. The next year, the U.S. Army and West Point were too preoccupied with mobilizing for war.

In the years between the end of the sectional conflict and America's declaration of war against Imperial Germany, Gettysburg had evolved from an obscure county seat to a town of national and international renown. It had not modernized as rapidly as nearby major urban centers, notably Baltimore, Philadelphia, and Pittsburgh, but it most certainly had felt the change brought about by Progressive Era legislation, especially federal laws that allowed a national income tax; regulated the banking industry, permitted federal inspection of meat products and forbade commerce in adulterated food and poisonous patent medicines, and regulated the railroads. Gettysburg also felt the increased presence of the federal government when Gettysburg National Military Park was created, and a Supreme Court decision focusing on a Gettysburg commercial interest set a precedent for the U.S. government to condemn private property if it was in the interests of the American people. Thus, the people of Adams County were becoming accustomed to the federal government's amplified role in their lives, perhaps even more so than the nearby cities, at least on a per-capita basis. Nonetheless, when the Great War exploded in Europe and spread to much of the rest of the world, Adams County residents, with their universally celebrated county seat, still could bask in their rural environment, which was relatively isolated from the bustle of its urban counterparts and all the concurrent problems associated with city life. The only war they were concerned about was the one that had been fought in their own backyards a half century earlier. They would have only three more years to enjoy peacetime and their small-town lifestyle, for war once again was coming their way.

CHAPTER TWO

"The Whole Structure Crumbles"

Gettysburg and the World, 1914–1917

"Humanity is the keystone that holds nations and men together," Atheltics' coach Connie Mack once said. "When that collapses, the whole structure crumbles. This is as true of baseball teams as any other pursuit in life." Mack and his lineup certainly held their stuff together in 1914, slugging, fielding, and pitching their way to another American League championship. Their closest competitor, the Boston Red Sox, finished eight and a half games behind in the standings. Gettysburg Eddie, despite turning thirty-nine years old in August of that year, still was in top form, finishing the regular season with fifteen wins and seven losses, for a winning percentage of .682. Also in baseball that year, George Herman Ruth, a native of nearby Baltimore, began his professional career in the minors with the hometown Orioles of the International League. He was elevated to the Red Sox in July and helped them to their second-place finish.[1] By the time the "Babe" had donned his Boston uniform, Europe and its empires were on the precipice of war. To paraphrase Connie Mack, the keystone of humanity was being chiseled away, and the whole structure was crumbling.

On April 8, the *Gettysburg Times* ran a front-page headline exclaiming: "Cadets Coming in Early May: Senior Class of the Military Academy at West Point Will Visit Gettysburg May Fourth and Fifth to Make Study of the Field." Arriving on a special train from the Hudson River Valley, the cadets were scheduled to tour and study the battlefield for a day and a half before returning to the Academy. Once they were back in their West Point barracks, reported the *Times*, "the cadets write criticisms of the conduct of the Gettysburg fight with suggestions on the conduct of the same battle according to the development of the war game and the practices of modern warfare." In past years, according to the newspaper, "One of the pleasant features of the trip . . . ha[d] been the game of baseball between the coming defenders of the country and the local college nine." The home team could not host the cadets in 1914, however, as it had a game already scheduled against the University of Pittsburgh.

Though Adams County residents and middle-class America might have been looking forward to the new baseball season that April, events in war-torn Mexico were drawing the United States closer to a possible conflict with its southern neighbor. On April 2, 1914, the American gunboat USS *Dolphin* steamed into the harbor of Tampico and fired several twenty-one-gun salutes to the Mexican flag, an honorable gesture, considering the ongoing internal turmoil in that country and especially since Woodrow Wilson still was angry about the military coup that had elevated Gen. Victoriana Huerta to dictator the previous year. Wilson even had removed the American ambassador the previous July for recognizing Huerta as the president of Mexico.

Then on April 9, crew members of the *Dolphin,* on an official assignment to procure fuel, were arrested in Tampico by Huerta's soldiers, setting the stage for a diplomatic confrontation. The American commander on the scene called for an apology and insisted that Mexican batteries fire a salute to the American flag, among other demands. The *Gettysburg Times,* which had been keeping its readers informed of the ongoing turmoil in Mexico, reported the incident in its April 14 edition. "Must Salute Flag Says the President," ran the headline on page 2. Four days later, it printed a story titled "Town Boys on Way to Mexico," listing the men from Gettysburg and the rest of the county who were serving on ships that at that time were steaming toward Mexico—four sailors and three marines were included in the group. In addition, the article mentioned that one Adams County citizen was then serving in the army on the Texas border.

Meanwhile, the Mexican government apologized, but the Huerta regime refused to salute the national colors, so on April 20 Wilson asked Congress for permission to use military force: "I come to ask your approval that I should use the armed forces of the United States in such ways and to such an extent as may be necessary to obtain from Huerta and adherents the fullest recognition of the rights and dignity of the United States, even admit the distressing conditions now unhappily obtaining in Mexico." The *Times* ran the headline, "General Huerta Refuses to Salute Flag: Wilson Asks Congress for Power. War Seems Certain. More Warships Go South to Join Fleet." It later announced that it had discovered that other men from the area were serving on the Mexican border or in the fleet heading for the Mexican Gulf Coast. Two were graduates of the college, one now a captain in Texas with the 4th U.S. Infantry, the other a surgeon on the USS *Des Moines*. One enlisted sailor from the county also was discovered to be in hostile waters, on the battleship *Minnesota*.[2]

On April 22, after deliberation, Congress granted Wilson his request to use military force. In reality, the Germans had been supplying arms and ammunition to Huerta and his government, and now Wilson had an alibi to invade and cut off the weapons trade. While Congress debated, marines and naval landing forces stormed the major port of Veracruz on April 21, where a German merchant ship with a cargo of arms was headed, and casualties (one hundred U.S., five hundred Mexican) were taken on both sides. A *Gettysburg Times* headline for April 23 declared, "Vera Cruz Is Held by Marines: Mexicans Driven from Seaport." The *Star and Sentinel* ran a similar page 1 headline but also noted in the accompanying article, "The approaching arrival of ammunition for Huerta on a German ship was responsible for action without waiting for Congress." Moreover, the *Times* also reported that a large U.S. force was mobilizing to invade the country and in a headline on April 24 announced, "College Boys to Respond to Call: Mexican War Arouses Patriotic Spirit at College and a Call for Volunteers Has Been Issued." Sgt. Adolph Weidenbach, who as a soldier in the 5th U.S. Infantry had been present at the fiftieth anniversary of the battle the summer before, was now a student at Gettysburg College. "He will give the students the regular training, prescribed by the army for recruits," the reporter noted, "with which he is thoroughly familiar." But the students' services would not be required. The marines and sailors captured the customs house, and an army brigade arrived to bolster the naval force. During most of the crisis, the *Times* not only ran daily stories about the ongoing events at Veracruz, but also highlighted the top navy, marine, and army commanders in Mexico and the senior staff officers in Washington, complete with photographs. The Americans remained in Veracruz through November. In the meantime, Venustiano Carranza replaced Huerta, but relations between the United States and Mexico remained strained. Carranza, also not happy with the American intervention, would be plagued by his own internal problems, including a revolt by a former Mexican general nicknamed Pancho Villa. A few months later, Villa would bring problems to the Wilson administration as well.[3]

If things *had* gotten out of hand in Mexico, National Guard units from across the nation would have been mobilized to augment the Regular Army and safeguard the international border. Gettysburg residents had witnessed summer training of the Pennsylvania National Guard even before the creation of Gettysburg National Military Park (GNMP), but the Guard would be absent the summer of 1914. The April 16 edition of the *Times* announced, "No Camp Here This Summer: National Guard Will Not Camp as a Division, Part Going into

Big Maneuvers and Balance Camping as Separate Brigades." In the years since the establishment of GNMP, the old battlefield had hosted the Guard's divisional maneuvers, not just on government property but on privately owned land as well. An early historian of the Pennsylvania National Guard later wrote about the 1908 Gettysburg divisional encampment: "Brigades were given opportunity to maneuver independently and on separate ground, 3,600 acres having been tendered free by the owners." In 1910 and 1912, divisional maneuvers again were held in Gettysburg.[4] However, not even a war against Mexico would have brought a return of the guardsmen to Adams County for mobilization, because plans already had been made to ship all National Guard property, which for several years had been stored in Gettysburg, to the Pennsylvania National Guard training facility at Camp Gretna, in Lebanon County. Even the timber-framed storage building, located on the battlefield along the Round Top Branch rail line, was razed and transported to Mt. Gretna, where it was rebuilt. By the autumn of 1914, the transfer of supplies, equipment, and building materials had been completed.[5]

In Europe that spring, the Germans and British continued expanding their battle fleets, in what came to be called the "naval race"; the German general staff fine-tuned the Schlieffen Plan, its military strategy for waging a two-front war; and the Serbian government gave its tacit support to the Black Hand terrorist organization, a committed group of Serbian nationalists determined to unite all Serbs, including those in Bosnia, then under the rule of Austria-Hungary.[6] Of far less consequence but nonetheless significant to the people of Gettysburg and the remaining veterans of the Army of the Potomac, Joshua Chamberlain, Civil War general and renowned hero of Little Round Top, former Maine governor, and retired Bowdoin College professor and president, had died in Portland, Maine, on February 24, 1914, most likely of complications from his wartime wounds. It had been nearly fifty-one years since, on the rocky hill a few miles south of Gettysburg, Chamberlain had performed the feats of courage and leadership that eventually garnered him the Medal of Honor.[7] Also in 1914, several new monuments were placed on or near the battlefield, including a bronze memorial statue for New York's James Wadsworth, commander of the First Division, First Corps, as well as markers designating Union hospital sites.[8] Most of the Union regimental markers had been erected in the late 1880s and early 1890s, but monument construction would continue through the Great War and beyond, especially those memorializing the Confederates. As war clouds appeared on the far side of the Atlantic, America continued to look backward to remember its soldiers from an earlier conflict.

Then everything unraveled in Europe. On June 28, 1914, Black Hand militants assassinated Archduke Franz Ferdinand and his wife, Sophie, in Sarajevo, Bosnia.

Among its many demands on the little Balkan country, Austria-Hungary called for an apology. The Serbs met most, but both nations immediately mobilized their armed forces. On July 28, Austria-Hungary declared war, and the fighting erupted. Then, Europe's capricious alliance system went into effect. Serbia allied with Russia, Austria-Hungary with Germany, and France with Russia. Russia mobilized its huge army in support of Serbia. Germany's Schlieffen Plan depended on rapid mobilization of its own armed forces. Its blueprint for a two-front war—against France and Russia—relied on railroad-system timetables to shuffle troops to the war fronts and from one theater to another. With so much at stake and with so many pieces that had to fall into place, Germany mobilized, intent on defeating France first and dealing with the Russians afterward. The French, still reeling from the aftermath of their 1870 war against Germany, and thus fearing another attack and yet loss of more territory, prepared their forces to implement Plan XVII, which called for a preemptive assault to regain the lost provinces of Alsace and Lorraine. The United Kingdom was committed to ensuring Belgian neutrality, which most assuredly would be violated when Germany set in motion the first part of the Schlieffen Plan. If Britain was sucked into a conflict, its dominions also would be, including Canada, Australia, New Zealand, and South Africa, as well as the United Kingdom's most important colony, an undivided India.[9] The United States, insulated by two oceans and thousands of miles of distance, watched and waited. And then it happened.

The *Adams County News* reported on August 1, 1914, "Declared Mobilization Could Not Be Stopped." Also that day, the *Gettysburg Times* ran its standard local stories on page 1, but headlining the international section on page 2 were the attention-grabbing lines: "GERMANY ARMS; RUSSIA MOBILIZING. THE KAISER DECLARES MARTIAL LAW. GENERAL WAR CERTAIN. CZAR AND GERMAN AMBASSADOR CONFER. SERBS HOLD AUSTRIANS." After the initial confrontations between the Serbians and Austro-Hungarians, the first big battles on what became the Eastern Front and Western Front began in August. The weekly paper *New Oxford Item*, published in eastern Adams County, exclaimed, "The Hostile Armies Ready to Grapple: Germans Move Forward in Belgium." Fighting broke out when the Belgians resisted the German invasion. Next, France attacked Alsace and Lorraine, but German machine guns and field artillery slaughtered its soldiers. To the north, the large Belgian fortress cities began to fall, one by one, to large-caliber German artillery, Krupp howitzers, and Skoda siege mortars. The British sent a military expedition across the English Channel and put up a heroic defense alongside the Belgian field army. On August 22, the French army suffered some twenty-two thousand killed in action in two separate but related battles while the next day the British Expeditionary Force (BEF) tenaciously defended Mons, Belgium. The *Item* announced in its August 27 issue, "Allies Are Driven Back into France: Germans Win First Big Battle."[10]

Meanwhile, the British dominions and colonies mobilized their forces. Next, the oceans became battlegrounds, as did the European powers' African colonies. Japan, hoping to expand its own Pacific empire, declared war on Germany on August 23, the same day as the Battle of Mons. The German 8th Army staged a holding action on the Eastern Front against the Russians, hoping to keep its foes at bay until France and Britain were defeated on the Western Front. Despite Russia's initial advantages, the Germans inflicted a major defeat on the Czar's armies at the battles of Masurian Lakes and Tannenberg in late August, almost annihilating the Russian 2d Army. Afterward, both sides dug trenches and the front stabilized. Back in France, the Germans nearly succeeded in taking Paris but were stymied at the Marne River, about twenty miles east of the City of Light. Then, in a series of maneuvers intended to outflank their opponents, the contending forces slashed toward the North Sea. By November, the Allies and Germans had reached a standstill.

As on the Eastern Front, trenches appeared in Belgium and France. The Germans, intending to hold their gains, built strong defenses. The French, Belgian, and British, hoping to regain the offensive and recapture lost territory, constructed trenches that were not quite as sound and dry as they should have been, as they were not intending to occupy them for very long. And because the Germans had taken most of the ridges, hills, and high ground (what little there was, especially in Flanders), their trenches, for the most part, were much drier and more habitable than those of the Allies. (The area between the opposing lines came to be known as "no-man's-land," a new military term now added to the English-speaking lexicon.) Then, also in November, Turkey entered the war on the side of the Central Powers, thus opening yet other military fronts from the Middle East to the Turkish Caucasus bordering Russia. By November 7, 1914, the German colony of Tsingtao, China, had fallen to a combined British-Japanese force. In the Balkans, back where it all began, the Serbian army stopped an Austro-Hungarian force, at great cost to both sides. The result, once again, was stalemate.[11]

The first Adams County man to fight in the war, though not as a soldier in the American army, grew up on Baltimore Street in Gettysburg. C. H. Allen joined the 6th U.S. Cavalry in 1889, in time to participate in the shameful massacre of the Lakota Sioux at Wounded Knee Creek, on the Pine Ridge Indian Reservation in South Dakota, in 1890. He served for more than five years on the frontier and was discharged in 1895. Then he enlisted in the Royal Artillery of the British army and fought in the Boer War in South Africa. When the Great War erupted, Allen left England with the BEF and participated in the Battle of Mons, the First Battle of the Marne, and the so-called Race to the Sea. Allen and his blokes finally settled into trench warfare near Ypres, Belgium in November. Another Adams County native, forty-year-old Mary Katherine "Kate" Wolf, originally from the Cashtown area, just west of Gettysburg, was a trained nurse working in New York City in 1914 when the war began. She soon volunteered for overseas duty, sailed for France in September, and served at the American Ambulance Hospital (a volunteer organization of American doctors, nurses, ambulance drivers, and administrators) in Paris, just in time to care for French and British soldiers wounded in the First Battle of the Marne.[12]

The *Gettysburg Compiler*, a Democratic Party newspaper, which seemed more preoccupied with local news and domestic politics, did not mention the outbreak of war until its August 15 issue, when it printed a summary of events titled "Progress of the War," covering the diplomatic and military headlines from the Archduke's assassination on June 28 through the opening military movements up to August 15. An editorial in an adjacent column included a political cartoon depicting the Republican elephant and Democratic donkey peacefully grazing in a meadow, with the words "PARTY UNITY" superimposed in the grass. The cartoon's title was "Good Pastures: Watchful Waiting—An Example to the World." Concerning the outbreak of the European War, the writer postulated,

> The world is aghast at the spectacle of destruction that looms in Europe. . . . All because proud rulers and vain diplomats had not the patience or the fortitude to submerge selfish ambitions and racial prejudices until the first burst of angry passion could abate. . . . Contrast the outcome of European diplomacy and the attitude of European government at this critical time with the calm, patient, forward-looking policy of the American government under the trying conditions of the Mexican crisis. . . . A single lapse from the high ideals and upright purpose of the patient man in the White House . . . would have plunged half this hemisphere into bloody strife and would have caused sorrows and losses and entanglement and problems that baffle the imagination.

Not really. Wilson used the affront at Tampico to enforce the Monroe Doctrine and thus curb German influence in Mexico. As in 1846–47, the Mexicans were no match for the Americans, and the Mexicans knew it. Wilson was just as belligerent and proud as the European leaders whom the editor had blasted, but he was characterized as the moral, upstanding "patient man in the White House." Most especially he was a Democrat—like the *Compiler*'s editors.

The allusion to "racial prejudices" was not, however, a reference to skin color. Instead, the editors were suggesting that Austrians felt superior to Serbs; Germans believed they were more racially and morally pure than the French, Belgians, and Russians; and all European white folks thought they were better than those people who lived in their own African, Asian, Pacific, and Caribbean colonies. Americans were no better in this regard. Wilson and his administration's actions toward Mexico and its "white man's burden" attitude toward its colonial residents in the Philippines, Puerto Rico, Guam, Hawaii, and other possessions is ample evidence that Americans were just as prejudiced as citizens of the Old World—to say nothing of the U.S. government's treatment of its own indigenous population and the second-class status it assigned its black citizens.

Moreover, the white people of Gettysburg and Adams County were no more virtuous than the majority of the rest of the country—despite having experienced a momentous battle in a victorious war that led to passage of the Thirteenth, Fourteenth, and Fifteenth Amendments. Gettysburg's school system was segregated; it had its own black ghetto—several square blocks surrounding the intersection of South Washington and Breckinridge Streets. Further, it had a separate cemetery for its black citizens. (But unlike U.S. National Cemeteries in the South, Gettysburg's Soldiers' National Cemetery was not segregated by race.) Pennsylvania outlawed educational segregation in 1881, and in 1887, the Commonwealth passed legislation that prohibited segregation in public accommodations, but communities across the state, including Gettysburg, generally ignored both laws.[13] Perhaps this popular attitude was part of the reason the African American population in Adams County decreased in the last decades of the nineteenth century and first decade of the twentieth, although de facto segregation was common throughout the North.

Nonetheless, more and more outside groups of black tourists traveled to Gettysburg during the same period, most especially for emancipation celebrations sponsored by Baltimore's black GAR posts. On some excursions, which daily passenger rail transport made possible, thousands of black tourists would congregate at Gettysburg's Round Top Park, next to the Harrisburg & Gettysburg Railroad / Gettysburg Electric Railway terminal. Sometimes they went into town to revel—and got drunk, became rowdy, engaged in fights, and drew the ire of Gettysburg's white population, which stomached these excursions because it made economic sense, not because the townsfolk were racially tolerant. In his book *Gettysburg: Memory, Market, and an American Shrine* historian Jim Weeks concludes that "it was not the sacred, but the secular, aspects of Gettysburg that worked to counter racial discrimination." Baltimore's black-owned newspapers regularly chastised the African American pilgrims for their excesses, noting the bad press they had received in Gettysburg. Yet, "when propriety discouraged excursionists, the market welcomed their dollars." These outings continued through 1916 but came to an end when the United States entered the Great War.[14]

The women of Adams County, both black and white, likewise faced discrimination, although white women were held in higher esteem than their African American counterparts. As a result of the Fifteenth Amendment, black men had gained the right to vote, but on the eve of the World War women in Pennsylvania still were denied it. The *Gettysburg Compiler,* whose racially biased reporters had been quick to condemn the black excursionists' rowdy behavior in their town, nonetheless urged its readers to support women's suffrage *and* prohibition, reforms supported by Progressive politicians. As early as 1914, *Compiler* advertisements and political cartoons regularly reminded Gettysburg residents to support constitutional amendments to ban the sale and consumption of alcohol and allow women to vote. Adams County even was the adopted home of one of the most outspoken suffragists of the era, Miss Lavinia Dock, who was born in Harrisburg but lived in Graffenburg Hills, a hamlet on the county's western

Lavinia Dock (second from right) and fellow suffragettes protesting in February 1913 (Library of Congress)

fringe. Dock's militant actions in support of women's suffrage eventually landed her in the notorious women's prison in Occoquon, Virginia, along with her fellow suffragists Alice Paul and Lucy Burns.[15]

As the Great War continued into the final months of 1914, the local newspapers reported more frequently on its progress, and Adams County residents had taken notice. On November 21, the *Compiler* reported, "On last Friday afternoon a number of women of the town met in the law library of the Court House to organize a movement to collect and send material to the War Relief Committee of New York, acting under the Red Cross Society." Subcommittees were formed that were responsible for collecting or fabricating surgical bandages, bed socks, petticoats, and nightshirts. An additional committee was created to oversee knitting tasks. The organization also requested donations of clothing, yarn, muslin, linen, and other similar materials for sewing projects. "That Gettysburg will do her part in a creditable way in relief for the horrible condition in the war zone is a foregone conclusion," noted the *Compiler*'s reporter.

The autumn of 1914 was not a happy one for local baseball fans. The underdog Boston Braves had stunned Eddie Plank and his Athletics, sweeping them, four games to none, in the World Series. Although Gettysburg Eddie pitched better than any of the other Philadelphia starters in the fall classic, giving up only one run in the top of the ninth inning of game two, the A's lost the game and the series.[16] Afterward, Connie Mack was so frustrated that he broke up the Athletics and traded away his star players. Considering his age, it was no surprise that Plank was swapped, too, to the St. Louis Terriers of the new (1913), but short-lived, Federal League. Mack's rash move was so devastating that the Athletics did not appear again in postseason play until 1929—but Mack was still at the helm and would remain so for another twenty-one years.[17]

In the last week of December, as a front-page story, the *Compiler* ran a dispatch from its new, unlikely hometown hero, the volunteer nurse Kate Wolf. Under the headline "The Christmas Thought for the Nations at Awful War Is Peace on Earth," the editor opined that Wolf's letter stirred "the heart and soul to the depths to which no other answer can be given than the intense desire, the appeal for Peace on Earth." Her words illuminated the gruesome sights in a military hospital during the midst of a campaign: "When one sees these dreadful wounds one wonders how civilized men can make war on each other. How they can bring themselves to kill and mutilate their own kind. No war has ever seen such wholesale butchery as this." Because Wolf was raised in an area where one of the bloodiest battles in recent history had occurred, her impressions carried added weight. She was not exaggerating: the industrialized warfare brought by breech-loading, rapid-fire cannons, huge mortars, massed machine guns, and bolt-action rifles was unimaginable in the Civil War. And neither the Allies nor the Central Powers had yet unleashed poisonous gas.[18]

By the time Wolf wrote her letter, on December 6, 1914, the contending forces already had dug into the earth, causing a different type of misery, what one British soldier called "a troglodyte world."[19] And it brought more than just horrid living conditions. "Life in the trenches is unspeakable," she wrote. "Our first frozen foot case said he had not been able to lie down for thirteen days owing to so much water. Each batch [of casualties] now brings us frozen foot cases from the trenches." (This war coined another new medical term: "trench foot.") Wolf marveled at the spectrum of races and nationalities among her patients, from "French, Arabs from Algeria, Tunis, and Morocco, blacks from the French Soudan, Senegals (black), and some British, with every known and hitherto unknown kind of wound." She took particular interest in one colonial soldier, a Moroccan named Abbas:

> I put Abbas in his bed and took his dirty, blood-soaked clothes off of him. I often wondered what went on in that brain back of those beady black eyes. Surely it was not for love of France that he was giving his life; an alien race and religion. The French subjects have no choice in the matter. England's Indian troops are better here because they asked to come. Abbas had shrapnel in the pelvis which was removed but nothing could control the green bug infection. The Arabs are either like children or fiends. A few days usually civilizes the fiends, though a few have remained fiends. Abbas accepted everything with true Oriental fatalism, though nothing escaped his beady eyes until the last few days.

Her description reflected the naïveté of a woman who had been raised in a rural community and dripped with the typical paternalistic, racist attitude that prevailed among whites toward non-whites in that era. Then, Wolf returned to her gruesome description of battle wounds and their treatment:

> The dental surgeons are performing miracles. Only the pictures could convince anyone what work is being done here. Some of these men come in with their jaws hanging in a mass of splintered bone and teeth. Just one case, for example. The bullet entered at the corner of the right eye next to the nose, came out under the chin. The roof of his mouth was smashed, both jaws broken so badly pieces came out, tongue pierced. [After surgery the] . . . only noticeable scars are a slight drawing down of the lower eye lid, a constant tear in that eye owing to the closing of the duct into the nose; sight same as ever, a scar under the chin and a slight impediment in speech. Have him open his mouth and you see the most

> intricate arrangement of silver plates, wires and springs, and a scarred tongue. Four weeks, that man's face was in a plaster cast, changed every week until his face was brought into proper shape—it spread out like a dish. He has been here since September and will be six months before the work is finished. He is one of the many who are more than grateful to the American Ambulance. In no military hospital is there such work done as here. That is being said by every military authority that comes here.

Adams County residents in their late fifties and older in 1914 certainly remembered men with similar wounds from the Battle of Gettysburg, but this hospital imagery would have awakened younger generations to the horrors of warfare about which they only had heard from secondhand accounts. Then, in the same newspaper column following Wolf's letter, a public announcement exclaimed, "The Community Christmas Tree is ready for the girls and boys of the town. The celebration service will start upon the arrival of Santa Claus."[20] And thus, 1914, with all of its jarring contrasts, had come to a close.

On December 25, Kate Wolf was too far from the now-stabilized Western Front to have seen the spontaneous truce that materialized the first Christmas in the trenches, but perhaps the rumors of the holiday fraternization made it to Paris by New Year's Day 1915.[21] In Gettysburg on January 2, the *Compiler* ran an unrelated news brief titled "Risks of Red Cross Work: Doctors Who Operate on the Field Under Fire Require Nerves That Are Steady," as well as another story describing "What the Horses Carry: French, German and Austrian Horses Are Taxed More Than English or Russian," and two other war-related stories.

On the front page of its February 6 issue, the newspaper printed another uncensored letter from Wolf, written on December 17, almost two months earlier. Her descriptions of the wounded continued to be heartrending. She wrote that, although the poor *"blesse"* (French for "wounded") were pleased over news that they had been given tickets for shows in the Paris theaters, they nevertheless were pitiable souls: "It was a sight to see their smiling faces but so pathetic to see the poor things, some on crutches, with and without two legs, others without an arm or an arm in a sling, others with heads bound up, everyone more or less battered, and the variety of uniforms, infantry, cavalry, zouave, etc., different regiments of zouaves have different uniforms, some red trousers, some white, some blue with gilt braid, all showing the hard service and blood stains." Nurse Wolf probably did not realize that she just as well could have been describing the sights around a field hospital in Gettysburg in July 1863—the Army of the Potomac had several Zouave regiments at the battle. She also recounted the story of an Arab soldier, whom she called a "Moor," who had lost his comrades to a huge artillery shell, labeled a "Jack Johnson" (nicknamed for the black American prize fighter who in 1914 was the reigning world champion): "He is out for revenge," Wolf surmised. "He and twenty other Moors were sitting around a soup kettle when a Jack Johnson burst, the twenty were blown to fragments, he escaped with a smashed arm and a lot of little cuts." The rest of her letter was just as disheartening.[22]

Back in Wolf's home state, the Pennsylvania Legislature was debating the merits of women's suffrage: after passing the house in February, and the senate in March, the measure was placed on the ballot as a referendum for the November election—for Pennsylvania's voters (all of whom were male) to decide. Perhaps on her return from the war zone, she might at last be allowed to vote. The *Compiler*'s editors ran a cute political cartoon on February 20 titled "GIVE MOTHER THE VOTE," featuring marching babies, with one tot even carrying a banner emblazoned "Votes for Our Mothers." The image was captioned: "Our Food Our Health Our Play Our Homes Our School Our Work Are All Regulated by Men's Votes. Think It Over!" (This upcoming vote concerned Pennsylvania women only; on January 12, the U.S. House of Representatives had rejected a proposal for nationwide women's suffrage.)

In the *Compiler*'s next issue, one of the headlines was far less important, but it was a juicy one—on page 1: "Eddie Plank Married: Announcement Is Made a Month after the Event." Eddie took as his bride a local lady, Miss Anna C. Myers of New Oxford, having tied the knot on January 20. The newspaper quoted Plank: "Yes, I am married. I suppose you will hear it all to-morrow, but I wanted to keep it a secret until I left for spring training. Mrs. Plank will meet me and go along south where we train." Spring training for the St. Louis Terriers, was in Havana, Cuba. The *Compiler* snidely noted in the last sentence of the article, "Plank is 40 and his bride is 20 years old."[23]

Before spring arrived that year, several notable events occurred in the United States. On January 28, the U.S. Coast Guard was created, when the existing Revenue Cutter Service and Life Saving Service were combined. During wartime, the Coast Guard would come under the command of the U.S. Navy, and it would play an important role in defending merchant vessels against enemy submarines—a German strategy that in early 1915 was just beginning to bear fruit.[24] Then, on February 8, D. W. Griffin's Civil War and Reconstruction–themed film, *Birth of a Nation,* premiered in Los Angeles. In it, Griffin portrayed African Americans as imbeciles or brutes, white southerners as victims, northerners as corrupt politicians and carpetbaggers and the masked thugs of the Ku Klux Klan as heroes. Despite the film's historical inaccuracy, whites widely praised it, because it conveyed middle-class America's skewed understanding of the era's history. Ironically, four days after the film's premier, the cornerstone for the Lincoln Memorial was laid in Washington. A month later, Woodrow Wilson hosted a private showing of *Birth of a Nation* in the White House, but it is unclear from the historical record whether Wilson enjoyed the film or even commented on its historical reliability.[25] (A year later, the film was shown in Gettysburg at Walter's Theater on York Street on May 1–2, 1916. Immediately afterward, the *Gettysburg Times* gave it a rave review, under the headline "A Great Picture: Gettysburg Given a Rare Treat in 'Birth of a Nation.'" The reviewer gushed: "The picture is highly spectacular, the story is intensely interesting, and the whole attraction a masterpiece which is destined not to be surpassed in the world of motion picture drama for many years to come."[26] Sadly, this view probably was typical of most white Americans who saw the movie. Either the *Times*'s reviewer was not aware of his own town's early history or he failed to make the connection: one of the "villains" of the film was Congressman Austin Stoneman, whose character was based on none other than Radical Republican Thaddeus Stevens, who had lived and worked in Gettysburg from 1816 through 1842. The film's success and its reception in Gettysburg were remembered half a year later, when Gettysburg College's Phi Kappa Psi fraternity held a masquerade ball in the college's Glatfelter Hall. It was described in the December 2, 1916, edition of the *Adams County News:* "After the guests had assembled, the members of the fraternity had left the hall for a few moments and suddenly reappeared dressed in the garb of the Ku Klux Klan. The trumpet call made famous by 'The Birth of a Nation' announced their approach and the white robed figures, with the typical helmet, made a most unusual scene. Decorations about the hall were featured by the insignia of the Ku Klux and a march about the room by the members and their guests made a very pretty sight." It is hard to imagine that at a place made famous by a bloody battle that helped to turn the tide of the war, and where a momentous speech redefined the meaning of that war, a local college fraternity could mythologize a terrorist organization.)

The arrival of spring 1915 meant a renewed season of offensives in the theaters of war, although fighting had continued through the winter months, especially in northern France. On March 10, the BEF commenced the Battle of Neuve Chapelle, near the Belgian border. Gettysburg's lone combatant at that point in the war, Sergeant Allen of the Royal Artillery, participated in the conflict's largest sustained bombardment to date, and he might have gotten a first-time look at military aircraft in action. The British military historian Martin Gilbert wrote, "At the start of the battle, 342 guns launched a thirty-five minute barrage on the German trenches, the artillery fire in part being directed by eighty-five reconnaissance aircraft. More shells were fired in that short opening barrage than in the whole Boer War, an indication of the terrifying transformation of the nature of war within a period of fifteen years."[27] For comparison, at the Battle of Gettysburg on July 3, approximately 260 cannons—U.S. and C.S. combined—blasted each other for two hours preceding Pickett's Charge, expending only a fraction of the shells fired by the British alone on March 10, 1915.

The battle lasted three days. The BEF had achieved some of its objectives and gained two kilometers of land (a little more than a mile), but it did so at great cost of life, including thousands of Indian soldiers.[28] This battle, the first large-scale fight on the Western Front that year, was not given any notice in the Gettysburg newspapers. But on April 17, the *Compiler* ran a rather bizarre story, titled "No Germs on the Firing Line: At Least Soldiers, Hourly Exposed to Death, Have One Advantage over Civilians." The article's author reported that even though soldiers were exposed to death every moment in the trenches, "infectious diseases are usually at a minimum, on the firing line, so says Col. Valery Harvard of the United States medical corps." The soldiers were tired, stressed, exposed to the elements, shelled and shot at, surrounded by filth, and usually wading in mud, "but infectious diseases are not included in this list." Since soldiers with infectious diseases were medically screened and prevented from serving in the trenches, "those on the firing line have little chance to become infected at all." This thinking would change within three years. (For now, Adams County's citizens, especially dairy farmers, livestock producers, and butchers, were more concerned about the nationwide hoof-and-mouth disease epidemic which had started in the fall of 1914. By January 1915, fourteen Adams County herds had been destroyed.)[29]

The rules of war had changed by the spring of 1915, too. On April 22, 1915, the German army unleashed chlorine gas, a choking agent, against a four-mile sector of Allied trenches near Ypres, Belgium, sending the French and their colonial frontline infantry into a frenzied retreat. With no gas masks to filter out the deadly poison, the Allied troops did not stand a chance, but the complete rout likewise surprised the Germans, who did not have enough reserves positioned nearby to follow the breakthrough. French and Canadian troops counterattacked and stopped the hemorrhage. The Allies quickly developed their own chemical warfare, and soon gas attacks became commonplace, but chemical agents did not break the stalemate of trench warfare. Later that year, the Germans employed phosgene, another choking agent, and in the summer of 1917 the Kaiser's army introduced yet another chemical, dichloroethyl sulfide, more commonly known as "mustard gas," a blister agent that, unlike the choking gasses, could linger for long periods of time.[30] (Adams County men who fought at Belleau Wood and in the Argonne Forest in 1918 experienced firsthand the horrors of *moutarde,* as the French called it.)

While nothing about the gas attacks appeared in its columns, the *Adams County News* did run a lengthy story about the fiftieth anniversary of Lee's surrender to Grant at Appomattox.[31] Then, on April 27, 1915, Italy entered the war on the Allies' side, with dreams of territorial gain should the Central Powers lose the war. The Allies had hoped that the opening of still another front, this one in the Italian Alps, would draw Austro-Hungarian and German troops away from the Eastern and Western Fronts. In the end, the Italian Front did not make much of a strategic difference elsewhere.

In the midst of these shattering military events, the senior class of the U.S. Military Academy came to Gettysburg in May 1915 for the annual staff ride. One of those cadets, among many other future general officers in that class, was a terrific varsity baseball player hailing from a small Missouri town. Thirty years later, he would be one of the few Americans ever to pin the five-star cluster on his uniform. Cadet Omar Bradley remembered, that even though the World War had been raging for ten months, "the conflict seemed remote from our cloistered world." He wrote in his autobiography,

Class of 1915, U.S. Military Academy, on the steps of Christ Lutheran Church, Chambersburg Street, Gettysburg. Cadet Omar Bradley is seated fourth row up, second from right; Cadet Eisenhower is seated third row up, just to the left of the right-side bannister. (Adams County Historical Society)

> We received no official documents or reports on the war. Everything we knew about it—and that was very little—came from newspapers and periodicals. None of the new tactics or technology employed in Europe caused the slightest change in the curriculum at West Point. We continued to study the men and campaigns of the Civil War for the most part and, as first classmen, spent three days at Gettysburg, thoroughly grounding ourselves in that battle.[32]

So, despite the history unfolding an ocean away, the West Point curriculum remained focused on past wars, with little thought about their relevance to trench combat, machine guns, and industrialized slaughter. Concerning this new style of warfare, the learning curve of the Long Gray Line's alumni and the rest of the professional officer corps would be very steep, indeed.

Regarding naval warfare, the German high command definitely was forward-thinking and had decided in early 1915 to blockade the United Kingdom with its submarines (or *unterseeboots,* which the English-speaking Allies shortened to "U-boats"). The German government even took measures, by posting notices in major U.S. newspapers, to warn possible passengers of the dangers of sailing on Allied ships destined for the British Isles. One such caution was directed at ticketholders for the Cunard Line's RMS *Lusitania.* Nonetheless, on May 7, the vessel was stuck by a single torpedo forward of the bridge. A well-known Gettysburg personality, Samuel Knox, president of the New York Shipbuilding Com-

Contemporary print of RMS *Lusitania* being hit by torpedoes off of Kinsale Head, Ireland (Library of Congress)

pany, was aboard the doomed ship. According to the *Compiler*, Knox was "one of the most prominent of the Philadelphians aboard the *Lusitania*. He went abroad alone on a mysterious errand, probably to get war orders." His brother, J. Charles Knox, lived in Gettysburg, and his sister, Kate Horner, resided a few miles to the west, in the hamlet of Knoxlyn (named for the family). Samuel Knox survived the ordeal, but nearly 1,200 other passengers perished, including 128 American citizens. All told, 61 percent of the souls on board were fatalities.[33]

The *Compiler* reprinted a cablegram Sam Knox had sent to the *Philadelphia Ledger*: "Shortly after two . . . a heavy concussion was felt on the starboard side, throwing the vessel to port. She immediately swung back and proceeded to take on a list to starboard, which rapidly increased." He noticed that the passengers remained calm, many returning to their cabins to fetch their life belts. Knox also witnessed "preparations being made to launch the [life]boats." But the ship was rapidly slipping beneath the waves. "I found the outside of the [life]boat deck practically even with the water and the ship was even farther down by the head." He got into a lifeboat, but the mechanism that lowered it into the water was stuck, and the boat could not cast off. At this point, Knox jumped. "I went overboard at once and attempted to get clear of the ship, which was coming over slowly." Then he almost lost his life. As Knox attempted to swim away from the doomed luxury liner, he recalled, "I was caught by one of the smokestacks and carried down a considerable distance before being released. On coming to the surface I floated about for a considerable time, when I was picked up by a little raft." After transferring to two other rescue craft, he finally set foot on terra firma at Queenstown, Ireland.[34] The *Lusitania* had gone down in eighteen minutes. The United States delivered a strong protest to the German government, which Adams County's newspapers printed verbatim. Three days after the sinking, President Wilson spoke in Philadelphia and proclaimed, "There is such a thing as a man being too proud to fight."[35]

Wilson's most avid apologist in Adams County, *Compiler* editor William A. McClean, wrote in the May 15 edition, the "United States has been through a wonderful experience during the past week. The nation, thrilled with the *Lusitania* horror, is exercising great self-possession. . . . The burden of steering the Ship of State is in the most capable hands and President Wilson has the confidence of the people and their support that he will do the right thing at the right moment."[36] The president made several demands in three separate notes to the German government over the next two months. The last, dated July 21, hinted that any further sinkings could result in a break of relations and possible American belligerency. Less than a month later, the British passenger liner *Arabic* was sunk, and three Americans died. (The *Arabic* was owned by the White Star Line, the same company that had owned the *Titanic.*) This time, the Germans agreed to stop attacking unarmed passenger ships without first giving a warning. At this point in the war, the Germans could ill afford to bring the Americans into the conflict.[37] On September 11, the *Compiler* printed the headline "Germany Yields to U.S. Pres[ident]. Wilson Wins Great Moral Victory. Recognized as Greatest Victory for American Diplomacy in a Generation." Wilson indeed had triumphed without going to war. Public opinion of the Germans dropped to a new low, however, and U.S. military preparedness became a national issue.

With the sinking of the *Lusitania* fresh in their minds, ordinary Americans began to question the military's ability to defend against an enemy attack from the sea. On August 7, the *Compiler* ran a story with the headline "Conditions of U.S. Army: Coast Defense Entirely Inadequate. A New Military System Needed to Effectively Protect This Country."[38] Within the next few months, an already burgeoning "preparedness campaign," spearheaded by none other than former president Teddy Roosevelt, would sweep the country. Although the *Lusitania* sinking had heightened tensions that prompted Americans to think about the efficacy of their own military and naval forces, life went on in Gettysburg and elsewhere.

The Philadelphia Athletics, minus Gettysburg Eddie and the rest of their stars, were on their way to a last-place American League finish, ending the season a whopping fifty-eight and a half games behind the first-place Red Sox. Over in the Federal League, Eddie Plank and the St. Louis Terriers would finish in a virtual tie for first place, without winning the championship, having finished .001 percent behind the Chicago Whales. It was the second and final season of the Federal League, but it also was the year Plank gained his three hundredth major-league career victory; he was the first left-handed pitcher ever to reach that milestone. (When the Federal League folded, Plank signed with the American League's St. Louis Browns.)[39]

At the height of the 1915 World Series, back at Gettysburg National Military Park, near the High Water Mark memorial, a bronze statue in memory of Brig. Gen. Alexander Webb, one of the Union heroes who bravely led a counterattack when Confederate troops broke the federal lines at the "Angle" during Pickett's Charge, was unveiled and dedicated on October 12.[40] As old veterans, politicians and townsfolk applauded the keynote speaker, events of a more momentous nature were happening a half world away, on a battlefield straddling the Dardanelles Strait in Turkey. Earlier that year, British, Australian, New Zealand, Indian, Newfoundland (a separate Dominion until 1949, when it joined Canada), and French troops had staged an amphibious assault on both sides of the strait that needed to be secured to allow free passage of Allied shipping bound for Russia's Black Sea ports. Like on the other fronts, what was called the Gallipoli campaign had bogged down in trench warfare. By autumn, the Allies decided to cut their losses, and a withdrawal began in late November. The last British and French troops were evacuated by the second week of January. On the Western Front, in December 1915, Sir Douglas Haig assumed command of the BEF in France and Belgium. Back home in Pennsylvania, voting-age men denied women of the Commonwealth the right to vote when they cast their ballots in November against the women's suffrage referendum. But, despite setbacks in 1915, the movement was gaining momentum, as was public awareness of the state of U.S. national defense. President Wilson addressed the latter topic at great length in his annual address to Congress on December 7, the entirety of which was printed in the *Compiler* four days later.

Early in his speech Wilson reminded his listeners, "We have stood apart, studiously neutral. It was our manifest duty to do so." He continued: "Not only did we have no part or interest in the policies which seem to have brought the conflict on; it was necessary, if a universal catastrophe was to be avoided, that a limit should be set to the sweep of destructive war and that some part of the great family of nations should keep the processes of peace alive, if only to prevent collective economic ruin and the breakdown throughout the world of the industries by which its populations are fed and sustained . . . if they could do nothing more." Wilson discussed the situation in Mexico (and the other Latin American countries) at great length. About its neighbor to the immediate south, he said, "We have been put to the test in the case of Mexico, and we have stood the test. Whether we have benefited Mexico by the course we have pursued remains to be seen. Her fortunes are in her own hands." But the largest part of his address was about the state of American preparedness.

Wilson then gave a short history lesson about America's reliance on a small standing army augmented by militia forces, concluding, "Our confidence has been that our safety in times of danger would lie in the rising of the nation to take care of itself, as the farmers rose at Lexington." But in the current international environment, it was time for change:

> War has never been a mere matter of men and guns. It is a thing of disciplined might. If our citizens are ever to fight effectively upon a sudden summons, they must know how modern fighting is done, and what to do when the summons comes to render themselves immediately available and immediately effective. And the government must be their servant in this matter, must supply them with the training they need to take care of themselves and of it. The military arm of their government, which they will not allow to direct them, they may properly use to

> serve them and make their independence secure,—and not their own independence merely but the rights also of those with whom they have made common cause, should they also be put in jeopardy. They must be fitted to play the great role in the world, and particularly in this hemisphere, for which they are qualified by principle and by chastened ambition to play. It is with these ideals in mind that the plans of the Department of War for more adequate national defense were conceived which will be laid before you, and which I urge you to sanction and put into effect as soon as they can be properly scrutinized and discussed. They seem to me the essential first steps, and they seem to me for the present sufficient.[41]

Wilson was telling Congress that changes were needed and plans would be laid before them in the coming year, plans that would result in policies to enlarge the army and the navy and prepare the nation for war, if it came to that.

Until the *Lusitania* sinking the Democrats had downplayed the idea of individual military preparedness, and now Wilson believed that the time had come to compromise with his political opponents, men like Roosevelt, Leonard Wood, and Henry Stimson. Wood was the original commander of the "Rough Riders" of 1898 before being promoted to command of a cavalry brigade in that war. From 1910 until 1914 he was chief of staff of the U.S. Army. Henry Stimson was a Harvard-educated lawyer who served as President Taft's secretary of war. These men, especially Teddy, were the nation's most prominent advocates for individual preparedness based on what came to be called the Plattsburg Movement. It should be recalled that as soon as the Fiftieth Anniversary of the Battle of Gettysburg ended, by direction of General Wood one of the first military-preparedness training camps for male college students was held on the GNMP, the other at Monterey, California. The response from student-participants and educational administrators was so positive that the policy continued with four camps in the summer of 1914 (but not at Gettysburg). Although Leonard Wood's term as chief of staff had come to an end by the time the world went to war, he stayed on active duty as commander of the army's Eastern Department. In 1915 Wood beefed up the summer training by allowing businessmen to volunteer for his instructional program at Plattsburgh, New York, one of four camps that summer, with a combined enrollment of more than four thousand volunteers.

Business, religious, professional, and even labor organizations had sponsored the 1915 encampments. These camps became so popular that in 1916 some ten thousand men volunteered, attending at their own expense or receiving grants from sponsoring groups. The U.S. Army furnished the equipment and trainers, but successful completion of the program did not guarantee a wartime commission. Military historians Allen Millet and Peter Maslowski concluded that what was now called the Plattsburg Movement "stressed values that no true Progressive could reject: increased civic awareness and public responsibility, the role of military service in reducing class, ethnic, and regional antagonisms, and the preparation of American youth for leadership."[42] What began in the remnants of the "Great Camp" of the Fiftieth Anniversary at Gettysburg in 1913 had blossomed into a full-blown preparedness crusade, spurred on by the 1914 Veracruz crisis and the 1915 *Lusitania* sinking.

As the year 1916 dawned, much of the world had been at war for nearly a year and a half. Millions of casualties already had been sustained on the battlefields of Europe, the Middle East, Sub-Saharan Africa and even the Far East. Sailors had perished in gigantic sea battles or drowned when their submarines or surface vessels were sunk. Aviators died horribly: burned to death, shredded by enemy pilots' machine guns, or plummeting to their doom. Civilians had paid the price, too. Belgian, French, Polish, and Serbian innocents became collateral casualties and sometimes deliberate targets. Noncombatants died when their passenger vessels were torpedoed. The British blockade of German ports was causing significant malnutrition in the Fatherland. Armenians were the subjects of genocide at the hands of the Turks. And yet, the real bloodletting was yet to come, beginning in February, when the Germans launched a massive assault on Verdun, the historic French fortress city, in an attempt to "bleed the French white," as Chief of the General Staff Erich von Falkenhayn described this strategy of attrition. When the battle finally ended in November, the total of French and German dead in that campaign approximated three hundred thousand; overall casualties approached seven hundred thousand. In an effort to help their French allies, by starting their own offensives elsewhere, the British, Italian, and Russian armies likewise were slaughtered, as were their enemies at the Somme River in northern France; the Isonzo region in the Italian Dolomites of the Alps; and near Vilna (Poland) in what came to be called the Brusilov Offensive. None of the Allied efforts were successful, except at increasing the butcher's bill.

Thanks to the ongoing coverage in the local newspapers, the people of Gettysburg and the rest of Adams County thus were well aware of the tragedy unfolding across the globe. The various newspapers continued to announce women's meetings for the gathering of supplies to be sent to the suffering noncombatants in France and Belgium. Even the local Camp Fire Girls got into the act: a front-page article in the *Adams County News* on March 18 publicized an upcoming meeting of the girls' local organization, the Jenny Wren Campfire, during which the young ladies would celebrate the fourth anniversary of the national organization in a special way by "the packing of a 'baby kit' for some little children in the war-zone and to contain all the things that would be most needed and appreciated." This was not the first time the Gettysburg girls sent supplies overseas: "Not long ago the Jenny Wren Campfire sent a similar kit, the receipt of which was acknowledged by the 'New York World' which said that Gettysburg led all the other towns and cities in the country in giving this aid." Even if the people of Adams County, many of whom were of Germanic ancestry, wanted to send aid to the Germans, the British blockade of the North Sea ports prevented any attempts. However, Gettysburg College students and professors showed their sympathy by organizing a German Choral Society, which, according to the *News*, "promises to become one of the most active of the college associations. . . . The purpose is not only to acquaint the members of the organization with popular German music, but also to give them training in the ready pronunciation of the language." About fifty students had signed up for the chorus.[43]

Literate Americans everywhere read about the European slaughter in their hometown papers. The weekly *Adams County News* reported that the "sound of the heavy guns in the Battle of Verdun was undoubtedly the loudest man made noise that the world has ever known. The noise was heard . . . 188 miles away, even indoors with the windows closed."[44] By July 3, 1916—the fifty-third anniversary of Pickett's Charge—only two days after the British and French assaulted the German lines along the Somme River in France, the daily *Gettysburg Times* had reported on the progress of the campaign. "Along the British front the forces of Sir Douglas Haig have been meeting stout resistance, the Germans having rushed reserves to the vulnerable points along the twenty-five mile front, but the advance continues." On the same page were reports about the continuing bloodbath at Verdun and the fighting between the Russians and the Austrians on the Eastern Front. However, during the summer of 1916, most Adams County residents were more concerned about events along the Mexican border than they were about the turmoil in Europe.

Shortly before the Americans departed Veracruz in November 1915, the United States officially recognized President Carranza and his administration as the rightful government of Mexico. Pancho Villa and his followers, who had fought against Huerta but also had broken off relations with Carranza, had been given some measure of support from the Wilson administration. Villa now felt betrayed and vowed to retaliate against the Americans. His revenge came at Columbus, New Mexico, on March 9, 1916, when he led approximately five hundred of his soldiers across the U.S. border and attacked the town and its small garrison of the 13th U.S. Cavalry, killing ten American soldiers and eight civilians and torching the buildings.[45] The *Gettysburg Times* reported the incident on March 11 with the headline, "To Get Villa Dead or Alive: U.S. Troops Are Ordered into Mexico. Gen. Funston in Command. 'To Capture or Kill'

Are Instructions to War Department—Carranza Notified, But Permission Not Awaited." Funston, who had been promoted to major general, supervised what came to be called the Mexican Punitive Expedition, commanded by Brig. Gen. John J. Pershing, a rising star in the U.S. Army. Pershing named to his staff a young lieutenant who only three years earlier had been assigned to assist with the Fiftieth Anniversary of the Battle of Gettysburg: George Patton.[46] During the unsuccessful campaign to capture or kill the Mexican revolutionary, at least fifteen men from Adams County served with the Regulars during the raid into Mexico or, if they were in the National Guard, along the southern U.S. border. (Three of these men later would be killed in action in France.)[47]

Captain William Long, a Gettysburg man in Company B, 6th Infantry, Pennsylvania National Guard, wrote home from El Paso, Texas, "If you know any person thinking of coming to the border, try and keep him there for he will wish he was back home again. We have been up against hardships ever since we came down, but have the nerve to stand for everything that comes our way." His nephew Lt. James Long, likewise posted in El Paso with another National

Brigadier General John J. Pershing and staff, near Casas Grandes, Mexico 1916. Pershing is in center front, and Lieutenant George Patton (in necktie) is just behind him. (Library of Congress)

Guard regiment, also wrote home. "This certainly is some place—no vegetation, nothing but sand, sage brush, snakes, lizards, horned toads, and in fact bugs of all kinds," he mused. "It is real western country and you can just imagine you are back home reading one of those western novels."[48]

One Adams County family with sons then in the service, but which also had a strong connection to the 1863 Gettysburg campaign, was the Sandoe clan of Biglerville, a small-town fruit-producing/canning center in the northern section of the county. In a headline of the July 1, 1916, *Adams County News,* it was reported that two sons were serving in the Regular Army, and two others had just joined the National Guard, "so that four boys of the one family are ready for immediate service along the border or in Mexico if needed." The fifth son, Ralph, the oldest of the siblings, "bears an honorable discharge from the United States Army after serving with distinction in the Philippines. He is a pensioner, his service having impaired his health." Luther, one of the brothers still serving with the Regulars, had been assigned as an instructor to the Plattsburg preparedness camp in 1915. According to the story, "The Sandoe family has had an honorable record for many years in providing men for the service of their country. George W. Sandoe, an uncle of these boys and a brother of their father, was the first man to fall mortally wounded during the Battle of Gettysburg." (Actually, George Washington Sandoe was killed on June 26, 1863, before the battle, when Confederates first passed through the town on their way to the Susquehanna River.) The same article also noted that two residents of another small town in the northeastern part of the county, York Springs, were then serving with the Regulars in Mexico. In the summer of 1916, while young Americans sweltered in the heat of the desert Southwest and the Sandoes continued their tradition of military service, the country witnessed the symbolic passing of the torch from the Civil War generation to the next cohort of soldiers when, in August, Maj. Gen. John Clem, the famed "Johnny Shiloh" and "Drummer Boy of Chickamauga," retired from the U.S. Army at seventy-five years of age.[49]

Though fruitless in its intended mission, the U.S. Army gained valuable experience during the Mexican Punitive Expedition, especially in the areas of motorized transportation and scouting, as well as aerial observation. Likewise, U.S. intervention in the Caribbean by the navy and Marine Corps in Haiti in 1915 and the Dominican Republic in 1916, sharpened the wartime skills of these services, especially the USMC.[50] At least one Gettysburg man, Robert Jones, "is in the United States Marine Corps and is now located in Santo Domingo [Dominican Republic]," noted the *Adams County News* on July 8, 1916, "where a recent uprising demanded the landing of the Marines." Within the next two years, the USMC would see a fundamental shift in how it would be organized and employed in combat, although it still would see its fair share of fighting in "small wars" in the Caribbean and Latin America. But the conflict in Europe raged on. In the midst of the Mexican crisis, the *Compiler* announced that "Ordean Rockey, a senior in Gettysburg College, left . . . to make final arrangements to sail at an early date to France. He will join the American Ambulance Corps at Paris."[51] Ordean was the younger brother of an earlier Gettysburg College graduate, Lt. Keller Rockey, USMC, who still was serving with the Marine detachment aboard the battleship USS *Nevada.*

While servicemen across the country were chasing revolutionaries, guarding the southern border, serving on the world's oceans, or intervening in the Caribbean, the policy makers in Washington were crafting new legislation for the future expansion of the army and National Guard, with the National Defense Act of 1916. The act doubled the size of the army and quadrupled the organized militia / National Guard over a period of five years; furnished a means of training new officers by establishing a Reserve Officers' Training Corps in colleges with its graduates forming an Officers' Reserve Corps for wartime emergencies; endorsed the Plattsburgh summer-camp programs; permitted the army to grow from 108,000 to 175,000 men during peacetime, expand to 285,000 men during war, and gave it the authority to form brigades and divisions. The National Defense Act also allowed the use of Guardsmen outside the continental borders of the United States during national emergencies, but they would mobilize and deploy as Guard units and not be used to fill the ranks of the Regular Army.[52] Then in August, in separate legislation, Congress authorized the funding of new battleships as part of a three-year naval modernization program.[53]

Gettysburg businesses and merchants jumped on the preparedness bandwagon, not to support the movement, but to take advantage of public awareness and thus make money. For example, the Gettysburg Department Store took out an advertisement in the August 5, 1915, *Compiler* that announced in bold letters: "Preparedness: The most used word today. We use it in our business also and are preparing for the needs of our customers by keeping a good supply of merchandise on hand—in spite of scarcity and a tendency for higher prices." This was not a case of false advertising. According the U.S. Bureau of Labor Statistics, "inflation was modest in 1914 and 1915, around 1 percent, but accelerated sharply in 1916," due in part by the Great War, even though the United States was still a neutral country.[54] Nonetheless, life went on in the historic little town. On July 8, 1916, while men from the British Empire were being slaughtered in the Somme River Valley, the *Gettysburg Compiler* blissfully reported, "Wedded High in the Air: Dan Cupid Makes Use of the Battlefield Tower." It seems that three years earlier, during the fiftieth anniversary of the battle event, "the great Peace Celebration of 1913 was responsible for many things and what more natural than that Dan Cupid should have come aflying on the wings of peace for his harvest of hearts. At any rate on July 3, 1913, the 102 steps of the tower on top of Culp's Hill were climbed by Miss Rose Browning [thirty-seven years old] and W. H. Barnhart [thirty-one], both government employees of Washington, D.C." One year later they again "climbed the . . . tower while the leaves of the trees crooned a wedding march in the upward processional until they stood before Rev. J. B. Baker and were united in marriage by him." Mr. and Mrs. Barnhart began their honeymoon with "an auto ride over the battlefield, then on to Atlantic City." Also that summer, news of a different sort arrived in the county seat on August 29 when the Gettysburg Fire Department received its new motorized fire engine, yet another sign of the town's impulse to modernize. The *Compiler* reported, "A fire alarm proclaimed the approach of the engine and its appearance on the streets was greeted with cheers and applause. The Boyd fire engine is the latest thing in auto fire engines, a wonderful and powerful apparatus . . . [and] can race to a fire at 45 miles an hour."[55]

Now two years into the Great War, a *Compiler* journalist authored an article titled "European War at Point [of] High Water Mark Tide Reached at Gettysburg." The subtitle read: "Initiative Now with the Allies and Germany Busy to Meet Offensives." Attempting to compare the two conflicts, the local pundit surmised, "For two years the South kept the initiative. . . . She failed, and with Gettysburg and . . . Vicksburg she lost the initiative forever. It took nearly two years after Gettysburg to bring Appomattox. . . . Now this is in sum what the allies expect to happen in the case of Germany."[56] The reporter was wrong. Each side struggled to replace its losses. By late summer of 1916, the Russians were on the ropes. The French, British, and Italians were absorbing enormous casualties. But so were the Germans and the soldiers of the Austro-Hungarian Empire, and the Turks. Rumania and Bulgaria had entered the war, and so had tiny Portugal. They suffered horrendously, too. The irony is that Gettysburgians of 1916 still were looking to their biggest moment of fame—July 1863—for lessons about the future.

Cashtown native Kate Wolf continued her service at the American Ambulance Hospital in France in the summer of 1916, the French government already having awarded her a medal for her efforts. On September 9, the *Compiler* published excerpts from several of the letters she had sent to some of her local friends. In one, she wrote about the time she was allowed to fly: "I went in a big fighting plane. I was strapped in the observer's seat in front. I am going again to do corkscrews and loops a mile up, that will be some sport. . . . If I was a young man there is where I'd be hunting Boch vermin." ("Boch" was the name the French assigned to their German adversaries.) Later, she recalled when the British wounded from the Battle of the Somme began to arrive early one morning as she lay in her bed:

> The ambulances coming in one after the other and being unloaded near my window roused me thoroughly. Night and day the trains arrive. A doctor from one of the dressing stations on the Somme front told us . . . they dressed 9,000 in 48 hours and sent them on. Where do the men come from? Every man from one British battalion was down on the Somme and the Boch trained their guns on them. Now the English take no German prisoners, one must exterminate such brutes. When I get home I'll tell you some stories that will make a fighting woman out of you. I'm peace loving but I'd gladly work a machine gun trained on such Bochs. I've seen and heard enough for that. To see little children brought into town with no hands sets every drop of blood bursting with the desire to kill.

Two years of nursing in an Allied hospital had hardened the woman from Cashtown. The war had changed her; gone was the idealistic nurse who had rushed to the sound of the guns in the autumn of 1914.

A world at war. German violations of one of the United States' traditional foreign policy principles: neutral rights and freedom of the seas. Rising inflation. Military preparedness. Agitation over women's suffrage, prohibition, and other Progressive reforms. These issues defined the 1916 presidential campaign, which pitted Wilson against the Republican Supreme Court justice Charles Evans Hughes. When Wilson and Vice President Thomas Marshall were renominated at their national convention in Saint Louis, the Democratic Party conceived their campaign slogan: "He Kept Us Out of War." World events, however, made this a pipe dream. Hughes challenged Wilson's labor policies and diplomatic failings. Wilson assaulted Hughes and his followers for alleged pro-German sympathies, and he accused anyone who attacked him for his own pro-British leanings of being disloyal to the United States.[57] The Democrat-aligned *Compiler* reprinted a political cartoon from the *New York World*, depicting Marshall dressed like the Kaiser, with the caption "Caught in the Wire Entanglements" of no-man's land, with the accompanying commentary: "As the Supreme Court Candidate cannot say what he would do if in President Wilson's place, or what he will do if he succeeds him . . . [w]ill it be a change to suit Germany, or have the country get into some sort of fighting?"[58]

The Republican was the favorite to win, but Wilson pulled it out. Nationwide, the election was fairly close: Wilson won with only 49.4 percent of the popular vote. In the Electoral College, he received 277 votes to Hughes's 254.[59] In Adams

County, Wilson had a larger margin, with 3,963 (52.7 percent) of eligible men casting their ballots for him while Hughes received 3,290 votes (43.7 percent).[60] Pennsylvania as a whole, however, showed a sizeable majority (54.25 percent) for the Republican candidate. This was the last presidential election in the Commonwealth—and other states without universal suffrage—where only men could vote. In its postelection edition, the *Gettysburg Compiler* triumphantly *crowed*—there was a cock-a-doodling rooster depicted between photographs of Wilson and Marshall in the page-wide headline—"HURRAH! WILSON WINS!"[61]

Within two weeks of Wilson's victory, the monarch of Austria-Hungary, Emperor Franz Josef, died at the age of eighty-six. Franz Josef had ruled his empire for nearly seven decades, and now his grandnephew Karl I ascended to the throne. Also, the Battle of Verdun was coming to an end. The French claimed victory, having regained all of the territory that it had lost since February. But the combat had taken its toll on the Republic's soul; another slaughter like Verdun could finish the French army. In December, Gen. Robert Nivelle replaced Joseph Joffre, who was elevated to the mostly symbolic position of "Marshal of France," from whence he could do no more harm. The Battle of the Somme likewise had come to an end. The British also believed they had "won"—having gained about seven miles of ground. Haig, however, being friends with King George V, stayed in command. On the Alpine front, the Italians had just lost the Ninth Battle of the Isonzo and major military operations ceased in that region until the following spring. On the Eastern Front, the Russian army was on the brink of collapse. And just before the year came to a gory end, Rasputin, the overly influential spiritual advisor to Russia's royal family, was murdered—poisoned, shot, and finally drowned. Russia was on the threshold of revolution. But, Wilson had "Kept Us Out of War."

Indeed, earlier in the year, he had done just that. After U-boats sank the unarmed French steamer *Sussex* on March 24, and two Americans were killed, Wilson gave the Germans an ultimatum on April 18: either cease attacks on merchant vessels without giving fair warning, or the United States would sever diplomatic relations. The Germans bowed to pressure and issued the Sussex Pledge, promising that U-boat captains adequately warn the crews of merchantmen before torpedoing a vessel or shelling it with its deck gun. Wilson's stance of "being too proud to fight" thus seemed vindicated for the time being.[62] The *Gettysburg Times* gave the German admission of guilt and repentance center stage on its international news page on Thursday, May 11, 1916. Much had happened in the war zones, however, since the Imperial German government made its pledge six months earlier.

With his election victory in hand and the military stalemate on all the warring fronts a harsh reality, Wilson attempted to mediate an end to the world conflict. He announced his aims to the American public on December 18, saying neither side was at fault for starting the war. His attempts fell on deaf ears with the Allies, although the Germans and Austrians halfheartedly hoped for peace. Wilson even infuriated some American religious leaders. *The Gettysburg Times* ran a January 1, 1917, story with the headline, "Churchmen Condemn Wilson Peace Move: Condemn Pacifism as Indifferent to Justice." The *Times* also noted in its New Year's Day edition that there were "few parties on New Year's Eve" and "but one watch meeting" at a local church. With no end in sight for the World War, and with the U.S. Army not having much luck chasing Villa in Mexico, Americans in general had little to celebrate.

The *Adams County News*, however, put a positive spin on the previous year in a column titled, "1916: A Year Full of Events That Will Live in the Nation's History." According to the editors, military history was made in the United States when the president ordered a punitive expedition into Mexico and then federalized the National Guard of all the states and sent them to stand watch on the international border. The *News* also applauded the passage of the National Defense Act and sundry pieces of Progressive legislation, modest as the number was. The editor congratulated Wilson's diplomatic efforts for once again scolding the Germans' continued violations of America's neutral rights. In an amazing admission of its seemingly pro-German bias—or perhaps in its attempt to appear balanced—the newspaper extolled the exploits of the merchant submarine *Deutschland* for making two transatlantic trips and safely docking at American ports. But the editors tipped their hand as apparent Anglophobes when they chastised the British government for its heavy-handed conduct in dealing with an Irish revolt the previous April—the Easter Uprising. Despite the World War's horrible battles (which the editors found appalling), and the suffering from man-made and natural disasters, all in all, the *Adams County News* remembered 1916 as a fairly good year.[63] President Wilson was optimistic, too. On January 4, 1917, he disclosed to his friend and trusted advisor, Col. Edward House, "There will be no war. This country does not intend to become involved in war."[64] The changing world situation would make a liar out of the president in a very short time.

On January 22, 1917, Wilson addressed Congress and presented an outline for peace in what has come to be known as his "Peace without Victory Speech." He still clung to the hope that the warring nations would accept his offer to mediate "a just and secure peace," meaning an end to hostilities without forging a new balance of power.[65] Although the president was not aware of it, the German high command already had decided to put an end to Wilson's fantasy. Kaiser Wilhelm had been convinced by his admirals to resume unrestricted submarine warfare against all merchant vessels, regardless of the flag they flew and the cargo they carried, even if this meant that the United States would come into the war on the Allied side. On February 1, 1917, the *Times* informed its Gettysburg readers that "Germany, in a note on President Wilson's recent peace speech in the senate, served notice on the United States that because of the failure to open peace negotiations with the allies, it would open unrestricted warfare on the seas."

The Kaiser's acquiescence to launching the new U-boat campaign had an immediate impact on Adams County and its agrarian-based economy. In the Friday, February 2, edition of the *Gettysburg Times,* the big headline read, "County Farmers See Wheat Drop: Headlong Plunge on City Markets is Quickly Reflected at Local Warehouses." The price of wheat, which had been declining steadily, dropped twelve cents a bushel in one day, from $1.75 to $1.63. "The trouble is, of course, due to the German submarine program as announced and anticipated," reported the *Times,* "which sent stocks on a downward slide in all markets on Thursday until everything far below the prices of the day preceding. . . . [Warehouse] owners in Gettysburg and other places in the county this morning at once adjusted the local market to conditions in the big cities." As if to put an exclamation point on the local farmers' bad news, a day later an American ship, the *Housatonic* (another sister ship of *Titanic*), carrying a cargo of grain, was sunk near the southern coast of Britain. That day Wilson broke diplomatic relations with Imperial Germany.[66] In Russia, meanwhile, the situation was unravelling and civil war was beginning, buoying hopes in the Fatherland that if the Russians could be knocked out of the war, and if the new submarine campaign was successful, it would not matter if the Americans declared war against them. By the time the United States mobilized, the war would have been won.

Meanwhile American Regulars and National Guardsmen still were serving in the American Southwest and Mexico, vainly chasing Pancho Villa and his revolutionaries, but not for long. With the looming prospect of the United States becoming a Great War belligerent, U.S. troops began leaving Mexico at the end of January. The *Gettysburg Times* ran a headline on January 29 that announced, "Pershing's Men Start North: Orders to Withdraw from Mexico Announced." So the local boys in in the Pennsylvania National Guard came home and those in the Regulars returned to their home bases, including the Fourth U.S. Infantry's Edgar Sandoe of Biglerville. Sergeant Bugler Sandoe, however, did not yet know it but he likewise would be returning to Adams County, as the Fourth soon was ordered to GNMP for training and reorganization.

Despite that the United States was easing its diligence along the international border and abandoning its pursuit of Villa, Mexican–American relations would not leave the headlines. About the same time of the American withdrawal, British intelligence intercepted a message sent from Arthur Zimmerman, the German foreign secretary, to his ambassador in Mexico. Decoded, it read:

> We intend to begin on the first of February unrestricted submarine warfare. We shall endeavor in spite of this to keep the United States of America neutral. In the event of this not succeeding, we make Mexico a proposal or alliance on the following basis: make war together, make peace together, generous financial support and an understanding on our part that Mexico is to reconquer the lost territory in Texas, New Mexico, and Arizona. The settlement in detail is left to you. You will inform the President of the above most secretly as soon as the outbreak of war with the United States of America is certain and add the suggestion that he should, on his own initiative, invite Japan to immediate adherence and at the same time mediate between Japan and ourselves. Please call the President's attention to the fact that the ruthless employment of our submarines now offers the prospect of compelling England in a few months to make peace. Signed, ZIMMERMANN.[67]

It was the final straw. First, Germany disregarded U.S. foreign policy by violating American neutrality rights and freedom of the seas. Now, it threatened to encroach on another of its diplomatic tenets by ignoring the Monroe Doctrine and cajoling Mexico to attack the United States. When on February 25 the British ambassador presented Wilson with a decoded copy of the intercepted message, it was more than the president could bear, and it brought the United States of America one step closer to war.

On March 5, 1917, the president delivered his second inaugural address. Wilson's most recent biographer writes, "the address was as unlike his first inaugural as was the spirit infusing the occasion. In 1913 he had spoken not a word of foreign affairs, only of his optimistic domestic agenda. Now he talked almost entirely 'of the thirty months of vital turmoil. . . . ' With that, Woodrow Wilson commenced his second term, delivering the nation to a place it could not even have imagined four years ago."[68] Nor could the crowd at Gettysburg's great "Peace Jubilee" in the summer of 1913 have *ever* foreseen that the United States would be in such a place on the world stage by the spring of 1917. On March 24, the *Compiler* ran the headline, "U.S. Practically at War—The Status of the United States on Germany To-Day. Congress to Meet on April 2nd When Official Declaration Will Come." On the same page, another story carried the news that "the Battlefield Council

N. 717, Order of Independent Americans, at their regular meeting on Monday evening passed a resolution to the President pledging him their loyal support in the impending national crisis." Although their symbolic act was equivalent to holding a candlelight vigil to end poverty and crime, it made the fraternal club's members feel like they were doing their patriotic duty. And on the same page, the *Compiler* gave equal space to the obituary of yet another Civil War veteran. This one, however, was a bit special. Corporal Daniel Reigle, late of the 87th Pennsylvania Infantry, whom President Lincoln *personally* had awarded the Medal of Honor, "died at his home in Cumberland Township on Monday a few hours after being stricken with apoplexy, aged 76 years and 1 month." Soon, epitaphs of a new generation of soldiers would appear in the *Compiler* and the rest of Adams County's newspapers. Gettysburg was going to war again.

CHAPTER 3

War and "Invasion," 1917

Brothels, Bars, but No BARs

In early 1917, American inventor and manufacturer John M. Browning introduced two new automatic weapons to the U.S. Army Ordnance Department in Washington. The first was a water-cooled, crew-served heavy machine gun that became the standard heavy machine gun for the U.S. Army. After testing and classification, it received the official nomenclature "Machine Gun, Caliber .30, Browning, M1917." The second, a much lighter, one-man weapon, was a magazine-fed, air-cooled automatic rifle. After its adoption, it became known as the "Rifle, Caliber .30, Automatic, Browning, M1918," more commonly identified by its initials, "BAR." The Browning Automatic Rifle was much superior to any light automatic rifle then in use by the Allies, but it, like the Browning Machine Gun, would not see battle until the late summer of 1918, and then only in limited numbers.[1] The BAR's procurement, testing, fielding, and employment were symptomatic of the U.S. Army's ill-prepared condition in 1917 despite previous years' increasing calls for "preparedness" and the "on-the-job training" the army had received compliments of General Villa in Mexico. The readiness of all of America's armed forces, and that of the entire nation, was about to get its big test.

On April 6, 1917, Congress declared war on Imperial Germany, President Wilson having addressed the lawmakers for this purpose four days earlier. Emblazoned across the front page of the *Gettysburg Times* for the Friday, April 6 edition were the words, "STATE OF WAR DECLARED." On the same page was an article titled "Will Be Ready to Do Their Bit: Gettysburg College Boys Can Be Counted on Says Their Own Publication." Quoting the school's newspaper, the *Gettysburgian,* the *Times* reported, "The publication tells that twenty-eight men have enlisted for one or other of the United States Army training camps this summer. Most of them will go to Plattsburg." Another story revealed that just across the southern border of Adams County, at Mount St. Mary's College in Emmitsburg, Maryland, "patriotism [was] at a white heat among the students. . . . All are hot for the war and for getting into it. The mere matter of having no guns with which to drill cuts no figure at all, broomsticks being plenty and, in the absence of the enemy, quite as effective as good training." The *Compiler* likewise announced on the front page of its weekly edition, also published on April 6, "UNITED STATES ENTERS WAR," with a bust photo of President Wilson above the headline. War fever had struck, and with it, a bit of hysteria. The April 14 *Star and Sentinel* dispelled rumors of espionage and subversion in the town with a front-page headline: "WILD RUMORS BRING UNJUST SUSPICION AND PROVE A HOAX." The article concluded that "it would be [better] for persons, before starting such stories, which they know will spread like wild fire to appeal to their reason and consider the effect they might have." And so it went across the county, the Commonwealth, and the United States.

The race to get into the fight had begun, and the nation was poised at the starting line, anxiously anticipating the drop of the flag. The federal government's role in everyday American life was about shift into much higher gear. Progressive Era legislation had somewhat greased the government gears and ever since the battle and especially since 1895, the people of Gettysburg had learned the pattern of the national government perhaps much better than other rural American communities. The town fathers would not wait for the conflict to come to them; they would solicit the federal government to bring war—or at least training for war—back to Gettysburg. A group of prominent citizens, including the mayor, county president judge and the presidents of the Lutheran Seminary and Gettysburg College, sent a petition to President Wilson and Secretary of War Newton D. Baker (a native of nearby Martinsburg, West Virginia), requesting that a training camp be established at Gettysburg National Military Park (GNMP), citing the ample maneuver space and the area's healthy conditions and satisfactory railroad facilities.[2]

The precedent for turning a national military park into an army training ground had been set at Chickamauga in 1898, and the Pennsylvania National Guard and sometimes Regulars had been using the Gettysburg Battlefield for years, even before the site became a national park. A report in the *Gettysburg Times* stated, "It was apparent to many of our people that the Gettysburg National Military Park would offer a site of great value to the government for the mobilization and training of troops. About two weeks ago it was decided by a number of our business men to get busy and push the claims of Gettysburg. . . . The officers

Congressman Andrew Brodbeck, D-PA (U.S. Congress)

training camps had been designated, so a mobilization camp was asked for." A select committee even had been designated to visit Washington to plead Gettysburg's case, but Andrew R. Brodbeck (D), representing the Twentieth Congressional District, of which Adams County was a part, pulled the right strings and GNMP was designated a military cantonment.[3] The people of Gettysburg got their mobilization camp, which the *Times* earlier had reported was more desirable than an officers' school "because it would bring a larger number of men and they likely would stay a longer period of time."[4] The presence of the camp obviously had more to do with the influx of capital than it did the patriotic fervor of Gettysburg's leading citizens.

On May 14, 1917, the townsfolk of Gettysburg received good news, headlined on the first page of the *Times:* "GETTYSBURG WILL GET LARGE CAMP FOR NEW TROOPS. War Department Selects National Park Ground for Mobilization Point." The story reported that "the regiments to be mobilized and trained at Gettysburg will be the Fifty Eighth, Fifty Ninth, Sixtieth, and Sixty First Regular Infantry. Each regiment will have as its nucleus a number of trained Regular Army men. In most cases one regiment of already trained Regulars will be used as the basis for the formation of two regiments of recruits." The story also enumerated the volume of troops that possibly could be assigned: "This will mean a camp of between 7500 and 8000 men. The war strength of a regiment is 1942 men which includes a machine gun company of 74, a headquarters company of 58, and a supply company of 10." Finally, the reporter noted that the Quartermaster Department immediately received orders to assemble the necessary shelter materials for shipment to Gettysburg, as troops were expected to arrive within a week and a half.[5] No doubt, town merchants and souvenir dealers stocked their shelves and reordered merchandise to prepare for the onslaught, but they pledged, in writing, not to arbitrarily raise prices just to take advantage of the economics of supply and demand. Hotel owners promised the same.[6] The town government and local law enforcement officials also had to plan ahead, but their experiences of the anniversary in 1913 surely gave them the confidence to handle such a large flood of people. Then, however, the visitors had been only temporary guests, and more than fifty thousand were elderly veterans. In 1917, the guests would be staying for a still undetermined amount of time, and they would be energetic, virile, youthful men, many away from home for the first times in their lives. Luckily for the ordinary citizen, but to the dismay of Gettysburg's saloon keepers, the Prohibition Era was about to dawn, and the U.S. Army, not afraid to experiment with new social ideas on its captive, regulated audience, would ensure that no American soldier would be authorized to imbibe alcoholic spirits of any kind, at least not while in uniform.

Lieutenant Colonel John P. Nicholson, the original and still-serving chairman of the GNMP Commission, received the same news from the War Department, although somewhat belatedly. Desiring to know which regiments would be posted on the park, on May 21 Nicholson fired off a letter to the assistant secretary of war. Two days later, the local papers announced the designated regiments, and about a week after that Nicholson got the same information from Washington.[7] Now it was official: his beloved shrine was in danger of being abused and maltreated, the same way Chickamauga had been damaged in 1898. (Chickamauga was getting another go-round in this war, too.)[8]

In the interim, both the Commonwealth of Pennsylvania and Adams County sprang to action, with state and local government agencies, benevolent organizations and public service groups mobilizing for the nation's impending participation in the conflict. Pennsylvania's "Council of National Defense" was organized soon after war was declared, with subdivisions for each of the Keystone State's sixty-seven counties. In Adams, the council's duties were to advise or oversee a variety of war-work tasks, including food and fuel administration; management of the county's Red Cross chapters; war-stamp sales and war-bond drives; morale and propaganda; civilian service and labor; and several other areas of local concern. An additional category, one that applied to few other Pennsylvania communities, was called "war camp community service."[9]

Shortly after the declaration of war, the *Compiler* printed the text of a resolution of the "Lutheran bodies of America," asking its members—especially significant, considering the presence of the Gettysburg Lutheran Theological Seminary—to pledge their loyalty and support to President Wilson and Congress and to help in the organization of Red Cross chapters across the country. Whether by chance or plan, the editor positioned an article directly following the Lutheran plea that announced, "Red Cross Organized Here."[10] The Gettysburg Chapter of the American Red Cross, founded on April 17, 1917, represented all of Adams County. The executive committee, comprising prominent citizens, organized eighteen auxiliaries in the smaller communities and towns. By the end of the war, the county chapter had enrolled 5,095 members and was responsible for several workrooms for the manufacture of surgical supplies and other hospital expendables. After the creation of the training camp, reading and game rooms were established in town for the soldiers, and a Home Service Department was organized to help the camp's visiting wives and families and assist the families of local soldiers whose own enlistments had caused personal hardships. In addition, the Adams County Red Cross provided sandwiches and refreshments to military truck convoys traveling the Lincoln Highway, entertained wounded soldiers hospitalized at Carlisle Barracks, provided jams and flowers to the local camp hospital, gave first aid classes, recruited nurses for the Red Cross, sent Christmas gifts to troops overseas, collected used clothing for Belgian and French refugees, organized a "Junior Red Cross" for school students, and, of course, raised funds totaling more than $46,000 by war's end.[11]

Despite the initial *rage militaire* in Gettysburg and across the nation, it was apparent to the army brass that conscription would be necessary to fill the ranks of the size of a modern land force required for overseas duty. President Wilson, initially opposed to a federal draft, signed the Selective Service Act on May 18, 1917. The new law was seen as a Progressive measure, more fairly administered than the federal conscription legislation of the Civil War, because it disallowed the hiring of substitutes or paying commutation fees to avoid service. The new statute also stipulated local, civilian control of the draft boards. All men—black, white, and immigrant—initially between the ages of twenty-one and thirty (in 1918 the age range was broadened to eighteen to forty-five), were required to register for the draft, after which they were given one of five classifications, with Class I being the most eligible for military service and Class V being totally ineligible. Registrants with critical wartime occupations were in the higher classifications, thus ensuring that skilled industrial and transportation laborers would be taken in the draft later rather than sooner. Men still could volunteer, but only for the Regular services and the National Guard, not for "National Army" divisions, the combat organizations that would comprise the bulk of the fighting forces. (Army divisions would be categorized by Regular divisions, numbered One through Eight; National Guard divisions, Twenty-Six through Forty-Two; and National Army divisions, Seventy-Six through Ninety-Three, with the Ninety-Second and Ninety-Third called "Negro divisions." Because the Army was segregated, the latter two organizations were a hodge-podge of African American draftees, volunteers, and National Guardsmen.)[12]

In Adams County, the draft was administered by a three-man board that included the sheriff, a physician, and the county clerk. On June 5, all men between twenty-one and thirty years of age were required to register for the draft in their respective voting districts. After the initial registration, the county draft board determined that 2,441 of their fellow citizens were eligible for possible conscription, and each man was assigned a number between 1 and 2,441. The numbers were allocated from lowest to highest, in alphabetical order by district. Districts were assigned by alphabetical order, too, so the number "1" registrant in the county would be from the Abbottstown district and his last name would start with the letter "A." The numbering continued through all thirty-two districts, with the last man in the last district—York Springs—numbered 2,441. The numbers were drawn at random at a national lottery in Washington, D.C. Each potential draftee was allowed to apply for an exemption during the registration process. The *Adams County News* commented "that comparatively few stated they had reasons for asking exemption. Those who did fill out this portion of the blank were generally men with dependents who would suffer by their being taken from their current occupations. Some asked exemption on ground of physical disability, and a few were engaged in occupations of special benefit either to the United States or one of its Allies." But that information proved false. *The Star and Sentinel* reported on June 16 that 1,558 of the registrants claimed exemptions. The draft board would have just over a month to get everything in order before the national lottery took place, on July 20.[13]

As far as the Allies were concerned, the declaration of war and the mobilization of American forces came none too soon. The Russian czar abdicated on March 15 and was replaced by a provisional government. With this, continued Russian military participation was in doubt. A week after America's entry, the French launched a disastrous offensive against German positions along the Chemin des Dames in the Champagne region of France, resulting in a gain of five hundred yards of land at the cost of more than 250,000 French casualties. The French soldiers were all but finished, and mutiny soon followed.

The British and their dominions, despite horrible losses on the Somme and the continuing stalemate in the Ypres Salient, still had some fight in them, but the citizens of the British Empire nonetheless breathed a collective sigh of relief now that their former colonials had joined the fray.

Yet the Americans were far from ready. British military historian Martin Gilbert has observed, "It had become clear in the Allied capitals that the United States' entry into the war would not have any influence on the battlefield for at least a year. This was a grave setback for the Allies, especially as Germany, the country whose indiscriminant submarine warfare had forced America into the war, continued to operate at sea with impunity." To safely transport American matériel and troops to Europe and deal with the deadly U-boat threat, a convoy system was devised and then implemented beginning May 24, 1917.[14] Horace Stewart, a young Gettysburg civilian mariner serving on the SS *Berwind,* wrote home to his parents in the summer of 1917 to tell them of his harrowing trip through the war zone before docking at Saint-Nazaire, France. Stewart related that his own convoy's ships ran with "lights out" and that during the last three nights of the voyage "we slept in our clothing, but I did not lose any sleep over it. . . . I was pretty nervous the first couple of night watches I stood, but soon got over that and by the time we got in the supposed war zone I did not mind it a bit. Really, I believe I was disappointed because we did not see anything at all."[15] He was lucky; the German U-boat campaign had proven efficient and deadly.

Another Gettysburg resident was not so fortunate. Albert R. Jacobs, assigned to the 158th Aero Squadron, made the Atlantic crossing in late January 1918 on the SS *Tuscania,* a sister ship of the ill-fated *Lusitania.* Sailing out of Hoboken, New Jersey, the *Tuscania* joined a convoy of other vessels protected by a small British cruiser and, eventually, seven British destroyers. The trip was uneventful until they neared the Irish coast. On the night of February 5, just after supper, in anticipation of landing the next day Jacobs went to the washroom to bathe and shave. "While I was awaiting my turn at the basin we were surprised by a violent lunge of the ship," he later wrote, "and a peculiar sound of explosion which we would expect to hear if an enormous chandelier were to fall from a great height." The *Tuscania* had been mortally struck by a torpedo from the German submarine UB-77, killing instantly thirty-nine merchant sailors stoking the boilers. The order was given to abandon ship, and Jacobs recalled the ordeal:

> The explosion damaged several life boats on the starboard side; a number of remaining boats were wrecked in launching; the rest of the convoy steamed away at full speed as soon as they knew we were struck and for the time being things looked very serious. One life boat was about fifteen feet from the water and loaded

> with men, most from our Squadron, when the rope broke on one end and spilled out. Another life boat dropped from considerable height on one that was loaded and previously launched killing and injuring a majority of those in the lower boat. Not many lifeboats got away safely.

Several destroyers came up to rescue survivors, and in the confusion of the darkness, men already in the water "were crushed between . . . [a] destroyer and . . . [the *Tuscania*] when the former came along side." Jacobs finally made it to an overcrowded lifeboat. "We were barely half a mile away when she [*Tuscania*] disappeared under the waves." The sea was rough and threatened to swamp his congested boat. Jacobs remembered that "the waves were so high that they kept washing in over the sides and it became urgently necessary to bail out, as we had nothing else we were compelled to use campaign hats." Eventually, he and his comrades were rescued by a minesweeper, then put ashore on Islay Island at 6:00 A.M. the next day. The U-boat attack had cost 166 American and British lives.[16] Enemy submarines threatened Allied convoys for much of the rest of the war. Perhaps the U.S. Navy would make a difference.

The United States' fledgling submarine force participated in an anti–U-boat campaign beginning in late 1917, and one of the sailors was a young man from Adams County. On its way to the war zone off the southern coast of Ireland, a flotilla of U.S. boats in Submarine Division 5 got caught in a hurricane off the Azores. On January 21, 1918, eight-year Navy veteran Royal A. Leese of the New Oxford area, assigned to the USF *L-10,* was swept overboard during the storm. His mother received a telegram from the Navy's Bureau of Navigation on Thursday, January 31, 1918: "The Bureau regrets to inform you that your son, Royal Allen Leese, gunner's mate, first class, U.S.N., was lost overboard . . . and the remains were not recovered."[17] In the postwar tribute *Adams County in the World War,* the authors wrote, "Leese has the distinction of being the first Adams County man to make the supreme contribution. He was 23 years, 11 months and 24 days old."[18] (This proved false: Leese was the *third* Adams County serviceman to die during the war. The first, Pvt. Clarence J. Strausbaugh of McSherrystown, died of convulsions on November 20, 1917, at Walter Reed Army Hospital. The second, Earl Joseph Myers of the tiny hamlet of Brushtown, allegedly had drowned on January 1, 1918, while undergoing training with the 4th U.S. Infantry at Camp Greene, North Carolina. [Myers had enlisted with the regiment while it was stationed at Gettysburg the previous summer. It later was revealed, however, that the drowning was a cover-up and the young man had been beaten to death.] So, Leese was the first county man to die in the line of duty.)[19]

Throughout the conflict the U.S. Navy's primary contribution to the American war effort remained focused on antisubmarine warfare and convoy operations. The mission of projecting America's might in Europe fell primarily to the U.S. Army with limited help from the Marine Corps, ill-prepared as both services were in the spring of 1917. With the announcement that Gettysburg would be the site of a new mobilization and training camp, the historic town and the surrounding area was set to become a cog in the burgeoning military machine for the great overseas adventure, hosting and providing support for training thousands of troops, lovingly called "dougboys" and "Sammies" (for Uncle Sam) by the American public and "Yanks" by the people of the British Empire. Ready or not, most of these soldiers eventually became part of the American Expeditionary Forces (AEF), the first U.S. combat organization ever to fight on the European continent.

As it turned out, two other army camps would be located on Civil War battlefields. Chickamauga (with its military camp now dubbed "Fort Oglethorpe") would be called on again as a training ground, and another, Camp Lee, would be located on the Petersburg Battlefield, although that site was not yet designated a national park. All three locations were chosen because of good road networks, the proximity of rail transportation, and, in the case of Camp Lee, the relative closeness to the ocean terminals in Hampton Roads.[20]

As expected, when Gettysburg was selected as a mobilization and training camp, businesses and merchants eagerly expected to profit from the arrival of thousands of new customers. A May 17 report in the *Adams County News* predicted,

> Gettysburg will be brought more prominently into the limelight. To its prominence as a battlefield town, there will be added the distinction of a military center. It should mean a new era of prosperity for Gettysburg and this section of the state. Its value as a tourists' resort will be greatly enhanced. That Gettysburg should experience an immediate real estate boom and a general business revival was the opinion of certain of its citizens when they were informed last night of the action of the War Department.

Another section of the article laid out the reasons GNMP was a good site for a mobilization camp: pure, existing wells initially dug for the fiftieth anniversary commemoration, adequate railroad facilities for off-loading supplies, and gently rolling ground expansive enough for a large cantonment, as had been proven during the Peace Jubilee of 1913 and the various National Guard encampments and maneuvers. Continuing, the story noted:

> Included in the many things about which there is conjecture is the attitude of the government regarding the distance the camp must be from a hotel. It has generally been published that no mobilization camp be located within two miles of a licensed saloon. If this is followed out here, one of three things may happen: the camp may be put out of the two mile limit and proprietors instructed not to sell to men in uniform, or the town may be put under martial orders and the licensed places closed by Army orders.

Obviously, owners of local establishments selling alcohol would not be happy to read this. But while rowdy, inebriated soldiers might somewhat benefit the saloon owners, their presence would contribute to public drunkenness, vice, crime, and the spread of sexually transmitted diseases. Not to be forgotten was that temperance advocates were pushing hard to nationally outlaw, through a constitutional amendment, the manufacture and sale of all liquor/alcohol products. One such organization, the Adams County Dry Federation, within a month of the soldiers' arrival, expressed its apprehension: "The war has not only made the liquor situation most serious on account of the grain it consumes, but it has made the local situation acute by establishing a training camp here." Of immediate concern was the report "that the soldiers are getting liquor somehow and it is one of the aims of the Federation to put a stop to this."[21] The local temperance advocates would get some special help from their Uncle Sam.

To ensure that business owners complied with the rules and that communities near training camps enforced the federal policies, the War Department created and oversaw the Commission on Training Camp Activities (CTCA), a consortium of civilian benevolent organizations and public services like the YMCA, Salvation Army, Knights of Columbus, and similar groups. The *Gettysburg Times* reported the federal backing of such efforts: "The war department means to spare no effort in the vicinity of big training camps where hundreds of thousands of American boys will be taught soldiering." Raymond J. Fosdick, a lawyer, Wilson confidant, and trustee of two Rockefeller philanthropies, was placed in charge of the CTCA at the national level. His mission, and the CTCA's, was to promote athletics and other wholesome activities and divert the doughboys from drinking, gambling, and prostitution and toward avoiding vice in general. The CTCA also became responsible for the Army's anti–venereal disease campaign. The *Times* article carried the warning that communities that failed to comply with army policy risked having the camps moved elsewhere, but in cases where that option proved impossible, "the government could place the districts immediately surrounding the training camps or even large portions of the city under military law, the threat of which alone would probably be sufficient to bring about a change."[22] If its citizens were not yet aware of this policy by the summer of 1917, the town of Gettysburg and its surrounding townships thus had been placed on notice.

Four camps designated for the mobilization and training of Regulars had been established in the eastern and southern parts of the United States. In addition to Gettysburg and Chickamauga, camps were organized at Syracuse, New York, and Westfield, Massachusetts. In the West and Southwest, existing forts served the same purpose. The new regiments to be activated at Gettysburg, the 58th through the 61st U.S. Infantry, would be built around cadre drawn from the 4th and 7th Regiments of the Regular Army. The 4th U.S departed on five special trains from its cantonment at Brownsville, Texas, on May 28 and arrived in Gettysburg on June 2. The 7th Infantry left El Paso on four trains on May 28 also, but because it traveled a longer distance it pulled into the Gettysburg station on June 4.[23] The lead article in the June 2 edition of the *Times* reported, "In five long trains the Fourth Regiment United States Infantry, numbering 2240 men with full equipment, arrived in Gettysburg last night and to-day. The Seventh will come in late Sunday night or early Monday morning, and the camp will be busy from now on for a period of several months." Gettysburg was transformed into a garrison town literally overnight, reminiscent more of the finely orchestrated fiftieth anniversary event in 1913 than of the chaotic 1863 battle. One khaki-clad soldier reflected on his recent service in Texas to a *Times* reporter, "Oh, it was awful down there. Sage brush and cactus, rattlesnakes and tarantulas." Instead of the hot, sandy, desert environment, the soldiers now would be quartered on a revered, finely manicured national park, with amenities that already were in place to cater to this new breed of "tourists." The army commanders made no attempt to immediately establish the camp when the troops arrived: "The men were allowed to leave the train and meandered about town" as a welcome respite from their cross-country train trip.[24] A *Compiler* article concluded, "The soldier boys are glad to be in what they enthusiastically call God's country . . . from sand and sage brush to our garden country has proven delightful to the boys."[25] The rapid mobilization of the armed forces inspired an American composer and a duo of lyricists to write the tune "We're in the Army Now."[26] In June 1917, Gettysburg might have adopted the popular new song as its own mantra.

While the town prepared for its new guests, it bade farewell to an increasing number of Gettysburg College and Lutheran Seminary students who were leaving school to join the armed forces. Most were undergoing training at Fort Niagara, New York, to become army officers. By the first week of June, more than a hundred Gettysburg College students had enlisted. On June 2, the *Adams County News* reported, "The departure of the college boys has cut into the enrollment there most noticeably . . . [, and the high number of enlistments] is said to constitute the largest proportion by any similar school in the State. The vacancies are most apparent in chapel, class room, and at the drills of the [ROTC] battalion where the shrinkage is very perceptible." Nonetheless, few people in the town of Gettysburg probably even noticed their absence. Instead, everyone waited in anxious anticipation for the Regulars to arrive. Everyone, apparently, except the editors of the *Star and Sentinel;* that publication's only mention of the new camp was in two small articles buried deep in the pages of the June 9 edition.

The first train to arrive, from Texas, contained thirteen stock cars of horses and mules accompanied by five passenger cars. According to the *Gettysburg Times,* on Saturday morning, June 9, "the [live]stock was unloaded and the first real touch of the military was given when a long wagon train proceeded over the streets from the Western Maryland freight depot to the camp site south of town." The old storage facility for the trolley service, which ceased operations in 1916—in May 1917, Congress finally approved the funds to purchase the right of way of the Electric Railroad on GNMP—was leased by the Quartermaster Department and stocked with provisions and fodder. "Load after load of baled hay had been stored there," announced the reporter. "Dozens of barrels of potatoes, crates of onions, and many other supplies have been stacked in the car barn and there is enough room there to house supplies for weeks to come. It will be one of the busiest places in connection with the entire encampment."[27] Local merchants must have been euphoric when the Quartermaster Corps' point of contact, a Sergeant Moore, had earlier announced to the local press, "As many of the supplies as possible will be purchased here." Alas, not all the commissary stores that the Army required could possibly be obtained locally. Moore admitted, "It is altogether probable that most of the food will be shipped in by special express trains, bringing enough to last for days at a time."[28] Nonetheless, the local economy was primed to make a lucrative profit from both the war itself and the immediate presence of the U.S. Army.

The area's crop growers already were beginning to feel the impact of the U.S. declaration against Germany. On May 7, the *Times* revealed, "Wheat was recorded at three dollars a bushel in Gettysburg this morning. This is within ten cents of the high water mark of Civil War days and far ahead of any record attained since then. And many think the end is not yet in sight." There was a downside, too. The cost of flour, an important staple in the daily diet, was steadily mounting. "With the rise in wheat has gone the climb of flour . . . to $1.85 a sack," noted the *Times* reporter. "The day laborer or the unskilled workman earning the wages usually paid here have to put in a full day's labor to buy a single sack,

Herbert Hoover, Food Administrator (Library of Congress)

and it is difficult to see how the other expenses are met, with all provisions at the top notch." (As a comparison, one dollar in 1917 equaled approximately $17.78 in 2017, and a sack of flour thus would cost nearly $33.00.) Sugar and other staples had been rising in price ever since Europe went to war, and now that the United States had entered the contest, consumer costs would continue to rise. Wartime inflation, coupled with increased demand for foodstuffs, munitions, and raw materials, already was shaking the economic foundation of the United States, and these tremors were felt immediately in Adams County. Although the federal government would not impose rationing, it did encourage food production and conservation by appealing to Americans' sense of patriotism. The government's reach also extended locally in its propaganda efforts, war financing measures, homeland security legislation, and, of course, conscription and recruiting. Naturally, federal agencies were created to oversee these broad areas of government control, and the first to be formed was the Food Administration, headed by Republican Herbert Hoover.[29]

Even before the federal government began to use price-fixing to mandate agricultural control measures, citizens of Adams County's communities sprang forward to meet the projected need. To prove their patriotism while also attempting to save money and feed their own families, the local populace—together with citizens across the nation—began planting Liberty Gardens. A report in the April 27 *Compiler* informed citizens that they could obtain copies of the official U.S.

publication "The Small Vegetable Garden" (Farmers' Bulletin No, 818), from their congressman's office in Hanover: "By the exercise of care and forethought . . . it is possible to grow considerable quantities of vegetables in limited areas and to supplement the family food supply." Town dwellers also cultivated staple crops just about anywhere that there was green space. For example, a short blurb in the May 5 *Adams County News* told its readers that in the southeastern edge of the county, the "unoccupied land on the rights-of-way of the Hanover and McSherrystown trolley line is being farmed this year. Potatoes are being planted and when the crop is gathered it will be sold to the employees at cost." Even parts of the battlefield that had lain fallow since the Civil War came under the plow's chisel. A May 17 *Times* article reported:

> For the first time in many years the slope of East Cemetery Hill is to be used for the raising of crops. Much of the sod has been turned and the ground has generally been prepared for planting, a large section being ploughed and made ready for use. The portion of the ground so set aside lies between the Baltimore Pike and the [park] avenue at the eastern side of the slope, the land to be cultivated lying east of the [Civil War artillery] batteries, and the hill along the pike not being touched. The ploughed ground will be used by school boys who have signified a willingness to do their share of the country's production of foodstuffs. After the war is over and things are back to normal once more it is expected that the tract will again be put in grass and gotten back to its former condition as soon as possible.

A Gettysburg real estate entrepreneur, eager to capitalize on the high cost of food, urged his fellow citizens to purchase one of his vacant town lots, "to avoid the high cost of living. . . . Then raise high-priced potatoes, onions, cabbage and other vegetables at half the selling price. The saving as compared to other high priced vegetables ought to go a great way towards paying for the lot of ground."[30] To prevent price gouging of foodstuffs and fuel and to control important resources, Congress passed and Wilson signed the Lever Food and Fuel Act of 1917. It gave the president the authority to fix the price of wheat and established the U.S. Grain Corporation (funded with $150 million) to guarantee the stabilized price. The Lever Act also gave the president control over petroleum prices.[31]

For the most part, however, the government was not all that controlling. The eminent historian of American society and World War I, David Kennedy, has written of the wartime Wilson administration: "They avoided unilateral exercises of government power; they sought the barest minimum of statutory bodies; they doggedly diffused administrative responsibility; they relied whenever possible on the time-honored principle of contractual agreement; and they affirmed repeatedly the *temporary* character of those few naked instruments of authority they were reluctantly required to grasp."[32] (Herbert Hoover, the director of the Food Administration, later would feel the wrath of that "time-honored principle of contractual agreement" when the "Bonus Army" of disgruntled World War veterans marched on Washington during *President* Hoover's administration in the midst of the Great Depression to claim *their* fair share of that contractual agreement.)

The June 2 edition of the *Gettysburg Times,* the same issue that carried news of the 4th Regiment's arrival, was chock full of war-related bulletins. The front page had a story about the ever-growing number of memberships in the Gettysburg Red Cross chapter; an article about the National Guard divisions being trained for shipment to France before the onset of winter; and one story concerning a philanthropist's son serving in France with the American Ambulance. (Paul B. Kurtz, a Harvard man, whose grandfather had been a Gettysburg resident decades earlier, had opted to drive ammunition to the front lines, a very dangerous endeavor. In 1914, his parents had donated land and funds to build the Kurtz Memorial Playground—in memory of Paul B.'s grandfather—an extensive recreation and athletic complex, just east of Baltimore Street in Gettysburg.) Finally, the *Times* reprinted a letter from a local man attending the officers' training school at Fort Niagara, New York.[33] Although the conflict had been raging for almost three years, America's involvement was in its infancy. The people of the area could not get enough war news and the *Gettysburg Times,* published six days a week, had cornered the market. The *Star and Sentinel,* which began publishing daily in 1914, printed its last daily edition on August 31, 1917. It continued as a weekly publication thereafter.[34] Then, the Republican-affiliated *Adams County News,* owned by W. Lavere Hafer, who also owned the "neutral" *Gettysburg Times,* merged with the *Star and Sentinel* a week later.[35]

The *Gettysburg Compiler,* one of the remaining weeklies, was the lone Gettysburg newspaper on which the Democratic Party always could count to support the Wilson administration's policies. Like other Progressive newspapers across the country, it now had to defend the anti-Progressive stance of going to war—especially in light of the 1916 campaign slogan, used to such positive effect less than six months earlier. The Democratic congressman representing Gettysburg put those policies in a positive light. Responding to interview questions, Andrew Brodbeck defended the new wartime measures in a front-page *Compiler* story on April 21 under the headline "The Selective Draft Bill Will Be Supported by Congressman Brodbeck. President Wilson and Army Board Have Correct Idea in Selective Draft." Brodbeck's task was to support the administration's universal military training and conscription policies. According to the article's author, "Brodbeck believes leaving out the training for militarism, the youth of the country will be greatly benefitted as to their physical condition if the bill for universal military training is enacted into law. . . . On the military end the congressman stated emphatically that he is against war as a general proposition."

Then the side-stepping and rationalization really began. Paraphrasing Brodbeck: "The best way to avoid war, unless all nations agree to disarmament," would be for the nation to be adequately trained and militarily prepared so that prospective enemies "would not care to provoke a destructive warfare." Brodbeck's defense of individual preparedness now stooped to the level of the ludicrous: "He argues that the open air life which these boys would have for the period mentioned ought to be of very material benefit to them in having helped to build a strong constitution. . . . [and] the exercise that they would undergo in addition to the outdoor life, would really place them in a position of enjoying a vacation with their expenses paid by the Government." Brodbeck's rationale for the pending Selective Service Act was just as convoluted: "The fact [is] that one who studies this matter usually comes to the conclusion that not only for the best interests of the country, but for the individual as well, a system of this kind would result beneficially." In other words, war is bad, military service is healthy and builds character, and conscription is progressive.

Brodbeck's blustering rationalizations meant nothing to the thousands of 7th Infantry doughboys arriving in Gettysburg on Monday, June 5, after their arduous trip from Texas. The trains that brought them to town were immediately sent to Columbus, Ohio, the rendezvous point for recruits being assigned to the 58th through 61st Regiments. The *Gettysburg Times* informed its readers, many of whom were associated with businesses hoping to cash in with their new-found customers, "But little time for recreation is to be allowed the men now in camp south of town, according to the schedule of duty announced to the Fourth on Sunday and to the Seventh after its arrival today. There are now about 4400 men in camp and, when the recruits arrive, the number will be increased to between 10,000 and 12,000." The story continued, "Gettysburg looked quite war-like on Sunday with the men in khaki roaming over the town, and many remarked, 'If 2200 make this big a crowd, what will it be with 12,000 here?'" Indeed, could the town's infrastructure support the incursion of so many soldiers? The superintendent of the municipal water company assured his customers that as long as people were not wasteful, there was an ample supply, as the Peace Jubilee four years earlier had plainly validated: "The Gettysburg Water Company always has had, and always will have, enough water to supply all the needs of the town. We demonstrated this most clearly in 1913 when our reservoir was running over, day and night. The burden of supplying 10,000 or 12,000 additional people—as is made necessary by the camp—is a burden of which we will be able to take with equal success if we have a bit of cooperation." What goes in must come out, so the soldiers' camp would have its own means for sewage and trash removal, but if needed the town government would coordinate with the camp authorities to ensure the proper disposal of any surplus "overflow."[36]

By the end of the same week that the soldiers arrived, the camp was beginning to take shape. It would be called, officially, the "Camp, United States Troops, Gettysburg, Pennsylvania." One hundred carloads of lumber had been ordered for the construction of latrines, mess halls, kitchens, offices, stables, storage buildings, and tent floors. On June 7, want ads were posted about the town for five hundred carpenters to be employed in the camp construction, to work ten-hour days at twenty-five and thirty-five cents an hour, depending on skill level. A *Times* story printed that same day alluded to the hope that the camp would become permanent and that upon departure of the Regulars it would become a training camp for drafted men. The same article carried news that the doughboys, so far, had conducted themselves well. "Frequent comment is made over the fine behavior of the men while in town. Every evening hundreds of them thronged the streets and, as yet, there has not been the slightest semblance of disorder or of any trouble with them." It proved to be wishful thinking.

The very week of the troops' arrival, the Virginia Memorial, the first ex-Confederate state monument placed on the battlefield, was dedicated with great fanfare to the delight of throngs of onlookers, who included more than a thousand Confederate veterans, some of whom had fought at, and bore scars of, the great battle of fifty-four years earlier. The regimental band and one battalion from the 4th U.S. Infantry took part in the June 6 celebration. As the Rebel veterans looked out from Seminary Ridge, where their memorial had been sited, they saw a sea of modern-day soldiers working feverishly to build a camp on the same fields that some of them had crossed during Pickett's Charge. "On either side of this scene they found to-day encamped the men of North and South, under row after row of canvas shelters, all engaged in the common cause of preparing to defend the rights of a united nation," related a June 7 *Gettysburg Times* piece. The story's author opined, "Doubtless not a few of the men of the South here to-day had grandson or nephew among the soldiers of the Regular Army now encamped on Gettysburg's field." The governors of both Virginia and Pennsylvania attended the ceremony, as did the Corps of Cadets of the Virginia Military Institute. Reconciliation. A common enemy. Brothers in arms. The huge memorial even was draped in U.S., not C.S. flags. The ceremony was staged in the spirit of a reunited, Caucasian-dominated nation, still grappling with issues surrounding the country's rapid postwar growth in the Jim Crow era. When the observance ended and the guests departed, the focus once again was on the current war and the activities of the khaki-uniformed doughboys, not the gray-haired, gray-clad veterans who had fought *against* the United States.

Due to a shortage of trained carpenters to erect the camp's buildings, the wages were raised to sixty cents an hour to attract workmen with the prerequisite skills. The pay was so good that local men quit their regular jobs to work at the camp, even though these positions were temporary. Laborers likewise came to Gettysburg from outlying areas to gain employment at the camp. The local economy was about to boom. "Not only are the carpenters and laborers reaping direct returns from this activity in building but stores are furnishing supplies, people having [horse or mule] teams are supplying them at lucrative figures, and there is very generally chance for getting 'good money,'" reported the *Times* on June 7. The June 16 edition of the *Star and Sentinel* related that the force of laborers already at work on the camp "was augmented . . . by the arrival of more than a hundred carpenters from nearby cities." This caused a layoff of the local workers at one of the regimental camps, "for when the out of town workmen arrived, being union men, they refused to work with non-union laborers. In addition to the [union] carpenters who arrived Saturday night a hundred or more negroes, to be employed for general labor, came to Gettysburg." One construction firm was contracted to perform over $100,000 worth of work. And it already had cost the federal government more than $200,000 to bring the troops from Texas to Gettysburg.[37] By midsummer, the Bell Telephone Company had laid cables and wires and installed a telephone exchange with three civilian operators to service the various regimental headquarters, hospitals, commissary, quartermaster, and other important offices. Sewer lines were excavated, and sewage treatment plants also were built, their construction employing a hundred men from nearby York working at $3 a day plus board.[38] The U.S. Post Office in Gettysburg had to hire three new clerks to handle the mail burden created by the soldiers' presence, and each regiment designated one of its men to carry mail to and from the camp.[39]

To pay the bills for what obviously would be an expensive war, Treasury Secretary William G. McAdoo told his supporters in Congress to introduce the Liberty Loan bill and War Revenue bill. By McAdoo's estimate, some $3.5 billion was initially required to fight the war. Much of this amount would be financed through the sale of Liberty Bonds (available at local Adams County banks), and the rest would be raised by tweaking the federal income tax on individuals and corporations, which was made possible a few years earlier by ratification of the Sixteenth Amendment. To sell the war bonds, the interest of which was less than that paid on commercial bonds, McAdoo, like Hoover, relied on patriotism and peer pressure. Bond drives were characterized by entreaties to the public from movie stars, sports heroes, and local dignitaries. The county newspapers also did their patriotic duty. On May 5, in a front-page headline, the *Gettysburg Times* urged its readers, "SUBSCRIBE HERE TO LIBERTY LOAN," followed by "Gettysburg Banks Report Local People Ready to Take Government Bonds." The last sentence of the story was both revealing and instructive: "Some people are trying to get the bonds as an investment while others see in their subscriptions one way of 'doing their bit.'"[40] Nonetheless, because the bonds were less valuable than other investments, it would take a good deal of promotion and advertising to make sure those citizens did "their bit." For citizens without the means to purchase the bonds, such as schoolchildren and low-wage workers, war savings stamps went on sale in early 1918. Public schools, post offices, and prominent places of business across Adams County sold the stamps.[41]

In addition to newspaper and other print advertising, direct appeals, made by local "four-minute men," stimulated the sales of Liberty bonds and war stamps, promoted recruiting for the armed forces, encouraged food production and conservation, and boosted home-front morale. The idea came from the mind of George Creel, a Progressive "muckraker" whom President Wilson had appointed to head the wartime agency known as the Committee on Public Information (CPI), which, in essence, was the federal government's propaganda machine. David Kennedy characterized the four-minute men as "a small, fast-talking army of patriotic speechifiers" selected by three prominent citizens from their own communities, then sent forth to enthuse the populace about the American war effort.[42] The head of the Adams County contingent was Charles E. Stahle, a prominent attorney and grandson of the *Gettysburg Compiler*'s founder. An article in the *Gettysburg Times* stated that the speakers were given their moniker because "in cities . . . the speeches are made in theaters and like places, where only limited time is allotted . . . [but] in Adams County, where there are comparatively few theaters or stated places of entertainment or public gathering, the work of this organization will be done as opportunity presents . . . [and] the speeches will not necessarily be restricted to so brief a period as four minutes."[43] With a large army camp now in their midst, the people of Gettysburg and the rest of the Adams County and northern Maryland would need little reminder that there was a war going on.

The first regiment to arrive, the 4th U.S. Infantry, had a long and storied history. Its military linage dated to 1792, and it had served in every American war since its inception. The regiment even fought at Gettysburg on July 2, 1863, suffering horrible losses. Its most recent campaign was the Mexican Punitive

Expedition, but the combat it would see on the Western Front would be far different than the type of fighting it had experienced in Mexico. The regimental commander was fifty-eight-year-old Col. Everard E. Hatch, a Maine native and 1884 West Point graduate. Commissioned into the infantry, by 1917 he had served in a variety of positions in his already long career, including service in the Philippines during the War with Spain and soon thereafter during the Philippine-American War. He also served at Vera Cruz in 1914 and commanded the 4th U.S. along the Mexican border from 1916 until its departure for Gettysburg in late May 1917.[44]

Soon after his arrival, Hatch appealed to the men of Gettysburg and the surrounding area to flock to the colors of the 4th Infantry and enlist. "To the Patriotic Young Men of Gettysburg and Adams County," he wrote in a letter printed in the local newspapers, "There are now six Infantry regiments of regular soldiers encamped on the Gettysburg National Military Park. Each one of these regiments have [*sic*] vacancies in their ranks . . . [but] this appeal is especially made for the 4th Infantry." He told the prospective recruits that his regiment was looking for "strong, healthy, honest young men," then presented a short history of the command and reminded readers that there was a monument honoring his regiment on the Gettysburg Battlefield. He concluded by announcing that a recruiting booth and the regimental band would be in the Gettysburg town square on Saturday, June 16: "The 4th Infantry, and the other regiments encamped at Gettysburg, extend opportunity to the young men of this section to serve their country." The 4th and the 7th Regiments were compelled to enlist new recruits to fill ranks vacated by two-thirds of their personnel, who were reassigned to become the nuclei of the four new regiments—the 4th soldiers going to the 58th and 59th and the 7th infantrymen assigned to the 60th and 61st. Within two weeks of their arrival from Texas, the old troops laid out camps for the newly organized commands, and they did so none too soon. On June 16, the *Adams County News* reported, "Nine hundred new recruits for the United States Army will arrive in Gettysburg this week as the first of numerous contingents which will be sent here to become parts of the regiments now forming. Others will follow as rapidly as they can be sent from the different stations and as soon as accommodations here are ready to receive them."[45] It must have seemed that Uncle Sam—his most famous manifestation being that of artist James Montgomery Flagg's 1917 portrayal—was pointing his finger at the town of Gettysburg and saying, "I WANT YOU."

With the arrival of Col. Frank B. Jones, the 7th Regiment's commanding officer, Hatch passed overall command of the camp to him. Jones was born in Mississippi before the Civil War and graduated from West Point in the Class of 1879. He served on the western frontier in the 22d U.S. Infantry from the time of his commissioning through the War with Spain and was wounded on July 1, 1898, during the Battle of El Caney in Cuba, exactly twenty-five years after the first day's fight at Gettysburg. After his recovery, Jones rejoined the regiment, which had been sent to the Philippines, where he was wounded again in 1899 in a battle against insurgents. He served in a number of other infantry regiments after more than twenty-two years of service with the 22d, then deployed to China as commander of the 15th U.S. Infantry during the Boxer Rebellion in 1912–13. Afterward, he was assigned to lead the 8th U.S. Infantry back in the Philippines until 1915, when he was reassigned to command the 7th U.S. at El Paso. When Jones arrived in Gettysburg, he was completing his thirty-eighth year of service to the nation and was sixty-one years old. During his long career, he had fought against Native Americans, Spaniards, Filipinos, Boxers, and Mexicans, and now he was in charge of training young men to fight Germans.[46] During the next several weeks, he soon would be joined by four more colonels, to command the 58th through the 61st Regiments.

Command of the 58th went to Col. Lutz Wahl, who upon graduating from West Point in 1891 was commissioned in the infantry, serving on the frontier, the Philippine-American War and various other assignments. Col. Benjamin F. Atkinson, commissioned as an infantry officer from civilian life in 1883 at the age of thirty-four, led the 59th. Atkinson spent his entire career in various infantry assignments and graduated from the Army War College in 1913, then was promoted to colonel in 1916. Col. Michael J. Lenihan, USMA Class of 1887, also commissioned in the infantry, would lead the 60th. Like others of his rank when the United States declared war, Lenihan, age fifty-two, had served on the western frontier and fought in Cuba and the Philippines. He was one of the first officers assigned to the War Department General Staff when it was created in 1906. Just before assuming command of the 60th, Lenihan graduated from the Army War College in 1917. Col. Samuel E. Miller, USMA 1879—graduating one place higher on the Academy's "order of merit list" than the 7th Infantry's Frank Jones, his classmate—would command the 61st. Miller likewise was commissioned in the infantry and served on the frontier and the Philippines and had a military career similar to Jones's. All four of the new regiments' commanders were seasoned veterans, with more than three decades of service each. By war's end, all would wear general officers' stars.[47]

Gettysburg was becoming more martial by the day, not from old Civil War veterans tottering around in their GAR or United Confederate Veterans (UCV) uniforms but from U.S. Army troops carrying guns and getting ready for war. Trainloads of recruits continued to arrive on a daily schedule, as did the provisions to sustain them. "In order to guard the stores of supplies in various buildings about town a guard was placed Sunday night," stated a newspaper report. "A tent for the soldiers has been located in the rear of Hotel Gettysburg [on the square] and this will serve as Headquarters."[48] Someone had been seen prowling around the premises of the buildings that the army had rented, and the camp commander was taking no chances. Neither was Congress. During the war, the federal government enacted several federal laws to curb enemy spying and sabotage, stop illicit trade, and even crush dissent: the Espionage Act (June 1917), the Trading with the Enemy Act (October 1917), and the Sedition Act (May 1918). The threat was real, as several incidents of espionage and subversion were uncovered during the conflict, and some real damage to defense activities occurred.[49] The Enemy Alien Act of 1798, dating back to the Quasi War with France during the John Adams administration, was dusted off in 1917 and used against German citizens residing in the United States. As it turned out, four Adams County residents remained German citizens; in early 1918, the four documented enemy aliens living in the county would be required to register their status with the federal government.[50] But the expansive security measures also led to abuses. Luckily, none occurred in Gettysburg. In Adams County, the soldiers would lead to an escalation in crime and vice, not German spies or those Americans sympathetic to the Fatherland.

The local citizens who had not been around for the 1863 battle, though accustomed to seeing soldiers and marines in town for training exercises and ceremonies in more recent years, had never witnessed so many troops at one time, not even during the 1913 Peace Jubilee or the Pennsylvania National Guard encampments. On Sunday, June 10, soon after the doughboys' arrival but before the onslaught of new recruits, hundreds of civilians gawked at the veterans of the Punitive Expedition as they prepared for the flood of new trainees. Lost in the rush to set up camp was the fact that the ground being occupied had once been a bloody battlefield and now was an important national historic site. One newspaper article observed, "[Every] day sees many machines occupying that portion of the battlefield, and the [town] occupants watching the operations of construction, the drilling of the troops, and the many other camp activities."[51] Army trucks and motorcycles plied borough streets, county roads, GNMP avenues, and the newly laid company streets in the camp. Horses and mules continued to arrive by the hundreds in July, requiring thousands of tons of fodder and forage, while depositing an almost equal amount of manure.[52]

Certainly the historic significance of where they were camped was not lost on the soldiers. Joseph J. Stone, a private in Company L, 59th U.S. Infantry, kept a detailed journal of his time in service. He was very literate and had a historic-mindedness, which is apparent in his entries. He noted that "the men who formed the nucleus of the organization came from Co. 'L' 4th Inf. Grant's old regiment. They were mostly N.C.O.s., all of the old army school and hardened into the service through years of experience in the old Regular Army." After describing their arrival in Gettysburg and his initial experiences with the other new recruits, Stone wrote: "Drill now began in earnest. The old battle field of Gettysburg became alive with men seeking to master the art that made the name of Gettysburg historic." Then he philosophized on the exploits of other American soldiers of a half century before and the historical importance of the land on which he and his comrades were living and training:

> The place, too, was ideal for the purpose and aided much in keeping and developing the martial spirit in the company. Who could drill or march on the ground made famous by Lee's charge and not feel in his bones the martial influence of that veteran hero of the Southland? And who could stand on the same ground made sacred by so many of our fathers and not feel, as Lincoln did, that these brave dead have died for things and principles that we ought to live for and die for as they have done before us. It was a patriotic atmosphere that Company L was surrounded with and the boys who made the company became full of the spirit and devotion that made sacred the place on which they drilled.[53]

In late summer, laborers found tangible evidence of the grim toll of that battle when they uncovered the remains of a Rebel soldier who had been killed in action more than a half century earlier. An article in the *Harrisburg Telegraph* revealed,

> Workmen digging in the camp of the Sixty-first Regiment unearthed part of what is thought to be the remains of a Confederate soldier killed during the battle. It is probable the man was one of Pickett's men, for it was over the ground where the find was made that the Virginia division marched to attack the center of the Union line. A portion of the skull and some of the hair and two teeth, one of them a gold one, were found, and with them were eighty-three Confederate bullets, part of the cartridge box, one minie ball [probably the one that killed him], a part of the soldier's woolen blanket and part of his gum poncho or coat.[54]

The contract laborer made the discovery while deepening the camp's water-supply lines to ensure that they were beneath the frost line. The *Gettysburg Times* reported that the doughboys "took a great interest in the news of the discovery and that many of them joined in the hunt for more bullets," which, they declared, they would take with them to France as souvenirs of the earlier war. The very next day, workmen uncovered the remains of a Union soldier, identifiable by the vestiges of his uniform and equipment, who then was reburied in the National Cemetery.[55]

Gettysburg National Military Park was suffering a severe environmental impact, and its cultural resources were endangered. Excavation of the historic landscape for structural foundations, latrines, and sewage lines and the grading of the land for building sites and camp roads changed the topography of the battlefield where the Confederate onslaughts of July 2 and 3, 1863, took place. Not to be forgotten was that a modern railroad grading bisected the training ground and its very existence already had disturbed the lay of the land. Modern camp detritus would mingle in the earth with Civil War relics for generations to come, possibly frustrating future archaeological studies. Parts of the battlefield were closed to visitors for security purposes. Hundreds of board-and-batten structures, including office buildings, stables, mess halls, latrines, and bath houses occupied the battlefield. Monuments and memorials were surrounded by the hustle and bustle of a modern army training area and cantonment, and thus susceptible to damage from vehicular accidents and vandalism from bored doughboys.

Photo of Camp, U.S. Troops taken from observation deck of the Pennsylvania Memorial, summer 1917 (GNMP Archives)

Camp stables, 1917 (GNMP Archives)

Captain Stuart A. Howard, USMA Class of 1903, in temporary command of the newly activated 61st Infantry, sent a note to GNMP Commission chairman John Nicholson in early summer to allay his fears about damage to the park: "You may be sure that every effort will be made by myself to see that enlisted men of the 61st Infantry do not molest in any way the monuments, trees, shrubbery, woods, etc. of the Gettysburg National Park. I personally hold this park to be sacred, and through the battalion and company commanders to see that this nuisance is abated. This regiment already has four noncommissioned officers on duty in the park to assist the park police in regulating the conduct of the soldiers."[56] A week later, Col. John Nicholson sent a letter to the War Department about military construction that continued to expand the size of the camp, requesting it be limited to the west side of the Emmitsburg Road, noting that it already "covers one of the most historical positions of any battlefield in the country: Longstreet's Assault and Pickett's Charge." Continuing, he warned, "To erect buildings on the line East of and along Hancock Avenue is to destroy the terrain . . . on the scene of Pickett's Charge, and whilst the Park land to the East is used for Parades and Drill, it but destroys the grass which can grow again, but buildings are unsightly and damaging."[57] Despite Nicholson's warranted apprehension about the damage to *his* park, at least the tracks of the old Gettysburg Electric Railway were being removed. Congress finally approved the funding, $30,000, to put into effect what the Supreme Court had ordered more than twenty years earlier.[58]

Military discipline was a sure way to keep bored soldiers under control. Providing for their welfare and off-duty entertainment was another. To keep the doughboys occupied and out of trouble, local government, businesses, the Red

Cross, YMCA, YWCA, YMHA, Knights of Columbus, and civic-minded citizens, all under the auspices of the CTCA, sprang to action. By the third week of June, plans were being formulated to remedy the situation. The local Red Cross chapter agreed to provide rest and reading rooms for the troops, complete with government-furnished phonographs; that a swimming area would be built; and the Kurtz Playground would be made accessible to the soldiers during certain daytime hours. An *Adams County News* story reported,

> Other things suggested . . . were the erection of a bandstand in Centre Square where band concerts and programs by the chorale society, and other like organizations, could be given during the summer; the holding of socials for the soldiers, the entertainment of one or two in each home of town, and the enlargement of the commercial activities looking toward the soldiers' entertainment. This would include the moving picture shows, bowling alleys, pool rooms, and so on. Already several of the churches have offered their lecture rooms to be used as centers for the soldiers, and others will follow.

Since there were about four hundred soldiers of the Jewish faith in camp, a representative of the Young Men's Hebrew Association attended the meeting, as did an employee of the YMCA. "The few Jewish families in Gettysburg have consented to open their homes to the soldiers of their faith," noted the reporter. As of June 18, there was only one Christian chaplain assigned to the camp, "and there is a specially heavy burden of caring for the idle moments of the young men."[59] The local churches were well attended by the troops, and as more uniformed clergy arrived, sometimes the camp's chaplains taught Sunday school for the town's various congregations. A report in the *Star and Sentinel* recounted that at St. James Lutheran on June 10, "the church was crowded with the boys in khaki. . . . [W]hen the Rev. Baker called for converts . . . about seventy of the men arose in their places."[60] Even Pennsylvania's "Free State Library Commission" lent a hand by sending books and magazines to Gettysburg and other military activities in the Commonwealth.[61] By the middle of July, The Red Cross had established a reading room on Chambersburg Street and a pool room on the town square. St. James Lutheran Church set up a reading room, and Father W. F. Boyle of St. Francis Xavier Church arranged several club rooms "with piano, writing tables, magazines, dance floor, and stage for minstrel shows and vaudeville shows." The Presbyterian Church on Baltimore Street and Trinity Reformed Church on High Street likewise established reading and recreation rooms for the soldiers.[62] Try as the various agencies might, the soldiers nonetheless would find ways to get into trouble, despite liquor having been outlawed for men in uniform.

It did not take the doughboys very long, however, to find their much desired spirits. On June 20, only two weeks after the soldiers' arrival, the U.S. district attorney issued warrants for the arrest of two Gettysburg saloonkeepers for selling liquor to the troops and one Philadelphia man for buying alcoholic drinks for uniformed soldiers. According to a newspaper report, "All three are liable to a year in jail or $100 fine, or both, if convicted."[63] A week later, Colonel Hatch announced that he would "furnish all the necessary assistance in the rounding up of persons furnishing liquor to men in uniform." Then, on Saturday, June 23 in Hanover, in neighboring York County, a Lancaster cigar maker was arrested for selling booze to soldiers assigned to the Gettysburg camp. A day earlier in the Borough of York, "Two young men were taken into custody. . . . Friday evening upon charges of having furnished liquor to U.S. Soldiers in uniform," reported the *New Oxford Item*. "Many of the soldiers going to York from the camp at Gettysburg have been getting liquor by some means, altho the law forbids selling liquor to a man wearing the uniform of the United States."[64] The troops had not been posted in Gettysburg for even a month, and it was apparent that the problem was getting out of hand.

Local police already were shorthanded and not equipped to handle the tidal wave of young soldiers. To make matters worse, the Gettysburg police chief, Horace C. Smiley, had joined the Regular Army when the United States declared war.[65] To remedy the shortfall, "members of the State Police force are now stationed in Gettysburg," stated the *Item* on July 19, 1917, "where they will remain as long as the United States Army camp is located there." Their specified purpose was to enforce traffic laws, but "any other duties that ordinarily would fall to the lot of the State men will be undertaken by them." The state police presence was none too soon, because the soldiers received their overdue pay on July 12. According to the *Item*, "there was a rush to spend some of the currency. Taxi drivers could not handle the demand for cars to take trips to York, Hanover and nearby places. Telephone calls to outlying districts brought many more automobile owners and throughout the afternoon and night, the soldiers were coming and going." That edition of the newspaper also ran a spate of stories about the arrests of both soldiers and civilians for breaking the liquor laws and for other crimes of vice, rowdiness, and negligence. For example, an automobile of carousing soldiers collided with a Hanover trolley, knocking it off the track. The troops sustained only minor injuries.[66]

The ongoing sale of booze to soldiers continued throughout July and into August. Almost every edition of the local news broadcast the arrests of drunken solders and boot-legging civilians. Even with the help of the Pennsylvania State Police, local law enforcement was overwhelmed. A big row broke out in

McSherrystown when Private First Class Lloyd Hayes, a 4th Regiment soldier, pulled a knife on a bartender and then "took charge of the drinks." After finishing off the whiskey, Hayes and his small mob of soldiers departed for next-door Hanover, where they were accosted at the town square by three law-enforcement officers. A melee ensued. Hayes bit two of the cops and then was subdued by a blow to the head. The *Item* covered the story in extraordinary detail:

> The offender was taken to the lock-up and Chief Smeach [Hanover Police] tried to communicate with one of the commanding officers at the Gettysburg camp, but failed. In the meantime, a Sergeant from the camp who was in Hanover, volunteered to take charge of the prisoner and take him to the guard-house at the camp. While Hayes was confined at the lock-up, some of his comrades, raw recruits, and Sergeant Houser, of the Hanover recruiting office, it is alleged, tried to start a riot, declaring that they would tear down the building to get him out. They, however, were calmed by some of the men who had been in service for some time and are accustomed to wearing the uniform with dignity.

It was later reported in the same newspaper that some of the soldiers had returned to camp, picked up their rifles, and gone back to Hanover before they changed their minds and surrendered. All eventually were court martialed. As it turned out, Hayes, the instigator, was a repeat offender and a bad apple.[67] Back in Gettysburg, in another incident, a drunken soldier struck the Adams County sheriff with a bottle.[68]

With so many soldiers assigned to the cantonment and with their regimental commanders preoccupied with training and organizing their units, the U.S. Army assigned a brigadier general to command the camp and oversee the myriad tasks associated with running the equivalent of small city. The *Official Bulletin* (a publication of the Committee for Public Information) announced in its July 12, 1917, edition that Chase Wilmot Kennedy had been ordered to Gettysburg to assume command.[69] General Kennedy was an 1883 graduate of West Point who had spent thirty-four years as an infantry officer on the frontier, Cuba, the Philippines, the Mexican border, and various stateside assignments. He was born nine months before John Brown's raid on Harpers Ferry, and at age fifty-eight was one of the army's older line officers, although he still was younger than Colonel Jones. Kennedy had been promoted to brigadier general on May 15, 1917, and took command of the Gettysburg camp on July 15.[70] He took immediate action to restore order and clean up the vice.

Kennedy believed the municipal police were overwhelmed and, as he explained in an August 11 letter to Maj. Gen. J. Franklin Bell, commander of the

Army's Eastern Department, "The Military Police can do good work in certain lines, but when it comes to arresting civilians outside of camps, they are without authority. Their uniforms, their inexperience and their restricted sphere of action preclude their doing effective detective work." What Kennedy believed was needed were "a few Secret Service Men and Deputy U.S. Marshals and an assistant U.S. Attorney." He continued:

> By their efforts the boot-leggers could be detected, arrested and bound over for trial, and the illicit traffic in liquor made so difficult and rare as to be practically harmless. I can and have put known houses of prostitution out of business by preventing soldiers from entering by means of Military Police, but this is only a temporary remedy, as they can open up elsewhere, and carry on their business until detected. It will need the work of the civil officials to ferret them out, arrest the proprietors and bring them to trial. By this means only can they be driven out of the prohibited zone.

Kennedy finished his letter by ensuring that the military authorities in the Gettysburg camp would cooperate with federal law-enforcement officials to the fullest extent of the law.[71]

Not aware of Kennedy's entreaty to Bell, the *Gettysburg Compiler* ran a story, also on August 11, under the headline "TOWN NEEDS PROVOST GUARD: CAMP COMMANDER'S OFFER OF ONE SHOULD BE ACCEPTED." The writer opined, "Gettysburg has become a small city since June 1 but this fact does not seem to have seeped into the appreciation of some of our people. They behold it as the same old town to be handled in the same old way, that new conditions do not evolve new problems to be solved in some other manner." The reporter correctly observed,

> The borough of Gettysburg with a population of nearly five thousand souls has become with the khaki cantonment a place of about 15,000 souls. . . . Every evening our streets are crowded with vehicles and the pavements with throngs. . . . Many of the stores become crushes at times and this condition lasts hours and hours. There is no complaint on the part of our people with this condition. It was to be expected. Our business people are reaping a harvest. Our people speak enthusiastically of the soldier, in large measure, as well behaved. . . . At any rate, Gettysburg has not had demonstrations of rowdyism to complain of as the other towns have noted. The condition of the town in August is not what it was in June, however.

The author believed that the difference in the middle of August—as far as the soldiers' collective behavior—was that there were many more new recruits in the camp. Back in June, the two regiments comprised disciplined veterans. Now, two regiments had multiplied into six, their ranks filled primarily by disorderly neophytes. And local law enforcement, even with state police backup, could no longer control the situation. It was time, the reporter concluded, to accept the earlier offer of the camp commander to allow a provost guard in the town.[72] General Kennedy complied, and a small MP force consisting of a sergeant, two corporals, and ten privates began patrolling borough streets.[73] Meanwhile, the army promoted Kennedy to major general and transferred him to Camp Dix, New Jersey.[74] Once again, Frank Jones found himself the senior commander at the camp.

In the third week of September, Jones deployed a much larger MP contingent, sixty mounted men, to Hanover to round up troops who had violated orders not to travel to the town due to a recent typhoid outbreak there. Nonetheless, the annual Hanover Fair proved "too great an inducement and a great crowd [of soldiers] finally decided to take chances," reported the *Times* on September 21. The MPs snatched between 175 and 200 doughboys, turned the local ballpark into a temporary lockup for the night (the soldiers had no choice but to sleep on bleachers and the grandstand), and then marched the prisoners some sixteen miles back to camp. The *Times* concluded, "The trip home saw the men tired, listless, disgusted, and disheartened and they were on their way from six o'clock until almost noon. Their punishment will be meted out in due time and doubtless their experience will put a crimp in further Hanover journeys until the ban is lifted."[75]

Finally, the U.S. government lowered the boom, as Kennedy's earlier entreaty to General Bell had borne some fruit. Although Gettysburg did not get all of the law-enforcement personnel the general had requested, the attorney general did send one agent from his investigative bureau, with another agent promised if additional help was needed. The appointment of a deputy U.S. Marshal and an assistant U.S. attorney, however, was not deemed necessary.[76] Then, on October 2, 1917, U.S. Attorney Rogers L. Burnett issued orders to the federal marshal to close all saloons within a five-mile radius of the camp. A report in the *Gettysburg Times* the next day specified, "The execution of the order will put Gettysburg in the 'dry' column, as all of the saloons . . . and at least one wholesale house are within the prescribed zone."[77] The *Compiler* commented, "It can hardly be said that the order came as a bolt of lightning out of a blue sky." Some of the hotel owners even predicted back in May that alcohol-related problems could make Gettysburg "bone dry." As a result of the federal order, Gettysburg's seven hotel bars, a liquor store, the Eagles Club, the Elks Club and the "Colored" Elks Club were closed. The *Compiler* placed most of the blame for Gettysburg's dilemma on York, Hanover, and Emmitsburg, and believed it only fair that the army should not allow its men to travel outside of the five-mile limit.[78] In other words, punish all the soldiers for the sins of the guilty. The army, however, would not play that game.

Despite the new regulation, thirsty soldiers went elsewhere, just as the *Compiler* had predicted (and as many of the doughboys had been doing all along)—to McSherrystown, Hanover, Emmitsburg, York, and even Carlisle—and problems caused by alcohol continued to plague Gettysburg and the regimental commanders. Private Hayes went back to McSherrystown about six weeks after his first encounter with authorities, got drunk again, and started another ruckus. The *Item* reported, "Hayes, who is known as a bad actor when he mixes brands, started a disturbance. . . . It is said his intimacy with young girls in McSherrystown has caused considerable comment and ill feeling." This time, the military police were called. When Hayes tried to flee, a fight broke out. Hayes finally was felled by a blow to the face.[79] And while the Gettysburg area was made "bone dry," and the law made it illegal to sell liquor to men in uniform anywhere, soldiers could still get booze. One enterprising doughboy acquired civilian clothing and traveled to New Oxford and bought spirits, not just for him but for uniformed soldiers, to whom he then sold the booze for a profit. He was caught and arrested.[80]

There was money to be made from the doughboys in many ways, not just in liquor, food, postcards, and taxi rides. A recipe for disaster starts with young men. Add a limited amount of free time. Then, mix in alcohol. Top off with hormones. The end result was the quest to fornicate. The *Item* conveyed to its readers on July 19: "Gettysburg authorities, with the assistance of members of the State Constabulary, raided a disorderly house along the Bonneauville Road, about two miles from Gettysburg, at 11:30 pm on Tuesday night and the inmates [prostitutes] were lodged in jail to await a hearing. . . . All the inmates gave their homes as Harrisburg and the addresses they gave are in the 'red light' district of that city."[81] With so many bored, young men in the Gettysburg area, enterprising "businesswomen" made their way to the historic town from the larger cities to take advantage of the laws of supply and demand.

But even if the local authorities stayed on top of the problem in and around Gettysburg, soldiers would go elsewhere to satisfy their sexual appetite. York, a much bigger town, was a favorite place. Two soldiers, from the 7th and 60th regiments, were arrested at the Gettysburg camp on July 30 and "charged with enticing York girls to Hanover." Both young women were underage. The soldiers went to York on July 14, having just been paid two days earlier, and convinced the two girls, ages sixteen and fourteen, to accompany them to Hanover. There, the foursome was arrested. The girls were sent back to York and placed in a house of detention. The soldiers likewise were carted to York, where they were jailed and faced charges before they were allowed return to Gettysburg. The authorities came to the camp two weeks later to haul them back to York to stand trial.[82] Nonetheless, the Gettysburg soldiers continued going to York; in mid-September, police in that city busted a bawdy house and arrested two soldiers and four women. Three cases of empty beer bottles also were seized as evidence.[83]

The *York Gazette* printed a scathing editorial about the bad behavior of the Gettysburg soldiers, and one of their commanders, Capt. B. B. McCloskey of the 60th U.S. Infantry, responded with a letter that was printed in the *Star and Sentinel:*

> Your article relative to carousing soldiers was read by me with considerable interest. Your reporter has a marvelous faculty for drawing word pictures. I could close my eyes and see the Bacchanalian revels. But one point was obscure to me—how much of this is due to the soldiers and how much is due to the sins of omission of the good people of York? In plain English, why don't you shut down on your bootleggers and bawdy houses? All violations of decency and morality so luridly described originate from the lawlessness that is directly under the control by the citizens of York. Let me tell you a little secret about soldiers. They are a pretty orderly set of men. Imagine yourselves what ten thousand lumber jacks, hay balers, or yes even students, so when they have their pockets full of money. . . . These men voluntarily enlisted to defend their country. The City of York happens to be the largest town in the vicinity of the camp. Naturally they go there. Don't the people of York believe they have some duty to perform, that for instance, to at least see that illegal bad booze and illegal cheap strumpets are kept from the soldiers? Parents are failing in their duties when they allow young daughters to run about with strangers.

McCloskey railed at the York newspaper for several more paragraphs. He concluded by sarcastically postulating whether the article "was written by a German, Pacifist or I.W.W," the latter reference an abbreviation for the International Workers of the World, a socialist, antiwar labor organization.[84]

Carlisle was another favorite haunt of the doughboys. The Cumberland County seat of government had been an army town since the birth of the Republic, the home of Carlisle Barracks. The town was about thirty miles due north of Gettysburg and easily accessible by train or automobile. After the Gettysburg bars were closed down, more and more soldiers from the camp visited Carlisle. The Cumberland County district attorney ordered State Police to raid a well-known bawdy house operated by Miss Cora Andrews. In addition to busting the prostitutes and four soldier-customers of the 59th U.S. Infantry, officers also confiscated a large stash of beer and whiskey. According to the *Carlisle Herald*, "The house has been noted as a resort for years, officers say, and special complaints have been made in recent weeks of soldiers frequenting the place. According to the officials it is the nearest approach to a cabaret that Carlisle possesses."[85] By that time, early November 1917, army brass had decided to send the six regiments to North Carolina, so the soldiers who had been nabbed did not stand trial in a civilian court.

In what seemed a futile effort to keep the Gettysburg soldiers occupied with *legal* off-duty activities, the CTCA continued to work diligently with local government, churches, and county agencies to provide various forms of entertainment, including sporting events, dances, speakers, concerts and visits to local family homes.[86] The *Gettysburg Times* ran a story in its July 9 edition under the headline "PROTECT MORALS OF MEN IN ARMY," which highlighted the CTCA's efforts in training camps across the nation. "In the neighborhood of each camp is stationed a trained community organizer, whose function is to promote recreation of the right sort for soldiers on leave," the article stated. The camp had its own baseball and football teams, which played other camps and nearby colleges. Track and field meets were held at the college. Boxing smokers were arranged, as this sport was pugilistic in nature and thus prepared the men for hand-to-hand combat.[87] Connie Mack even brought his lousy Philadelphia A's to town for an exhibition against the 7th Infantry.[88] The 7th lost 7–1 on the Gettysburg College field, and the game was less than spectacular, but several thousand soldiers and civilians attended. Ten percent of the ticket sales went to the Army Relief Fund. Eddie Plank, recently retired, umpired the game. The *Gettysburg Times* expounded, "The Seventh Regiment Band played between each half inning, the crowd itself was gay, and the affair one of the most popular since the opening of the camp."[89] Although the soldiers could clandestinely wager their money on the athletic contests, these competitions—unlike poker and other card games—weren't held for that specific end purpose.

Soldiers' clubs opened in other nearby localities, and the YMCAs of York and Hanover provided rooms for visiting soldiers.[90] The Women's Club of York organized dances, and the doughboys picked to attend were "carefully selected for their moral standing, from a different regiment for each dance," reported the *New Oxford Item*, "and will go to York in automobile busses, accompanied by a number of their officers, and will return to Gettysburg immediately after the dances are over." Back at the camp proper, a concrete, in-ground swimming pool was built, with dimensions of 110 by 50 by 10 feet, near the famed High Water Mark of the Confederacy monument and the massive Pennsylvania Memorial. Unfortunately, its construction was not completed until autumn. And a swimming hole

Swimming pool for Camp, U.S. Troops under construction, summer 1917. The pool was about a hundred yards southwest of the famed High Water Mark Memorial. (GNMP Archives)

was created by building a dam where Willoughby Run flowed into Marsh Creek.[91] The army, the CTCA, and local agencies were doing everything possible to fulfill the War Department's directives for the soldiers' "wholesome entertainment."

Regardless of the best efforts of the community and government agencies, the boys persisted in being boys, as the *Item* noted in its October 18 edition: "The 12,000 soldiers in the Gettysburg camp received their pay, $750,000, last week, and Gettysburg merchants and auto drivers experienced the usual rush following the compensation of the troops. Thousands of dollars were sent home by the boys, thousands were deposited in the bank, while thousands upon thousands went for amusements of various kinds, including the ever popular army crap game." Some troops spent their money on items that made their camp life more comfortable. The Gettysburg Department Store took out regular advertisements in the local papers aimed directly at the doughboys, claiming, "We have made special efforts to have a large stock of goods on hand, articles that will make camp life more comfortable and homelike," such as flashlights, camp stoves, wrist watches, safety razors, even bicycles.[92] But soldiers who spent their money on illegitimate goods ran the risk of facing both civilian judges and military justice.

The local papers continued to carry news of soldier arrests and convictions in almost every issue, despite the CTCA's exertions. Possession of booze or displaying public drunkenness, fighting, frequenting bawdy houses, and enticing underage girls for sexual favors were the most common offenses. In proximity to the camp, on private property just to the south, a theater company erected a huge tent that could seat more than thirteen hundred patrons. In reality, the productions were glorified "girlie shows," intended to make money off of the doughboys, charging twenty-five cents per person or thirty-five cents for a reserved seat.[93] The Garden Girls company ran afoul of the law, however, for posting advertisements for its shows within the confines of the cantonment. The company's owner appeared before the U.S. commissioner and received a fine. Back in town, at least one soldier was arrested for passing forged checks. Another stole $2,000 from the camp quartermaster office. One local driver was beaten and robbed by several soldiers. Some of the bored doughboys intentionally uncoupled a rail car and sent it plummeting into Plum Run where the trolley bridge had been removed. All these incidents and more occurred despite the presence of an additional twenty-one military policemen at the camp.[94] Finally, the CTCA and the "Gettysburg Ministerium" went to the town council on October 2, 1917, to ask for a curfew law and the employment of a policewoman, measures they found "absolutely vital at this time to correct evils that are already in evidence and to protect the morals of the town." Soldiers, however, were exempt from the curfew, as the ordinance was intended to keep boys under the age of sixteen and girls under the age of eighteen from being corrupted. The law, as passed on October 5, made it illegal for adolescents in those categories from being outside from 9:00 P.M. until 4:00 A.M.[95] Yet, as Captain McCloskey had written earlier in his combative reply to the *York Gazette,* the situation would have been no different, and perhaps worse, if the same number of lumberjacks or students or plowboys were let loose on the local communities. Nevertheless, the U.S. government, hand in hand with local and state authorities, had clamped down.

The presence of thousands of temporary guests also led to public health issues in addition to the obvious spread of venereal disease. As for the camp itself, a sanitary inspection report dated July 31, 1917, stated that the "general sanitary condition of the camp proper is excellent. There is no criticism in regard to any feature except as to prevalence of flies and mosquitoes." Nonetheless, the medical officer reported, the kitchens and dining facilities "are screened so that there is comparatively little contact between the flies and food except in companies where fly traps, fly paper and fly swatting have not been diligently resorted to." It seems that the real fly nuisance was located outside of the camp's perimeter:

> One source of flies and probably the main one is the manure piles in the stables of six or seven farm houses in proximity to the camp. One barn within twenty

> yards of a mess building showed accumulations of manure in the yard, and manure quickly covering half a dozen adjacent cow stalls; a pig pen in the same yard contained pigs black with flies. On the walls and wire screening off the adjacent mess building myriads of flies had collected so that it was impossible to open the door without admitting many of them.
>
> The condition of this barn and its surroundings is typical of half a dozen others in more or less close proximity to the camps. This is however not the most dangerous sanitary feature.
>
> The camps of the 60th and 7th Infantry Regiments are situated across the street from private residences in Gettysburg. In these houses the privy system of excreta disposal is in use. Within fifty yards of the camp, open privies were found with excreta freely exposed to visitation by flies, and these vermin were present in plentiful numbers. . . .
>
> Inspection of the back yards and stables in this part of town showed numerous places where garbage and manure had been allowed to collect and where flies were undoubtedly breeding.

The inspecting officer, Lt. Col. Henry H. Shaw of the Medical Corps, concluded, "These conditions have been reported by the local military authorities to the State Board of Health and some attempt has been made to clean up one of the barns but the results are not permanent or satisfactory." Within the borough, although some clean-ups had occurred, "no thorough-going methods have been adopted."[96]

Although engineers had installed a sewer system in the camp proper, it carried only liquid waste from the shower facilities and kitchens to the two sewage treatment plants that had been installed in 1917, both located within the confines of GNMP. Once the water was treated with chemicals, it was released into Plum Run, the historic watercourse that flowed through the Valley of Death and around Devil's Den before dumping into Rock Creek south of the battlefield. The disposal of human waste was a bit more complicated. There were 111 multi-seat latrines in the camp, none of which were connected to the sewers. This meant that soldiers had to be detailed to empty the contents of the pails located beneath the seats and also the receptacles that were connected to the urinal troughs. The urine was deposited into designated soakage pits, but the excrement was hauled to one of twenty incinerators built especially for such a purpose. According to a military medical journal of the era, "To be efficient incinerators must be of such a type as to destroy completely and rapidly all material without emitting odorous gases in or about the camp. Closed incinerators are mostly used as in these it is possible to produce a hot fire before introduction of the material to be

Tents, stables, and other buildings along Hancock Avenue on Cemetery Ridge. Note how close the camp comes to the "Angle" and the "Copse of Trees" at the top left of the photo. (S. Boardman Collection)

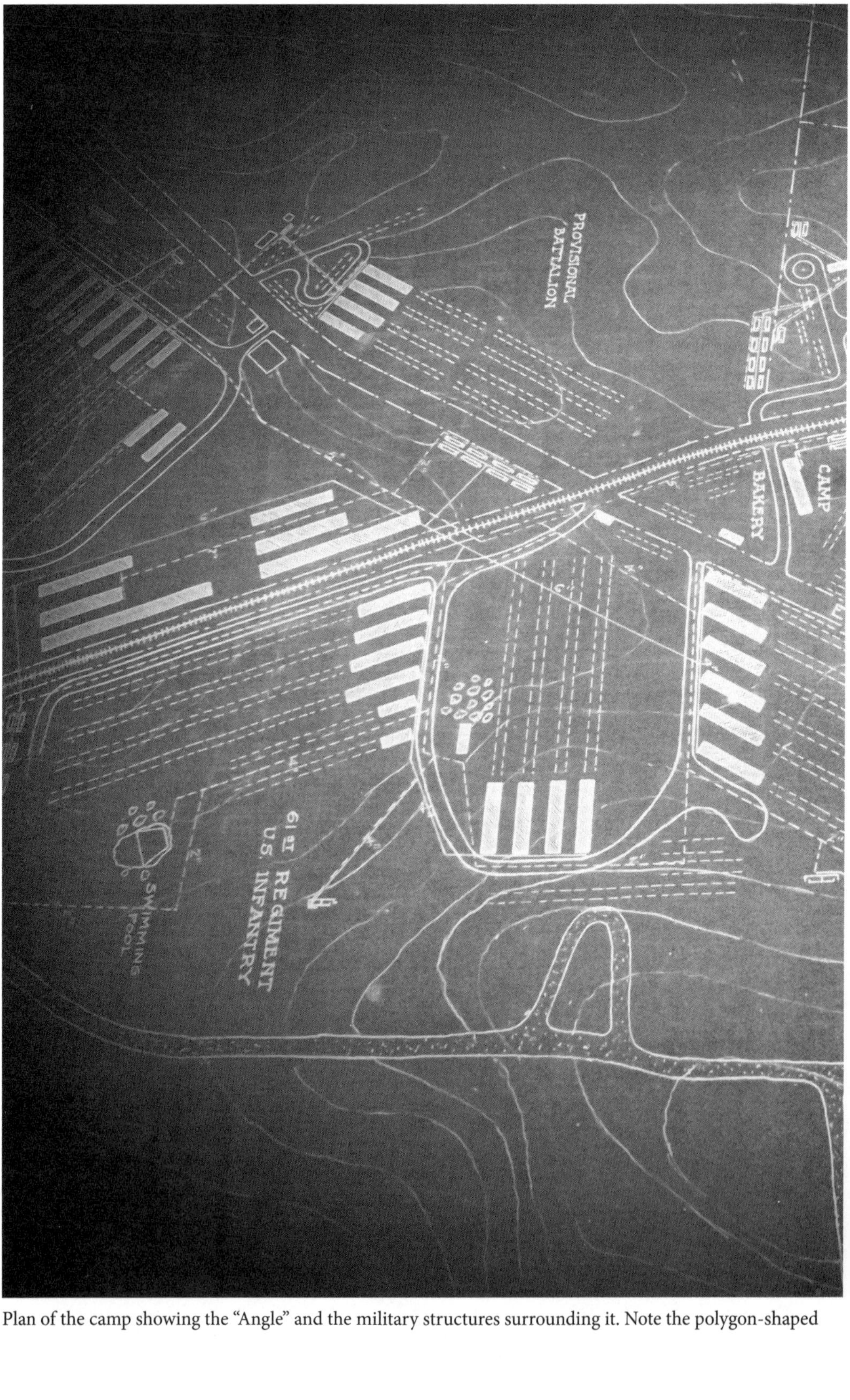

Plan of the camp showing the "Angle" and the military structures surrounding it. Note the polygon-shaped

swimming pool to the left of the inscription "61st Regiment U.S. Infantry." (GNMP Archives)

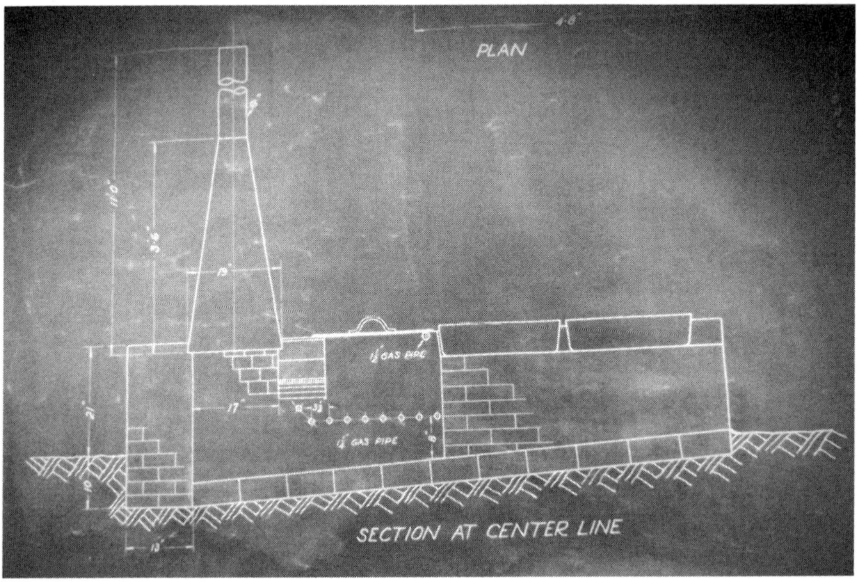

Plan for human waste incinerators (GNMP Archives)

burned." (Blueprints of the type employed at the Gettysburg camp indicate that they were closed incinerators.) As it took at least ten hours to burn the waste of each thousand men, the incinerators would have been in constant use, causing a pall of odd-smelling smoke to waft across the cantonment.[97]

The army, through military discipline, toiled to keep the camp in good sanitary condition, but it was up to the local government to remedy the sanitary issues within the borough limits. Thus, when the town council, through its own board of health, failed to fix the sanitation problems, officers at the camp complained to Dr. Samuel Dixon, the state commissioner of health. In early August, Dixon notified the town council to take the necessary actions to rectify the nuisances. When they did not, the Commonwealth took control, in true Progressive fashion. The *York Daily* reported on August 16 that a team of ten public health officials, under the supervision of the state's chief medical inspector, had been sent to Gettysburg. According to the story, "the state and army authorities have objected to the failure to require regulation of piggeries, to abate surface drainage conditions, to clean up refuse, take steps to get rid of pools of water, offensive barnyards and stables and to abate the fly and mosquito nuisance. Some of the places complained of are close to the encampment of the regulars. Hotels and restaurants will be inspected." The town council fought back, to no avail. The *Times* wrote indignantly, "Locally the action of the State Department of Health will be a matter for severe censure and criticism. Gettysburg does not regard conditions as unsanitary as representatives of the Department would indicate . . . and the State is stepping in—according to belief here—after the necessary work has been done."[98] Nonetheless, local government was forced to yield to state control, as Gettysburg stunk, was dirty, and buzzed with flies by day and mosquitos by night.

Talk surfaced at town council meetings to sue the State Board of Health to relinquish its control. One of the state inspectors told the council that if the town enforced its own regulations concerning piggeries in the borough limits, if homes and businesses with access to sewers abandon their outhouses and connect to the sewers, and if property owners without sewer access ensured that their "surface closets" conformed to the local board's regulations, "then the Commissioner of Health will restore the local board." The councilmen, however, rejected the restrictions that the state board wanted to be placed on piggeries, and the impasse continued.[99] Next, the state board ordered the town council to build a sewage disposal plant for the borough, reversing an earlier order that the town build two septic tanks, the work of which was just about completed. This directive, of course, had been given before the arrival of more than ten thousand soldiers.[100] Then, the borough-council president accepted the resignation of one member of the board of health, fired the rest, and appointed new members.[101] The state board would not recognize the new board, however, and announced that when it relinquished control, it would be to the old board.[102] By year's end, the bureaucratic problem still had not been resolved.

With all of the social problems that had transpired with the deluge of thousands of young men into what had been a rural, yet well-traveled town, it was easy to forget the primary reasons the soldiers were there in the first place. The camp's dual purposes were to organize four new regiments and train their men to fight. A typical day included drill and ceremonies, physical exercise, bayonet training, weapons familiarization and maintenance, small-unit tactics, chemical-warfare training, signaling, and map reading. With no suitable firing ranges in the vicinity, plans were made to transport the soldiers to the Pennsylvania National Guard training facility at Mount Gretna, some forty miles distant, for marksmanship training.[103] The doughboys dug trenches and machine-gun pits on the historic Trostle Farm, where severe fighting occurred on July 2, 1863, and archeological evidence exists indicating that at least some trenches were dug and barbed wire was strung in the camp near the southern edge of the town.[104] Under CTCA guidance, troops also received training in the prevention of venereal disease[105]

The first new recruits to reach the Gettysburg camp received their uniforms shortly after their arrival, consisting of an olive-drab woolen uniform jacket with a standing collar, with two brass, circular disks attached, one with "U.S." and the other with crossed rifles (for infantry) or, if they were assigned to another Army branch, the insignia of that branch (such as a caduceus for medical, a flaming cannon ball for ordnance, etc.) Each recruit also was issued matching pants, canvas leggings or woolen leg wraps (called puttees), brown, ankle-high leather boots, along with shirts, underwear, neckties and a round campaign hat, as well as belts and other sundry items. Field gear would have included a cartridge belt, canteen with cover, mess kit, first aid pack, backpack, haversack, poncho, blankets, ration tins, entrenching tool, and bayonet with scabbard.[106]

One new recruit at the Gettysburg camp was destined to be unique in the entire U.S. Army during the war as its youngest soldier. Ernest L. Wrentmore had stowed away on an eastbound freight train from his home in West Farmington, Ohio, and landed in Altoona, Pennsylvania, where he found a recruiting station and enlisted in the Regular Army. A half-century later, he recalled, "The day I stepped into an Army recruiting office to tell a tough-looking individual my desire to enlist, I was twelve years old. The date was September 29, 1917." Smart, large in frame, and mature for his age, Wrentmore indeed was not even a teenager and had convinced the recruiter that he was eighteen years old. He signed an alias on his enlistment form: "Henry E. Monroe." His ruse worked, and soon he was on

Ernest Wrentmore, aka "Henry Monroe," the youngest soldier to serve in the American Expeditionary Forces (Courtesy of Ernest Wrentmore III)

another train, this time as a legitimate passenger, destination Gettysburg. Wrentmore wrote in his memoirs, "The campsite was situated on the memorable battlefield, Gettysburg! Our eyes were met with an endless sea of tents and low buildings. It was a thrilling site, never to be forgotten." He subsequently was assigned to Company I, 60th Infantry. Now going by the name "Henry," he described the training regimen of an infantryman:

> The training began, an endless routine of learning to become a combat team—individually and collectively—in learning how to save our necks in hand-to-hand fighting. Perpetual drill—miles of hiking—utter exhaustion. It seemed that the drive of the officers and noncoms would never cease. Following a few weeks of this training, I discovered that I was putting on weight—good, hard muscle. I found that I was having no trouble staying right in there with the rest of them. I liked bayonet drill, and I hit the dummy with as hard an impact as any of the boys. I was fast becoming a good combat soldier.[107]

The recently adopted .30 caliber Browning machine gun and the BAR had not even gone into production when the infantry camp was established at Gettysburg, so recruits like Pvt. Henry Monroe trained on the Lewis-Savage light machine gun and the Hotchkiss M1909 Benét-Mercié machine gun that had been brought with the 4th and 7th Regiments from the Mexican Border campaign. Their rifle was the caliber .30–06 (or "ought-six" as the soldiers called it) U.S. Springfield, which they also had used against Pancho Villa's bandits, and the recruits were issued the same rifle. Officers, noncommissioned officers, and soldiers in non-infantry specialties, such as bandsmen, usually carried the M1911 .45 caliber Colt semiautomatic pistol. When the Gettysburg doughboys finally arrived in France in May 1918, they exchanged their rifles for the newer U.S. Enfield Model of 1917, the same caliber as the Springfield and to an untrained eye very similar in appearance. They also received their individual gas masks after disembarking in France.[108] There is no record of the troops being issued their steel helmets while encamped at Gettysburg.

Of course, whenever weapons and live ammunition are brought together, accidents happen. Several doughboys were wounded or killed in the Gettysburg camp from carelessness. The first fatality, however, was the result of suicide. Within a month of his arrival from Texas, Pvt. Samuel Gettman, a Russian immigrant who had settled in Chicago, took his own life by hanging himself from his tent pole. Originally assigned to the 7th Infantry, Gettman had recently been reassigned to the 60th. According to a report in the *Compiler,* "As a foreigner he did not mingle freely with his fellows and had been unusually quiet of late and it is believed the act followed a fit of despondency." He was given a full military funeral in the nearby National Cemetery.[109] Gettman was one of almost a half-million first-generation immigrants (of forty-six different nationalities) who either had enlisted or were drafted into the American army. These foreign-born men comprised approximately 18 percent of the entire force.[110]

In September, two separate firearms incidents wounded four soldiers and killed a sergeant. In the second week of that month, an officer demonstrating a machine gun's operation mistakenly thought the weapon was not loaded. When he pulled the trigger, it discharged a bullet, which wounded four 59th Infantry soldiers and passed through a book that a fifth soldier was then reading, the deflection undoubtedly saving his life. One of the wounded men suffered an amputated leg as a result. In a separate accident a few days later, supply sergeant John Lucas, also of the 59th, was killed when a rifle accidently fired. According to the *New Oxford Item,* "Struck while asleep in his tent by an army rifle which was accidentally discharged during a demonstration to recruits . . . the bullet entered the top of the sleeping man's head, coming out through the roof of his mouth." Yet one more death was averted on September 24, when quick thinking by a corporal and his swift kick knocked a rifle out of the hands of another supply sergeant in the 59th Infantry, who was intent on suicide by blowing his brains out. The men tussled afterward for the rifle, when it accidentally discharged and the bullet nearly struck men drilling outside of the sergeant's tent.[111] Another soldier, twenty-two-year-old Pvt. Sidney Delaune, died of liver and kidney cancer on September 28. A reporter for the *Gettysburg Times* wrote, "Delaune is the third soldier to die here since the opening of camp in June. This is considered a remarkable record as the enrollment has been as high as 12,000 and the normal death rate in such a community is much higher." The writer chalked it up to the "fine and sanitary condition of the camp and town" and the youthfulness and "good physique" of the soldiers.[112]

But little more than a week later, on October 8, another soldier committed suicide, this one a twenty-year veteran of the army. While serving on mess duty early one morning, when none of his comrades were looking, the 7th Infantry's Jacob Weber "took a rifle, placed the barrel to his head, and then pulled the trigger," reported the *New Oxford Item.* "The full force of the load hit him squarely in the side of the head, and mutilated it terribly. . . . His death is the fourth which has occurred since the opening of the camp and the third . . . from unnatural causes."[113] Five days after Weber's demise, two soldiers were injured and a third was killed in a collision between an automobile in which they riding and a freight train at a crossing on the Lincoln Highway in New Oxford. According to the *Star and Sentinel,* "Daniel Richardson, the soldier, was instantly killed. His body was thrown to the side of the road. . . . Richardson was a member of Company B, 60th Infantry. His home is in Milwaukee." The reporter noted that the driver, a local civilian who also was hurt, was hauling the soldiers back to Gettysburg from York in the early morning hours of Saturday, October 13, and was driving too fast to see the approaching train. Three other doughboys in the car escaped unharmed, even though the automobile was a total wreck.[114] The unfortunate Richardson was the last of the Regulars at the Gettysburg camp to perish that year.

The days were getting shorter and the nights colder, and the camp did not have winter barracks. The War Department thus moved the six regiments to a new cantonment, Camp Greene, near Charlotte, North Carolina. Before their departure, however, the infantry regiments were restructured once again, this time to create a battalion comprising trench mortar and machine-gun companies, in keeping with an army divisional reorganization of August 1917.[115] Private Stone of the 59th Infantry, who earlier had marveled at drilling on the fields of Pickett's Charge, scribbled in his journal, "Not many weeks went by [after our arrival], however, before the advance rumors of a move reached the camp. Boxes were made and packing up began the latter part of October. Supply Sgt. Campbell became the most important figure in the company. He had more jobs to give away than anyone, but everybody worked and soon the property was packed and marked for Camp Greene, N.C."[116] The *Times* publicized the impending transfer on Thursday, October 25: "All six regiments of the United States Regulars are to be moved from the Gettysburg Camp as soon as the railroads can provide the necessary facilities. This announcement came on Wednesday evening, and regimental officers were advised to be in readiness for breaking camp on short notice." The writer of the article expressed surprise that the move was announced so suddenly, but he allayed townsfolk's fears by explaining that it could take several weeks to transport all of the soldiers to North Carolina: "The railroads are now taxed to their utmost to provide facilities for the movement of troops and conscripts and it is predicted that it will take the better part of a month to get 12,000 or 15,000 men out of here." The article concluded with the encouraging news that it was likely that another camp would be established in Gettysburg in the spring, as "several new storage houses have been rented [by the Army] in Gettysburg within the last few days, and all things point to the opening of the camp very early."

The onset of colder weather was not the only reason that the "Camp of the United States Troops, Gettysburg, Pa." was disestablished. The *Times* announced in bold letters on the front page of its November 2 edition, "CAMP NEXT YEAR IS ENDANGERED . . . Intoxication and Certain Diseases Will Not Be Permitted, and Question Is Up to Communities." The U.S. Army would flex its muscle and not allow another camp at Gettysburg in the spring if the local authorities and businesses did not clean up their acts:

> That the liquor and evil social conditions in Gettysburg and surrounding towns were in part responsible for the removal of the troops to the South earlier than had been anticipated, was the statement of an Army officer at a conference Thursday afternoon, attended by representatives from Gettysburg, Hanover, and Emmitsburg. That these same conditions, if not remedied, will prevent the re-establishment of the camp in the spring was brought clearly to the attention of those in attendance. . . . Attention to conditions surrounding the town . . . was directed by the September medical report which showed an increase in cases of intoxication of 100 percent over that of August, while the number of cases of diseases resulting from vice was more than 100 percent. . . . The War Department is determined that an army of strong young men shall be sent abroad, and that this army dare not be menaced by the ravages of liquor and vice. *If Gettysburg, and the towns in this neighborhood, do not take the necessary steps to safeguard the soldiers during the remainder of their time here, and make necessary arrangements for them next spring their return in 1918 will be out of the question.* The number of men here is small compared to other places and accommodations can readily be found for them.

The message was fairly straightforward: the responsibility for stamping out vice and liquor lay with the community, not with the army. If the citizens of Gettysburg and the surrounding area wanted to continue to profit from the soldiers' presence, they must take the appropriate measures or risk losing next year's camp to another locale.[117] Gettysburg civilians were indignant about the accusations that the army leveled and believed the army itself was partly to blame for allowing the soldiers to travel to other towns to get booze and solicit prostitutes. Yet, wrote a *Times* reporter, "the situation largely resolves itself into a necessity for better conditions in towns and cities near Gettysburg, that this place gets a minor share of the blame but that it also has something to do in order to protect the soldiers."[118] The town leaders would have about four months to come up with a plan for improvement.

One man who undoubtedly hoped the soldiers *would not* return was GNMP Commission chairman Nicholson. In September, he received a letter from his friend and fellow Union veteran, Col. Henry S. Huidekoper. "I hope you are quite well," he remarked, "and as happy as one can be with 12,000 soldiers injuring your beautiful park." He snidely concluded, "They had better have gone elsewhere, even to honoring another southern general by naming the camp after him. My mind reverts to the sentiments of fifty years ago." Despite the passage of time, the efforts at reconciliation characterized by the 1913 Peace Jubilee and a common enemy in "Kaiser Bill," old grievances and hard feelings persisted more than a half-century later. In early November, Nicholson sent a note to U.S. District Attorney Rogers L. Burnett asking him to "not let up on the liquor business with the hotels and rum houses at Gettysburg." Nicholson suggested that the military police were not doing their job; if they had been, "there would have been much less liquor there, and less confusion and vandalism. Our Guards in one day collected more liquor by holding up automobiles on Hancock Avenue than was gathered by the military police during their whole service here." The soldiers' relocation to North Carolina could not come soon enough for Nicholson.[119]

The army's transportation officers were able to move the soldiers, their equipment and the horses much faster than anticipated. By the end of the second week of November, only a rear guard remained in the town. Soldiers whose dependents had come to Gettysburg also had to make arrangements for their wives and children to accompany them to Charlotte, return to their homes, or remain in Gettysburg. While stationed in camp, at least eighty-two soldiers applied for marriage licenses from the Adams County Clerk of Courts. Many of the doughboys married local women, but some brought their old girlfriends to Gettysburg and tied the knot before embarking for Camp Greene. The *Times* noted in its November 28 edition that the "first eleven months of this year have broken all previous records on the issuance of marriage licenses. . . . And many of the Sammie bridegrooms did not get their licenses here. A number were married in York, Harrisburg and Baltimore, so that Cupid was evidently losing little time in his target practice among the troops stationed here." The six regiments that had been posted at Gettysburg in 1917 would comprise one brigade each in the Third, Fourth, and Fifth Divisions of the American Expeditionary Forces. These divisions would participate in the horrific, bloody campaigns of the summer and fall of 1918, including Château-Thierry, Second Battle of the Marne, Soissons, Saint-Mihiel and the Meuse-Argonne offensive. Undoubtedly, many of those army brides who had been married in the summer and fall of 1917 would be grieving widows by the end of 1918.

Although most of the soldiers would leave Gettysburg by Thanksgiving 1917, they left behind, in the care of the Quartermaster Department, numerous temporary buildings that had been constructed during their stay in a camp that measured approximately four hundred acres of government-owned or -leased land. The structures included 111 mess halls of various sizes, 115 bath houses, 115 latrines, 8 hospital shelters (wards and administration), 1 bakery, 18 animal shelters, 1 motor shed/stable, 6 hay-storage sheds, 1 headquarters building, 1 telephone exchange, 3 sleeping barracks (for quartermaster troops remaining in Gettysburg),

Partial view of the camp from Cemetery Ridge, looking west. Note the derelict streetcar of the defunct Gettysburg Electric Railway in the foreground and troops marching on the Emmitsburg Road. The fenced monument next to the truck is that of the 8th Ohio Infantry, marking the position where the regiment fought on July 3, 1863, during Pickett's Charge. (S. Boardman Collection)

2 sewage disposal plants, 20 waste incinerators, 1 grease storage shed and 2 pump houses—all together, more than 400 structures.[120] Colonel Nicholson certainly was happy that the great majority of the soldiers were moving to North Carolina, but the landscape of his beloved battlefield had been drastically altered and obviously could not be rehabilitated to its shrinelike appearance until after the war.

The Regulars spent a dull Thanksgiving in their new training area. Many wished they were back in Gettysburg. Although the North Carolina camp had better amenities than their old cantonment, they missed the congeniality of Gettysburg's citizens. The *Times* informed its subscribers, from "many letters received from soldiers who spent the summer here and are now at Camp Greene, there is a general desire that they may all return to Gettysburg at as early a date as possible." The infantrymen complained that, although the daytime temperatures were warmer, the nights were just as cold as in Gettysburg. Camp Greene had a much larger soldier population, and while its infrastructure was much improved over the Gettysburg camp, "they would rather be in a smaller camp where the civilian population is more in evidence." The residents of Charlotte also were not as congenial, and there was "much less tendency among the people . . . to open their homes and hearts to the soldiers than was shown here. . . . One boy writes to friends here that the people in the southern city act as though they are afraid of the soldiers." The soil underfoot was clay, and when it rained everything turned to sticky, red mud. The end result, according to the soldier who had written to the *Times,* was that "there is not one of us that would not rather be freezing at Gettysburg than be here."[121]

The Regulars, however, would not be coming back to Gettysburg. After spending five months in North Carolina, at the end of April 1918, they entrained for Camp Mills, Long Island. Shortly thereafter, the Sammies left for New York Harbor and boarded ships that took them first to England and thereafter to France. Private Stone of the 59th U.S. Infantry noted that his own command embarked on the White Star Liner *Olympic* (sister ship of the ill-fated *Titanic*) at 3:00 P.M. on May 5, 1918. The *Olympic* had an encounter with a U-boat during the Trans-Atlantic voyage, but the liner rammed the submarine and apparently sank it. According to Stone, "The Olympic sailed on in its zig-zag course and on May 12th arrived at South Hampton Harbor." After a few days in England, the regiment embarked at Dover, crossed the English Channel, and shortly thereafter arrived at Calais, France.[122] The great adventure was about to begin.

CHAPTER 4

Goodbye Gettysburg, Hello France—

"We're Going to Square Our Debt to You"

With the exodus of the six U.S. Infantry regiments, their animals, and much of the equipment from the historic battlefield cantonment, things began to settle down in Gettysburg. Even before all of the troops had departed, the bars were permitted to reopen on November 9, as only the soldiers of the 61st U.S. Infantry, the camp hospital, the machine-gun battalion and trench mortar battery remained, and all were camped on the battlefield outside of the half-mile radius of the closest bars.[1] Once these men entrained for North Carolina, a small detachment of quartermaster and ordnance soldiers stayed behind to account for, maintain, and guard the surplus equipment, as well as the structures that had been built for the Camp of the U.S. Troops. The buildings were not heated, and thus the remaining doughboys were forced to find lodging in Gettysburg until warmer weather arrived. That these men still remained in town buoyed the hopes of the local citizens that another camp would be established in the spring. For the winter of 1917–18, however, the people of Adams County watched and waited as they sent their own sons and a few daughters off to the killing fields of the Western Front.

The biggest problem Gettysburg citizens faced that winter was the shortage of coal, needed for fueling furnaces and stoves. People felt the pinch even before Christmas. In reality, there was no dearth of anthracite—the problem lay in transportation foul-ups that stranded trainloads of coal in marshalling yards. It would take months to sort out the mess. Meanwhile, the folks in Gettysburg were getting cold. A concerned citizen sent a telegram to Congressman Brodbeck in mid-December to see if he could intervene with the Fuel Administration and get some badly needed coal delivered to Adams County. His reply was printed in the *Gettysburg Times* on December 19: "Telegram received. Have conferred with Dr. Garfield who will intercede with the Fuel Administrator of Pennsylvania, Mr. Potter, who is in Washington to-day." (Harry Garfield, president of Williams College and son of President James Garfield, was the nation's Fuel Administrator during the war, responsible for the production, distribution, and pricing of coal.) It was a cold winter in Gettysburg, and until the coal situation was fixed, citizens burned wood rather than freeze.

By January 1918, the "Yanks"—mostly Regular Army, National Guard, and a contingent of the Marine Corps—had arrived in British and French ports by the tens of thousands. A popular American song celebrated the deployment of these troops, and its lyrics captured the mood of the nation and its soldiers. The last line of the chorus even harkened back to the Treaty of Alliance between France and the fledgling United States, signed in 1778, which brought the French army and navy into America's War for Independence:

> Goodbye Broadway, Hello France,
> We're ten million strong,
> Goodbye sweethearts, wives and mothers,
> It won't take us long.
> Don't you worry while we're there,
> It's for you we're fighting too,
> So Goodbye Broadway, Hello France,
> We're going to square our debt to you.[2]

The French alliance contributed to America's independence. It was widely believed that the Battle of Gettysburg preserved the Republic. Now, young men from the Gettysburg area were on their way to Europe to help save the Allies and participate in their modern-day crusade against the Central Powers. Sailors of the navy and Coast Guard already were doing so by performing convoy and antisubmarine duty to ensure that the Sammies reached foreign shores safely. Once there, the American Expeditionary Forces' regiments and brigades deployed to "quiet sectors" of the Western Front, alongside seasoned British or French units, to get a taste of trench warfare—with its incessant shelling, raids, and occasional attacks. Meanwhile, the division, corps, and army staffs shook out their wrinkles, and training camps in Britain and France were established with host-nation staffs to instruct the Americans in the "proper" way to fight. The First Division (Regular Army) received its baptism of fire in November 1917, when three of its soldiers became the seminal American troops killed in action.[3]

Back home, the first draft call had taken its quota—240—of eligible Adams County men, and many of them were engaged in basic training during the late summer and autumn of 1917. A parade in their honor was staged the first week of September, led by Civil War veterans from the Gettysburg GAR post.[4] Most of the county's conscripts were sent to Camp Meade, Maryland, just north of Washington, D.C., where they were assigned to the Seventy-Ninth Division, a National Army unit comprising primarily draftees from eastern Pennsylvania, Maryland, and the District of Columbia.[5] Adams County men also signed up for the six regiments that had been camped on the battlefield. Local boys likewise had enlisted in the Pennsylvania National Guard, whose units would comprise the Twenty-Eighth Division on the Western Front. This organization, like the Regular divisions, would fight in some of the most horrendous battles of 1918. And naturally, there were men who had enlisted in the navy and Marine Corps, as well as non-divisional army units such as the Air Service, Coast Artillery, Quartermaster, Ordnance, Engineer, Medical, and Signal Corps. Adams County women served, in far lower numbers, with the Red Cross and Army Nurse Corps. The few African American men from Adams County who served, but in equal proportion to their small segment of the overall county population, were relegated to labor battalions or the Ninety-Second and Ninety-Third Divisions.

The initial contingent of 120 white conscripts from Adams County boarded rail cars on Thursday, September 20, 1917, set for Annapolis Junction, Maryland, the closest station to the recently established and still under-construction Camp George Gordon Meade. The drafted men paraded through the streets of Gettysburg with the 4th U.S. Infantry Band in the van, cheered by hundreds of their fellow citizens. "The youths themselves were gay and happy," reported the *Times* that day. "One or two who were taking final leave of members of their families were a bit moved but, as a general rule, they were all in high spirits." As the train pulled away from the station, the band played "National Emblem" while the crowd shouted approval and threw their hats in the air. On October 6, the second group of draftees, this time only twelve men, left for Camp Meade with very little fanfare. The *Times* headline stated, "QUIET FAREWELL TO DRAFTED BOYS. No Music, No Cheers to Send Second Contingent to Camp Meade." The war finally was becoming personal to the people of Gettysburg and Adams County, and already the enthusiasm was wearing off.

A few weeks later, another parting took place in Gettysburg with great fanfare but to a smaller crowd than what had amassed for the first departure of draftees. What would appear a racist headline to modern eyes was heartfelt appreciation to the white subscribers of the *Gettysburg Times:* "SEVEN NEGRO BOYS TO CAMP. Happy Farewells and Cheers when the Colored Contingent Leaves.

Showed Proper Sprit. No Sadness to Send These Boys on Their Way." One of the conscripts in this group, John S. Williams, had been employed as a laborer at Gettysburg National Military Park. He was accompanied by his older brother, Joseph, who likewise had been drafted. Knowing the men would not arrive at Camp Meade, where elements of the so-called Negro divisions were forming, until nightfall, mothers and wives packed them boxed lunches. What certainly *was* racist was the reporter's remark: "The things that taste specially good to the negro boy were in those boxes and it is a safe bet that there was a happy time when the boxes were opened on the way."[6] In modern parlance, the writer was implying that there were enough fried chicken and collard greens to go around.

By now, Gettysburg College and the Lutheran Seminary had sent a fair number of alumni and current students off to war, most as army officers. The college ROTC detachment, meanwhile, was busy training students in basic military skills and leadership. College faculty even offered courses to the Regulars during the fall semester of 1917 at little or no cost. An article in the September 26 *Gettysburg Times* related, "Specially attractive to the soldiers is a course in Military French which will be given Mondays and Wednesdays from seven to eight o'clock in the evening. . . . The instruction given here will, it is believed, be of inestimable value when those who take it get on the other side." Captain Keller Rockey, Class of 1909, already was speaking to Frenchmen, as he was one of the first marines to arrive in France in the summer of 1917. Another Gettysburg alumnus, the naturalized German immigrant 1st Lt. Adolph Weidenbach, U.S. Army, likewise had been serving in France since the summer.[7]

Meanwhile the local draft board continued examining and inducting men for the National Army. By October 3, according to the *Times,* the board had examined a total of 1,488 men. Of that number, 200 asked for no exemption, 375 were found physically unfit, 146 asked for occupational exemptions, 700 requested exemptions due to dependent family members, and 67 "did not answer call." Despite the disparity between those called and those who answered, in addition to the Sandoes (mentioned in chapter 2), another Adams County family contributed all four of its sons to the military by the autumn of 1917, albeit in noncombatant roles: Col. Henry D. Snyder commanded the U.S. Army Medical Supply Depot in New York; Lt. Cdr. John J. Snyder served aboard the SS *Leviathan,* probably the most famous American troopship of the war, as its senior medical officer; 1st Lt. William R. Snyder was stationed at Camp Thomas, Kentucky, as a dentist in the Dental Reserve Corps; and 1st Lt. George A. Snyder, also of the Dental Reserve Corps, was posted at Fort Kearney, in Luna Vista, California. All were veterans of the Spanish-American War.[8] Likewise, a McSherrystown clan contributed four brothers to the armed forces: Preston,

Claude, Guy, and Earl Weaver. The first three were drafted into the army, while the fourth enlisted in the naval reserve. Preston and Guy both were assigned to Company I, 316th Infantry Regiment, Seventy-Ninth Division, and Claude was sent to Kelly Army Airfield, Texas, to work in an aero supply squadron before being shipped to France in January 1918.[9]

By October 11, approximately 20,300 other new troops had joined the Adams County conscripts at Camp Meade. Most of the local soldiers were assigned to Company A, 316th U.S. Infantry Regiment. That unit was assigned to the 158th Infantry Brigade, under the command of recently promoted Brig. Gen. Everard Hatch, who previously commanded the 4th U.S. Infantry Regiment at the Gettysburg camp. The rest of the local men were spread among the 304th Engineer Regiment, the 310th and 311th Machine Gun Battalions, and division auxiliary troops. Some of the Gettysburg College men who had graduated from officers' training at Fort Niagara likewise were assigned to Camp Meade, to become junior officers in the Seventy-Ninth Division. These young lieutenants, along with reassigned Regular Army noncommissioned officers, faced a gargantuan task. According to the Seventy-Ninth Division historical committee, "They had been brought together suddenly to constitute the framework of a combat division and to direct its training—the training of thousands of men who had never before marched in formation, shouldered a rifle, obeyed orders, or had the slightest knowledge of military life and discipline." The junior leaders' mission was daunting, considering that the Seventy-Ninth comprised men from many different nationalities and religions, with varied occupational and educational backgrounds. The division history illuminated this important fact by citing evidence "secured in a statistical census taken by the 310th Field Artillery." According to this report,

> In this one regiment there were fifteen nationalities . . . [and] four different religious beliefs, while twenty-five men of the regiment asserted they had no religious adherence. As to educational attainments, but fifty men in the regiment had ever attended college while 114 had no education of any sort. Others had been to elementary, grammar and high schools. These statistics are typical of other units in the Division. They indicate the heterogeneity of the regiments and the mammoth task it was to weld these thousands into a fighting unit.[10]

Although accustomed to seeing such a large volume of people from different parts of the country (as a result of the 1913 Peace Jubilee and the constant flow of American and international tourists over the years), the boys from the Gettysburg area nonetheless experienced quite a culture shock at Camp Meade. Not only were they being indoctrinated with the U.S. Army's warrior ethos, at the same time they were being exposed to a variety of languages and ethnicities on a scale that they possibly could not have imagined just a few weeks earlier. Unlike many of their new comrades, however, all of the Adams County recruits at least could speak English.

John S. Williams, the former GNMP employee, was not acclimating well to army life. Assigned to Company C, 368th Infantry, Ninety-Second Division, one of the two African American divisions, Private Williams wrote his old boss, Chairman John Nicholson, a letter from Camp Meade. "I dont like it any to well down here an wish I was back home an they have not give us any clothes yet an it rains down here about every day an it is wet getting around." He asked Colonel Nicholson to send him his last paycheck as well as his sweater and scarf "for down here they dont give the men anything." A few months later, Williams was desperate to be discharged. He pleaded with Nicholson to pull some strings to get him out of the Army. He offered to pay "200 dollars to get back home again to my place of work . . . I would be willing to work for nothing if I would get back home . . . Colonel when you rite to me please tell me about it for I thought because you had lots to do with the Government so I thought it would not be any harm to ask."[11] There is no record of whether Nicholson even tried. Considering the army's benign neglect of its black soldiers, it is not surprising that Williams wanted to return home. Insufficient clothing, a shortage of overcoats, and inadequate housing and bedding were common complaints. Then, to allay fears among white civilians, the Ninety-Second Division's subordinate units were trained at several different stateside camps and did not come together as an organized combat division until its various regiments and support battalions reached France.[12] A Gettysburg native then working in Hagerstown, Maryland, was heading for Camp Meade about the same time. John Lane, whose mother still resided in Gettysburg, had been drafted in the summer of 1917. He would become, as the *Gettysburg Times* later reported, "the only colored man to be commissioned from Adams County," rising to the rank of first lieutenant in the Sanitary Corps.[13]

Regardless of skin color, the Camp Meade troops were given military instruction very similar to that administered to the Regulars at the Gettysburg camp. Because of the intense training schedule, passes were limited, as were the number of visitors to the camp.[14] During their first few weeks of military service, in what the Army called the "school of the soldier," the recruits were taught how to wear the uniform, salute, march, and acquire other basic skills. They also received a solid dose of physical conditioning.[15] In a letter printed in the *Gettysburg Times* on December 3, 1917, Pvt. Percy Eichelberger of northern Adams County, assigned to Company A, 316th Infantry, recounted a typical training day: "Drill begins at 7:30 A.M. and continues until 4:30 P.M., with one hour for dinner. . . . The training program is as follows: marching, physical exercises, bayonet charging, war games then marching before mess, the afternoon is devoted to chiefly semaphore (signaling), bomb throwing and manual of arms. The bombs are thrown from real trenches according to present skill will take some time before we are ready to throw effectively 'over there.'" By early November, combat training had begun in earnest. In addition to what Eichelberger mentioned, recruits received training in rifle and pistol marksmanship, automatic weapons, and chemical warfare. Also, schools were established for first aid, intelligence, engineering, and artillery.[16]

More arrivals from later draft calls continued to swell the Seventy-Ninth, which, since its inception, was commanded by Brig. Gen. Joseph E. Kuhn, an 1885 graduate of West Point who until his appointment as division commander had spent his entire career in the Corps of Engineers. By February 1918, conscripts from West Virginia and Ohio were added to the Seventy-Ninth's ranks. Field training and large-scale maneuvers were conducted in the early spring, and more men arrived in May, from as far away as New York and Connecticut. The division slowly was losing its regional makeup, but its ranks still were filled primarily with men from the District of Columbia, Maryland, and Pennsylvania. The Adams County soldiers and the rest of the Seventy-Ninth Division embarked for France in July 1918.[17] By then, several U.S. divisions had been engaged in intense fighting near the Marne River east of Paris. Strategically, it seemed like 1914 all over again. Since March, the Germans were throwing everything into their effort to win the war before the Americans could get into the fight.

The first Adams County native killed in action was Cpl. William F. Gehring of New Oxford, assigned to Company A, 149th Machine Gun Battalion, Forty-Second Division.[18] (At the time of his enlistment, however, he lived and worked in Hanover.[19]) Gehring was felled by shrapnel on March 9, 1918, in a quiet sector of the front near the Vosges Mountains. 1st Lt. John J. Halliday, the chaplain of Gehring's regiment, wrote the fallen soldier's mother a letter in an attempt to assuage her grief:

> As chaplain of the 166th Infantry, it is my duty to convey to you the details of the death and burial of your son. . . . William was on duty in the trenches and an exploding shrapnel shell took its toll of his life. On March 11, the funeral was held from a chapel in a village back of the lines. Full military honors were accorded to your son. The body was laid to rest in the cemetery along with the fallen heroes in the French and American armies. The grave was appropriately marked and the exact location is on file with the Graves Registration Service. . . . Mere words are too inadequate vehicles to express my sympathy to you in your hour of bereave-

ment. Death is a distressing thing, but death in action for one's country has its reward of glorious achievement. William died a hero. Surely the All-Wise Father will receive this fallen hero. May I be of service to you?[20]

Before the year's end, Halliday and hundreds of other American chaplains would compose thousands of similar notes to distraught mothers and wives, just as Union and Confederate chaplains had written fifty-five years earlier from the battlefield at Gettysburg.

A few weeks later, on April 3, nineteen-year-old Wilford Rupprecht, a native of McSherrystown, also made the supreme sacrifice. (Like Gehring, at the time of his enlistment Rupprecht resided in Hanover.) The previous summer, he had joined the 7th U.S. Infantry, when it was training in Gettysburg. He then transferred to the 2d Trench Mortar Battalion, Second Division. Rupprecht was killed while serving near the Toulon Sector of the Western Front, another so-called quiet sector.[21] Pvt. Albert J. Lentz of Company D, 18th Infantry, First Division, was the first Gettysburg soldier to be killed in action when he fell near Cantigny, France, on April 26, 1918. Lentz had moved to Chicago about

Left: General Joseph E. Kuhn, right, talking to officers of the Seventy-Ninth Division at Camp Meade, Maryland, 1917 (Library of Congress); *right:* Albert J. Lentz, first Gettysburg man to be killed in action. (Adams County Historical Society)

three years earlier, but his parents still resided in Gettysburg. He had even spent part of his childhood living in the house known as General Lee's Headquarters. While working in Chicago, Lentz enlisted in the Regular Army and served in the Mexican Punitive Expedition. His unit was one of the first American divisions to sail for France in 1917.[22] Ironically, the first three Adams County men to be killed in action—but, not surprisingly, considering the ethnic backgrounds of the county's residents—were of German ancestry.

General John J. Pershing, commanding the AEF, was determined to keep his American army intact and not feed brigades or divisions piecemeal to the French and British to serve under their commands. In the spring of 1918, however, the strategic situation forced Pershing to alter his stance. Back in Gettysburg, on February 12, the locals learned of Russia's withdrawal from the war with this *Times* headline: "RUSSIA IS OUT. NEWS CONFIRMED." The Bolsheviks had gained the upper hand and had called for peace. The headline was a bit premature, but the handwriting was on the wall. On March 3, it became official. After the Russians and Germans signed a separate peace agreement—the Treaty of Brest-Litovsk—German troops no longer were needed on the Eastern Front, so Kaiser Wilhelm approved the launching of Operation Michael, Imperial Germany's last great attempt to win the war. The limited Allied gains made in 1917 were all but eradicated, and on March 25 the Germans broke the Allied line near the French city of Amiens. In this emergency, Marshal Ferdinand Foch was named the Supreme Allied Commander. The situation was perilous, and soon the Germans again were threatening Paris. On May 2, the British prime minister, David Lloyd George, reminded Pershing that since the beginning of the German offensive, British Empire casualties totaled 280,000 and French casualties exceeded 340,000. Bowing to pressure, Pershing agreed to put some of the AEF into the line, but most of his force, about two-thirds of the expected 650,000 Americans that would be in Europe by the end of May, would be held in reserve to constitute a separate American army. The other third of Pershing's forces soon would be needed. On May 27, the Germans renewed their offensive. By May 28, they had driven a huge wedge in the Allied lines, fifteen miles deep and forty miles wide. It was time for the Americans to step up to the plate. At Cantigny, where Albert Lentz had been killed more than a month earlier, the First Division withstood the German onslaught and counterattacked. They held the town and demonstrated to the Germans that the Sammies were a formidable force.[23]

On Thursday, May 30, while the AEF was receiving its baptism of fire, the good people of Gettysburg were commemorating Memorial Day with its annual ceremony in the Soldiers' National Cemetery. The speaker that day was Bishop

William F. McDowell of the Methodist Episcopal Church, who delivered an address titled “Gettysburg and Its Relation to the World War.” With a sizeable crowd of Civil War veterans in attendance, McDowell focused his remarks on North–South reconciliation, the similarities between the Battle of Gettysburg and the current battles, the pride that Americans should feel in the present conflict for fighting on principle and the confidence that all should have in the ultimate triumph of democracy over the “Hun.” Delivering a speech that was long-winded, self-righteous, xenophobic, and rife with historical errors, McDowell nonetheless knew his audience. At one point, he told the crowd, “The memories and spirits of the men of Meade, and Reynolds and Hancock, the men of Lee, and Longstreet and Pickett are crying across the seas to the men of Foch, and Haig and Pershing, to stand fast . . . to stand fast in the mighty utterance that Lincoln here made for all the sons of men everywhere.” A reporter for the *Gettysburg Times* believed that the oration was “one of the best of recent years.” Most certainly, the First Division soldiers who had just fought at Cantigny would have laughed at the bishop as he ranted about Hindenburg and the Hun and the Turk.[24]

On May 23, in the midst of the Allied crisis, the British armed merchant-cruiser RMS *Moldovia,* carrying companies A and B, 58th U.S. Infantry, was plying the English Channel en route to a French port when a German U-boat sent a torpedo into its portside hull at the dark hour of 2:40 A.M., near the sleeping berths of Company B’s doughboys. A terrific explosion rocked the ship, killing fifty-four men outright. In the ensuing confusion, two more soldiers drowned. Many of the dead men had trained at Gettysburg the year before. The *Gettysburg Times,* reporting the news of the sinking on May 25, noted in a subhead, “Many Well Known in This Place Go Down to Death in English Channel.” A list of the dead was printed in the story, the author surmising that it “will be anxiously scanned by Gettysburg people to whom many men are known personally.”[25]

Two other regiments that had trained at Gettysburg already had landed in France and soon were involved in combat operations. The 4th and 7th Infantry, comprising the 5th Infantry Brigade, Third Division, were engaged at the bloody Battle of Château-Thierry during June. Gettysburg residents learned of the death of one of the soldiers who had trained on the National Military Park when the unfortunate doughboy’s sweetheart received a telegram announcing his demise. Pvt. Joseph P. Socia, whose home of record was Houston, Texas, was killed in action on June 10, 1918, in the midst of the Third Division’s dogged defense along the banks of the Marne River against a sustained German drive.[26] Two of the Sandoe brothers, Luther of the Twenty-Eighth Division and Edgar of the Third, also fought in this campaign, as did many other Adams County soldiers serving in those two units and other Regular Army and National Guard divisions.

Captain Rockey fought with the Marine Brigade of the Second Division at the Battle of Belleau Wood, only a few miles north of Château-Thierry, where, for his actions on June 6, 1917, he was awarded the Navy Cross and Distinguished Service Cross. The citation for the latter medal states:

> The President of the United States of America, authorized by Act of Congress, July 9, 1918, takes pleasure in presenting the Distinguished Service Cross to Captain Keller Emrick Rockey, United States Marine Corps, for extraordinary heroism while serving with the First Battalion, Sixth Regiment (Marines), 2d Division, A.E.F., in action at Chateau-Thierry, France, on 6 June 1918. Captain Rockey performed distinguished service by bringing up supports and placing them in the front lines at great personal exposure, showing exceptional ability and extraordinary heroism. He was indefatigable and invaluable in carrying forward the attack and organizing and holding the position.[27]

A few months later, Rockey, who had since been promoted to major, wrote a tongue-in-cheek letter to the *Gettysburg Times* to deny rumors that he had been killed in action. According to Rockey, "The reports of my death are considerably exaggerated. . . . I speak French like a native—of Pennsylvania—can't seem to speak the 'orrid language beyond a pleasant bonjour to the mesdemoiselles." In conclusion, he assured the *Times,* "If you don't see me around Gettysburg directly after the hostilities cease you will know I've been planted [in the ground] because that's one town I'm going to break for."[28]

Rockey was lucky to have survived, but the Battle of Belleau Wood brought grief to a well-known Gettysburg family when it suffered the loss of twenty-one-year-old Sgt. Paul J. Altoff, USMC, a York native, who died of wounds received in action on June 11, 1918. Likewise, Biglerville native William Benton Thomas, USMC, was wounded above the left eye on June 6. Family members told a *Times* reporter that they hoped "the skill of the American surgeons will bring him back to health and that he will be able to resume his duties and finally return home safe." The navy doctors did their jobs well, and Thomas returned to duty and served through the end of the war.[29] Another marine with Gettysburg connections was not as lucky. Capt. Edward C. Fuller, a 1916 graduate of the U.S. Naval Academy, had befriended many Gettysburg residents during a two-month Marine Corps training course held at GNMP shortly after his graduation. Fuller was killed in action on June 6, during an enemy counterattack. A *Times* writer compared him to a famous Civil War general: "The Germans plunged heavily. Captain Fuller stood like Stonewall Jackson, superintending the shelter for his men, meanwhile ordering them to hold back the Huns." During the attack, Fuller was killed by an enemy shell. At the time of his son's death, Col. Ben Fuller was commanding the U.S. Marine Barracks in Philadelphia.[30] (Later in his career, then General Fuller became the fifteenth commandant of the Marine Corps.)

Littlestown native Monroe Feeser had been drafted in the summer of 1917; departed with the Adams County men for Camp Meade in September; and subsequently was assigned, like so many other local boys, to Company A, 316th Infantry, Seventy-Ninth Division. He was part of a large group of Seventy-Ninth soldiers transferred to the Third Division at Camp Greene, to help that division push its personnel strength to its authorized levels. Feeser was severely wounded in the Allied counterattacks of July 1918, the Aisne-Marne offensive. His injury was catastrophic and led to the amputation of his right leg at the thigh. He also suffered a fractured left foot and other injuries. He underwent several surgeries, endured transfers from one hospital to another, and suffered through rehabilitation. By war's end, Feeser had not recovered enough to travel back to the United States; he would not do so until March 1919. By 1921 he still was receiving treatment in a U.S. Army general hospital. One of his Adams County comrades, Willis D. Lauver of Arendtsville, had a similar military career: he was drafted, was initially assigned to the 316th Infantry Regiment, and then volunteered for immediate overseas service with the 4th Infantry Regiment, Third Division. Lauver likewise sustained a severe shrapnel wound at Château-Thierry and spent the rest of the war in various hospitals. Feeser and Lauver were two of at least fifty-seven Adams County men who were wounded during the war and lived to talk about it.[31]

Gettysburg College student Percy Eichelberger of Gardners, a small town in the orchard country of northern Adams County, was another drafted man originally assigned to the Seventy-Ninth Division. Like Feeser and Lauver, he was transferred to the Third. Eichelberger was present when the division defended the Marne River crossing points at Château-Thierry in June and July 1918. On July 15, "the Hun tried to make a crossing of the river. At many points he failed to reach the water's edge," Eichelberger recalled a few years after the war. "At others he was checked in the attempt to cross, while at other points he crossed only to be swallowed up by the ever-present Yank."[32] The German juggernaut thus had been stopped at Belleau Wood and Château-Thierry, and soon the Allies went on the offensive. Belleau Wood went down in Marine Corps history as one of its most famous battles, and the battlefield was renamed by the French Government, "*Bois de la Brigade de Marine*" (Wood of the Marine Brigade.) For its stout defense of Château-Thierry, the Third Division received the nickname, "Rock of the Marne," and thereafter was called the "Marne Division."[33] Now, it was time for the Americans, French, and British to go on the attack.

Lloyd Garretson, a Biglerville resident who had enlisted as a musician in the 4th Infantry Regiment when it was posted at Gettysburg a year earlier, wrote home to his sister soon after the end of the war. On February 3, 1919, the *Gettysburg Times* reprinted the letter: "I don't know what the American papers had [written] about the Marne drive, but from what I hear the Marines were getting all the credit for it. Well, don't you believe that, for it was the old Third Division that stopped the Dutch at Chateau Thierry. Our machine gun battalion just piled them up on the bridge as they tried to cross before it was blown up." Still, Garretson gave the sea soldiers due respect: "The Marines did good work in Belleau Woods, which is north of Chateau Thierry." Due to the censorship policy of the AEF, war correspondents could not provide the designation of regiments, divisions, or branches of the army, but they could differentiate between the army and the Marine Corps. As a result, the Marine Brigade of the Second Division got the lion's share of the news coverage during the summer of 1918.[34] When Garretson wrote home after the war had come to a close, the censorship policy already had been lifted, and he was free to laud the accomplishments of his own Third Division.

The *Compiler* ran a short story a few weeks after the outcome of the campaign had been decided. "Many military writers are comparing the Second Battle of the Marne to Gettysburg as the high water mark of Hun barbarism and from this point the Hun will recede until ultimately defeated." The writer obviously knew his Gettysburg readers would understand the comparison. The story was mostly propaganda that characterized the sensationalized wartime reporting of the American press, but its author was correct in his assessment of the German army's decline and the significance of American participation: "The important part taken by the American boys in this Gettysburg of the World War is one of the brightest chapters of the war yet written."[35] By this time, the German high command was well aware of the fighting abilities of the Americans, and it would not have to wait very long before the AEF struck back.

The new mission was the reduction of the Aisne-Marne salient, a bulge in the Allied line between the Aisne and Marne rivers formed by the German offensives of late May and June 1918. Two American and one French corps would carry out the assault. The U.S. I Corps was under the command of Maj. Gen. Hunter Liggett, who five years earlier had commanded the Army contingent supporting the Gettysburg Peace Jubilee. The other major American force, III Corps, included the Twenty-Eighth Division, comprising primarily Pennsylvania National Guardsmen (with a sizeable body of Adams County men), and the Fourth Division, which included two of the regiments that were formed at Gettysburg in 1917, the 58th and 59th Infantry. The French XX Corps also had two American units assigned, the veteran First and Second Divisions.[36] During the upcoming campaign, sailors assigned to USN railway-artillery batteries, manning huge, fourteen-inch naval cannons mounted on railroad carriages, provided pre-assault gunfire support. A Gettysburg native, Quartermaster Second Class John H. Menchey, was a noncommissioned officer assigned to one of those batteries.[37]

The attack began on July 18. The next day, Cpl. Roy M. Kesserling of Biglerville, assigned to the 26th Infantry Regiment, First Division, received a gunshot wound. He recovered and returned to his unit in late summer. About the same time, a soldier in the 4th Infantry Regiment of the Third Division, who had trained at Gettysburg the year before, bore witness to an aerial dogfight that made the national headlines back in the United States. More than a half century later, Sgt. Dominic Pence recalled, "On July 18, 1918, I was at the Marne River watching two German fighters and one American fighter. The two Germans downed the American fighter . . . [which] went down on the enemy side. After we crossed the river when the Germans fell, we saw there was a grave and a wrecked airplane. The grave was of Quinten [*sic*] Roosevelt."[38] Twenty-year-old 2d Lt. Quentin Roosevelt, the fifth and youngest child of President Teddy Roosevelt, had been assigned to the 95th Pursuit Squadron, U.S. Army Air Service. He shot down his first German on July 10 but met his own demise four days later at the hands of a pilot from the squadron of the famous "Red Baron." Pence got the date wrong but his description of the dogfight was absolutely correct. American patrols, perhaps even Pence's, actually found Roosevelt's marked grave on July 18.[39]

During the next month and a half, the Aisne-Marne salient was totally reduced, but at great cost. Gettysburg native Louis S. Bushman, who had enlisted in the 4th Infantry when it was training on GNMP, was serving as a medic in the Third Division when he was gassed on July 26. Likewise gassed was Cpl. John Crim of Gettysburg (who earlier had resided in West Virginia), who joined the 4th Infantry Regiment six days after war was declared. He later was transferred to the 58th Infantry while it was training in his hometown. James F. Howe, also of Gettysburg and assigned to the 109th Infantry, Twenty-Eighth Division, was struck in the hand by a bullet from a machine gun on September 6. Another Gettysburgian and soldier in the Twenty-Eighth Division, Cpl. Earl J. Smith was captured in July and spent the rest of the war in a German prison camp. Pvt. Harold J. Angell of Littlestown was wounded in the left leg on July 25, ending his combat service. Pvt. Alphonsus A. Carbaugh of New Oxford, assigned to the 8th Machine Gun Battalion of the Third Division, was slightly wounded on July 18. John C. Neff of Gettysburg, a private in the 58th Infantry, Fourth Division, was wounded in the back by a shell fragment on July 19. During the same period, Pvt. Calvin Cullison of Cashtown, assigned to the 108th Machine Gun Battalion, Twenty-Eighth Division, received a gunshot wound to his left knee.[40] Many other Adams County soldiers were slightly wounded or gassed. Far less fortunate were four Adams County men who made the ultimate sacrifice during the summer of 1918.

Boyish looking Cpl. Francis E. Rider of East Berlin was killed in action on July 15 near the Marne River while serving in the 109th Infantry, Twenty-Eighth Division. He was a week shy of his nineteenth birthday. Another doughboy from the Twenty-Eighth, Pvt. Clair Richwine of Gardners, was wounded near Château-Thierry while fighting with the 112th Infantry Regiment. He subsequently was captured and died in captivity on August 31 from the wounds he had received in action. John W. Jobe, who was born in Missouri but claimed Gettysburg as his home of record, had served with the 4th U.S. Infantry along the Mexican border in 1916. When the unit arrived in Gettysburg in 1917, he was reassigned to Company I, 58th Infantry. In September, he was transferred to the 308th Infantry of the Seventy-Seventh Division, a National Army organization composed primarily of drafted men from New York. Before leaving for his new assignment, however, he married Miss Mabel Galbraith of Gettysburg. Jobe, then only eighteen years old, was killed in action on September 5 near the town of Fismes. The *Times* reported his death a month later, after his young bride was notified of his death: "Sergeant Jobe was very successful with his work, and while here made many friends who will regret to learn of his death." Jobe's remains were repatriated to the United States after the war, but Rider and Richwine are buried in the Oise-Aisne American Cemetery, near Seringes-et-Nesles, France, along with 6010 other Americans.[41]

Joseph Stone of Company L, 59th Infantry Regiment, Fourth Division, who only one year earlier had marveled at the experience of training on the famed Gettysburg Battlefield, was now engaged in his own battle to collapse the Aisne-Marne salient. He continued to chronicle—in somewhat bombastic fashion—his unit's adventures in his historical journal:

> About 4:30 pm of the 17th of July the company moved forward. All night long the boys marched thru muddy swamps. They were in heavy marching order too—burdened with 100 pounds of junk. They arrived in the rear of the fighting line next morning and took up positions in the trenches near the little village of Chepy. That same morning the boys of the 58th Infantry went over the top against strongly entrenched German positions, a stunt which dumbfounded as well as stampeded the Germans. But they were due some surprises for all along

> the lines were American Divisions with a win or die look on their haughty faces. The Dutch were up against the very spirit of Liberty itself for never in history did a nobler army advance against a foe.[42]

In the short space of three months, the AEF—or a portion thereof—had demonstrated its mettle, first in a last-ditch effort to thwart a sustained enemy assault, and then by launching a counteroffensive that erased all of the gains the German army had made in the spring of 1918. The cost, however, was approximately fifty thousand American casualties in the counteroffensive alone.[43] Although the 59th Infantry was actively engaged only four days, Private Stone noted that "'L' Company went into the fight with five officers and 257 men; all but 105 were killed, wounded, or missing, a casualty rate of 40 percent. Several officers in the company were wounded. All but 2 sergeants and most of the corporals were missing—they had "done their bit."[44] (In actuality, had Stone's arithmetic skills been better, he would have been chagrinned to discover that his unit suffered a casualty rate of 60 percent.) The entire Fourth Division suffered roughly 2,100 casualties in just three days of battle from July 18 to July 21.[45] In the wake of the fighting, Stone reflected, "The spirit of Gettysburg showed itself in the remarkable bravery of the boys who did their first soldiering on her fields."[46]

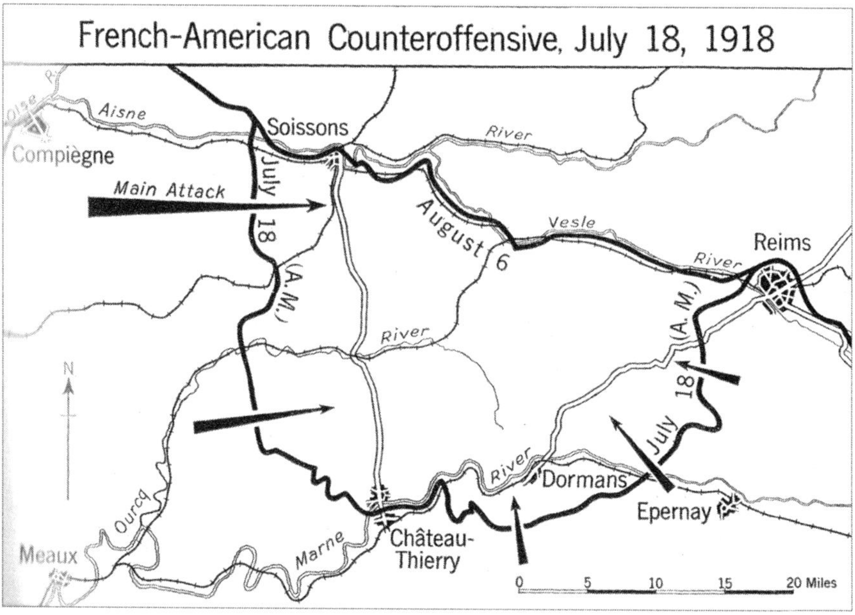

Map of the Aisne-Marne Counteroffensive, July–August 1918 (American Battle Monument Commission)

The counteroffensive continued into early September. Pvt. Francis E. Miller, a drafted man who later was transferred to the Machine-Gun Company, 109th Infantry, Twenty-Eighth Division, wrote about the exploits of his unit—which by now had earned the nickname "Iron Division"—in a letter to his mother. Like so many other missives from servicemen and nurses, this one found itself on the front page of the *Gettysburg Times*. "I have been on the front lines since July 4th, but September 4th, Wednesday afternoon at three o'clock beats the climax," Miller mused. "We went over the top. It was a terrible struggle between machine gun fire and artillery action. I succeeded in killing a German lieutenant and three others, besides taking four prisoners." He then listed the German units to which his prisoners had been assigned, but the Army censor cut it from his letter. Continuing, Miller wrote, "One of my best friends was knocked off, one who came down from Camp Meade with me. He was Charles Cool from Fairfield." Cool, likewise assigned to the Seventy-Ninth Division before being transferred to the Twenty-Eighth, was wounded by shrapnel but quickly recovered and was able to rejoin his unit. "I am one of the luckiest boys on the line, I can say without fear of contradiction," Miller pondered. "A bullet hit my steel helmet and dinged it, but I only got a black eye. The doctor said it was a bruised bone, and would take some time before it would heal up."[47] Miller stayed with his unit till the end of the war. Despite being on the front lines for more than two months, he and his comrades would get only a short respite before the next campaign.

Major John B. Duckstad, age twenty-eight, graduated from West Point in 1915 and was commissioned in the infantry. He served on the Mexican border with the 4th Infantry Regiment until it was transferred to Gettysburg in June 1917. Duckstad was subsequently reassigned to the 58th Infantry as part of the corps of cadre needed to train the new volunteers. While stationed at Gettysburg he met and fell in love with a Gettysburg woman, Miss Dorothy Zane, and shortly thereafter she became pregnant. He came back to Gettysburg from Camp Greene, and on December 26, 1917, they were married in her grandparents' home on Carlisle Street. Duckstad sailed for France with the Third Division in early May 1918. He fought in the Second Battle of the Marne and subsequent counteroffensive, only to be severely injured in a motorcycle accident while riding in a sidecar on September 4. He died the next day, leaving back in Gettysburg a young widow and baby son whom he had never seen.[48]

Pershing and his staff, meanwhile, were planning a major offensive operation that would see the American Expeditionary Forces fight as a unified army for the first time. But until then, other Adams County residents serving in noncombatant roles contributed their labor to winning the conflict. When the Americans had declared war a year earlier, the American Ambulance Hospital, where nurse Kate Wolf had been working since 1914, became "Base Hospital No. 1, AEF" Now under American command, Wolf subsequently was transferred and assumed the leadership of the American Red Cross Station at Angers, about 190 miles southwest of Paris.[49] Her friends in Adams County started the "Kate Wolf Fund" to subsidize her efforts to provide personal-care items, food, and cigarettes to American troops passing through Angers. On February 9, 1918, the *Compiler* printed Wolf's letter of thanks telling the fund's donors that their money was being put to good use: "I had occasion to bless you good people last night for I had forty-five dear boys for the night, not one had a sou [a low-denomination French coin], they had no pay recently." The soldiers had stopped at Angers on their way to pick up a trainload of mules. She was able to put them up for the night, treated those men who needed minor medical care, and bought them food and cigarettes using money from the fund. "If all the folks interested in the 'Fund' could have seen and heard those boys they would feel their money was well spent. It did not take much for the forty-five—less than three dollars." By this time, Kate was not the only Adams County nurse serving in France; she had been joined by several others, and more were on the way.

Malissa A. McElheney of Gettysburg, who was working as a nurse in Baltimore's Mercy Hospital when the United States declared war, joined the Army Medical Department and sailed for France on June 30, 1917. She served with an American medical unit assigned to the British army on the Western Front and did not return to the United States until the spring of 1919. Pauline M. Sherman of Littlestown signed with the Army Nurse Corps in March 1918 and arrived in France in August. She served with the AEF until April 1919. New Oxford native Mary Wagner entered the service in March 1918 and sailed for Europe in July. She worked at Base Hospital No. 16 in Chaumont (Pershing's Headquarters) and later at Evacuation Hospital No. 9 at Vaulecourt, where she was assigned as a surgical nurse. Wagner returned to the United States in March 1919. Another New Oxford woman, Agnes S. Smith, joined in March 1918 and departed for overseas service in June. She served at eleven different base, camp, and station hospitals in France before returning home in July 1919. Smith served near the front lines in three separate campaigns, the Champagne-Marne, Aisne-Marne, and Meuse-Argonne offensives. Finally, Beulah Armor of Gettysburg entered the service in September 1917 and shortly thereafter left for France, where she spent her entire stint at Navy Base Hospital No. 5 in Brest. She returned to the U.S. in February 1919.[50] These women were some of the more than ten thousand American nurses who served overseas during the war. They were joined by other women who worked alongside men in YMCA and Salvation Army organizations serving the AEF.[51]

Because she worked at a navy base hospital in France, which received Marine Corps patients from the Belleau Wood battle, one Gettysburg nurse saw first-hand the horrors of that fight. On July 10, 1918, the *Gettysburg Times* reported, "Miss Beulah Armor has been in one of the American hospitals helping to nurse the United States Marines who were wounded in the recent heavy fighting. She tells of their wonderful courage and their willingness to get back into line." In a letter the newspaper reprinted, Beulah wrote a letter to her parents on June 16, while the fighting still raged and Belleau Wood had not yet been conquered:

> We have been very busy here up until yesterday and to-day. It is the most pathetic thing seeing these boys coming in, some of them shot almost to pieces. We have two operating teams here and the first few days after our arrival we were kept busy night and day. Now I am on duty from 12 noon to 12 midnight, so I won't have more than twelve hours duty. We have seven of our doctors, five nurses and two boys [navy corpsmen], in our two teams. One of the boys with us is George Snyder, of New Oxford, you know he is the boy who is with our unit.

When Kate Wolf had written earlier about taking care of her forty-five dough-boys who had been tasked to fetch a trainload of mules, she wrote, "I feel all we American women over here should do our best for every boy we meet. I try to impress this same thing . . . forget yourself and be a bright spot on every boy you meet, he needs it and you may be the last American woman he will ever see."[52]

The affection felt by the soldiers toward their nurses and other women war-workers serving near the front lines inspired the popular ballad "The Rose of No Man's Land." Its final stanza aptly summarized the spirits of women like Kate and Beulah:

> It's the one red rose the soldier knows,
> It's the work of the Master's hand;
> Mid the War's great curse,
> Stands the Red Cross Nurse,
> She's the rose of "No Man's Land."[53]

Historian Lyn MacDonald has commented that the nurses themselves specially liked the song, particularly when it was sung at concerts for their patients. While a handsome young tenor crooned the verses "with one eye fixed meaningfully on a row of nurses [who], . . . forgetful of their aching feet, their broken fingernails, their weary muscles and their red, chapped hands, exchanged deprecating giggles and were secretly flattered and delighted."[54]

Coincidentally, the *Compiler* printed a letter from Gettysburg resident Maurice Weaver, a surgeon serving with the 11th U.S. Infantry, Fifth Division, then posted in a quiet sector in the Vosges Mountains, in which he related a story about collecting real roses in no man's land: "The Captain and I went out into No Man's Land one evening about dusk and picked some roses from an old garden once part of a French home. . . . Rose leaves from No Man's Land I've sent back will be quite a relic." Certainly the symbolism was not lost on Weaver, who undoubtedly had come to depend on nurses in the operating rooms and recovery wards. Whether unintentionally or by editorial design, the young surgeon's letter appeared in a column directly adjacent to one of Kate Wolf's letters.[55]

In July, the Seventy-Ninth Division, the organization to which so many Adams County men were assigned, was zigzagging across the Atlantic on troopships at the height of the fighting. By August 1, the division was undergoing intense combat training in the French regional department of Haute-Marne. Latecomers who had missed marksmanship training at Camp Meade finally were afforded the opportunity to become familiar with their weapons. Steel helmets and individual gas masks were issued for the first time. It was in late August, while the division still was training, that a deadly virus—which would come to be called the Spanish influenza—struck for the first time. The Seventy-Ninth suffered about six hundred cases, with a 4 percent mortality rate.[56] (The only Adams County serviceman to die that early from the Spanish influenza was Navy Hospital Apprentice First Class George E. Snyder of New Oxford, posted to U.S. Navy Base Hospital No. 5, the same unit to which Gettysburg native Beulah Armor was assigned as a nurse. Snyder contracted the flu and died on September 20, 1918.[57]) The flu would raise its ugly head again about a month later. For now, however, the Seventy-Ninth Division's soldiers continued to gear for war. They would need it.

"The training period of the Seventy-Ninth Division . . . came to an abrupt termination on September 7, 1918, when in the early hours of the afternoon, a telegram from General Headquarters [of the AEF] at Chaumont came ticking into the Division telegraph office at Prauthoy," wrote one of the division's doughboy-historians. "It was concise and it was welcome." The message ordered the division to entrain for its new assignment, which would bring it under tactical French control, in the front lines near Bar le Duc, about fifty miles southwest of the embattled city of Verdun. (During the 1916 Battle of Verdun, Bar Le Duc had become known as the rear area and main French logistical base, and the French had come to call the road between the two towns La Voie Sacrée, or "Sacred Way," as it was the only artery for replacements, food, ammunition, and medical supplies for the French defenders.) The 316th Infantry had the farthest distance to march to get to its point of embarkation, where soldiers and animals were crowded into the notorious *Quarante Hommes et Huite Chevaux* (Forty Men and Eight Horses) boxcars, so named because they could hold eight horses or mules comfortably or forty men uncomfortably. The Sammies arrived at Robert et Espagne, west of Bar le Duc, while the newly created First U.S. Army went on the attack to crush the Saint-Mihiel salient, about twenty miles south of Verdun. The regiment's soldiers could hear the Allied artillery booming in the distance as their French colonial truck drivers—Vietnamese—drove them to the front where the Americans relieved French troops on September 14, 1918. The 316th Regiment would remain there with the rest of the Seventy-Ninth Division for about a week. On the distant horizon, the doughboys could see a prominence of ground named Montfaucon, which served as a major German headquarters and observation post in the Argonne Forest north of Verdun.[58] The Adams County boys and their divisional comrades did not know it yet, but they had been placed in position in anticipation of the next big campaign, one that would come to be called the Meuse-Argonne offensive. In that operation, the Seventy-Ninth would get to know Montfaucon exceptionally well. For now, however, a good chunk of the AEF was fighting about thirty miles to the south, around Saint-Mihiel.

Adolescent soldier "Henry Monroe" of the 60th Regiment, Fifth Division, likewise remembered the terrific barrage that preceded the Saint-Mihiel ground assault. "From opposite Verdun to St. Mihiel, and east to Pont-à-Mousson, there roared the greatest concentration of artillery fire the world had ever known. Cannon of all sizes rained steel upon every known point on the German line."[59] Although he was wrong about the barrage being the "greatest concentration of artillery fire the world had ever known" (the Somme bombardment by the British army in late June 1916 was longer and more intense), the ferocious fusillade *was* the greatest barrage the U.S. Army ever had experienced—dwarfing the two-hour bombardment in the afternoon of July 3, 1863, between Seminary Ridge and Cemetery Ridge. Joe Stone and the survivors of his Company L also participated in the Saint-Mihiel offensive. "September 5, 1918, the co. resumed its march towards the St. Mihiel front and took its positions in the front line trenches the following day," he chronicled in his journal. "In the great 'All American' offensive that followed on this sector the company did its part." Besides the Fourth Division, two other American divisions with Gettysburg connections would participate in the assault: the Twenty-Eighth and the Fifth. In all, nine American and four French divisions would launch the offensive beginning September 12. The salient was shaped like a triangle, with its northern point at Verdun, its western apex at Saint-Mihiel, and its southern tip at Pont-à-Mousson, stretching twenty-five miles long at its eastern base and jutting sixteen miles into the Allied lines. It had remained virtually unchanged in shape since the beginning of the war.[60]

Plan of the Allied attack during the Saint-Mihiel Offensive, September 12, 1918 (American Battle Monument Commission)

Henry Monroe was serving as the "runner" for his company commander, Capt. Edward Allworth, who also had been with the 60th Infantry during its brief stay in Gettysburg the summer before. Monroe (née Ernest Wrentmore) recalled the carnage of his first real battle: "Everywhere were signs of heavy fighting, dead Huns on every side, with an occasional Yankee who had given his 'all.' Seeing our own boys lying in cold death or being looked after by the medics brought this war damn close to home."[61] Now thirteen years old, Monroe was growing up very fast. The German army in that sector already was beginning to withdraw in a planned retrograde to straighten out its defensive line, so the initial combat operation of the First Army went better than expected. But the Americans paid a steep price nonetheless. In tangible, human terms, the Saint-Mihiel offensive cost the AEF some seven thousand casualties during the four-day battle from September 12 to 16. Four of the six regiments that had been organized at Gettysburg in 1917 paid a bloody toll in this fight. For example, the 60th and 61st Infantry, in the Fifth Division, suffered the loss of 17 officers and 354 enlisted men.[62] (Charles M. Sanders, who resided with his parents on Gettysburg's south side, was assigned to the 11th Infantry, also in the Fifth Division, and was severely wounded by shrapnel on September 13. A day later, Pvt. Ohrum C. Bond of New Oxford, also in the 11th Infantry Regiment, was wounded by a burst from a machine gun.[63]) The intangible price tag was the deal General Pershing made with Generalissimo Foch to keep the American army intact. To prevent Foch from attaching U.S. divisions to other Allied armies for the upcoming offensive that was expected to end the war, Pershing agreed to limit the Saint-Mihiel operation to a mere straightening of the bulge in the Allied line and then immediately move his army sixty miles northward to launch the new campaign by the end of September, thus taxing the logistical elements of the First Army to its utmost and taking a physical toll on the doughboys.[64]

Back in Gettysburg, the hometown *Times* ran a story with the headline, "ARE COUNTY MEN IN GREAT DRIVE?" The writer correctly speculated that the Seventy-Ninth Division was part of V Corps, and since it was the last of the corps to be organized, "it is regarded that it is unlikely that the units in it will be called upon to perform a very large share in the present operation, and for this reason it is the general belief that the Adams County unit [316th Infantry], together with other similar outfits, will be held in reserve." Continuing, the author noted that the six Regular regiments that had trained on the Gettysburg Battlefield had been actively engaged all summer, as had the Pennsylvania National Guard regiments comprising the Twenty-Eighth Division, now nicknamed the "Iron Division," for its martial exploits. "Whether these Regulars and these former National Guardsmen are being used in the present fray is a matter of conjecture."[65] In fact only the 60th and 61st Infantry in the Fifth Division participated in the Saint-Mihiel drive.

A unique aspect of the Saint-Mihiel offensive was the introduction of the 1st Provisional Tank Brigade to combat. The brigade, organized and commanded by Lt. Col. George Patton (who had called himself a "park policeman," when his detachment of the 15th Cavalry was assigned to support the Gettysburg Peace Jubilee in 1913), met the test of battle well. Patton had established the American tank school in Bourg, France, earlier in the year, and he was instrumental in developing the training, tactics, and tables of organization and equipment for the Tank Corps. When the 1st Provisional Tank Brigade was created, Patton was the logical pick to command it. Although the Saint-Mihiel battle had not been a particularly difficult one for the tankers, the operation did allow the brigade to work out its kinks, instilling confidence in the men for the more difficult campaign ahead. In fact, Patton and his tankers had been instructed to stand down only two days into the four-day battle so that the tanks could be transported by rail to the vicinity of their jump-off line for the Meuse-Argonne offensive.

Colonel Samuel Rockenbach served as director of the AEF Tank Corps and was Patton's superior officer. The organization and training of the Tank Corps back in the United States was the responsibility of Col. Ira C. Welborn, a Medal of Honor winner for his actions in Cuba in 1898. To Welborn fell the responsibility of establishing a tank-training school that would provide replacement soldiers for the tank battalions of the AEF and, eventually, for the deployment of entire stateside tank units. For this important mission, he chose a young officer from Abilene, Kansas.[66]

CHAPTER 5

"Treat 'Em Rough"

Camp Colt and the Genesis of an American Leader

He had visited Gettysburg National Military Park (GNMP) with the Class of 1915 only three years earlier. In March 1918 Capt. Dwight D. Eisenhower received the unwelcome news that he would be returning to the historic town. The twenty-seven-year-old infantry officer dreamed of making his mark as a combat leader in France, not by commanding a training camp on an old battlefield from fifty-five years in the past. At West Point, Eisenhower had not been a model cadet of the type characterized by the likes of Douglas MacArthur, Class of 1903, who in 1918 was commanding a brigade in the Forty-Second "Rainbow" Division in France and, at age thirty-eight, the youngest general in the AEF. MacArthur graduated at the top of his class and served as First Captain of the Corps of Cadets. Eisenhower, nicknamed "Ike," by his family and continued by his classmates, finished 61st academically, out of a class of 164. His conduct record pulled him downward on the order of merit list: Cadet Eisenhower was 125th in the class, having accumulated 211 demerits over four years.[1]

Not going to the Western Front was one of several disappointments Ike had faced in the three years since he accepted his Regular Army commission. Second Lieutenant Eisenhower requested the Philippines as his first assignment out of the academy but instead was ordered to San Antonio because of the ongoing tensions along the Mexican border. Though dissatisfied with his posting, he met Mamie Doud, his future wife, there. They were married in her hometown of Denver, Colorado, in 1916, and, now an army wife, she accompanied him back to Texas. After war was declared against Imperial Germany, Ike was assigned to the 57th U.S. Infantry, also in Texas. However, he soon received orders to Fort

Oglethorpe, on the Chickamauga battlefield, as an instructor at its officers' candidate school, yet another frustration—as he wanted to remain with his regiment. Mamie stayed behind in San Antonio, unable to travel, as she was by then expecting the couple's first baby. At Oglethorpe, Ike worked for Col. Henry Slocum, son of Maj. Gen, Henry Slocum, who had commanded the Army of the Potomac's XII Corps at Gettysburg. While assigned to his post in northwest Georgia, recently promoted Captain Eisenhower received a telegram announcing the birth of his first child, Doud Dwight, whom Ike nicknamed "Icky."[2] The new father was elated to receive the news but still exasperated that he was relegated to the training and instruction of officer candidates instead of fighting Germans. A half century later, Eisenhower wrote of his frustration, and then of unexpected jubilation: "Some of my class were already in France. Others were ready to depart. I seemed embedded in the monotony and unsought safety of the Zone of the Interior. I could see myself, years later, silent at class reunions while others reminisced of battle. . . . My elation, then, can well be imagined when I received orders in late winter to report to Camp Meade, Maryland, to join the 65th Engineers. This, I was told, was the parent group which was organizing tank corps troops for *overseas* duty."[3] Eisenhower returned to San Antonio to see his wife and baby son and then headed east, alone, to Camp Meade, Maryland, where he and his fellow officers were given the mission of organizing the 301st Tank Battalion (Heavy) which, the planners projected, would be using an American version of the British Mark V heavy tank.[4]

By the middle of March 1918, the 301st received orders for shipment to Europe, and Eisenhower was notified that he would *command* the battalion. He left for New York to reconnoiter the port facility where his battalion would embark. "Within two days I was back at Meade," he recalled—but unwelcome news waited. "The plan had been changed." Once again, Ike's ambitions were thwarted. "My chief said he was impressed by my 'organizational ability.' I was directed to take the remnants of the troops who would not be going overseas, and proceed to an old, abandoned campsite in Gettysburg, Pennsylvania, of all places."[5] Eisenhower was frustrated once more, but the people of Gettysburg were overjoyed. The Sammies were coming back, and with them, their monthly pay vouchers.

Stories concerning the prospects of another army camp pervaded the streets of Gettysburg during the harsh winter of 1917–18. On February 18, the *Gettysburg Times* printed an article titled "RUMORS ON CAMP MOST NUMEROUS." In it, the reporter chronicled the speculations of the townsfolk regarding the reopening of the camp. The writer concluded, "All . . . is street rumor for the truth of which The Times does not vouch, but several of the stories are apparently well founded." The wild tales came to an abrupt halt on March 8. "A telephone message from Congressman Andrew Brodbeck this morning told that all doubt about the opening of the Gettysburg camp had been removed," wrote a *Times* correspondent, "that it would be prepared for troops and that a regiment of engineers would be stationed here within a short time. This confirms the accounts published in this paper from time to time over the past few weeks." The newspaper reiterated that the earlier rumors had been mere gibberish, especially one that had alarmed white citizens about black soldiers being stationed in Gettysburg: "The old story of 10,000 negro troops being ordered to Gettysburg, and many other reports were stated, none of which were given credence by those in touch with the situation." So now it was official. Gettysburg would get another camp—for white soldiers—in 1918.

Since the departure of the Regulars the previous autumn, the people of Gettysburg and Adams County "did their bit" (a common American home-front catch phrase) to help win the war. Fruits and vegetables grown in Liberty Gardens during the summer were "put up" in mason jars and crockery to be consumed during the winter months. The citizens tolerated, at the urging of Herbert Hoover, "Meatless Mondays" and "Wheatless Wednesdays." The U.S. Food Administration also admonished Americans to limit their household sugar consumption to two pounds per month. Housewives pledged not to hoard flour and were compelled to fill out forms accounting for the amounts they kept in their pantries. The *Times* carried the government's guidance: "Your government does not want you to give up three square meals a day—nor even one. All it asks is that you eat less of the foods we need to keep the armies going and eat all you want of the

Food Administration poster, 1918, calling on citizens to substitute cornmeal and other grains for wheat flour (Library of Congress)

other things that we have in plenty. . . . America and her allies must not run out of meat, wheat or fats. If we let that happen, Germany will win the war."[6]

Schoolchildren once more planted gardens on the battlefield, again on East Cemetery Hill, but now in 1918 on Culp's Hill and Oak Ridge, too.[7] Liberty bonds and war savings stamps continued to be sold, with local businesses sponsoring patriotic newspaper advertisements urging residents to support the Third Liberty Loan Drive in the spring of 1918.[8] Four-minute men still gave patriotic speeches.[9] The county's Red Cross chapters raised money and sent supplies overseas and to stateside army camps. Men volunteered for the military or remained subject to conscription. Adams County families watched as their sons, brothers, and sweethearts departed for training camps. The newspapers printed the soldiers' letters mailed home from the Western Front and sometimes announced the fates of fallen soldiers or sailors. Army truck convoys on the Lincoln Highway used the town churches as waystations for overnight accommodations and the Red Cross supplied the drivers with food and drink. The *Times* summarized the efforts of the people of Adams County in a front-page article marking the one-year anniversary of the declaration of war. The reporter noted that the county

> has contributed more than 400 men to the various fighting branches. . . . Five young men from this county have given their lives in the service of their country. . . . In many lines of endeavor Adams County has made contributions of which she is justly proud. To the first and second Liberty Loans she subscribed more than $600,000. In the first Red Cross drive the contributions were more than $6800. . . . [as well] as shipment after another of supplies for hospitals and camps. Quantities of clothing were sent for use in war-torn countries. Men on the truck trains were fed and entertained on their way to the seaport. . . . To date more than $44,000 worth of thrift stamps and war savings certificates have been sold. . . . [and] the Young Men's Christian Association war fund [holds] about $2000. The Knights of Columbus reached its goal of $5000. To the Y.W.C.A. the county made gifts which totaled $750. To the fund for war camp activities and soldiers' recreation work more than $900 was given.

The article continued, ad nauseam, about county residents' efforts of to support the war effort. Certainly the locals had made a handsome profit in 1917 from the soldiers stationed at the Camp of the U.S. Troops, and they were poised to make more money from the throngs of doughboys soon to arrive. But the citizens also contributed to the war effort in many diverse ways, out of not greed but patriotism. According to an April 16 *Times* story, "Adams County's patriotic record has always been a proud one and . . . that it will continue will be a safe tradition."

Unlike other areas of the country, particularly the Midwest, where "coercive volunteerism," so named by historian Christopher Capozzola, took place, the people of Gettysburg and Adams County eagerly volunteered for the Red Cross, knitted socks, bought war stamps and bonds, planted Liberty Gardens and imposed self-rationing not because they were coerced to do so but because they wanted to, for either patriotic reasons, personal economic gain, or both. No vigilance societies were needed to police their patriotism, although the local newspapers included constant reminders of their duty to do their bit. Capozzola has noted, "If violence is as American as cherry pie, so, too, was the obligation of policing. Across America, citizens' leagues rounded up socialists, striking workers and suspected prostitutes, and during the war vigilant citizens engaged in acts of political violence that they believed were part and parcel of the war effort."[10] Despite the large number of Adams County citizens with German ancestry, there was little public sympathy for the Central Powers, even before the United States entered the war, and with perhaps one or two exceptions, there were no mad hunts for suspected German spies or sympathizers. When policing was required—not to coerce volunteerism but to fight vice and enforce sanitation and public health policies—local and state government agencies took control of the situation. When the soldiers created problems, the U.S. Army and other federal agencies stepped up. Beginning in March 1918, the arrival of thousands of more young men would usher in another economic boom for merchants, but it also would bring a new spate of headaches.

Meanwhile, the ROTC students at Gettysburg College were learning the way of war being waged in France and Belgium. Just west of Glatfelter Hall, one of the main college buildings, the cadets dug trenches to simulate life on the Western Front. At the same time, the U.S. government warned area farmers that if they claimed agricultural exemptions to avoid the draft, they had better "be actively engaged in farm work after April 15" or take the chance of being inducted. With thousands of soldiers soon arriving at the old campsite, the State Board of Health remained the overseer of Gettysburg's public health and sanitation, much to the chagrin of the town councilmen.[11] War was a grim business and all levels of government were clamping down, just as they had done with the enforcement of Progressive social legislation in years past.

The first contingent of soldiers from Camp Meade arrived on Friday, March 16. More doughboys were on their way from Camp Cody, New Mexico; Camp Upton, New York; Columbus Barracks, Ohio; Newport News, Virginia; and Allentown, Pennsylvania. The supply officer for the Camp Meade group, a Lieutenant Draper, obviously aware of the previous camp's alcohol-related problems, told a *Times* reporter, "I wish you would tell your people that the man who gives or sells liquor to a soldier is doing a distinctly pro-German act, in that he violates the law and helps to render that man unfit for the service he is expected to perform. We absolutely will not tolerate any bootlegging and any infractions of the law will receive immediate attention." Arriving troops were informed immediately about the prohibition of liquor in both camp and town.[12] The Gettysburg Borough Council even added a supplementary police officer in January 1918, and it elected a new chief, Officer Charles Culp, to replace Horace Smiley while the latter served in the army.[13]

Captain Eisenhower assumed command of the camp on March 29, 1918, replacing Maj. W. N. Vance, Corps of Engineers, the senior officer present when the camp was activated on March 23, 1918.[14] Eisenhower's stay at his new command was brief, since he still had to get the 301st Tank Battalion prepared for its overseas movement. He recalled in his memoirs: "I took a small detachment to the new campsite. . . . My mood was black. I decided to leave them in charge of a good man named [Robert] Garner, a captain who had been commissioned a year earlier from the non-commissioned ranks. I knew little about him but he seemed quite capable." Before Eisenhower departed for Camp Meade, he watched as his small contingent of troops raised the garrison flag on the existing flagpole, which had been used by the previous year's camp. Continuing his story, Ike reminisced about the incident many years later,

> As I was ready to get into an automobile to start the long drive back to Baltimore, I saw Captain Garner watching the flag flapping at the top. I paused and he said, "Captain, the last time I was on this ground was many years ago. At the time I was standing before a general court martial which sentenced me to six months in the guard house, and then suspended the sentence.
>
> "Now," he said, "I'm a captain in the same Army, and I'm standing here as temporary commander of the camp in which I was disgraced." As I looked up, this old, hard-bitten, gray-headed former non-com had tears streaming down his face. All I could manage to say was, "Look, Garner, I know you'll do a splendid job. Good luck."

Eisenhower compiled his memoirs almost fifty years after this episode, but it had a lasting impact: "To this day," the former five-star general and two-term president of the United States mused, "whenever we stand to salute the flag, that memory is with me."[15]

Although Ike could not recall Garner's first name so many years later, he evidently remembered the incident correctly. Captain Robert Garner was recommissioned as a Tank Corps officer from the infantry on April 3, 1918, and listed as second in command of Camp Colt during the month of April, with full

Camp Colt Headquarters (previously the Camp, U.S. Troops, HQ). Today, the area is occupied by the McDonald's and General Pickett's Buffet parking lots. The small monument adjacent to the HQ on the Emmitsburg Road (or Steinwehr Avenue) is in memory of the 4th Ohio Infantry. (S. Boardman Collection)

responsibility as commander of Company A, 302d Tank Battalion. Evidently, Garner had trained at Gettysburg as a Regular Army enlisted man during one of the joint exercises with the Pennsylvania National Guard, or perhaps he had been assigned to the 5th U.S. Infantry when it provided support for the 1913 Peace Jubilee.[16]

The new cantonment, unlike the infantry camp a year earlier, actually received an official name, designated "Camp Colt," for Samuel Colt (1814–1862), the man who invented and mass-produced the revolving-cylinder, six-shot pistol that both sides had used during the Civil War.[17] (The company that Colt founded also manufactured Gatling guns after the Civil War and at the time of the World War was producing the M1911 .45 caliber semiautomatic pistol as well as the BAR). Camp Colt occupied the same ground as the previous year's infantry camp, but more structures were authorized, and a target range was situated some two miles south of camp, near Big Round Top. Additional hospital accommodations, the conversion of some of the old stables and warehouses into personnel quarters, and the procurement of heating plants for the troops' bathing facilities were required, all to the tune of more than $17,000. Col. Ira Welborn requested funding for these projects on April 18. Two months earlier, $20,000 had been allocated, and Welborn indicated that the previous amount was "sufficient to partially prepare the Camp for 2500 men." He estimated that the supplementary funding would allow Camp Colt to accommodate four thousand soldiers.[18] As it turned out, the Tank Corps attracted some of the best of the army's existing soldiers and new recruits, and the cantonment eventually would swell in size to a peak strength of nearly sixty-four hundred men.[19]

Before he returned to Camp Meade, Captain Eisenhower took out an advertisement in the *Gettysburg Times* for "a five or six room house. Furnished or unfurnished."[20] The sooner he could find a temporary residence, the faster he could bring his young family to Gettysburg. "In April, not long after we established the camp, Mamie had arrived with our new baby, 'Icky,' and after several unfortunate trials we found suitable quarters in Gettysburg," he recalled.[21] The location of their first Gettysburg residence has not been determined, but Mamie remembered it as a damp, tiny home with two rooms upstairs and two downstairs, with the only heating source a potbellied stove on the first floor. The new commander's wife did not know how to operate the stove without instructions, as she had never seen one before. After a short time there, the family moved to the Alpha Tau Omega fraternity house on North Washington Street, whose members had vacated it after the May commencement. Although the accommodations there were much improved, the house did not have a kitchen, compelling Mamie and the baby to take their meals with Ike at Camp Colt. Finally, with the college's summer recess coming to a close, through the efforts of a local attorney, the Eisenhower family found a nice brick residence on Springs Avenue, adjacent to the Lutheran Seminary campus. According to their eldest granddaughter, Susan Eisenhower, "It was their first real home."[22]

For unknown reasons, in the spring of 1918 Ike apparently felt obliged to quarter his men under canvas rather than temporarily billet them in the existing structures built in 1917. "One bright spot was that tents were easily available," Ike reminisced in his memoirs. "We began to erect them, and although we had no materials with which to build tent frames and floors, we managed to make the men comfortable enough. Five or six men went into each tent, rather than the eight for which they had been designed." He also remembered that the Camp Colt staff "immediately established a personnel and records section. Within a short time the command was functioning, making its reports, and getting along." A late snow in early April created a mini-crisis that the quick-thinking Eisenhower was able to overcome. As the flakes fell, he made his way through deep drifts into town: "At the first hardware store I bought every stove that could fit into a tent. By the time I reached the last shop, I had cleaned the town out." Nonetheless, there still were not enough stoves to go around, so Eisenhower allowed his men to build fire pits in their tents. "These permitted modest fires inside the rest of the tents," Ike recalled, "although they required a patrol of men all night to keep the fires going and make sure that no tent burned down." A weather-related calamity was averted, the men amazingly did not gripe about "army negligence," and things soon returned to normal. "They seemed to take the storm as a splendid way to demonstrate their robust health," Ike believed. "To me the spirit of the men proved to be the best disease preventative."[23]

This was how Eisenhower remembered the incident nearly fifty years after the fact. In his published memoirs (1967), the former president warned his readers "to take all quoted material, particularly recollected across the decades, with the necessary grain of salt."[24] He should have cautioned readers about his own memories, too. According to a Special Sanitary Inspection Report of Camp Colt, dated April 12, 1918, the inspector wrote,

> Command at Camp Colt, Gettysburg, consisting of 1450 men, occupying mess halls used last year for summer camp. These mess halls totally inadequately heated by one, and occasionally two Sibley stoves. Several inches snow on the ground. Recommend Quartermaster General direct immediate shipment here by express of at least 60 wood heaters to prevent illness; also recommend no more tank organizations be sent here until camp is ready to receive them. Available supply [of] cots [already] in use. Couple hundred men forced to sleep on bed sacks on floor.[25]

Perhaps Captain Eisenhower did, in fact, quarter *some* of his men in tents, and conceivably he did brave the snow drifts to purchase stoves for his men, but the sanitary inspector's report indicates that Ike did the wise thing and sheltered his men from the snow and cold in existing structures and kept them warm—or attempted to—with the government-issued stoves already on hand.[26] In the waning years of his life, Eisenhower probably had recounted this story so many times that it morphed into his own mini-version of Washington at Valley Forge.

Nevertheless, the unexpected blizzard caused difficulties for Adams County citizens and businesses, especially those who relied on electricity, as the storm knocked out power lines. Telephone service also was disrupted. The weight of snow and ice on the power and telephone cables, coupled with gusting winds, snapped the poles or blew them over, creating obstacles that blocked road traffic. The area's orchards, an important part of the local economy, also were adversely affected. A *Times* reporter wrote, "Peach trees with the buds about ready to burst were caught. Apple trees, their limbs crushed by the weight of the snow and ice gave way."[27] The war already was causing hardships; now Mother Nature was also spanking the county's civilians.

Warmer weather soon followed, leaving Captain Eisenhower time to focus on establishing his new command and framing his training mission. The first tank units organized in the United States were the 1st and 2d Battalions, Light Tank Service, 65th Engineers, created at Camp Upton, New York, but transferred to Camp Colt in March. Likewise, the 2d Heavy Tank Battalion, 65th Engineers, was organized at Camp Meade in February and reassigned to Gettysburg in March. Eisenhower accompanied that unit from Meade to Colt. During the upcoming months, Ike would be responsible for forming the 303rd, 304th, 305th, 328th through the 338th, and the 346th Tank Battalions, as well as the 304th and 309th through 314th Tank Centers (administrative/logistical commands). Many of these battalions would deploy to the AEF, but none would see combat.[28] Of course, Camp Colt also would have its share of support personnel, particularly quartermaster troops (supply, transportation, and food service), ordnance soldiers (mechanics, repairmen, welders, machinists, and ammunition specialists), a headquarters section, and medical staff.

A company of casuals was formed for new arrivals awaiting assignment to one of the battalions (*casuals* are soldiers awaiting assignment). For men who did not meet the physical or mental standards for overseas service, a development battalion was created to give classes, exercise, and health monitoring. The casual company included a "venereal detachment," and the development battalion had a venereal company for men who had contracted any of those diseases. These unfortunates remained segregated until they recovered or received orders

Tanks Corps recruiting posters (Library of Congress)

for treatment at a general hospital. Unlike the infantry regiments from the year before, the Tank Corps was not authorized a regimental band, so Eisenhower sanctioned the organization of a drum, bugle, and fife corps from among his soldiers who possessed musical talent, probably as homage to the generation that had fought on the same ground fifty-five years earlier. The corps was assigned to Company A, 302d Tank Battalion.[29] (In early October, a real military band was organized from Camp Colt men who could play musical instruments.[30]) The Tank Corps also was approved to conduct its own officers' training school, and that, too, would be located at Camp Colt.[31]

Second Lieutenant Charles H. Phillips was one of the young men who attended the Tank Corps Officers' Training School. His experience probably was typical of other candidates'. He enlisted at Fall River, Massachusetts, on October 4, 1917, at the age of twenty-three. Until then he had been a grocery clerk and had served in the National Guard as a corporal from April 28, 1914, to March 30, 1916. He then served as an assistant supply sergeant after his enlistment in the Regular Army and was posted at Camp Devens in Company B, 302d Infantry Regiment until he volunteered for the Tank Corps on March 13, 1918. Concerning his weapons training, he recalled, "We had wooden rifles for a short period

Camp Colt Drum, Bugle, and Fife Corps (Pennsylvania State Archives, Harrisburg, Pa.)

and then [a] modified .30 cal. at Camp Devens. No Tank Corps training at Camp Colt, Gettysburg, Pa. We were supposed to get that at a Tank camp in England, but we were sent to France direct." Phillips remembered that the "food rations were satisfactory at both Camp Devens and Camp Colt." Concerning his officers' training, he recalled, "I attended the Tank Corps Officers' Training Camp at Camp Colt, Gettysburg, PA. This was for 4 weeks, afternoons only. Consisted of Inf[antry] close order drill & lectures on Army Regulations & Articles of War. We were given some homework to do at night on administration. But this was never checked. My National Guard training was what qualified me for my commission."[32] In other words, once a candidate was deemed qualified to become an officer and selected for officers' training, it was pretty difficult to "wash out."

Eisenhower's most immediate training problem had nothing to do with officers' training. It was his lack of tanks. His ordnance personnel fabricated a sheet-metal, moving mockup dubbed the "Battling Lizzie." Because it was modeled on the Mark V heavy tank, Ike's soldiers at least could use it to get a feel for being inside one of the steel monsters. A short announcement in the June 7, 1918, *Brooklyn Daily Eagle* reported on the Brooklyn men assigned to Camp Colt: "Corporal Neville B. Hart of 329 Linden Avenue, Brooklyn, directed the

"Battling Lizzie" (Pennsylvania State Archives)

building of an imitation tank recently and it is being used by members of the 328th Battalion. It is mounted on an old chassis and runs along in excellent style." If nothing else, "Battling Lizzie" made a great backdrop for group photographs.[33]

No heavy tanks ever were delivered to Camp Colt, but on June 6, 1918, an FT-17 Renault light tank arrived at the Western Maryland depot in Gettysburg. "With the cheerful cynicism of soldiers," Eisenhower recollected, "we had not expected to see one until we reached Europe."[34] A *Gettysburg Times* reporter wrote, "The long expected tank is here. Camp Colt's officers and men are as happy as a playground full of children with a new toy. This morning one of the small French tanks was received by freight from an automobile factory 'Somewhere in America.' It was soon unloaded and driven through town while scores of people watched it with the greatest interest." The tank had been built in France but delivered to an American manufacturer for study, most likely the Maxwell Motor Company (forerunner of Chrysler) of Dayton, Ohio, which had received a contract, along with several smaller companies, to supply forty-four hundred tanks of the Renault design to the Army.[35]

In his memoirs, Eisenhower alleged that two more tanks were shipped to the Gettysburg camp: "Three small tanks were sent to us. . . . each weighed about seven tons, and each, in combat, carried either a machine gun or a small one-pounder cannon, mounted in a revolving turret. Each *was* to carry, I should say; the tanks arrived without weapons." Once again, Ike's memory was hazy. None of the local newspapers ever reported the appearance of the two other tanks, which would have arrived at one of the town's two train stations. As evidence that only one tank was assigned to the camp, the *Gettysburg Times* affirmed soon after the armistice that "the *lone tank* with which the Camp Colt men got their practice rolled through the streets of town this afternoon."[36]

Photographs of the Camp Colt tank indicate that it was a first-production model, mounting a cast iron turret (later models were designed with riveted, steel-plate turrets). Eventually, Eisenhower's tank would be armed with a Hotchkiss machine gun. Tanks with machine guns were categorized as "female" tanks; those armed with the one-pounder (37mm) cannon were called "male" tanks. Although the new tank's presence obviously was not a military secret, the June 11 issue of the *Times* reported that the "machine is stationed in an isolated part of the camp and visitors are not allowed to get a sight of it."

The drive train was powered by a four-cylinder, water-cooled, rear-mounted thirty-nine-horsepower gasoline engine, which allowed the FT-17 to travel at a lethargic four to six miles per hour, with a maximum range of forty miles per tank of gas. (In contrast, the United States' World War II Sherman tank had a sustained speed of twenty-six miles per hour, while the modern M-1 Abrams tank can reach forty-five miles per hour.) The Renault could be started with an external hand crank or, if under fire, an internally mounted one. The fuel reservoir was installed forward of the engine and separated from the crew compartment by a firewall. A driver and a commander/gunner manned the tank, the latter crew member firing the weapon, rotating the turret (capable of a 360-degree rotation), and giving directions to the driver. The tank had no internal communication system, so the commander would employ a series of signals by lightly kicking the driver in the back to indicate direction and speed, since the noise from the engine and the tracks prevented oral commands from being understood. The tank's armor was nearly an inch thick, bolted onto a steel chassis. It also mounted a curved, detachable, rear "tail" to facilitate trench crossings and was propelled by rear-drive sprocket wheels mounting caterpillar-style steel tracks that passed around large, wooden, steel-rimmed, forward-mounted wheels. Its tactical mission on the battlefield was to support the advance of infantry over no-man's-land.[37]

The British had pioneered the use of tanks in combat, first employing them—with little effect—during the Battle of the Somme in 1916. Their first *successful* use against the Germans had been the Allied breakthrough at Cambrai in November 1917, when 324 tanks were engaged as the main assault force, with infantry and horse cavalry providing support. Historian Martin Gilbert writes, "The first day of the Battle of Cambrai marked a decisive success for the tank and strategy of using it to create a decisive breach in the enemy front line. The German defenses had been broken, five miles gained, and more than 4,000 German

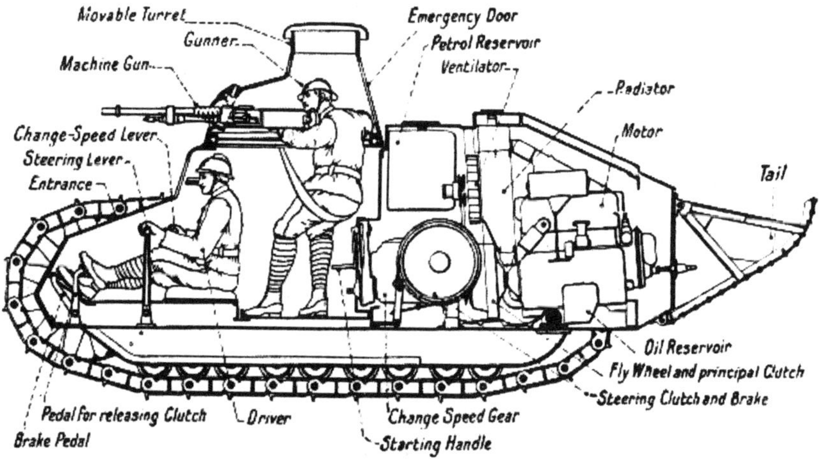

DIAGRAMMATIC SECTION OF A FRENCH LIGHT (OR "MOSQUITO") TANK.

Schematic cutaway drawing of a Renault FT-17 (*The [London] Times History of The War,* Volume 19)

soldiers taken prisoner." After the initial breakthrough, however, mechanical failures and accurate enemy artillery fire decimated the tank force, thus preventing the initial German defeat from turning into a total rout. Nonetheless, the successful massed-tank assault had changed the complexion of warfare.[38] Even German army chief of staff Paul von Hindenburg recognized the tank's future capability to spearhead an attack:

> The English attack at Cambrai for the first time revealed the possibilities of a great surprise attack with tanks. We had had previous experience of this weapon in the spring offensive, when it had not made any particular impression. However, the fact that the tanks had now been raised to such a pitch of technical perfection that they could cross our undamaged trenches and obstacles did not fail to have a marked effect on our troops. The physical effects of fire from machine-guns and light ordnance with which the steel Colossus was provided were far less destructive than the moral effect of its comparative invulnerability. The infantryman felt that he could do practically nothing against its armoured sides. As soon as the machine broke through our trench-lines, the defender felt himself threatened in the rear and left his post.[39]

The heavy tanks' shock-power facilitated the British victory at Cambrai; once the defenders recovered from their initial surprise and fear, however, they were able to repulse the attack. But Hindenburg recognized the tank's potential, and some twenty years later, it would be a resurrected German army that perfected the employment of the steel behemoths on the battlefields of the next war.

Captain Eisenhower was fortunate to welcome to Camp Colt two British advisors who had commanded tank battalions in the Battle of Cambrai. One was forty-six-year-old Lt. Col. Frank Summers, who had been awarded his nation's Distinguished Service Cross for bravery in action in March 1915 and the Distinguished Service Order for his actions during the Battle of the Somme in the summer of 1916 as a tank company commander. (Sadly, his son Cyril, a Royal Navy officer, had been killed in action a month earlier, during the historic Battle of Jutland.) Lieutenant Colonel Summers took command of a tank battalion in 1917 and led it during the Third Battle of Ypres and the Battle of Cambrai, where his unit fought with great success. Transferred back to the United Kingdom in 1918 to organize tank training, he soon departed for the United States and was assigned as a liaison officer at Camp Colt.[40]

The other British officer sent to Gettysburg was Maj. Philip Hammond, who had served with Summers at Cambrai as a fellow battalion commander and had been awarded two Distinguished Service Orders (one during the Second Boer War and one in 1914) and the Military Cross (1914). Hammond's tank battalion at Cambrai nearly exploited the British breakthrough, but the Germans succeeded in partially destroying a bridge over the San Quentin Canal at the town of Masnières; the span's structural integrity now jeopardized, the weight of Hammond's lead Mark IV tank collapsed it.[41] The experience Hammond and Summers brought to Camp Colt's training program would be immeasurable. Decades later, Eisenhower recalled their arrival: "At about the same time [that we received the tank], two British officers appeared as advisers. Thus began my connection with allies, a word that became vitally important to me as the years rolled on. The British officers helped us to understand the uses of these new, armored weapons." Continuing, Ike remembered, "In their conversations, I heard about a British political figure named Winston Churchill. According to the two officers, this Churchill had a hand in producing the first tanks. They admired him extravagantly. And I must say that from their descriptions, he sounded like a good chap."[42] Indeed, the tank concept was Churchill's brainchild; in January 1915 as First Lord of the Admiralty, he recommended to Prime Minister Herbert Asquith that "special mechanical devices for taking trenches" should be developed.[43] Thus, long before they came to know and trust each other during another world war, Eisenhower and Churchill shared an experiential bond.

Incredibly, a Gettysburg native actually participated in the Battle of Cambrai. Lt. Herbert A. "Harry" Bream, who grew up on Confederate Avenue straddling

From left: Captain Dwight D. Eisenhower at his Camp Colt Headquarters, with Colonel William H. Clopton Jr. (Tank Corps), and British advisors Lieutenant Colonel Frank Summers and Major Philip Hammond. Note Summers's black armband, worn in memory of his son killed at Jutland (Eisenhower National Historic Site)

Seminary Ridge and graduated from Pennsylvania College in 1910, was assigned to the 11th U.S. Engineer Regiment (Railway), attached to the British army.[44] In a letter home that made its way to the March 26, 1918, edition of the *Gettysburg Times,* Bream boasted, "Now, we like to be called experienced soldiers, having been behind the line, in the line and—at Cambrai—over the line. When the British broke the Hindenburg Line on the 20th of last November we were there and crossed with them." The 11th Engineers had been instrumental in transporting the British tanks by rail to the vicinity of their jump-off line for the assault. On November 30, 1917, the Germans counterattacked and penetrated to the area where the Americans were repairing the rail line, and the engineers were forced to fight back with their picks, shovels, and any discarded weapons they could find. One American engineer was observed felling five enemy attackers with his shovel before he was killed.[45] The 11th Engineer Regiment thereafter proudly proclaimed itself the first American unit to engage the foe.[46]

Prior to the tank's arrival, Eisenhower and his staff devised a broad training program for the Camp Colt doughboys that included rifle marksmanship, mechanical maintenance instruction, drill and ceremony, tactics, and even telegraphy. But more importantly, machine-gun and direct-fire cannon training were required. According to Eisenhower,

> I went to Tank Corps headquarters in Washington to ask for small-caliber cannons. Only a few Navy guns, of the swivel type (we called them "three pounders"), were available. We drilled with these anyhow, even though we lacked ammunition and sufficient backstops. A number of machine guns came in and we trained the gunners until they could take them apart blind-folded and put them together again. Then someone had the notion of mounting them on truck trailers or flatbed trucks, and so we were able to train the men to fire from mobile platforms at both moving and still targets. The only satisfactory place for firing was Big Round Top. . . . Its base made a perfect backstop. Soon, soldiers were shooting from moving trucks at all kinds of targets there and the firing might have been heavier than during the great battle fifty-five years earlier.[47]

The *Times* noted in an article on July 6, 1918, "Some target practice this week with machine guns back of the Round Tops gave the impression that there was a regular battle under way there, but it was only a little demonstration." The idea that an important terrain feature on a national park was used for target practice might shock the senses of modern-day, historic-preservation-minded people, but then again, the notion of using the revered Gettysburg Battlefield as a training camp is equally bewildering.

Once the tank arrived in Gettysburg, recruits were trained to drive it on normal terrain as well as over obstacles. To learn how to negotiate a steep rise with an abrupt drop, drivers used the earthen ramp of the destroyed Bliss Farm barn. To get a feel for driving across a shell-cratered battlefield, drivers took the tank into the basement cavity of the Bliss farmhouse. (On July 2, 1863, the 14th Connecticut Infantry Regiment had burned to the ground the house and barn of William and Adeline Bliss to prevent Confederate sharpshooters from using the buildings. Although the Blisses filed a claim with the federal government, they never received a penny in reimbursement.) In 1918, all that remained of the farm structures were the bank barn's ramp and the depression where the farmhouse's cellar had collapsed. The destruction caused by the grinding of steel caterpillar tracks over this historic, cultural feature has not been measured, but the ramp and cellar are still visible today, indicating that any damage was slight.

Camp Colt's lone FT-17 negotiating the bank of the razed Bliss barn (National Archives)

Left: The FT-17 emerging from the ruins of the Bliss barn, followed by a platoon of doughboys (National Archives); *right:* The FT-17 resting in the cellar cavity of the Bliss farmhouse (National Archives)

Because of the technological nature of mechanized combat, the Tank Corps sought recruits with general mechanical skills, as well as heavy-equipment operation and automotive and machine-shop backgrounds, but it also accepted men who had been cooks, clerks, motorcyclists, and telegraphers, among several other civilian occupations, to fill support roles. An article in the July 4, 1918, issue of the popular magazine *Motor Age* informed its readers,

> If you are one of the mental and physical aristocrats of American citizenry—if you are the owner of a sound body, a clear head, an executive, mechanical mind—if you seek vigorous service—if you want to ride to Berlin instead of walk—if you want to do utmost damage to the Hun—join the tank service—it will give you experience, rank, training and excitement to your heart's content. . . . [The Tank Corps] still requires 3000 tractor drivers, heavy truck drivers and motor car engine mechanics

> who have physical strength, mental strength and executive ability—men without a single physical defect, who can think quickly and clearly and if need be, think for others. These men can be between eighteen and forty-one years of age.

An application form was included at the end of the article, for potential recruits to complete and mail to the director of the Tank Corps in Washington, D.C.[48] The June 1 edition of the *Times* ran a similar article that basically stated the same thing, but it also reported: "The examinations for induction into the Tank Corps are especially rigid, both mentally and physically. Particularly good eyesight is required to pass the necessary examinations."

One recruit, Pvt. John B. Kimberly, articulated in a letter to his wife back home in Iowa, "a few questions they ask you here when you are up before the Personal [*sic*] Board for your final exam to become a Tanker." His answers were exactly what the examiner wanted to hear:

> What did you join the Tanks for? 'answer'—To fight.
> Do you care if you never come back? ans.—No.
> Do you realize that you are entering the most dangerous division in the army? ans.—Yes.
> Did you bid everybody good-bye before you left? ans.—Yes.
> You will be alright for a tanker, then, report to your co[mpany] so & so (Now that is just what they ask you only a whole lot more. They ask such questions as those more to test your nerve more than anything else.)

Private Kimberly had been talking to a battle-seasoned corporal who had just returned from France, who told him that the Tank Corps "was the finest branch of the service to be in."[49] Apparently, to have the mettle be a tanker, the correct "attitude" was just as important as the physical and mental attributes.

Eisenhower convinced himself that the quality of the average soldier assigned to the Tank Corps was superior to other army troops. "At Camp Colt, because our enlisted personnel were volunteers showing exemplary zeal, our troops were a few cuts above average. . . . Illiterate men were few; in fact I encountered none." The standards for admittance to the Tank Corps were high, but men obviously not qualified for this branch of the Army nonetheless slipped through the cracks. With more and more men being assigned to the camp, some were not physically fit or mentally prepared for the highly technological (for 1918) nature of tank warfare. Men who needed to be brought to a higher standard prior to embarking on tank training were assigned to the Development Battalion. To command this organization, Eisenhower called on the services of

Captain Eisenhower, first row, center, and part of his HQ staff. On Eisenhower's immediate right is Norman Randolph; Robert Garner is the second officer to Eisenhower's left, first row. (Pennsylvania State Archives)

one of his Academy classmates, twenty-seven-year-old Philadelphian Norman Randolph, whom his West Point chums had nicknamed "Baldy" and "Dutch" because of his thinning hair and a slight Pennsylvania Dutch accent. "He had a genius for training," Ike remembered. "The men liked him and so it was sensible to give him command of the new battalion. Two or three hundred men were transferred to it." Those who were too "physically defective" were discharged from the army. "But those who were slow or inept or, as the expression became later, oddballs, Randolph and his assistants did a great deal." The majority of the soldiers assigned to Randolph's command eventually were transferred to line battalions. Eisenhower even recalled that twenty-one of Randolph's reformed "oddballs" were sent to officers' training school, with eighteen of the candidates earning promotions to second lieutenant.[50]

The Development Battalion, organized on July 18, comprised two companies and a headquarters. According to a report by 1st Lt. Elisha S. Lewis, the battalion medical officer, men inflicted with venereal disease were assigned to Company A, while Company B held "the incapacitated and 'Misfits'; i.e., those who do not get along well with their officers, and associates and those who had no opportunity to drill, on account of special duties or illnesses." Lewis wrote that Captain Randolph attempted to bring the "misfits" assigned to Company B up to military standards through drills, exercise, special gymnastics, and lectures on military subjects, as well as a "class in English for illiterates and those of foreign birth who have a scant knowledge of our language." (Eisenhower's recollection about not encountering any illiterates obviously was clouded by time.) Camp Surgeon Lt. Col. Thomas H. Scott, Medical Corps, supervised the rehabilitation process for men with physical problems, "embracing Medicine, Surgery, Mechanically Applied Gymnastics, [and] Electro and Hydro-Therapeutics." In addition, Lewis reported that organized athletic competitions, including boxing, baseball, basketball, and volleyball were regularly conducted, with the athletic equipment supplied by the Knights of Columbus and the YMCA, the latter organization also furnishing "a well-appointed tent and moving pictures."[51]

Company A—the Venereal Company—had its own special rehabilitation regimen. Its soldiers received regular lectures about sexually transmitted diseases and underwent a medical procedure known as chemical prophylaxis. The Army Medical Department directed that upon reporting to the medical tent this category of patients would first urinate and then wash their genitalia with soap and water, followed by another washing with bichloride of mercury (today considered a poison), all under the watchful eye of a medical attendant. Next, the medic would inject a solution of paragol into the urethra, which the patient held for five minutes before expelling. The patient then rubbed calomel ointment onto the penis, then wrapped the organ in waxed paper. The patient was instructed not to urinate for at least four hours, lest the treatment be ineffective, which would necessitate its repetition.[52] If this process was not humiliating enough for all involved, Company A's billeting area was quarantined from the other troops, cordoned off with a ten-foot high, barbed-wire perimeter, like a stockade.[53]

Lieutenant Lewis noted that the battalion also was responsible for overseeing the suppression of prostitution in the surrounding area. As of October 21, 1918, Lewis reported, "One hundred women who either lend or sell themselves to soldiers have been apprehended, taken before a magistrate and found to be suffering with either gonorrhea or syphilis." They were given treatment until the symptoms abated. Lewis reported that the "method of finding these women was simple. The men for the most part were very willing to give full information regarding the source of their misfortune, and the girls finding themselves in disgrace were eager to involve others pursuing the same occupation. In this way, the list of names multiplied very rapidly, with the result that both prostitution and disease is receiving a drastic check." Tracking down and arresting the prostitutes was carried out simultaneously with a campaign to educate the public. "Officials of the towns in the environment of Camp Colt have been interested to work in cooperation, and lectures have been given at public meetings of the citizens, where venereal questions and issues have been thoroughly discussed." Lewis reported that back in camp, the men had been fully indoctrinated in instruction on disease prevention, "hav[ing] been brought face to face with the exigencies of the venereal problem." By the third week of October, of the 588 troops assigned to the battalion, 404 were treated for gonorrhea and 49 for syphilis.[54] It is not known how many of these men had contracted the diseases before entering the army, as opposed to those who "caught the clap" while serving in the military.

Doctors throughout the armed forces determined that five out of six infected servicemen had contracted sexually transmitted diseases before they entered the service. Several medical reports indicated that nearly 25 percent of the new soldiers at some camps already were inflicted. One historian who has chronicled the social history of venereal disease has observed, "Military physicians and officials concluded that, in spite of the effectiveness of the programs to combat venereal disease in the camps, the problem had first to be addressed in civilian life.... These findings became the basis for transforming the CTCA's battle against venereal disease into a truly national campaign. . . . The citizens' campaign became an effective means of engaging the civilians to do their 'bit' for the war effort."[55] Thus, Lieutenant Lewis's public outreach program for the Gettysburg area was in keeping with Army policy to involve the civilian populace in combatting the problem.

The CTCA, through the YMCA, also arranged lectures about the dangers of sexually transmitted diseases to the Camp Colt soldiers who were *not* assigned to the Venereal Company, with the hope that expert instruction would educate them—and scare them enough that they would not engage in unprotected sex and would avoid prostitutes and "loose women" altogether. Iowan John Kimberly wrote to his wife about one such presentation:

> We heard some lecture last night at the Y.M.C.A [tent]. It was about taking care of yourself while you are in the army. I managed to get one of the books he lectured on, and will send it in this letter if I can find room.... I marked what he talked the most on, and it would do any one man or woman good to hear it. Sure would open your eyes, as about 1/3 of the diseases we think are common are only caused by the vernearel [*sic*] sickness. He said about ½ of the men and women in the world are affected with it, and sometime during their life it will show out on them or on their children. He was one of the country's best physicians and came from Washington, D.C. [He] sure gave some talk [I] would like to write one statement he made but this letter might get opened, and such stuff is not allowed to be sent in the mail.[56]

That CTCA publication, *Keeping Fit to Fight,* undoubtedly was the book to which Kimberly referred, as it was the military's most widely disseminated pamphlet concerning the dangers of venereal disease. The medical doctor making the speech—who personified the Progressives' reliance on so-called experts to diagnose and fix societal problems—used his knowledge and experience to paint a graphic portrayal of the horrors of sexually transmitted diseases, so distasteful that the Hawkeye soldier was afraid to put it on paper lest his letter be censored. One historian of medicine has written, "Photographic exhibits especially illustrated the most devastating effects of untreated syphilis: twisted limbs, open lesions, and physical deformities. Some lecturers prided themselves on their ability to send chills through the ranks."[57] Without a doubt, the doctor made quite an impression on the young Iowan.

The U.S. Army clearly took venereal disease very seriously and made its contraction a military offense. Eisenhower's adjutant published the post's sanitary regulations on April 12, soon after Camp Colt was established. Paragraph 16 outlined the necessary steps to be taken for men who had contracted any of the maladies:

> The cause of these diseases is a matter of common knowledge. They are entirely preventable, and the Army punishes those who exposed themselves and contract venereal diseases by stoppage of pay and restriction of privileges while under treatment. The soldier will apply at the Organization Infirmary immediately after returning to camp. If he fails to apply for preventative treatment and contracts the disease he will be Court-martialed. Venereal prophylaxis must be performed effectively and must be available day and night. All venereal cases will be segregated in separate quarters, where they will be under the care of a Medical Officer.[58]

Despite this stern warning early in the command's existence, the Tank Corps soldiers would prove just as adept at getting into trouble as their infantry predecessors had a year earlier. Nonetheless, all levels of government were cracking down. To set a stern example, on June 1, 1918, the Adams County Court sentenced Tom Amprazes, arrested in 1917 for maintaining a house of prostitution, to a $500 fine and one year in jail. However, because Amprazes previously had been a model citizen, the charges were to be commuted if he departed the county by sunset on the day of sentencing and donate $100 to the Red Cross War Fund. He complied.[59] Still, the problems associated with vice and bootlegging continued.

Progressive social hygienists believed alcohol consumption lowered the soldiers' abilities to fight off their sexual impulses, which led to fornication and the possible contraction of venereal diseases.[60] As a result, Captain Eisenhower sought to control the drunkenness that had prevailed among so many of the soldiers in the 1917 camp. On opening Camp Colt, he immediately put his military police to work. On March 25, the *Times* ran a headline that proclaimed, "MILITARY POLICE ON EVERY NIGHT. Town Gets Service Promptly from Camp Colt Head. No Apparent Need Now. But Takes No Chances." The hotel managers and saloonkeepers signed a pledge not to sell to men in uniform and not to allow anyone to purchase liquor for off-premises consumption. In Hanover, liquor retailers committed to sell no booze for consumption off premises, and wholesalers agreed not to sell or deliver any alcohol after 6:00 P.M. Ike's military policemen also worked closely with civilian law enforcement and the U.S. district attorney. In late May, Deputy U.S. Marshal Harvey Smith hauled six local bootleggers, who had been caught selling booze to soldiers, off to U.S. District Court in Williamsport, Pennsylvania. Ike's soldiers, however, circumvented the clampdown by going to York, Hanover, Carlisle, and other nearby towns in Pennsylvania and Maryland. On June 11, the *Times* reported that the MPs were sent to Chambersburg, where widespread bootlegging was suspected. Although the military policemen did not apprehend any troops in violation of the law, two Chambersburg cops arrested a pair of inebriated Camp Colt men. A newspaper account stated that one of the drunks "had half his clothing off. Both were placed in jail to sober up."[61] Back in Gettysburg, it seemed that the majority of the citizens had learned their lesson from 1917—but not all.

"Most residents welcomed the soldiers," Eisenhower reflected, "if for no other reason than patriotism. A few saw in them a source of quick and easy profit, catering to all their appetites. In any community, this minority can cause endless trouble, sometimes seriously affecting, by a sort of contagion that runs through the ranks, an entire command." The young captain quickly established amicable relations with the civilian populace and its governing officials "to protect the community and the troops against the offensive few." Although he possessed the authority to close all saloons and other liquor-dispensing establishments within a five-mile radius of Camp Colt, Ike took the diplomatic route and allowed them to continue to do business in the usual manner; this would show the army's good intent. However, Eisenhower also was pragmatic about the situation: "My provost forces were well acquainted with all such places in the Gettysburg area and they thought it better to allow them to stay open and keep an eye on them, rather than close them down and cause a surge in bootlegging, a business they couldn't control." Things went smoothly until Ike received "a report that a man who owned a sizeable hotel with a bar had been surreptitiously serving liquor to men in uniform."[62] The time for a showdown had come.

Not quite sure if he had the authority to close the business, since it also catered to overnight guests, recently promoted Major Eisenhower placed the entire location "off limits" to soldiers and put a provost guard around the hotel. According to Eisenhower, "Naturally, with this restriction enforced, visitors who had come to see their brothers and husbands and sons and sweethearts would not go into the hotel either. The hotel owner came to see me, made a promise, and I gave him another chance." But the owner did not live up to his word, and Ike put the guards back in place. This time, the proprietor summoned Congressman Brodbeck, who accompanied the hotel owner to a meeting with Eisenhower. Undeterred, Ike stood his ground. In his memoirs, Eisenhower recalled the outcome of the contentious summit:

> After debate, the congressman said, "Well, we have means—we can go to the War Department. If you're going to be stubborn, I'll have to take up the question of replacing you."
>
> I said, "You do just exactly that."
>
> He looked a little startled.
>
> "Nothing would please me better than to be taken out of this job. I want to go overseas. If they take me out of here, maybe I can get there."
>
> The dialogue ended on this note and he left with his secretary and his constituent. Within minutes, the secretary came back and said, "Look, major, don't pay any attention to all this. The congressman had to do this because the hotel man is a very important supporter of his but we don't want to start a quarrel."
>
> "That's all right with me," I said. "Let it go."

Despite his secretary's assurance that the congressman was just putting on a show to appease his constituent, Brodbeck filed a complaint with the War Department, and the end result was that Eisenhower received a commendation from Secretary of War Newton Baker "for diligence in looking after the welfare and well-being of my soldiers." The defeated hotel owner was forced to grovel at Eisenhower's feet for forgiveness. The young major did not believe that the repeat offender deserved another chance, but he relented, warning the proprietor that he would send plainclothes MPs to ensure that the rules were being followed. If the hotel owner was caught breaking them again, Ike swore he would put him out of business. "We had no more trouble," Eisenhower recalled.[63]

Because of his standing in the community and Brodbeck's political support, the hotel proprietor thus escaped the consequences of his lawlessness. Less affluent citizens were not so fortunate. One was George Washington, a black man arraigned before the U.S. commissioner in Gettysburg on May 18 for selling a half-pint of whiskey to an undercover MP posing as an ordinary uniformed soldier. Washington worked as a chauffeur at the Lincoln Way Hotel on York Street.

(It is not known whether this was the same hotel owned by the man Eisenhower personally had confronted.) After the transaction, the whiskey was turned over to the Pennsylvania State Police, who then arrested the luckless Washington. He was held on $500 bail for his appearance at the U.S. District Court in Williamsport, Pennsylvania, on June 3, 1918.[64] His racial background, however, probably had nothing to do with the arrest, since the majority of the culprits arraigned along with Washington were white.[65]

In another bootlegging sting, the MPs sent a uniformed private to the home of a Gettysburg citizen, named J. Conti, under suspicion of selling whiskey to the doughboys. According to the *Times,* "Lieutenant Emmerick [of the military police] sent a soldier to the house of Conti . . . and the soldier purchased a small quantity of whiskey with which he returned to headquarters." After conferring with the state police, the lieutenant and two state troopers "went to the place to effect an arrest." Conti opened the door but then slammed it in their faces, compelling the officers to force their way in. "There was a brief but lively moment before the arrest was affected and Conti was soon on his way to jail." The officers also discovered additional evidence, a large cache of empty bottles and "stock on hand."[66]

The privately owned amusement park adjacent to GNMP's Little Round Top was a favorite hangout for Camp Colt's soldiers. A sanitary inspector from the U.S. Army Surgeon General's Office wrote about an interview with Col. John Nicholson of the Gettysburg National Park Commission concerning vice-related problems there:

> The condition described to me by Col. Nicholson is certainly very deplorable. He says that this resort is frequented by prostitutes, not only from Gettysburg but from the neighboring towns of York, Harrisburg, Chambersburg and Emmitsburg. These excursions bring in with them quantities of beer and whiskey which they give or sell to the soldiers. As a result of this debauchery the grounds . . . are used for association purposes. On a single evening over 50 couples were detected [by park guards] and driven from hiding places behind the tablets, monuments, rocks and trees of the [GNMP] reservation. On one occasion his officers found over 300 empty beer bottles scattered around their various hiding places. Colonel Nicholson further stated that he found it impossible to police this point.[67]

Since the prostitutes were bringing the booze, and it was not being supplied by the operators of the amusement park, Eisenhower could not shut down the resort. His only hope was that his soldiers would find other ways to occupy their free time, lest they face the stern hand of military justice if caught violating the regulations.

Continuing its work from the year before, the CTCA and its subsidiary organizations, such as the YMCA, Red Cross, and Knights of Columbus, did their utmost to provide wholesome recreation for the soldiers. George Le Roy Aldenifer served as the YMCA athletic director at Camp Colt from May through September, when he too was called to serve in the U.S. Army. "I shall never forget my first five weeks there," he wrote in his diary in September 1918, a few weeks after he had been inducted into the service. "It was a wonderful experience and I felt that I was doing 'my bit' just as well as my friends who had enlisted in the army or navy. I helped to organize the best base-ball team in camp and we played many games with teams from nearby towns. The people of these towns always gave the boys a welcome reception and furnished them with home cooked meals." Aldenifer was kind enough to donate the use of his automobile, an Oakland Roadster, to the YMCA, "as long as I was there to run it. Of course the expenses were charged to the 'Y' but they were light due to the fact that the men in camp were all mechanically inclined and did the repairing of the car free of charge." Because of the large volume of military traffic, Aldenifer found that the "roads into town were all cut-up from constant use of army trucks over them." Only two months into his Gettysburg assignment, Aldenifer received his draft notice. He had tried to enlist for officers' training in 1917, but because he was missing a thumb from an earlier accident, he was found to be physically unfit for military duty. One year later, the Army needed men, and, thumb or no thumb, he was called to serve. Before departing Camp Colt, he recalled, "I gave good-bye to my Christian friends of the red triangle [the insignia of the YMCA] and to as many of the tankers as I saw when packing up my clothes, took my car to 'Eddie' Plank's Garage where I told them to sell it for not less than $250.00 cash and boarded the train at five fifty-five A.M. July 23rd 1918 en route to Camp Syracuse." Aldenifer would finish the war as a private assigned to a stateside unit, the 10th Company, 1st Regiment, Ordnance Department.[68]

As it had during the previous year, the CTCA scheduled concerts, patriotic speeches, and athletic events at Camp Colt, which apparently were well attended by the troops. In late May, a professional wrestler with the stage name of "Americus" came to town to accept the challenge of Cpl. Frank S. Leavitt of Company B, 329th Tank Battalion, who before the war likewise had been a pro wrestler. The *Times* reported, "The Tank Corps giant has met Americus before, and it is virtually a toss-up between the two men. Just before he transferred from the infantry to the Tank Corps, he wrestled Americus in Madison Square Garden and the verdict was a draw after some of the fastest action ever seen in a mat contest."[69] During the Gettysburg rematch, the contest once again ended in stalemate.[70] In an unfortunate off-duty incident following a sponsored social event, twenty-four-year-old Nebraskan and Regular Army veteran Cpl. Thomas A. Richards, returning with several truckloads of soldiers from a dance at the York Out-Door Club, fell off the rear of the truck, fractured his skull, and died. He was a member of Company B, 337th Tank Battalion.[71]

In May 1918, Eisenhower authorized the publication of a weekly newspaper titled *Treat 'Em Rough,* as a way to disseminate Army and camp information, publish war news, report the scores of Camp Colt's sports teams, announce special events, spread friendly camp gossip, and improve morale. The title soon became the motto of the entire Tank Corps.[72] Thirty-six years later, a former Camp Colt officer hailing from the Territory of Alaska recalled how the motto came to be: "In Nome, Alaska, there was much playing during winter months of basketball teams. I was a member of the Arctic Brotherhood team. At every game, those Arctic Brothers and friends who were spectators, always yelled, especially when game points were not in their favor, 'TREAT 'EM ROUGH.' Above the words was a Black Fighting Cat." (The black cat was—and still is—the icon of the "International Con*cat*enated Order of the Hoo-Hoo," a service and fraternal organization founded in 1892 whose members are involved in the forest products/lumber industry. The Arctic Brotherhood was one of its lodges.) This officer, the originator of the motto for the newspaper, was Lt. George R. Goshaw, who at one point was the camp adjutant. (During President Dwight D. Eisenhower's administration, Goshaw served as U.S. Commissioner of Alaska, which remained a U.S. territory until it attained statehood in 1959).[73]

Life at Camp Colt, like many other rural Army camps in 1917 and 1918, could be boring. Drill, classes, chow, guard duty, and sleep occupied most of an enlisted soldier's day. On Sunday, June 16, 1918, Private Kimberly wrote a letter to his wife back home in Maxwell, Iowa, likewise a very pastoral community. Having stood guard duty the night before, and unsure whether he had to pull it again that evening, he told her, "A bunch here in our Co. are going out on a hike today, to look the old battle grounds over. Would go along if I was sure that I wouldn't be on guard tonight." Then, he admitted, "This sure is one dead place. Absolutely nothing going on." Kimberly was just getting started. Now the griping, in the best traditions of the U.S. Army, really began:

> They have a Y.M.C.A. here, but it don't amount to anything, but after a fellow has been working all day he don't care to roam around any I'll tell you. Gettysburg is not a very large place, some say about 2500 is the population but don't know myself. This is a pretty place though, as it is a rolling country here at the camp and lots of timber around it and the mountains are not far away, as they are very plainly seen. Believe me if you want the best end of the army don't *enlist,* just wait

> and be drafted. An enlisted man has to put up with ten times more than a drafted guy does. When you enlist you are lucky to get 3 square meals a day and a bed to sleep in, let alone a barracks. *Tents* are good enough for the *enlisted* man, I used to think that Camp Dodge [Iowa] was a hole, but that is a paradise [compared] to what we have to go thru.

Then, his hubris overcame his grievances:

> But never[the]less, and not bragging any, old Camp Colt is going to turn out some of the best fighting regiments that Uncle Sam has, as every man here has to pass the hardest physical examinations there is to get into the T.C., and they are learning us what the infantry, machine gun, and artillerymen has to know, besides our own little game of war. And they don't give us any feathers to sleep on when we come in tired of a night, if you haven't got a cot, just roll up your blanket and sleep on the floor. I am not kicking any myself but I don't want to hear any drafted guy kick when this war is over.

His prideful grousing went on for another four pages before he concluded, "Well I am running out of news and about everything else, will make an attempt to ring off. Sure is a fine day here, wish you were here so we could go out in the shade and enjoy life together again."[74]

The grueling training days, off-duty boredom, and high temperatures of a southcentral Pennsylvania summer were taking their toll on Camp Colt's soldiers, who began to grumble about what they considered unfair treatment by Gettysburg's businesses and residents, and finally they expressed their collective discontent in a mid-August issue of *Treat 'Em Rough*. The *Gettysburg Times* reprinted the scathing editorial on the front page of its August 22 edition under the headline, "TREAT 'EM ROUGH HITS GETTYSBURG: Current Issue of Camp Colt's Publication Scores Town on Numerous Accounts. Prefer Many Charges: Lack of Hospitality, High Prices, Benefit Dances, and a Number of Other Things Named." The tankers' complaints were numerous and stinging: being compared to Gettysburg College's rowdy students; being equated to the "roughneck" infantrymen of the 1917 camp; being "trimmed" of their money the same as tourists; as well as being shown a lack of appreciation "for the remarkable influx of trade due to the coming of the Tanks Corps." The soldier-editor did not stop there. He also griped about the doughboys' dearth of dinner invitations from the town residents and even censured the licensed battlefield guides for not offering to give soldiers free tours. Gettysburg's churches were the only organizations that were praised, for having "given unselfishly of their time and money to provide social entertainment to the Tankers." The author of this angry and sarcastic missive then stated the reasons the soldiers were in Gettysburg in the first place:

> The Tankers are not in Gettysburg because they love the town particularly. It's a nice town, but that isn't why the soldiers are there. Neither are they in the Army because they can't make a living any other way. The soldiers are in uniform and in Gettysburg in response to a national emergency. They are training for service—for hard, dangerous, grueling work that will make this world a decent place to live in. They are fine American boys and men who have left their homes and businesses at the call of Old Glory. They deserve at least good a treatment as is accorded the civilian. And "Treat 'Em Rough" is going to see that they get it.

He concluded by listing the ways Gettysburg might become "a fine place":

> IF the merchants would take about 25 percent off their prices, which should make prices about normal.
>
> IF the road to camp was repaired instead of spending money to build a perfectly elegant but useless park plot, or whatever it is, in the middle of the square.
>
> IF the jitney drivers would lower their prices (they could do it and make more money at the same time if the road to camp was repaired).
>
> IF Gettysburg citizens would wake up to the fact that the boys of the Tank Corps come from good American homes—at least as good as the homes in Gettysburg, and the Tankers are gentlemen and NOT rough-necks or home-wreckers.
>
> IF Community Dances were arranged, free to Tankers.
>
> IF some of Gettysburg's excess profits were diverted into channels which would be of benefit free to the soldiers.

In conclusion, the author snidely remarked: "At this point we desist. We have wandered into aimless chatter. The millennium has been, we understand, indefinitely postponed."[75]

Camp Colt's bored, homesick soldiers may have felt slighted, ripped off, and, most importantly, unappreciated, but hundreds of Gettysburg and Adams County families also had sent their sons and a few daughters off to war and were feeling the anxiety of separation and loss. Certainly unscrupulous merchants had taken advantage of the troops, but it is unlikely that the majority of citizens did not appreciate the sacrifices of the soldiers. (Le Roy Aldenifer, the YMCA athletic director, even mentioned that the citizens had invited the soldiers into their households for home-cooked meals.) The truth was that Gettysburg had become war-weary. Its citizens, likewise, had made sacrifices, and the basis of the economy—tourism—had suffered a major blow since the United States' entry into the war. The soldiers, in essence, had become the new "tourists."

The battlefield itself also had taken an ecological hit, with hundreds of structures; herds of horses and mules; and hundreds of trucks, cars, motorcycles, horse-drawn wagons—plus the tank—occupying the geographic center of the battlefield between Seminary and Cemetery Ridges, the scene of Pickett's Charge. To keep down the dust, eighteen thousand gallons of coal tar—Tarvia—was sprayed on the thirty-six thousand square yards of compacted dirt, cinder, or gravel roads bisecting the camp, leaving a black stain on the formerly bucolic national park and its once rolling farmland.[76] And even though the wastewater from the shower facilities and kitchens drained into sewage treatment plants, the filtration systems were not being properly maintained, thus polluting the park's streams. One of Colonel Nicholson's employee-supervisors inspected the plant on the Trostle Farm "and found that the filthy condition of Plum Run was caused by the waste matter of the Camp which should have been treated with Chloride of Lime." Rather than go through War Department channels to alleviate the situation, the park employee took matters into his own hands: "A supply of [Chloride of Lime] has been received and is now being used and the trouble corrected." But he took the process one step farther by having park laborers scatter "fifteen bushels of stone lime . . . in the channel from 100 yards north of United States Avenue to Devil's Den."[77] Tens of thousands of doughboys had called that area "home" since May 1917, and the environmental impact to the park was severe, although the soldiers had little control over the situation. Now, the current camp residents were asking the townsfolk not to compare them to the "roughnecks" from the previous year. In reality, however, the tankers and their support personnel had been just as mischievous as the infantrymen in 1917, albeit in smaller numbers.

The townspeople and the *Times* editors took offense at the tankers' charges, and a rebuttal appeared in the August 23 edition. The headline summarized the reaction: "TOWN REPLIES TO TREAT 'EM ROUGH: Most of Criticism Is Shown to Be Unfounded on Facts and Entirely Undeserved. CITIZENS RESENT CHARGES: Editorial in Soldiers' Paper Fails in View of Canvass of Conditions Here and Elsewhere." The author responded to each criticism, to the tune of two and a half columns of print, and even replied to the accusation that "the tankers have to live down the reputation of the last year's camp." In a less-than-honest reply, however, the editor wrote, "Gettysburg has most pleasant memories of the 14,000 boys stationed here for four or five months in 1917, boys who met every advance quickly and were most appreciative of every service done for them." The article concluded: "The Tank Corps is proud of the very high class of its personnel, but is it not possible that this very pride may make its members unreceptive to the advances of the townspeople who would willingly throw open their homes but whose hospitality has not always been gladly accepted as it was cheerfully tendered."

Coincidentally, rumors that Camp Colt would be closed arrived in town that very day. On August 24, the *Times* reported, "Rumor has it that Camp Colt is to be abandoned. . . . From a business point of view Camp Colt is of unquestionable benefit to the community. Without any war industries the town would be in a bad way if the camp were not to be continued here." It seemed that the editors no longer were indignant about the grumblings printed in *Treat 'Em Rough.* For the moment, however, the tales turned out to be false.

Nonetheless, the *Treat 'Em Rough* editorial staff published a rejoinder in its next issue (September 10) that is too lengthy and petty to summarize. It did, however, express regret for hurting "the feelings of a great many estimable people. For this we are sorry and we apologize. We have no desire to hurt anyone's feelings or hurt their sensibilities." The editors did not care if they "riled" any guilty parties, but "to those citizens who are really hurt, grieved, and to whom our editorial came as an unwarranted slap in the face, we apologize in all sincerity." Nonetheless, the soldier-editors did not back down. In a special sidebar slapped smack-dab in the middle of the lengthy editorial's first page, they proposed: "The Tank Corps at Camp Colt asks nothing of Gettysburg except a universal square deal. They are getting a square deal now—in spots. The Tankers appreciate what is being done now, but 'Treat 'Em Rough' wants, on behalf of the soldiers, a weeding-out of the things which are baneful. This can be achieved only through a cohesive organization of Gettysburg citizens. GET TOGETHER, GETTYSBURG."

Again the *Times* responded, this time on September 12, with very little commentary. Most of the article reprinted sections of the *Treat 'Em Rough* editorial when the writers admitted that they might have exaggerated or been flat out wrong. "The new outburst is in part a reiteration, in part an explanation, and in part a retraction of the former caustic criticism," the *Times* editor explained. Incongruously, on the same page of the *Times'* editorial was a news report reprinted from the *York Gazette,* titled "Camp Colt Men Included in Disorderly Conduct Charge," naming three Colt soldiers, a sergeant and two lieutenants, as well as two York women who had been arrested in the nearby city.

As summer days grew shorter and the daily temperatures slowly began to drop, bulletins on the war's progress continued to filter down from the battle zones to the Camp Colt soldiers and their civilian neighbors. The Adams County newspapers dutifully printed the casualty lists, promoted the sales of war bonds and stamps, announced additional draft calls, solicited funds for the Red Cross, recounted the outcomes of the ongoing military campaigns, and reprinted letters from local sons and daughters who were witnessing firsthand the overseas conflict. The constant fusillade of war-related news permeated Adams County. Not even Gettysburg College's ivy-covered walls could keep the war from taking center stage. On October 1, 1918, while many of its alumni were leading soldiers and marines on the Western Front and ROTC students dug trenches on campus, the entire school became an official U.S. Army post. Gettysburg College was not alone. All across the country, civilian colleges and universities came under the jurisdiction of the War Department, with all able-bodied males enlisted as army privates. They would constitute the Students' Army Training Corps (SATC) and would be subject to military discipline, required to wear uniforms and take military-related instruction in addition to their civilian courses.[78] "At the stroke of noon to-day Gettysburg College was officially taken over by the War Department and converted into a 100 percent military institution," reported the *Times* in its October 1 edition. An official ceremony marking the occasion was conducted in front of the "Old Dorm" building, which had been used as a Confederate observation post and field hospital during the 1863 battle. The college president, William A. Granville, spoke briefly to the 350 new inductees and reminded them that the first military training camp for civilian college students had taken place in Gettysburg just after the 1913 Peace Jubilee, setting the precedent for the entire preparedness movement that now had evolved into the SATC. Students enrolled in ROTC became part of the SATC for the duration of its existence, which proved short.[79]

In command of the Gettysburg SATC Detachment was 1st Lt. John E. Carney, a veteran of the 1918 summer campaigns, during which he was wounded and gassed. Granville later reported that since women students, men under the age of eighteen, pre-seminary students, and men physically unfit for military service had not been inducted into the corps, SATC presence required "the running of two quite distinct college curriculums simultaneously, a very difficult undertaking." Because the military students also were required to eat together, and as the college did not have a dining facility, Granville stated that "it became necessary to install kitchens and provide mess halls for the accommodation of more than 350, those of our students who are enlisted in the S.A.T.C." To accomplish this, Granville ordered the conversion of classrooms to kitchens and mess rooms on the first floor of Stevens Hall (named for Thaddeus Stevens), and added to the building a temporary 1,976-square-foot annex for use as a mess hall.[80] (Women from the community were hired as kitchen workers.[81]) Although the SATC "soldiers" were officially members of the U.S. Army, they would not come under the command of the Camp Colt authorities, who by then were preoccupied with their own problems.

The war continued, and Pershing's doughboys were involved heavily in the fight. Eisenhower, his staff and subordinate leaders had four major missions in support of the AEF: provide the recruits with basic combat skills, inculcate military discipline, and instill esprit de corps; provide them with an orientation to tank warfare; get them physically fit, keep them healthy, and provide for their welfare; and when their orders for overseas' service arrived, deliver the finished products to their ports of embarkation in a timely fashion. "Once the basic provisions of the Abbeville Agreement had been fulfilled," Ike later wrote, "we began to make monthly shipments of Tank Corps troops to Europe."[82] (The Abbeville Conference concluded with an agreement between the Allied nations that determined the allotment of manpower requirements, particularly the deployment of U.S. divisions on the Western Front.[83]) "Frequently, men from other camps, on reaching the embarkation depots, had gone absent without leave, or had imbibed too freely while roaming the eastern cities," recalled the conservative major. "Warned, we took measures to see that our men arrived at exactly the right moment, were put aboard ship, and all records were turned over without giving them any special opportunities for peccadilloes." His soldiers may not have appreciated Ike's concern for their well-being, but the Camp Colt commander truly believed he held their welfare at heart: "Happy or not, they may very well have been saved from a protracted tour of hard labor, a blot on their records, of if they had managed to get aboard ship in time, from the violent seasickness that can follow a spree on the town."[84]

Some eighty years later, one of Camp Colt's few remaining veterans wrote a short memoir about his time in Gettysburg in 1918 and also his voyage to France. Private Chester H. Beymer had trained to be a signaler while at Camp Colt, and he distinctly remembered practicing with his telegraph "buzzer," as he called it, "under a shade tree on the grass where the Union lines had been. The monument erected there to commemorate the place where the Union forces had turned back Pickets [*sic*] Charge . . . was almost within touching distance." Selected for the "October Automatic Replacement Draft" for overseas shipment, Beymer recalled what happened next:

> We had [our] uniforms updated by giving up our wide brimmed Stetson hats for the overseas cap. This was a small triangular cloth cap with no visor or brim. You put it on tilted a little to one side. It provided a little jaunty and devil-may-care look. It also provided a cushion between the top of your head and the steel helmet if you needed your helmet in a hurry. It could also be folded up and carried in your pocket

> easily. Stetson hats didn't fit inside a tank. We were issued two pairs of hob nailed boots to replace the . . . dress shoes. The advantage there was that the hob nail soles never wore out. They also should help you from falling on muddy or frozen ground.

Beymer and the other soldiers who were selected for the Replacement Draft received their orders on October 18 and left Gettysburg the same day. They traveled by rail to Camp Mills, New York. After a short stay of one night—outside, in the rain—they took an electric train to Hoboken, New Jersey, where they "boarded a British freighter, name unknown. It was known by the troops as a bucket of bolts." Next, he and his pals were assigned bunks "three tiers high. . . . The [sleeping] hold had apparently been disinfected by what smelled like creosote. It was strong, but since we hadn't slept the last two nights, we had no trouble going to sleep and slept the night through."[85]

According to Beymer's recollection, "The next morning when we came on deck we were out in the Atlantic and a convoy was forming up. . . . There were two battleships or heavy cruisers way out front on the horizon leading the way. Then there were three destroyers circling the pack like sheep dogs. They had to keep the convoy organized." (Beymer was mistaken about battleships leading the convoy, as the only U.S. dreadnoughts plying European waters had been attached to the British Grand Fleet.[86]) All told, Beymer reckoned there were thirty-five vessels in his convoy, most of them cargo ships and troop transports, "and they each had a special place assigned to them. The speed of the convoy was, of course, limited to that of the slowest ship."

If Eisenhower believed that expediting his troops' travel to the port of embarkation—without giving them time to get drunk—would prevent "a violent bout of seasickness," he was sadly mistaken. Beymer recalled that on the morning his convoy steamed away from the American coast, "Breakfast was brought out on deck in 30-gallon wash tubs. One look and I headed to the rail. I was seasick for the next six or seven days." The voyage across the North Atlantic proved mostly uneventful, for at that time of the war the German U-boat threat had all but dissipated. Nonetheless, Beymer remembered that when his transport was about halfway across the ocean, "we came on deck one morning to find our ship standing stock still and not another ship in sight. It seemed that the engine had broken down during the night. There was a lot of hammering and clanging down in the engine room." After an entire day of floating powerless, with all hands on deck searching the horizon for an enemy periscope, the engine was repaired, and just after dark "out of a fog bank came our little destroyer, working his signal lamp like crazy wanting to know what we were doing and to get moving. We went below feeling somewhat safer and the next morning we were back in our usual place in the convoy." Chester Beymer and his shipmates arrived in Liverpool, England, on October 31. After less than a week's stay in the United Kingdom, the contingent of tankers crossed the English Channel and landed at Le Havre on November 6, and three days later the soldiers were loaded on a train and headed to a training area. By the time they reached their destination, the war was over.

Beymer's experience would have been similar to that of hundreds of thousands of other soldiers who made the North Atlantic convoy crossings since America's entry into the World War more than a year earlier. The hundreds of Adams County soldiers who served on the Western Front, as well as the thousands of Regulars who had trained at Gettysburg in 1917, likewise made the perilous trip—and some were not so lucky, such as the men of Company B, 58th U.S. Infantry, who had lost so many of their comrades during a U-boat attack in the spring.

While Eisenhower prepared his tankers for war in the autumn of 1918, those men who had made the earlier crossings were girding their loins for the largest American battle ever fought to that time, much bigger and bloodier than when their forefathers had killed each other during the Battle of Gettysburg. For now, all eyes were fixed on a small, somewhat forested area of rolling hills and ridgelines just north of the blood-drenched, shell-cratered area around Verdun, a place called the Argonne.

CHAPTER 6

Into the Argonne

In late summer of 1918, as Maj. Dwight D. Eisenhower trained his tankers for overseas service and delivered them to their ports of embarkation on schedule, General Pershing's staff at American Expeditionary Forces (AEF) headquarters was laying plans for the final push of the war. With the rapid reduction of the Saint-Mihiel salient behind them, American commanders and staff officers struggled to move an entire army to the jump-off line north of Verdun for what history would remember as the Meuse-Argonne offensive, named for the right and left boundaries of the maneuver area, the Meuse River and the Argonne Forest. The survivors of this momentous campaign called it simply "The Argonne." And men from Gettysburg and Adams County, as well as those who trained on the Gettysburg Battlefield in 1917 and 1918, would be in the thick of it.

The French army had tried to conquer this area during the previous four years and had failed miserably, with unburied human remains and scattered temporary cemeteries marking the distance of their advance. The German army had spent the same time improving its trench lines, constructing steel-reinforced concrete machine-gun bunkers, siting and registering mortars and artillery, and laying belt upon belt of barbed-wire obstacles. The Huns also placed observation posts on all of the critical terrain features on both sides of the Meuse River. Moreover, the German army in that sector had planned for a defense in depth, with up to four major lines of resistance stretched across the area where the Americans were poised to attack. During the 1916 epic Verdun battle, the German crown prince ordered his own observation post built from the ruins of an old monastery on a hill known as Montfaucon.[1]

Complicating the operational situation was that a big portion of the same Allied force that had just fought in the Saint-Mihiel offensive would have to fight again two weeks later in the Meuse-Argonne offensive. Overseeing the massive logistical operation to move an entire army in the short space of less than fourteen days was another officer destined for greatness, Col. George C. Marshall, a native of western Pennsylvania and a 1901 graduate of the Virginia Military Institute. On only three roads, more than 428,000 men; 3,980 artillery pieces; 90,000 mules and horses; and all of their food, fodder, medical supplies, ammunition, and other provisions would have to be moved some forty to fifty miles northward in less than two weeks. Yet somehow, Marshall and others like him would get it done.[2]

Kate Wolf wrote home in August, in time for the *Gettysburg Compiler* to publish her letter, on September 14, just before the great offensive began. Her tone reflected her four years of grim work: "Isn't it horrible when men think only of how many other men they can kill and we women tell them to get all they can as though they were swatting flies, and then praise them when they have helped heap up German dead.—To such a pass has this world come." During the next campaign, the German dead would indeed be heaped high, but so would American.

The Seventy-Ninth and Twenty-Eighth Divisions, organizations to which so many Adams County men were assigned, were part of the force slated to make the opening assault. Likewise, the Fourth Division, of which the 58th and 59th Infantry still were assigned, also would be in the initial drive. Only one year earlier, many of the men who comprised those units had been camped at Gettysburg and had made friends in the surrounding community. Within a few weeks, the four other regiments that had spent time in Gettysburg in 1917, the 4th, 7th, 60th and 61st, would be committed to the offensive as well. The Seventy-Ninth Division was about to test its mettle, but it was heretofore untried. Its soldiers were rookies. As fate—or some very poor tactical planning—would have it, the Seventy-Ninth would be placed in the very center of the opening assault, up against the most formidable terrain the Americans would encounter.

The Seventy-Ninth Division's commander was Maj. Gen. Joseph E. Kuhn, an 1885 West Point graduate who had spent most of his career assigned to non-combat related engineering projects. However, he knew his adversary very well. Kuhn was an observer of the 1906 German military maneuvers and had served as an attaché to the German army from 1914 to 1916, when the United States was a neutral nation. He was considered an intellectual and had been assigned to the Army War College as its president. The Seventy-Ninth was his first true command, as he had served for only a month as the commander of the 1st Engineer Regiment at Brownsville, Texas in early 1917.[3]

One of the men in Seventy-Ninth Division was Ira Ellsworth Lady of Arendtsville, a small village in northern Adams County. Lady had graduated from West Chester Normal School (now West Chester University) in 1913 and was employed as a secondary school teacher before the war. Drafted in the fall of 1917, he found himself a private in Company A, 316th Infantry at Camp Meade, just like most of the other white draftees from Adams County. Volunteering for immediate overseas service, he subsequently was transferred to the 4th Infantry Regiment, Third Division, was promoted to sergeant, and sailed with that unit for France in early April 1918. Lady participated in the campaigns along the Marne River during the summer and in August was selected for officers' training school. He was commissioned a second lieutenant on September 25 and was reassigned to his original unit, the 316th, just in time for the campaign to begin.[4]

Like Ira Lady, Grover Cleveland Maus of Littlestown, whose parents' obviously were fond of the two-term president, was drafted and assigned to Company A of the 316th. And like Lady, he volunteered for immediate overseas service and was transferred from Camp Meade to the 4th Infantry Regiment, Third Division. Maus fought in the summer campaigns as well as the Saint-Mihiel battle.[5] Soon after the war he recalled, "After the success at St. Mihiel all energy was directed toward the great drive. . . . Of course for a time the enlisted men knew nothing about plans. All they knew was that they were being moved from one portion of the front to another, sometimes by trucks, at other times on foot." His description of the movement from the Saint-Mihiel region to the starting line of the next offensive deserves attention, especially since he recounted it shortly after the war, while his memory was fresh:

> It does not take long to tell about the movement of an army, but one must actually have been part of it to realize what it means. The hikes were made at night, and most of those September nights were rainy. To hike for the better part of a dark, rainy night, over long rough roads, across shell-torn fields, through forests, sometimes being compelled to stand on a road jammed with what appeared to be an endless line of trucks, artillery wagons, ambulances, and everything which goes to make up an army; drenched by a chilling rain from without and wet with perspiration from within is an experience never to be forgotten. At the end of such a hike you pitched your tent in some deep forest without the aid of daylight, lay down on the cold ground and envied your dog at home.[6]

Maus's experience echoed those of countless fellow doughboys who were about to embark on what was hoped to be the final campaign of the war. No doubt, Pvt. Bernard Althoff of Gettysburg, assigned to Company B, 145th Infantry, Thirty-Fifth Division, would have suffered a similar bad time, and the death of his cousin, Sgt. Paul Altoff, USMC, who had been mortally wounded at Belleau Wood, certainly weighed heavily on his mind. In a letter dated September 4, the young sergeant wrote to his parents "to let you know that I am still alive." After complaining about the lack of mail from back home, "which makes me feel as if I don't have a friend in the world," he wrote, "I have four tricks in the front line and went over the top twice. You have read about No Man's Land. There is nothing out there but barbed wire, entanglements and shell holes, but there are plenty of them. I have been over as far as the third line German trench and that's as far as I care to go at one time." He concluded his long, descriptive letter, "This war is Hell—hope it will soon be over."[7]

Some twenty miles west of where Althoff, Lady, Maus, and a hundred thousand other Americans were preparing to attack, several U.S. and French divisions were about to launch a similar offensive in the Champagne region, part of the same Allied grand offensive all along the Western Front that would begin on September 26. Men from Adams County, particularly the soldiers and marines in the Second Division, would take part in the Champagne attack, as would soldiers assigned to the three African American regiments of the Ninety-Third Division serving with the French army. Pvt. Joseph A. Williams of Gettysburg, who had been drafted in 1917, was assigned to Company F, 372d Infantry, Ninety-Third Division. (The 372d was attached to the French 157th Division.[8]) Because they were serving with the French, Williams and his comrades wore U.S. Army uniforms but carried French rifles and used French accoutrements and helmets. Since the French army already contained tens of thousands of black soldiers from its African colonies, the men in these three African American regiments were treated much better than the black doughboys assigned to the Ninety-Second Division, which was poorly trained and ineptly led by its white and black officers.[9] Three Gettysburg men were assigned to the hapless Ninety-Second: Reuben B. Lyles, of the 368th Infantry, and Freeman L. Stanton, likewise assigned to the 368th, and his cousin Jacob A. Stanton, assigned to the 350th Field Artillery.[10] The Ninety-Second would play only a minor role in the upcoming offensive, serving on the boundary at the western edge of the Argonne Forest as liaison between the U.S. First Army and the French Fourth Army.

Gen. John J. Pershing would lead the First Army while retaining command of the AEF. (The last time an American general had tried to wear two hats was when George McClellan commanded both the entire Union army and the Army of the Potomac during the first year of the Civil War, fifty-six years earlier.) The initial assault force, arrayed from west to east, comprised the I, V, and III U.S. Corps, containing nine divisions, three in each corps. Six divisions were held in reserve. Maj. Gen. Hunter Liggett remained in command of I

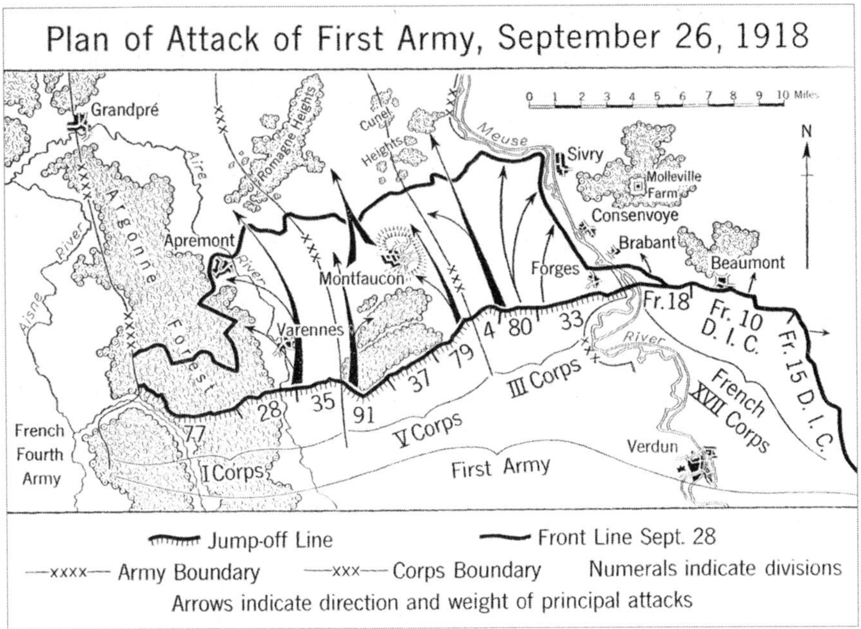

AEF tactical plan for the first phase of the Meuse-Argonne Offensive (American Battle Monuments Commission, *American Armies and Battlefields in Europe: A History, Guide, and Reference Book* [Washington, D.C.: GPO, 1938])

Corps, Maj. Gen. Charles Cameron led V Corps, and Maj. Gen. Robert Bullard commanded III Corps. The Twenty-Eighth Division, in I Corps, would attack through the eastern section of the Argonne Forest and along the western valley of the Aire River. The Seventy-Ninth Division, assigned to Bullard's corps, faced the formidable Butte de Monfaucon. The attack orders thus placed the inadequately trained Seventy-Ninth, with absolutely no combat experience, in position to storm and carry the most important and heavily fortified terrain feature in the entire initial phase of the operation. On that division's right flank, the III Corps lay in position. The Fourth Division, with its two regiments of Gettysburg-trained infantrymen, was assigned to III Corps, and its sole mission was to drive northward while protecting the right flank of the Seventy-Ninth during its assault on Montfaucon.[11]

The "Big Show" opened in the early morning darkness of September 26 after an intense but relatively short Allied artillery barrage. Joe Stone of the 59th Infantry, Fourth Division, succinctly jotted in his journal, "The barrage lifted at 5:30 A.M. and the advance started." The Seventy-Ninth Division attacked along a one-and-a-half mile front with the 157th Brigade, comprising the 313th and 314th Infantry, leading the assault while the 158th Brigade, with the 315th and

316th Infantry, followed about a half mile to the rear of the leading regiments.[12] A heavy fog; smoke; and difficult, shell-torn terrain caused considerable confusion and immediately triggered a breakdown of coordination between the various divisions and corps. Then, the creeping artillery barrage that preceded the advance of the Seventy-Ninth's infantry outdistanced the struggling foot soldiers as they endeavored to keep pace. The 157th Brigade soon encountered stout resistance from German machine guns and artillery and could not take Montfaucon, its first day's objective, by nightfall. The Seventy-Ninth had advanced nearly five miles on September 26 but had not accomplished its immediate mission. Joseph Kuhn, its commander, who now wore the rank of a major general, relieved the commander of the 158th Brigade and ordered the 157th to renew its attack on the morning of September 27. By noon, the Butte de Montfaucon was under American control.[13] During the assault on the German bastion, the 316th Infantry was heavily engaged and took severe casualties, but no Adams County soldiers were killed. The only known casualty from the county was an Arendtsville resident, Pvt. William A. Raffensberger of Company A, who received a machine-gun burst in the left thigh and was slightly gassed during the September 27 attack. He survived his wounds and returned to the United States on December 30.[14]

Capt. H. L. Haverstick, an officer in the 304th Engineer Regiment, assigned to the Seventy-Ninth Division, grew up in Adams County and after the battle wrote a letter that appeared in the *Gettysburg Times.* (It was his unit's mission to repair roads and bridges the artillery barrage had destroyed.)

> At 5 a.m. [on the twenty-sixth] we moved out and went over the line with the infantry, following the doughboys up and filling in the holes made by shells, and slowly across no-man's land we kept agoing, bridging such holes that were too large to fill, as many were forty five to fifty feet wide and twenty feet deep. We knew what our artillery was doing the night before. Tit tat tat tita tat tat, the spat of the machine guns kept up all day, and the air was never without high explosives and shrapnel, making life worth nothing any moment. It was Mountfaucon we were after and we got it.

However, the failure of the Americans to take Montfaucon on September 26 gave the Germans time to bring up reinforcements and strengthen their other defensive lines, setting the stage for a protracted campaign of attrition.[15]

About four miles west of Montfaucon, where I Corps was advancing, Gettysburg native Bernard E. Altoff (Company B, 145th Infantry, Thirty-Seventh Division), met the same fate as his cousin when on September 28 he was killed instantly by an exploding shell while directing his platoon's operations to silence a machine-gun nest. By September 29, the First Army had advanced approximately eight miles, but the momentum was grinding to a halt. Although they survived the struggle to take Monfaucon, Privates Charles C. Bucher of Bonneauville and Andrew E. Mickley of Gettysburg were killed on September 30. Both were serving in Company A, 316th Infantry. The next day, Pvt. William B. Hoke of Abbottstown, assigned to Company F, 109th Infantry, Twenty-Eighth Division, was mown down by a German machine gun. On October 4, Littlestown's Allen S. Hartman, the son of a preacher, assigned to Headquarters Company, 316th Infantry, was mortally wounded and died while being carried from the front lines. About the same time, Abbottstown native Jacob Markline, of the same company, was mortally wounded. On September 28, many miles away in the Champagne drive, twenty-five-year-old Joseph Williams of the African American 372d Infantry Regiment was killed by an exploding shell. The first week of the grand offensive had been tough on the parents, wives, and sweethearts of Adams County's soldiers.

On October, 1 Pershing replaced the divisions in V Corps with the more seasoned Third and Thirty-Second divisions, while in I Corps the First Division took over for the Thirty-Fifth and the Eighty-Second replaced the Twenty-Eighth.[16] Grover Maus of the 4th Regiment, Third Division recalled, "Now followed a period of comparative quiet for several days. Do not misunderstand the term quiet. It means simply that no attempt was made to advance on an extensive scale." Artillerymen moved their guns forward while teamsters hauled ammunition and other supplies from the rear areas to the front lines. Staff officers updated their plans and ordered the replacement of units. Medical personnel took the wounded to field hospitals. "All these things were done under the fire of enemy artillery," Maus wrote. "The infantry on the lines dug in and protected themselves as well as they could, but the casualties were heavy every day." Some of the Third Division's doughboys occupied abandoned German dugouts, but a direct hit by an enemy shell could be devastating. According to Maus, "No one, except one who has seen it, can realize the carnage caused by a shell exploding in a dugout filled with men. The very thought of it is like a nightmare to those who have witnessed such slaughter. Men in the rescuing parties have been known to have gone insane by the horror of it." He concluded, "It is not well to dwell on the awful side of war."[17] His fellow warriors would have agreed.

Quartermaster 2d Class Albert Menchey of Gettysburg, still serving with the huge Naval Railway Battery, helped provide fire support during the offensive. Though his battery was positioned near Verdun, far behind the front lines, he nevertheless bore witness to the war's destruction and desolation. In a letter to his mother, printed in the *Times* on October 17, the young sailor described the devastation around him:

> The short time we have been at the front has been without any casualties or any serious trouble from the enemy. Several times we sent him a few souvenirs to let him know that we were here and make him realize that he had a new and powerful weapon to face. . . . The country around us is nothing but a place of ruined villages and cities and houses. For miles there is nothing more than heaps of ruins. The fields are covered with shell holes, barbed wire entanglements, and trenches. The hills are covered by dugouts and trenches. German helmets, guns, and shells are plentiful.

Even before the Third Division took over for the Seventy-Ninth, Sgt. Percy Eichelberger of the former division's 4th Infantry Regiment was wounded by shrapnel. He was removed to a hospital in the rear to recover and while convalescing wrote a letter to the folks back home. The *Gettysburg Times* printed it on October 11. His description of the carnage was similar to Quartermaster Menchey's account: "One cannot imagine what it is like at the real front. To say it plain, it's regular hell. . . . A certain stream was so filled with dead Huns that one could trot across and the odor was something awful. Some of the villages are leveled to the ground, trees are mowed off and holes large enough to bury big teams [of horses] are everywhere. Equipment lies scattered around everywhere, mostly Boche. It is not uncommon to run across the unburied dead and graves are very dominant." Eichelberger closed by informing the *Times*'s subscribers that just because he had been wounded did not mean that he was out of the war, "for I have fond hopes of getting into it again."

Meanwhile, in the sector of advance to the west, where I Corps was operating, the Seventy-Seventh Division was pushed forward into the thick Argonne Forest to silence German artillery that was stymying the advance of V Corps. The 1st Battalion, 308th Infantry led the division's attack. In command was Maj. Charles W. Whittlesey, who in civilian life worked as an attorney in New York City. Whittlesey and his men, under orders not to relinquish any ground, held on to their advanced position while being reinforced by three companies from 2nd Battalion, 308th Infantry Regiment and a company from the 307th, bringing his total force to 670 men—seven understrength rifle companies and two depleted machine-gun companies. Soon, Whittlesey's hodgepodge command was cut off from the rest of the division, and it underwent a trying ordeal that lasted until the evening of October 7, when the rest of the Seventy-Seventh finally broke through and relieved what came to be called the Lost Battalion. Of the original 670 doughboys whom Whittlesey led into the Argonne, only 191 walked out.[18] The battalion's rescue was accurately reported—minus the unit's numerical designation—in the *Gettysburg Times* on October 9.

One of the most celebrated acts of heroism in the annals of American military history occurred during the attempt to relieve the Lost Battalion. On October 8, Cpl. Alvin C. York, a pacifist from rural Tennessee (who was forced to fight), assigned to Company G, 328th Infantry, Eighty-Second Division, was credited with silencing several machine-gun nests, killing 25 German soldiers, and capturing 132 more. For this exploit, he was awarded the Distinguished Service Cross and the Medal of Honor. However, York's heroics did not save everyone in his patrol.[19] One American soldier who had been killed during the fight was a young man from Hanover, just over the Adams County border. Private Ralph G. Weiler (also of Company G) was slain as he, York, and fifteen other doughboys attempted to silence the machine guns that had pinned down the rest of his company.[20] Weiler is buried in the Meuse-Argonne American Cemetery.

The second phase of the offensive actually had begun several days before Alvin York's feat, commencing at 5:30 A.M. on October 4, but it quickly bogged down because of intensive artillery fire coming from the heights above the east bank of the Meuse River. On October 5, with four French and one American division, Pershing ordered an attack against those heights. Back on the west bank of the Meuse over in I Corps, the First Division had pressed forward and nearly outflanked the German units in the Argonne Forest. On the morning of October 7, Liggett committed the Eighty-Second Division in a risky maneuver that required it to cross the Aire River, but the "All American" division pulled it off. The Germans began their withdrawal from the Argonne, and the Lost Battalion was saved.[21] During this phase of the offensive, Charles J. Kral of York Springs, a veteran soldier who had enlisted in 1916, fighting with the 58th Infantry, Fourth Division, was killed by machine-gun fire on October 6. Three days later, Paul Cole, of Buchanan Valley in western Adams County, assigned to the 127th Infantry, Thirty-Second Division, was mortally wounded by artillery fire.[22] Likewise, nineteen-year-old Cpl. Byron W. Alwine was wounded that day, though not mortally; he was a native of Irishtown who had enlisted in the 4th Infantry when it was posted in Gettysburg—two months before his eighteenth birthday.[23]

The next major objective would be to carry the main German line of resistance, the Kriemhilde Stellung, or what the Americans simply called the Hindenburg Line. Before launching the assault, Pershing created the U.S. Second Army, promoting Robert Bullard from III Corps to take its command. At the same time, Pershing relinquished command of First Army and turned it over to Hunter Liggett. Replacing Bullard as III Corps commander was Maj. Gen.

John Hines, formerly Fourth Division commander. Liggett turned I Corps command over to Maj. Gen. Joseph Dickman, who had commanded IV Corps during the Saint-Mihiel offensive (and was not engaged in the current offensive). George Cameron, commanding V Corps, was relieved at his own request and replaced by the First Division's commander, the acerbic Maj. Gen. Charles P. Summerall. Pershing now could focus all of his energy on commanding the entire AEF and allow the new First and Second Army commanders to work out the details of the upcoming attack, an assault on the Romagne Heights along the Hindenburg Line, about five miles north of Montfaucon.[24]

Summerall's V Corps, now comprising the Forty-Second, Thirty-Second, and Fifth Divisions, would spearhead this phase of the campaign. In the upcoming action, a feat just as amazing as Alvin York's—if not more so—was about to unfold near the village of Cunel. First Lt. Samuel Woodfill had recently taken command of Company M, 60th Infantry, Fifth Division. Woodfill was a Regular Army noncommissioned officer who had been commissioned at Gettysburg in the summer of 1917. On October 12, his company came under intense machine-gun fire from three different directions. Woodfill's Medal of Honor citation explains his subsequent extraordinary actions:

> While he was leading his company against the enemy, his line came under heavy machinegun fire, which threatened to hold up the advance. . . . When he got within 10 yards of the gun it ceased firing, and 4 of the enemy appeared, 3 of whom were shot by 1st Lt. Woodfill. The fourth, an officer, rushed at 1st Lt. Woodfill, who attempted to club the officer with his rifle. After a hand-to-hand struggle, 1st Lt. Woodfill killed the officer with his pistol. . . . Calling on his men to follow, 1st Lt. Woodfill rushed ahead of his line in the face of heavy fire from the nest, and when several of the enemy appeared above the nest he shot them, capturing 3 other members of the crew and silencing the gun. A few minutes later this officer for the third time demonstrated conspicuous daring by charging another machinegun position, killing 5 men in one machinegun pit with his rifle. He then drew his revolver and started to jump into the pit, when 2 other gunners only a few yards away turned their gun on him. Failing to kill them with his revolver, he grabbed a pick lying nearby and killed both of them.[25]

Woodfill thus singlehandedly killed at least thirteen of the enemy and captured three more.

Young Ernest Wrentmore (aka Henry Monroe) was in the same vicinity. Many years later, he recalled Woodfill's actions: "Over on our right, I saw . . . a few of our Gettysburg crowd slowly fighting their way into Cunel. . . . We could

Captain Samuel Woodfill wearing his Medal of Honor (Library of Congress)

also see that Company 'M' was giving the enemy hell, and having much success. There was vicious fighting in progress, and, led by Lieutenant Sam Woodfill, the boys of 'M' Company could not be stopped. Woodfill was awarded the Medal of Honor for his conspicuous bravery and leadership. He went wild!"[26] After the war, the *Gettysburg Times* ran a story about Woodfill's wartime adventures: "Along with the troops that came to Gettysburg from the Mexican border, was Lieutenant Woodfill, an unassuming, courteous soldier of the old school. He made many friends here and the description of his valor on the battlefields of France will be of especial interest here." The multi-decked headline ran, "GREATEST HERO OF WAR. General Pershing Commends Modest Soldier Who Flirted With Death in Facing Heavy German Fire." Indeed, soon after the war's conclusion, Pershing selected Sam Woodfill, not Alvin York, as the most outstanding soldier of the AEF.[27]

Finally, on October 14, the Romagne Heights were carried. They had been the objective of, and were expected to fall on, September 26, the first day of the campaign. Instead, its conquest took Pershing's men nineteen days. Two days later, on October 16, twenty-three-year-old Capt. Francis E. Dougherty, USMA 1917, was mortally wounded by an exploding shell and died in less than an hour. He was assigned to the 4th Infantry directly out of West Point and had spent the summer of 1917 in Gettysburg. He initially commanded a rifle company but then was ordered to organize and command the regiment's Headquarters Company. On October 15, he received temporary command of a battalion, which he led for less than a day before his fatal wounding. The shell that took his life also killed forty-six other soldiers.[28] The incident was a tragic example of the meat grinder the campaign had become.

The intense, sustained combat had taken its toll on the AEF. In addition, the Spanish influenza was killing or incapacitating men already suffering from exposure, fatigue, stress, and lungs weakened by the inhalation of poison gas. "Continuous fighting was maintained along our entire battle front, with especial success on the extreme left, where the capture of the greater part of the Argonne forest was completed," Pershing wrote in his official report. "The enemy contested every foot of ground on our front in order to make more rapid retirements farther west and withdraw his forces from northern France before the interruption of his railroad communications through Sedan." These losses created a personnel shortage that quickly became a crisis. "We were confronted at this time by an insufficiency of replacements to build up exhausted divisions," Pershing recalled. "Early in October combat units required some 90,000 replacements, and not more than 45,000 would be available before November 1 to fill the existing and prospective vacancies." To make matters worse, he was forced to send two of his divisions, the Thirty-Seventh and Ninety-First, to Flanders to assist the French Sixth Army.[29] Consider historian Edward Lengel's assessment of the effects of the fighting on the Third Division alone: "The 3rd Division's battalions had shrunk to the size of companies, and, and its companies to the size of platoons. Yet still it received orders to attack. The 4th and 7th regiments, their battalions combined into provisional formations, jumped off in the early morning [of October 18]. Neither of them got anywhere."[30] Nonetheless, the AEF continued to grind away at the German defenses.

In the Fifth Division, on October 18 thirteen-year-old Ernest Wrentmore's regiment, the 60th, along with its sister organization, the 61st Infantry, was ordered to attack again. Decades later, Wrentmore vividly recalled the moment of the assault. "Suddenly it was 8:30: zero hour had arrived! . . . The long, thin line of doughboys was once more on the attack." But the Germans did not melt away as they had done during the Saint-Mihiel fight. They pounded the two American regiments with artillery, machine guns, and rifle fire. "Men fell on all sides," Wrentmore recollected, "some never to rise again. My old Gettysburg buddies were catching hell. God! It made me sick." They pushed on despite heavy enemy fire:

> Many of our boys were down. Heavy shelling had made the soggy, muddy fields one huge sea of death, and it was most difficult for our medics and stretcher bearers, who were going like mad, caring alike for friend and foe. Even though the morning had broken bright and sunny, the air was now permeated with the sickening, sweet odor of the wounded and the dead, mingled with the powder fumes of bursting shells and the firing of thousands of small arms. Added to this, the Boche were firing poison gas, which made the pollution of the air even more complete. Gas masks went on and off, intermittently.

Wrentmore survived this attack and showed his mettle time and again. As a runner (messenger) for his company commander, he soon found himself in hand-to-hand combat, killing several Germans with his .45 caliber pistols as he made his way between command posts. Wrentmore's luck, however, was about to run out.[31]

On another mission to deliver a message, he was struck by a machine-gun burst. It knocked him down, but he was unscathed. His gas mask, however, was in shreds. The young soldier made it back to his own command and there got some needed rest, but the next day the Germans fired gas shells near his position, and his mask ruined, the deadly fumes overcame him. Wrentmore's comrades found him unconscious, and while carrying him to an aid station, they came under artillery fire—the thirteen-year-old imposter was wounded in both legs, but somehow the stretcher-bearers got him to safety. He woke up at the aid station. "How long I had been there, I do not know. It was a certainty I had come through a damn rough deal, and it was obvious that I had a long siege facing me," Wrentmore remembered. "I was terribly weak, and I continued to cough my insides out, terrific pain accompanying each effort. My lungs and throat were on fire, and my legs felt heavy as lead." From there, he was driven in an ambulance to a general hospital. "Henry Monroe" would survive, but the war was over for him.[32] Many of his "Gettysburg buddies" in the 60th Infantry would not be so fortunate.

Between the first and last day of October, U.S. losses totaled more than seventy-five thousand.[33] Among them were nineteen Adams County men, including fourteen who were killed in action or died of wounds and five who succumbed to the flu.[34] But the German army was being pushed back along the entire Western Front, and it too was losing men from combat and illness. The

Central Powers' alliance was falling apart. Bulgaria already had left the war. On October 3 Germany sent a note to President Wilson requesting an armistice; the next day Austria-Hungary likewise asked the president to negotiate a peace agreement. Both nations' leaders were hoping Wilson could broker an armistice with the Allies based on his Fourteen Points. Historian Richard Hofstadter summarizes the president's January 8, 1918 speech, which laid out his program for peace: "Wilson's liberal and generous statement of war aims in his speech to Congress made him the moral leader of the western world. His promise of a decent peace also undermined the will of the Germans to continue the bloody struggle, and when they sued for peace they did so on the basis of the Fourteen Points."[35] Before the end of the month, Germany ended its unrestricted submarine warfare campaign (October 21) as a show of good faith; six days later, Erich Ludendorff, the second-highest officer in the German army (and its operational planner) resigned; and on October 30 the Ottoman Empire signed a separate armistice. The handwriting was on the wall when Austria-Hungary signed an armistice on November 3. Germany was now alone. Yet the slaughter on the Western Front continued, especially in the Meuse-Argonne region.

Sergeant Henry Kolda was one of the few Tank Corps men who had trained at Camp Colt earlier in the year and had actually made it to the front. He was a Regular Army soldier who had first enlisted in 1909. During his short stay in Gettysburg, he met and married Maude Reed of Fairfield. Henry was assigned to the 316th Repair and Salvage Company, which had the mission of recovering battle-damaged or mechanically broken tanks, repairing them, and sending them back into action. In early November, he wrote a long, descriptive letter to his "girlie" to let her know what he had been doing and also to reassure her that he was safe. Occupying an old German dugout in a destroyed French town, he described his surroundings:

> I am almost 10 miles behind the lines in a city that the Germans held for 4 years. Every house in the town is built of stone but it looks as though an earth quake hit the place. Every building is down, nothing but a few walls left standing and there is not one house that has 4 walls up. But Oh Maude you should see what's under the town, all dugouts of stone and concrete with electric lights and stoves and beds, it sure is fine. I have one about 20 feet underground that I share with four other men and we sure are cozy. The German planes can drop all the bombs they want for all I care, they could never hit us. We have a real swell place, we even have two kinds of water (Dirty and Clean) Ha" Ha". We heat water with tin cans on the stove. Say Maude you say you are going to buy a trench hat, you ought

> to see mine, it's heavy tin [and] it feels like a brick on your head and if you was here I'd give you one. They are laying all over the field here. . . . There are a lot of German graves and also American graves here. We sleep among them, but you know a dead German is damn good company compared to a live one. Usually I prefer dead ones even if I have to make them good myself. . . . This thing will be over soon and we are going to eat Thanksgiving dinner in Berlin and right after dinner we are going to bury the Kaiser and the rest of his gang.

His lengthy message went on for several more pages, mostly questions about home and continued reassurances that everything would work out. In closing, he jokingly told his bride to "tell those wise guys up there [in Gettysburg] that if they don't cut out flirting with you that they will take part in a funeral when I get back." Kolda did not dare to tell her until December 1918—while he was hospitalized and after the war had ended—that he had been suffering from trench foot and the effects of gas.[36]

Hunter Ligget's First Army would deliver the death blow west of the Meuse. Liggett's command numbered more than a million men, about 90 percent of them American soldiers. The attack plan called for a frontal assault by the three corps that had opened the offensive in the last week of September. The doughboys jumped off on November 1. By November 4, they had taken all of their assigned objectives. The next day, Bonneauville resident Sylvester G. Miller, Company A, 316th Infantry, whose Seventy-Ninth Division had been recommitted to the fight on the east bank of the Meuse, was killed in action. Far to the north in Flanders, where Pershing had transferred the Ninety-First and Thirty-Seventh divisions, Charles A. Shuyler of Ortanna, a hamlet in the apple orchards of western Adams County, was mortally wounded. He was assigned to the Company M, 145th Infantry, Thirty-Seventh Division. After lingering for four days, he succumbed on November 4. He had been the only man from his little village to make it to France.[37]

Within a week, the armistice between Imperial Germany and the Allies would be signed in a railcar in the Compiègne Forest. Knowing this—and in spite of it—Pershing relentlessly pressed the attack, and men on both sides were killed needlessly. Then, at 11:00 A.M., on November 11, 1918, the Great War ended. Two days earlier, Ernest Wrentmore had turned fourteen years of age. Paul F. Cole of Buchanan Valley, who had been wounded more than a month earlier, died on Armistice Day. Lt. Ira Lady of Biglerville, wounded early in November, would linger for several days after the armistice went into effect before succumbing to his wounds on November 22.[38] (Before his death, he was attended by an old friend from Adams County, York Springs resident Jim Myers, a medic assigned to the hospital where Lady was a patient.[39]) Such was the terrible price of victory. But the dying was not yet done. Men continued to pass from their wounds long after November 11, 1918, and any more would perish from an invisible executioner, the Spanish influenza, striking those in and out of uniform without prejudice of age, gender, or race. Back home in Adams County, the flu had been taking a terrible toll since the last week of September, when a detachment of infected doughboys arrived at Camp Colt. Major Eisenhower had wanted to command soldiers in battle on the Western Front, but now he would be fighting another kind of battle at Camp Colt, one that proved deadlier than George Patton's foe in the Argonne.

CHAPTER 7

"The Whole Camp Had to Be Considered as Exposed"

The Ordeal of the Spanish Influenza

"An estimated one third of the world's population (or approximately 500 million persons) were infected and had clinically apparent illnesses during the 1918–1919 influenza pandemic. The disease was exceptionally severe. Case fatality rates were greater than 2.5%, compared to less than 0.1% in other influenza pandemics. Total deaths were estimated at approximately 50 million and were arguably as high as 100 million."[1] So goes a modern U.S. government (2015) explanation of the consequences of the monstrous Spanish influenza pandemic, which took more lives than were lost in the World War. Gettysburg and Adams County likewise suffered from its effects. The truth is, had the U.S. Army not located a training camp in Gettysburg in 1918, probably few people in Adams County would have died from the influenza. But in about seven months, Adams County alone, not including Camp Colt, would suffer at least 133 deaths from the flu. In contrast, the combined Union and Confederate armies in July 1863 would cause one immediate civilian death, that of Virginia Wade.

Ten days before the Meuse-Argonne offensive was scheduled to begin and while all eyes were on France, Colt received a detachment of 111 soldiers from Camp Devens, Massachusetts, an area already besieged by the influenza. Some of the Devens transfers were suffering headaches, but Camp Colt's doctors believed the symptoms were caused by the typhoid fever inoculations the doughboys had received prior to departing their Massachusetts post. "The next morning, alarming reports started to reach me," Eisenhower recalled. "Some of the new men, I was told, were registering high fevers and were obviously very ill. The camp surgeon immediately took countermeasures. Before noon, 'Spanish flu' was recognized. Because the men had not been confined to quarters and some of them were obviously carriers, the whole camp had to be considered as exposed." It was. And soon it would spread to Gettysburg and the outlying communities.

Historians and scientists have yet to determine exactly where the Spanish flu originated, but a consensus is emerging that it probably first appeared in January 1918 in Haskell County, Kansas, in the southwest corner of the state, eventually making its way eastward across the state, where it was contracted by soldiers stationed at Camp Funston, and from there it was transported with infected doughboys to their ports of embarkation on the East Coast and finally to the Western Front. Once in France, it spread through the rear areas and front lines of the Allies, across no-man's-land to the Central Powers' armies and eventually back to the combatants' native countries. Since the warring nations censored news reports about the flu's staggering effects on their armies and civilian populations, news of the pandemic went public only when it spread to Spain, a neutral nation. From then on, it was known as the Spanish influenza.[2] The pandemic erupted in three waves. The first began when a mild flu flared up in late spring / early summer of 1918, the second was the plague of severe influenza in the autumn, and the last occurred in the spring of 1919.[3]

The flu's symptoms usually included a temperature of from 102 to 104 degrees (sometimes climbing to 106) as well as a sore throat, headache, physical exhaustion, aching limbs, a severe cough, and even intense nosebleeds and dark skin blotches. Sometimes vomiting and loose bowels occurred. In such a weakened state, patients normally developed pneumococcal pneumonia and immense pulmonary hemorrhages, with death soon following. Whereas previous influenza strains typically struck children and the elderly, the Spanish influenza primarily affected people in the prime of their life, their twenties and thirties.[4] And it was especially deadly to the soldiers of both sides, already weakened by stress, fatigue, and exposure. A historian of American military medicine recently has noted:

> The influenza virus exploited conditions in military camps, battlefields and trenches to transform from a common winter ailment dangerous only to the infirm, into a lethal disease that could sicken at least a quarter of all people it came in contact with and could kill even the strongest. . . . The influenza epidemic was especially disastrous in the United States because it overlapped entirely with the American war experience. . . . Both were concentrated in September, October and November 1918. Once it arrived in its deadliest form in early September, the flu dramatically affected American war activities.[5]

The ordeal of Camp Colt during the pandemic was a microcosm of that unfortunate and deadly American military experience in the autumn of 1918. Making matters even worse, Colt's hospital was not prepared for such a calamity. A medical inspector's report, written to determine whether the camp was suitable for wintertime use—the inspector concluded it was not—gave an indication of the state of the camp hospital in late August 1918, one month before the outbreak: "Half of its bed capacity is in tents. There is no hot water for bathing. Shower baths and bucket latrines are from 250 to 500 feet from the wards."[6] The distance from the wards to the latrines alone would make it difficult, if not impossible, for weakened men with diarrhea to relieve themselves in a sanitary fashion. (Soldiers caught relieving themselves anywhere but in the latrines—unless they were bedridden—were punished. For example, on October 14, 1918, a second lieutenant in the 301st Depot Company disciplined three men who were "denied all privileges" and forced to "perform such extra duties as may be designated until further notice" when they were "caught urinating on the trees in back of the barracks."[7])

The influenza epidemic hit Camp Devens, Massachusetts, on September 8 and medical officers first reported it on September 12.[8] The contingent of troops from Devens arrived at Camp Colt four days later. The first person in Adams County to die from complications of the flu was one of the soldiers who had been transferred from Devens. On September 22, Pvt. Donat W. Boyceclaire of Rhode Island succumbed. The next day, a front-page story of the *Gettysburg Times* reported, "He was placed in the hospital immediately after his arrival from Camp Devens, last Monday, and died at 7 o'clock Sunday evening. He was 21 years old." Two other soldiers died the same night. Seventy more were hospitalized. The next day, two more men died, and the number of patients in the hospital doubled overnight. On Wednesday, September 24, the *Times* reported a fleeting glimmer of hope: "Influenza at Camp Colt is abating, according to reports from the camp hospital this morning." More importantly, the reporter noted, "So far, no cases have been reported among the town people." It was wishful thinking, and the death toll mounted. Three more soldiers died between September 24 and 25, and another three passed in the next twenty-four hours. The *Times* headline on September 27 blared, "INLFUENZA RAGES AT CAMP COLT." And so it did for the next several weeks.[9]

The number of deaths from the flu continued to rise. By September 30, twenty-six soldiers had perished. Nine more died within the next twenty-four hours, with the *Times* declaring on October 1, "WORST DAY FOR DEATHS AT CAMP." The headline proved wrong: on October 2, twelve soldiers died from the flu. Eisenhower and his army physicians were taking all possible precautions to thwart the spread of the influenza. To prevent men without official passes from leaving town, military police were stationed at all of the major roads leading out of Gettysburg. Troops who displayed any signs of sickness were quarantined, and soldiers were not permitted to congregate, lest they spread the influenza. Restaurant owners barred the doughboys from entering their establishments. In a futile attempt to cleanse the thoroughfares and gutters of the influenza, the Gettysburg Fire Department even hosed down the streets. St. Francis Xavier Church converted Xavier Hall, its parochial school, into a military hospital. Other churches followed suit. Father W. F. Boyle called on townsfolk to contribute pillows, sheets, and blankets.[10] "The people of the town realizing the needs of the situation responded in a way to delight those in charge of the hospital, making them feel that anything that Gettysburg could do would be done," reported the weekly *Compiler* on October 5. A teacher at a one-room school house in Littlestown asked her students to solicit donations from the townsfolk, and they quickly gathered $100, which bought hot-water bottles and other health supplies. Likewise, the Red Cross sent nurses to Gettysburg to assist at the camp. The Soldiers' Club House on Middle Street was converted to nurse's quarters for up to a dozen of the angels of mercy. But the death toll continued to climb. "The little town had no place to take care of the dead," Eisenhower recalled. "There were no coffins. We had no place to put the bodies except in a storage tent until they gradually could be taken care of more suitably."[11]

Nevertheless, Eisenhower and his subordinate commanders still continued the camp's training mission. On October 2, Pvt. G. M. Gilliland wrote to his wife back in California and filled her in on the camp's news. "We had a strenuous day. We hiked this afternoon with packs and rifles. We stand retreat at 5:00 and have 'mess' at 5:30." Later in his letter he confided, "You must not worry about me. I am in perfect health and don't expect to be sick. There is Spanish Influenza in camp but it is being checked and will be O.K soon." Then, he warned her, "You must not think of coming here. You could not stand the cold. I know you would catch pneumonia. There have been some deaths from it here. You are much better off and far safer right where you are."[12] Gilliland could not have been more prescient, because the worst was yet to come.

On October 3, the *Times*' main headline declared, "TWENTY ONE DIE AT CAMP COLT IN SINGLE DAY." In a related page 1 story, the newspaper conveyed the minutes of a citizens' meeting convened to discuss plans for handling an outbreak of the flu beyond camp boundaries. Although the local board of health denied that the flu had spread to the borough, some citizens attending the assembly disagreed: "Various men present said that while no official reports of influenza had been made, there were doubtless large numbers of cases in the town and a number of sufferers were named."[13] The very next day the first flu-related civilian fatality in Gettysburg passed away: twenty-two-year-old Mrs. Howard S. Bunting, a native Californian and wife of a Tank Corps soldier who only had arrived in town on September 30. She already was ill upon her arrival. Hers was just the first of many more flu-related civilian deaths.[14]

At a town meeting on October 11, a physician from the Pennsylvania Department of Health heard reports from two local doctors who said they were treating more than 150 flu cases in Gettysburg alone. Further, according to a front-page article in the October 12 *Gettysburg Times,* the area south of town between Two Taverns on the Baltimore Pike and Barlow on the Taneytown Road was "under the full force of the scourge." The reporter noted that there were some very severe cases in the borough, and it was not known how many of the lesser cases would turn critical. The town's physicians also were overworked, toiling with their patients until the dark hours of early morning. "Many in this section are critically ill. Several families were mentioned where four or five were sick in bed with the only care given by people from the outside," according to the reporter. "Well persons have become fearful and it is practically impossible to have the sick properly cared for."

There were several cases in Adams County when the flu took multiple family members, some even from the same households. Grief overcame a Littlestown family early in October. "The ravages of the deadly influenza pneumonia have fallen heavily on the family of Mr. and Mrs. William P. Robinson. . . . This morning, Hoy Robinson, a son, died after an illness of some days," noted the *Times* on October 5. "On Tuesday [Oct. 1] another son, Homer William Robinson, in the Navy, died at Puget Sound, Washington." Hoy was twenty-two and Homer was just shy of his twenty-fifth birthday.[15] A few days later, sorrow struck the hamlet of Barlow, about five miles south of Gettysburg along the Taneytown Road, the same thoroughfare that George Meade and his staff had traveled to get to the battlefield during the night of July 1–2, 1863. Grace Maring, thirty-six, died on October 10; three days later her husband Oliver, thirty-eight, likewise succumbed. Their passing orphaned two adolescent sons, John and Harry Maring.[16] In mid-October, the grim reaper visited the Gross family of Tyrone Township, near Heidlersberg, a village northeast of Gettysburg, when two brothers, Amos and Jacob, were lost three days apart, October 13 and 16, followed by their mother on October 17.[17] William, thirty-four, and Mary Noel, thirty-three, of Centennial, another hamlet in eastern Adams County, died six days apart, William on October 19 and his wife on the twenty-fifth. Mary's sister, the widow Louisa Smith, aged thirty-two, passed on October 23. The Noels

Above: Mr. and Mrs. Oliver Maring, of Barlow, Cumberland Township, who died three days apart (Courtesy of Gary Maring); *right:* Harry and John Maring, orphaned by the Spanish influenza. They survived and lived to old age. (Courtesy of Gary Maring)

left two sons and two daughters behind.[18] Harry Strevig of Littlestown suffered the loss of his son and two brothers from the flu.[19] Finally, Peter J. Smith of Centennial lost two family members within a week, his mother on October 14 and his sixteen-year-old daughter on October 19.[20]

During the month of October, at least seventy-one civilians who had resided within the borders of Adams County died from complications of the flu. Many more residents living elsewhere or who were traveling also died from the scourge. In one sad case, thirty-year-old Andrew Sheely of Cashtown died in Niagara Falls while on his honeymoon.[21] Joseph Busby, twenty-three, of McSherrystown, had taken a job in Chester, Pennsylvania, five months earlier. He caught the flu and died of pneumonia on September 30.[22] Miss Christina Swomley, a trained nurse living in New Oxford, traveled to Dillsburg in northern York County to care for her sister, bedridden with the flu. Swomley, aged nineteen, caught the flu and died in her sister's home on November 1. Ironically, her sister survived. They had three brothers in the armed forces, with two serving in

France.[23] Several new army brides from Adams County, who had followed their husbands to their new duty stations, contracted the disease and died in their transient homes. Ruth E. Leech Stanley, originally from Gettysburg, was the first to pass away. She had met her husband, a sergeant in the 59th Infantry, when he was stationed at the Gettysburg camp in 1917. She accompanied him to Yaphank, New York, where she caught the flu and died on September 24. She had just turned twenty and had given birth to a baby only a few days before her demise.[24] Another new army wife, Margaret Holder (née Bushman) of Gettysburg, contracted the flu and died of pneumonia while living at Camp Cody, where her husband, 1st Sgt. Charles R. Holder, was then stationed. He had been a soldier in the 60th Infantry and posted at Gettysburg in 1917, and they were married in January 1918.[25] County residents serving in the armed forces likewise perished from the flu, both stateside and overseas. In fact, almost as many servicemen from Adams County died (eighteen) from the Spanish influenza as were killed by enemy ordnance (twenty-six).[26]

Fifty-eight years after the crisis, an elderly veteran wrote a letter to the Gettysburg College president to convey his own recollections of Camp Colt. Walter L. Hand had been a medic in the 304th Medical Detachment back in 1918. After recounting his memories of Eisenhower and the camp in general, he recalled the influenza's deadly impact:

> In late September, we medics suddenly found our daily chores at our infirmary tents turn into a grim struggle to do what we could to save the lives of our tank corps men. While our buddies overseas were driving relentlessly to victory in the decisive 47-day Meuse-Argonne battle, a sudden onslaught of the deadly pandemic of influenza struck our camp with devastating fury. 175 died of it before it subsided in early October. (The figures are Ike's.) Quoting from my letters, "Most of the fatal cases in army posts have come as a result of pneumonia contacted under care for influenza. . . . We medics are all working hard, but [fellow medical corpsmen] Thumm and Sergeant Bradford are both on the verge of collapse. . . . Spraying throats is still in order. (We used chlorozone.) . . . Every man who has a temperature above 99.5° F is isolated in our "bull-pen" down at Co. C or in one of two special tents in Co. A. If he gets too badly off we send him to the camp hospital. . . . No crowds are allowed in the tents and barracks (this stopped the crap games). . . . We are allowed to fill up in only one side of each bench in the mess hall."[27]

Regarding the application of chlorozone, Eisenhower believed this remedy spared his family's life: "Even my wife and my youngster could contract the terrible disease," he remembered. "A doctor from Oklahoma, a Lieutenant Colonel

[Thomas H.] Scott out of the National Guard, had ideas of his own. In addition to isolation he used a number of strong sprays on patients." One, apparently, was chlorozone. "He told me he would like to experiment with my family and my headquarters staff which, including enlisted men, must have numbered forty or more." Ike approved, and each morning Scott "used two sprays on the throat and nostrils of each of us." The first, [chlorozone], "was intensely pungent and strong" and gave Ike the sensation of "the top of my . . . head going off." The second was "a sort of soothing syrup to follow the first." Eisenhower could not know for certain if the sprays actually weakened the effects of the flu, but he could not argue with the results: "Not a single person in my headquarters command or my family contracted the flu." In conclusion, he wrote, "Lieutenant Colonel Scott is another of those men to whom I will always feel obligated."[28] There is no medical evidence, however, that the chlorozone or similar sprays prevented the virus from killing the host or reducing the effects of the symptoms.[29]

The armed forces, the U.S. Public Health Service (USPHS), and local and state governments poured their resources into combatting the flu, but still the death count rose. The pandemic certainly had a detrimental impact on the war effort, both overseas and domestically. Congress passed legislation to make available a million dollars to the USPHS for public education, statistical-data collection and additional personnel. President Wilson signed the bill on October 1. Congress, however, allocated no additional funding to the War Department because the assumption was that war funding alone could cover the plague's expenses. At army camps across the United States, the worst week for mortality was from October 4 and October 10, when 6,160 recorded deaths occurred.[30] It also proved to be the worst one-week period at Camp Colt, with forty-two deaths from influenza or pneumonia. The flu devastated the AEF about one week later. Between October 11 and October 17, while some of the worst fighting in the Argonne was being waged, 1,451 men succumbed.[31] Oddly, only one Adams County serviceman, Luther H. Scott, an infantryman from Bendersville, died from its complications during that time, on October 14.[32]

Between September 16 and October 5, some 427 men were admitted to the Camp Colt hospital, while an additional 916 soldiers were isolated in battalion infirmaries. During that same period, 83 men died from pneumonia, according to a report by Col. S. J. Morris, Medical Corps, who performed a sanitary inspection of Camp Colt. His testimony provides a detailed examination of the steps undergone to ameliorate the dire situation:

> The measures taken to prevent the spread of this disease . . . have been excellent, but despite the precautions it had . . . [spread] very rapidly. Practically all the men

> in camp sleep in tents. Orders have been issued that not more than five men be allowed in one tent, but this is neglected in a few cases. . . . Men are required to sleep with head and feet alternating, and cubicles were arranged in tents [to isolate sections of the quarters] with shelter halves. Tents are furled each clear day and all bedding and clothing sunned and aired. Inspections of the entire command are made twice daily, at which time the nose and throat of every man is sprayed with a germicide solution and checked off on a company roster. Any man showing symptoms of disease is immediately isolated at one of five infirmaries, scattered over the camp. All serious cases are sent to the camp hospital, which consists of large hospital tents and frame shacks, or is transferred to a large hall [Xavier Hall] in the Town of Gettysburg, which is being used as a hospital. The Y.M.C.A. and Knights of Columbus buildings have been closed and all forms of entertainment and grouping together of soldiers are prohibited. One man from each organization is sent to Post Exchange daily to make purchases for all members thereof. All wooden floors are scrubbed daily with solution of Lysol and kerosene. Special guards are placed on duty at night to enforce ventilation of tents. The camp hospital is clean and well cared for. There is an ample supply of bedding, cubicles are arranged at all wards and patients' beds are placed with head and foot alternating. Masks are used by some attendants but are not in general use. Paper sputum cups are used in all wards; no paper bags or napkins are provided.

Morris went on to describe the hospital at Xavier Hall, noting that the floors were mopped daily with an antiseptic solution and that gauze masks were required to be worn by all visitors. "There is no overcrowding of patients in either hospital," he observed.[33]

Morris also reported that no autopsies had been performed; for that matter, "very little [had been] done in the way of laboratory work" except for forty-five sputum examinations. Records of the tests were poorly kept, he noted, due to "the great stress of work." Nonetheless, Morris praised Eisenhower and his line officers, who had "given every possible assistance to the Surgeon in the conduct of this episode." He also lauded the efforts of Lieutenant Colonel Scott, whom he characterized as a "very efficient medical officer." In conclusion, Morris wrote, "This epidemic has been very well conducted in this camp, the chief criticism being that pneumonia cases were not separated from the influenza cases early enough." He then made a list of ten minor recommendations for improvement for Eisenhower and Scott to follow, as well as suggesting to the Surgeon General of the Army "that eleven (11) additional nurses be sent to this camp for duty."[34]

Luckily for the sick soldiers, volunteer nurses and nurses' aides were streaming into Gettysburg to assist the medical staff, and a number of soldiers who had not shown any symptoms were detached from their battalions to help the medical staff.[35] Two women—one a sister and the other a wife—who came to the camp to care for their loved ones, remained at Colt to help care for the sick even after their own soldier boys died. According to the October 7 *Gettysburg Times*, "Both young women, though burdened with their great grief, applied for enlistment as nurses to help the other sick boys." Even Lavinia Dock, a radical suffragist who also was one of America's most authoritative nurses, came home to Adams County to assist at the camp. But nurses also were needed to care for civilian victims. On October 11, the *Times* ran the headline, "GETTYSBURG MUST ACT IMMEDIATELY. Women Called upon to Volunteer as Nurses in Homes. Need Is Urgent." Any women, whether qualified nurses or not, who were willing to volunteer were instructed to apply to the Red Cross headquarters as soon as possible. One trained nurse who answered the call, Miss Lydia Miller of Chambersburg, spent two weeks attending to patients in the Camp Colt hospital. She contracted the flu herself, returned home, and died on October 20.[36]

Although the emergency situation continued, and in an obvious response to the call for volunteer nurses, Major Eisenhower published a message of thanks in the local newspapers to express his gratitude for their assistance in caring for his soldiers:

> Headquarters Camp Colt,
> Gettysburg, Pa.
> October 11, 1918
> To the citizens of Gettysburg:
> On behalf of the officers and men of Camp Colt, as well as their relatives and friends, I wish to express to you our sincere appreciation of your timely assistance during the recent regrettable epidemic. It is gratifying to note the spirit of cooperation that has prevailed everywhere, and I am sure your kindness and sympathy will ever remain a bright spot in the memories of those who have suffered bereavement.
> D. D. Eisenhower Major, Tank Corps Commanding[37]

Colonel Morris, however, inspected the camp and submitted his report *before* the worst period at the camp, when in the week from October 7 to October 16, ninety-eight men perished from the effects of the Spanish flu. Assuming Eisenhower and Scott implemented Morris's recommendations to the fullest, those changes obviously did not remedy the disastrous situation in the least. The truth is, medical science had not yet evolved to allow physicians to do much about the flu virus. Not until the 1940s would scientists be able to identify viral pathogens, about the same time that antibiotics were being developed that could improve a pneumonia patient's chances for survival. Regardless of Eisenhower's efforts, as well as those of his officers and medical staff, there was not much *anyone* could do except contain the disease. Since pneumonia can be contagious, perhaps an earlier segregation of the pneumonia patients from those who had contracted the flu but had not yet developed pneumonia might have made a difference, but this hypothesis is nearly impossible to prove.

By mid-October, the flu crisis in Adams County was waning, yet it continued to take the lives of soldiers and civilians for the rest of 1918 and even into 1919. Still, by October 24 the situation at Camp Colt seemed to be on the upswing, and four military physicians were transferred from Gettysburg to attend to flu victims in other camps.[38] The October military death toll at Camp Colt was 117, making a total of 149 dead since the epidemic struck.[39] Seven more doughboys died from the flu in November, for a total of 156 fatalities overall. (In his memoirs Eisenhower claimed that 175 of his soldiers had died from the influenza. A report in the *Gettysburg Times* during the second week of January 1919 concluded that 160 soldiers had died. The lowest number, 156, and probably the most accurate, was derived from tabulating the soldiers' obituaries in the *Gettysburg Times* and *Gettysburg Compiler.*[40]) On Saturday, November 9, 1918, the *Times* reported, "Health Officer David M. Crist on Friday made a complete investigation of conditions hereabouts with regards to influenza." According to the article,

> He found that there were still about 200 cases in the county of which fifty were of recent origin. There is little serious sickness among the number of patients. In the town there are about thirty cases left, and here too, there are very few whose condition is at all critical. At Camp Colt about fifty were reported to be suffering from the disease. Two more deaths have occurred at the camp. . . . Four of the last five have occurred among men who have been here less than a week. The situation in camp is reported as so much improved that the flu restriction on the number of men in any store, hotel or restaurant has been lifted and today the various business houses presented the same appearance as in midsummer.

The last soldier passed of influenza on November 17, 1918. The majority of the doughboys had departed Gettysburg before the third wave of the influenza struck in late November and early December. The last civilian victim of the Spanish flu was a three-year-old girl from Butler Township, some five miles north of Gettysburg, who died on April 27, 1919, making a total of 133 civilian deaths from influenza/pneumonia in Adams County. With that final casualty,

Deaths by Age Group in Adams County, September 1918 through January 1919

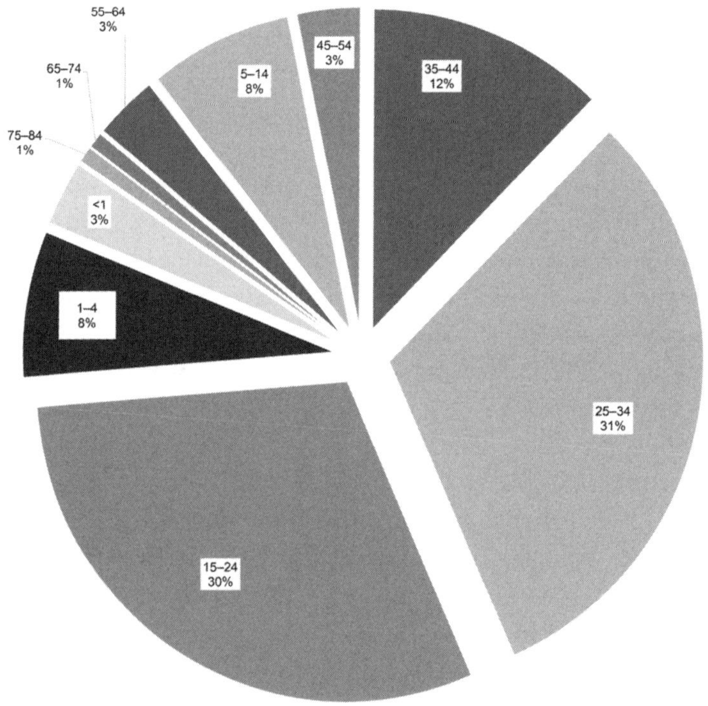

Note: Two adult women, whose ages were not found, are not included in this chart.

the ordeal was over, but it had cost at least 291 military and civilian souls within the county's borders. With a county population of approximately 33,000 in 1918, the civilian mortality rate in Adams County was a little more than 0.4 percent.[41] (As a comparison, approximately 0.6 percent of the U.S. population perished from the Spanish flu.[42]) Due to a lack of records, the civilian morbidity rate for Adams County cannot be determined.

Camp Colt fared about the same as other army posts and units in terms of its morbidity rate. The entire U.S. Army, which included stateside posts and the AEF, suffered a morbidity rate of 26 percent.[43] One historian has speculated, based on the snapshot view of Camp Colt summarized in Colonel Morris's October 6 report, that the morbidity rate at the Gettysburg camp likewise was 26 percent.[44] The influenza mortality rate in the U.S. Army was 1.6 percent, but at Camp Colt it was 3.3 percent, more than twice as high as the entire army.[45] Medical historian Carol Byerly has observed, "Sickness rates in U.S. camps ultimately ranged from

Spanish Flu Fatalities in Adams County, 1918 through 1919

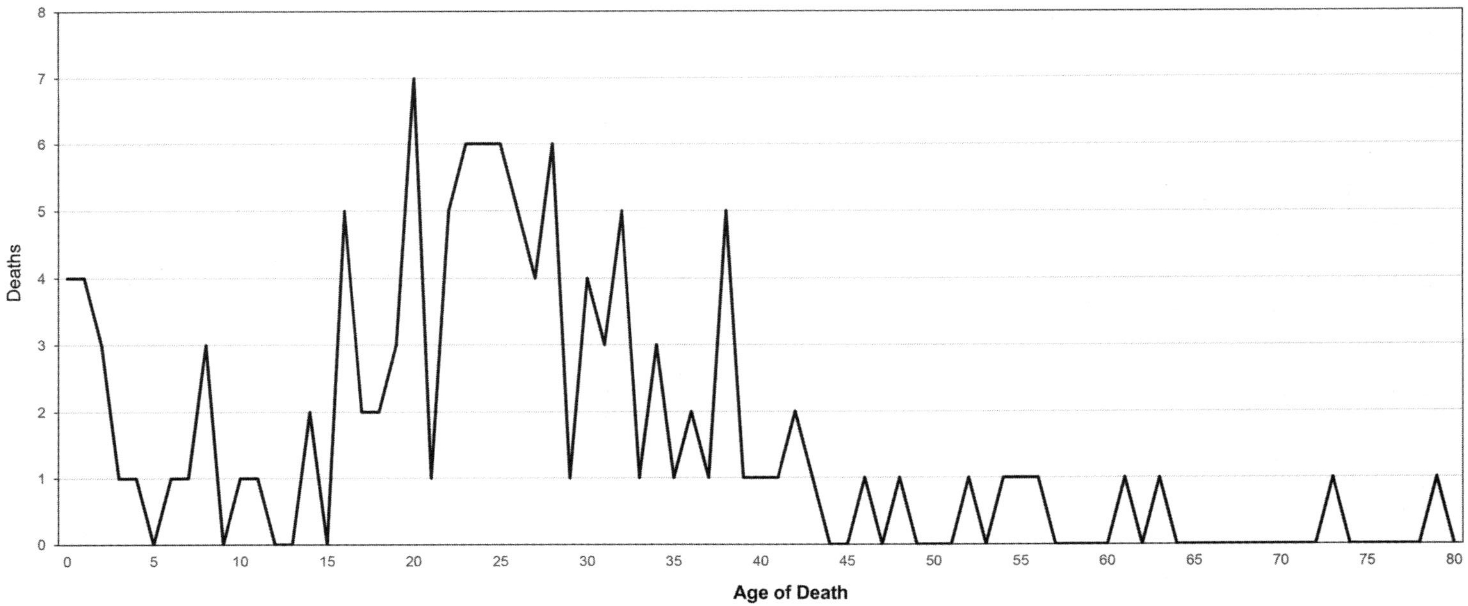

Note: Two adult women, whose ages were not found, are not included in this chart.

10% at Camp Lewis, Washington, to 63% at Camp Beauregard, Louisiana, averaging between 25% and 40%; death rates ranged from less than 1% at many camps to 3.3% at Camp Sherman, Ohio."[46] Camp Crane, another nearby Army cantonment, some 120 miles east of Gettysburg and half as populated as Camp Colt (averaging about 2100 personnel during the flu's second wave), occupied a fifty-acre area (roughly one-eighth the size of Camp Colt) in the middle of Allentown, Pennsylvania (population 73,500). Yet, according to a recent study (2012) by the University of Michigan Center for the History of Medicine,

> As was the case in many other military facilities, the vast majority of Camp Crane's influenza cases developed in a short, approximately eight-week window. Some 348 cases were reported between September 26 and November 4, 1918, with 51 cases of pneumonia and 12 resulting deaths. A few more cases developed throughout November and into December 1918. In the end, 355 cases of influenza broke out at Camp Crane. Of this number, 62 developed into pneumonia, and only 13 of these cases died.

Researchers concluded that the "experience of the camp during the 1918–1920 influenza epidemic was still . . . remarkable . . . given that the camp was located on a very small parcel of land in the middle of busy downtown Allentown, Pennsylvania."[47] Thus, the morbidity rate for Camp Crane was only 17 percent, and its mortality rate was less than 1 percent. So, aside from the aberration of Camp Crane, it seems Camp Colt was average in terms of its morbidity rate, but its mortality rate was among the highest of the stateside Army camps, despite its relatively low military population and rural location.

Numbers, percentages, and ratios are impersonal and do not reflect the widespread physical suffering of the afflicted or the mental anguish of surviving family members and friends. Soldiers who perished at Camp Colt could be buried free of charge in Gettysburg National Cemetery, but most were returned home at the request of their next of kin. Each flag-draped coffin was accompanied by a soldier from Colt, who immediately returned to Gettysburg at the completion of his solemn duty.[48] The uniforms and other clothing items of the deceased soldiers were destroyed on the orders of the camp surgeon, so the bodies were dressed in new uniforms, consisting of a wool coat and breeches, cotton underwear, a pair of stockings, a pair of leggings, and a pair of marching shoes.[49] Personal effects, other than uniform items, were packaged and mailed to the next of kin.

One soldier who died as a result of the flu, Scottish immigrant Pvt. Thomas B. Montguire, owned a Harley Davidson motorcycle that he kept in Gettysburg. He contracted the influenza while attending a training school elsewhere and during his return to Camp Colt fell ill and was admitted to St. Joseph's Hospital in Lancaster, Pennsylvania, where he died on October 13, 1918. His remains were transported back to Camp Colt. After his demise, trouble arose for his company commander, who had to decide to whom he should send the man's personal effects, including the Harley. Montguire had a romantic involvement with Mademoiselle Margaret Schléby, a French citizen staying with an acquaintance in Short Hills, New Jersey. Capt. R. R. Whittingham, commander of the 301st Depot Company, to which Montguire was assigned, responded to a telegram from Mademoiselle Schléby, who claimed that she was Montguire's fiancée and wanted information about his final resting place and the status of his personal property. In his October 16 reply, Whittingham wrote, "His personal effects, including a Harley Davidson Motorcycle, will be shipped at once by express collect to 231 Madison Avenue, New York City. Enclosed are two copies of inventory of these effects which you will please sign as a receipt and return."[50]

At some point during the same day, and obviously unbeknownst to Whittingham, another woman, who also claimed to be engaged to Montguire, signed for the deceased soldier's personal effects, including the motorcycle. This prompted Whittingham to send another letter to Schléby on the same day, in which he was forced to backtrack on his earlier promise:

> Your telegram dated yesterday has been received and, in accordance with your request the remains of Private Thomas Montguire will be buried tomorrow in the Gettysburg National Cemetery with full military honors. The expense of the entire funeral is borne by the government.
>
> In connection with his personal effects, there seems to be some uncertainty as to just who is entitled to them, as a certain Miss [Sarah] Drew, who is present here in Gettysburg, claims that she is his fiancée. She has no particular evidence to substantiate this statement and possibly you have, so in this event will you kindly advise in detail just what your relations with private Montguire consisted of. In the meantime, Miss Drew has cabled his mother in Scotland in an effort to establish her claim.
>
> Army regulations only give me authority to hold these effects [for] thirty days and if at the expiration of this period no satisfactory claimant can be secured they are sold at public sale and the receipts therefrom forwarded to the Adjutant General of the Army, who in this case, would turn them over to his mother, Mrs. Montguire.
>
> Be assured that you have my personal sympathy in your sorrow and possibly it

is some consolation to know that your fiancée died, for Liberty, in the service of his Country.

Awaiting your prompt reply, I am
Very respectfully yours,
R. R. Whittingham
Captain, T.C., U.S.A.
Commanding, 301st Depot Company[51]

But the drama was not over. In a letter in her native French, Mademoiselle Schléby not only anguished over the news of the death of her loved one but also expressed her incredulity that her fiancé was engaged to another woman. She pled her case:

> Being French and not being able to speak English as well as I need to, please Mr. Commandant excuse these few lines. Received this morning your letter of October 16 and was very surprised to learn that a certain Miss Drew is the future bride of Thomas Montguire—an impossible thing and incredible since I have been his fiancée for 20 months and we were to be married before [his] departure for France. I am unable to be present in Gettysburg since the receipt of your letter of October 14 as I have been suffering from the cruel loss of my dear fiancée. Dear Mr. Commandant I have no evidence or signed paper that Thomas Montguire was my fiancée, but several families in New York know of our relationship from his last two leaves that I spent with him there. So Mr. Commandant if you are not able to decide on the personal affairs of Thomas Montguire, I think it is fair to send the letters, pictures, and things belonging to him in my possession to his mother, Mrs. Montguire. Please believe, Mr. Commandant, of my deep sorrow and all my thanks to you.[52]

In the meantime, Sarah Drew had been in contact with Montguire's mother, and the motorcycle was shipped to a Harley Davidson dealer near Drew's New York City address, where it was sold for cash.[53] Captain Whittingham then informed Schléby that the motorcycle and Montguire's personnel effects were "converted into cash and the funds derived therefrom forwarded to his mother in Scotland." He also told her to keep the things Montguire had given her and also notified her to expect "a package containing the letters you wrote to him and a photograph case evidently given by you to him."[54] Private Montguire's infidelity and subsequent demise thus left two fiancées distraught and a mother in mourning.[55]

Although Montguire's story was unique, it was heartbreaking tale echoed over and over again in the autumn of 1918. Telegrams to the camp's soldiers

Grave of Private Thomas Montguire, in the Soldiers' National Cemetery (Photo by author)

from families stricken with the influenza sometimes arrived after their soldier, likewise weakened from the flu, already had died, normally from pneumonia. Records of the Development Battalion bear silent testament: on October 18, Pvt. Lawrence Richardson asked for leave to bury his wife; that same day Pvt. Samuel Di Basi requested leave to attend the funeral of his mother, and so did Pvt. William Fleming, who requested leave due to his sister's demise from the influenza. On October 23, Pvt. Charles F. Hammond of Company B filled out the necessary forms to allow him to visit his critically ill brother. And so it went across Camp Colt's battalions throughout October and into November.[56] For the people of Gettysburg and Adams County, the epidemic came at a time when the local newspapers, especially the daily *Gettysburg Times,* were routinely reporting on the casualties from the Meuse-Argonne offensive—and on the same page listing the names of its citizens who had died from the flu. It was a tale recurring on a regular basis across the Commonwealth and the nation.

The onset of the influenza epidemic had a sad and profound impact on the soldiers and nurses assigned to Camp Colt. Perhaps the greatest memorial bestowed on its dead was written for *Treat 'Em Rough,* the camp newspaper. Titled "'Gone West': A Tribute by a Comrade," the anonymous author, in the midst of this unprecedented biological disaster, eloquently articulated his sorrow:

> The Tank Corps is "in the shadow of a great affliction." The epidemic of Spanish Influenza which has been sweeping the country has taken from us some of our bravest and our best.
>
> Funeral platitudes appeal but little to the fighting man. Death is part of his business—almost his stock in trade, as it were. But in this case, death stealing on us like a thief in the night, hits hard and hits home.
>
> So, we are gladly forgiven for pausing a moment at parade rest, in the midst of our grueling, driving work, and choking back a most unmilitary lump in our throats as the bugles call Taps for our pals.
>
> They died no less bravely than if they had fallen on the field of battle. They died "in line of duty." No soldier, called upon to make the supreme sacrifice, does more. The tragedy of it all is that they cannot be with us, shoulder to shoulder, fighting for victory.
>
> To the families of these boys we tender our sincere sympathy. And if tears gleam suspiciously in our eyes, why—well, the boys were our bunkies and we loved them.
>
> We stand a moment with heads bowed and with heavy hearts, in silent tribute. Then, with heads up and eyes front, we send word to these, are bunkies, across the Great Divide:
>
> "We will carry on, fellows, we will carry on."[57]

And they did carry on, but not for much longer. In fact, none of Camp Colt's soldiers who had read that particular issue of *Treat 'Em Rough* would ever see combat in the Great War. In a few weeks, it would all be over "over there."

CHAPTER 8

The End of the War and Beyond

"I can hardly realize it is all over," wrote an astonished Harry Bream on November 12, 1918. Still serving with the 11th Engineer Regiment (Railway), Bream mused that the "unusual silence seems so strange, no roll of guns or no red glow in the sky. . . . The world seems to have suddenly stopped or headed backwards."[1] Adams County men assigned to the Seventy-Ninth Division, which had "jumped off" on September 26 at the beginning of the Meuse-Argonne offensive, found themselves back on the front lines when the war came to an end on November 11, 1918. Even that morning, when the senior leaders at all levels of the AEF were aware that the armistice ending the conflict would go into effect at 11:00 A.M., the Allied attacks nonetheless continued. A soldier-historian who helped to compile the Seventy-Ninth Division's history wrote, "While the Armistice message was passing through the various stages of its transmission to the front line battalions, the time for the morning attack had arrived." In the hours leading up to the armistice, thirty-six soldiers of the Seventy-Ninth Division were killed or died of wounds.[2] None were from Adams County. Lamentably, Cpl. Paul Cole of Buchannan Valley, who had been seriously wounded on October 8 while assigned to the Thirty-Second Division, died in his hospital bed as the armistice went into effect.[3]

In the last week of October, as the Spanish influenza catastrophe was ending at Camp Colt, Maj. Dwight D. Eisenhower was notified that he had been promoted to lieutenant colonel.[4] His advancement came so late in the war that he would not have much time to wear his new rank, as most wartime promotions were "brevet," or temporary. Ike had been promised command of a tank regiment in

France if the war dragged on, and he even refused a promotion to full colonel if he agreed to remain at Camp Colt, but he was determined to get into the fight. Now, his dreams of battlefield glory would come to an end. Then sorrow struck Ike personally. During the days leading up to the armistice, the Eisenhower family was notified that Mamie's younger sister, Ida Mae, nicknamed "Buster," had died from a kidney infection on November 9. Mamie and the baby boarded a train on November 10 for the long trip to Denver, Colorado, where they arrived on November 11, in time to attend the funeral.[5] Before they departed Gettysburg, Ike wrote a letter to his mother-in-law about the loss of Buster, who, with her father, had spent most of the summer in Gettysburg helping Mamie and the baby. "Mamie has repeated over and over, 'poor mother, poor mother'—and tomorrow she starts to you. I cannot come—duty prevents—but even now I know that the love you bear your children tells you that my heart and my love are with you." He closed his condolences with a touching reflection about his late sister-in-law: "To me it seems the truest monument our darling has left to her memory is the lesson of patience and sweetness she has taught us. I hope I have learned that lesson well enough that from this day on I may also show those traits in dealing with my fellow man."[6] Despite Mamie's grief, at least with the announcement of the armistice, she now knew her husband would not be going to the Western Front. It would be another nine months until the young family was reunited.[7]

Four days before the armistice finally brought an end the war, the United Press (UP) prematurely reported that the conflict had concluded. The *Gettysburg Times*, using Associated Press (AP) reports, announced that rumors of the war's cessation were false. The citizens of Gettysburg and Adams County, reacting to the UP stories, went wild with joy—and so did the rest of the nation. It seemed everyone had been misled.[8] Nonetheless, the end was in sight. But on November 11, when the armistice actually did go into effect, the *Times* got it wrong, with a headline, emblazoned across the top of the front page, screaming in bold, capital letters: "UNCONDITIONAL SURRENDER." However, the newspaper gave its readers the rest of the story in a subhead: "GERMANY SIGNS TERMS OF ARMISTICE; WAR OVER." Imperial Germany only agreed to a temporary termination of the fighting, pending the overall settlement of the peace discussions. Technically, Germany and the Allies still were at war (the other Central Powers nations already had capitulated), but for now, the Allies, and particularly the people of the United States—whose soldiers, sailors, and marines had made a significant contribution to victory but suffered more fatalities from the Spanish flu and other causes than from combat—were going to throw one hell of party.

The *Gettysburg Times* proclaimed on Monday, November 11, that the townsfolk "went into transports of enthusiasm this morning that far exceeded the premature celebration of last Thursday. . . . During the morning all places that had flags for sale were besieged. . . . Everywhere [in town] the flag appeared and some French flags also were to be seen." In an adjacent column, the *Times* announced the great town festival planned for that evening: "Gettysburg will celebrate formally at seven o'clock to-night. And every resident of Adams County is invited to come for the jubilee. . . . A parade, expected to be the best the town has seen for years, will be the big feature." The article's author asked the readers to put out all the flags they could find and to illuminate their houses and businesses "from top to bottom." Sadly, the same edition of the *Times* also reported that three more Camp Colt men had died since its November 9 issue.

The little town of New Oxford, in far eastern Adams—which had been home to Royal Leese, the first man from the county to die in the line of duty when he was lost at sea—likewise joyously celebrated the end of the World War. According to an article in the *Item,* its weekly news organ, "New Oxford along with the rest of our Glorious Country went wild with enthusiasm and patriotism, when the news was flashed over the wires on Monday to the effect that Germany had concluded an armistice with the Allies." Before daylight on November 11, the ringing of church bells and blowing of factory whistles signaled that the end had come. "Throughout the day everyone seemed to be overjoyed by the glad tidings." That afternoon, reported the *Item,* an impromptu parade marched through the town, "in which at least seventy-five automobiles, trucks, large farm wagons and other conveyances, all decorated with the National colors, participated." It also announced that the provost marshal general of the United States had suspended all draft calls, "stopping the movement during the next five days of 252,000 men and setting aside all November calls for 300,000 men"—much to the relief of the nineteen Adams County draftees, listed in another column on the same page, who had left earlier in the week for induction into the Army at Camps Meade and Crane.[9]

"Did Gettysburg Celebrate? She Surely did."—was one of the major headlines on the front page of the November 12 edition of the *Times.* The borough's leading citizens, however, understood that the conclusion of the war also meant the end of Camp Colt. On the same page that recounted the festive celebration of the previous day, a writer for the *Times* speculated, "Camp Colt will probably be a thing of the past within a very few weeks. No official announcement has been made but the abandonment of the National Park grounds for camp purposes is expected as a natural result of the end of the war." For now, however, the soldiers at Camp Colt, along with the citizens of Gettysburg and the rest of Adams County, were euphoric over the Allied victory.

Lieutenant Colonel (ret.) E. B. Cope, the Gettysburg National Military Park (GNMP) engineer and a veteran of the Battle of Gettysburg, wrote a letter about the end of the world conflict to Col. John Nicholson two weeks after the armistice. Both men had experienced the horrors of war as young men, both had been instrumental in the creation of the park and its evolution as a shrine, and both now faced the massive cleanup necessary to restore the park to its prewar state. However, Cope did not mention these subjects in his note to the park commission's chairman, instead reflecting only on the war's conduct and outcome:

> Dear Colonel Nicholson,
>
> Well the war is over, we have both lived to see the end which has been glorious in its results to the millions who have upheld the cause of righteousness and humanity, but has also brought disaster and oblivion to those who have caused more death, destruction and misery to the world than has ever been known. No punishment that can be devised and inflicted on these Devils could ever atone for the audacious villainy they have been guilty of, and for which their dupes for generations will feel the sting.
>
> Respectfully,
> E. B. Cope[10]

Fifty-three years earlier, in the debate over Reconstruction, the substance of this letter easily could have been written by a bitter Radical Republican about the defeated South in the wake of Lincoln's assassination and the devastating aftermath of the Civil War. Now, with the end of the Great War and the further unifying effects that the conflict brought to a once divided nation, the great issues of the Civil War—slavery, secession, emancipation, equality and, according to historian David Blight, "disloyalty and treason"—took a backseat to the reunification of North and South that had begun with the early veterans' reunions, had escalated during the War with Spain, was sanctified by the 1913 Peace Jubilee, and now was cemented by the World War and the defeat of the Central Powers.[11]

Once the fanfare over the armistice had subsided, everyone wanted to know when their soldiers would come home. The first bunch to return was the group of draftees who had reported to Camp Meade the same day the armistice was announced. They arrived back in Gettysburg two days later. On reporting for duty at the Maryland camp, the conscripts flatly were told to find their way home—at their own expense—as they no longer were needed. After a short discussion, they pooled their money and purchased tickets for the return trip. According to the *Times,* when the would-be soldiers got back to Gettysburg and explained to the local draft board what had happened, "steps were promptly taken to have them paid for the expense they had to incur to get back."[12] Although the draft board remained intact until March 31, 1919, to compile statistics and write reports, no further draft calls were made. Of the 6,376 Adams County draft registrants since conscription had begun a year and a half earlier, 548 actually were selected for military service, with only two dodgers who failed to show.[13]

On November 12, 1918, the *Gettysburg Times* correctly predicted in a front-page article, "Camp Colt probably will be a thing of the past within a very few weeks. No official announcement has been made but the abandonment of the National Park ground for camp purposes is expected as a natural result of the end of the war." Just three days later, the newspaper announced that the tankers would be leaving the next day, Saturday, November 16, on special trains bound for Camp Dix, New Jersey, to be mustered out of the service. The Tank Corps' officer candidate school was terminated, with the candidates receiving certificates but not commissions. New recruits and recent Colt arrivals immediately were sent home. Special Orders No. 237, HQ, Camp Colt, dated November 15, 1918, stipulated that the troops would board cars on the military siding of the Round Top branch and "proceed by rail to Camp Dix, Wrightstown, New Jersey, to arrive at that station not later than November 19, 1918." Four separate train sections comprised the rail movement to New Jersey.[14]

Lieutenant Colonel Eisenhower, his subordinate commanders, and the headquarters staff were overwhelmed with the tasks of a major movement and subsequent demobilization. "Nothing at West Point or in the forty months since graduation had prepared me for helping to collapse an Army from millions to a peacetime core," Ike recalled. "The new problem kept us even busier than we had been in the middle of the summer." Added to the tasks of packing up and shipping out was the supplementary complication of keeping his soldiers motivated to do the job at hand: "A new aspect of leadership was demanded of every commissioned and non-commissioned officer—the ability to explain, reasonably and persuasively, all the necessary measures that would have to be taken before we could fold up the camp and the war." Ike's subordinates had to precisely plan and execute the tasks associated with a major troop deployment; so, for example, his tents and mess equipment had not been shipped while the men still waited for their train ride to Camp Dix. Yet, they pulled it off. "We reached Dix with between five and six thousand people," Eisenhower recalled. "After the discharge of most of the men, we were left with between two and three hundred, the remnants of my command." Soon, Ike and his significantly reduced tank organization—now the size of a small battalion—were ordered to their new assignment, Camp Benning, Georgia.[15]

In the midst of the hustle and bustle of getting the soldiers moved from Colt to Dix, two bedridden patients still in the camp hospital died on Saturday, November 16, from the Spanish flu—the last troops at Camp Colt to perish from the malady.[16] (In early January, the *Compiler* reported that William McKeever, another Tank Corps soldier who had married a woman from Gettysburg, died of the flu at Camp Dix. His new wife was by his side as he passed.[17]) Sixteen men too sick to make the trip to Dix were transported in a special hospital car on November 22 to Fort McHenry General Hospital—the same fort that inspired the "Star Spangled Banner." One of Camp Colt's physicians and two enlisted medics, who would return to Gettysburg after delivering their patients, accompanied the ill soldiers.[18] A week later, fourteen women serving in the Army Nurse Corps who had been assigned to Camp Colt were transferred to U.S. Army Debarkation Hospital No. 1 at Ellis Island, New York, where they would attend to wounded and sick men coming home from overseas.[19] The influenza still threatened Adams County's citizens, particularly in the eastern part of the county and also in the town of Fairfield, about thirteen miles southwest of Gettysburg. The flu persisted in eastern Adams County even into the first week of December, with at least ten persons sick in New Oxford and twenty suffering in the little village of Hampton.[20]

Most of the men serving overseas would not return to the United States until the spring and summer of 1919. However, the Tank Corps soldiers from Camp Colt who had been shipped to a training camp in England about five weeks before the armistice would be some of the first to return. The *Times* reported on November 19, 1918, that "an official statement was given out in Washington Monday evening that the American troops now in England would be sent home within the next ten days. . . . It would accordingly appear that the tankers will be among the first to come home when the movement starts and this is promised for the present week." In a cruel twist, the doughboys in the six regiments of U.S. Regulars who had trained on GNMP in 1917 would be among the last to return to the United States in 1919, since combat organizations were slated to be some of the last to leave Europe—just in case Germany disregarded the terms of the armistice and hostilities recommenced.

Soldiers, sailors, and marines still undergoing training in the United States when the war ended were relatively easy to muster out and send home, but it was a much more difficult process for the doughboys of the American Expeditionary Forces. The soldiers and marines not on occupation duty came back to the United States during 1919 as soon as sea transport was available. The high command came up with a pecking order that determined the sequence of embarkation from the war zone: casuals (men not yet assigned to a unit); surplus and special service troops, which would include divisions that had been broken up whose personnel then were used as replacements for front-line units; men assigned to the United Kingdom; soldiers in the U.S. Army Air Service; troops assigned to Italy; combat divisions on the Western Front; and, finally, Services of Supply personnel (especially the grave registration units, normally called "pioneer labor battalions," whose troops were African Americans).[21] The U.S. Third Army, which did not come into existence until after the armistice, performed occupation duty in Germany until the peace treaty finally was signed in June 1919. By 1920, only sixteen thousand Americans remained as occupiers, with the last few departing in early 1923. Likewise, several thousand American troops had been part of an Allied force in North Russia and Siberia as a consequence of the Russian Revolution. They were withdrawn in 1919 and 1920, paving the way for Bolshevik victory and the eventual establishment of the Soviet Union.[22]

Soon after Christmas 1918—the first during peacetime since 1913—Cashtown's Kate Wolf wrote a letter home that made it to the front page of the February 8, 1919, *Gettysburg Compiler.* After describing the wonderful Christmas celebration she hosted for the soldiers at her hospital—thanks in part to donations from Adams County citizens—Kate ended by observing that "everyone is howling to go home and the joy of the boys when they start is boundless." (Kate finally would come home—after more than five long years in war-torn France—in September 1919.) Just below her letter, the *Compiler* published another missive from France, this one from the national religious secretary of the YMCA, Reverend Julius Wadsworth, who had encountered a young man from Gettysburg with whom he had shared a ride through the French countryside. Wadsworth then wrote to the soldier's mother to inform her that her boy—former Gettysburg police chief Horace Smiley—was doing well: "I enjoyed talking to your son. . . . He is a fine looking lad and so gentlemanly in his bearing and speech." Wadsworth continued, "He is anxious, like all the boys, to get home. These past seventeen months seem long to him and even yesterday he was happy in the orders that had just come, sending his outfit to Brest,—which looks as if it were a step closer in that Brest is near the Port of Embarkation." Then he concluded, "But really we cannot say just when the boys can come home. It may be several months yet before they can be spared from here."[23] As it turned out, Sergeant Smiley and his unit arrived in the United States in mid-April, and Smiley was discharged on May 4, 1919. Although the Borough of Gettysburg had kept his position open for him, Smiley returned only briefly to his job as police chief. Instead, that fall he ran as a Democrat for the position of the Register of Wills and Recorder of Deeds for Adams County and won the election.[24]

While the troops came home in dribs and drabs, the Gettysburg chapter of the American Red Cross routinely hosted rehabilitation patients from newly activated General Hospital No. 31, at Carlisle Barracks. Still recovering from wounds received in action, the disabled soldiers usually were given lunch and dinner and toured the battlefield with a licensed guide. A report in the April 26, 1919, *Compiler* explained that the soldiers "represented all kinds of wounded cases from slight to severe ones, shrapnel wounds, and those caused by high explosives. Many of the boys were from Pennsylvania and one at the Pennsylvania monument declared he had been over the top in France and would not be satisfied until he went over the top here and went over the high spots at the memorial." Nurses from the Carlisle-based hospital also frequented.

The end of the conflict also meant that Gettysburg College, still under War Department direction, soon would return to civilian control. On December 16, the 350 men enrolled in the Students' Army Training Corps (SATC) were discharged from the service.[25] This small, private institution contributed many of its alumni and some of its enrolled students to the war effort. At least 333 Gettysburg College alumni (and those who attended but did not graduate or had not yet graduated) had donned a uniform, including one woman, Cora D. Swartz, Class of 1907, who served as a nurse. The oldest alumnus to serve was Maj. (Reverend) Francis H. Weaver, Class of 1873, an army chaplain, one of twenty-one men who graduated before the turn of the century that served in the military during the conflict. Fourteen graduates and former students from the classes of 1905 through 1922 died in the service of their country during the World War.[26] On Sunday, June 8, 1919, the college remembered them during commencement exercises, with a Gold Star Men Memorial Service.[27] To commemorate in perpetuity its graduates who had made the supreme sacrifice, the college opted for a utilitarian remembrance, what Progressives called a "living memorial."[28] In 1924, the college began construction of its Memorial Athletic Field, completed a year later and named in memory of those Gettysburgians who died in the World War.[29]

Along with alumnus Keller Rockey, USMC, Class of 1909, who was awarded the Distinguished Service Cross for heroism, so was Capt. Frederick A. Muhlenberg, Class of 1908, as a company commander in the 314th Infantry, Seventy-Ninth Division, for his courageous actions near Nantillois, France, on September 26–30, 1918, at the beginning of the Meuse-Argonne offensive.[30] Colonel John S. Fair, Class of 1894, who as a career soldier fought in the Spanish-American War and the Philippine-American War, saw service on the Mexican border, and commanded a field artillery brigade during the World War, was awarded the Distinguished Service Medal.[31] Quite a few alumni over the age of forty served as medical officers or chaplains with the army or navy or directed YMCA operations at stateside camps and overseas, while the younger graduates and current students either enlisted or, prior to the establishment of the SATC, were drafted and served in a variety of combat, combat support, or service positions in the armed forces, many as commissioned officers.[32] Despite the strong showing of its alumni during the war, once the SATC was dissolved on December 21, 1918, the college faculty called on the Board of Trustees to eliminate the ROTC course as well, but the majority of the board voted to retain it. The Gettysburg College program was the first one reestablished in Pennsylvania after the war.[33] (Less than two years later, the National Defense Act of 1920 institutionalized the commissioning of junior officers on a continuing basis through ROTC and established a system of summer training camps for students not enrolled in the ROTC program.[34])

Except for a decrease in enrollments in 1917–18, the Lutheran Theological Seminary largely was unaffected by the war.[35] Nevertheless, many of its alumni, as well as those who had been enrolled when the United States declared war—and even future alumni—served in the armed forces during the conflict. Previously ordained seminary graduates who had enlisted performed their duties as chaplains; however, some men served as combatants, notably those who had yet to graduate but enlisted in 1917 or '18 and veterans who enrolled at the seminary after the armistice. First Lieutenant Edgar J. Eyler, from nearby Thurmont, Maryland, matriculated to the seminary after he graduated from Gettysburg College in 1915, but he joined the army before completing his studies. Eyler died of wounds received in action during the Meuse-Argonne offensive while serving with the 315th Infantry, Seventy-Ninth Division. Captain Albert D. Bell, who graduated from Gettysburg College in 1908 and from the seminary in 1911, served as a chaplain in the 310th Infantry, Seventy-Ninth Division. He perished from pneumonia after his lungs were weakened by poison gas during the Argonne fight.[36] Exactly three years after the end of the war, the seminary celebrated Armistice Day with a special service in the chapel. According to the seminary bulletin for November 1921, "the text was Luke 2:214, 'On Earth Peace,' and the sermon was a plea for disarmament as a Christian goal." Eyler and Bell were singled out as the two "alumni who gave their lives in the Great War."[37]

By the early winter of 1918–19, most of Camp Colt's quartermaster and ordnance troops were busy overseeing the disposition of the remaining equipment, supplies, and subsistence stores. These men, along with the hospital staff, were all that remained of the camp's personnel after the tankers' departure. The camp's lone Renault tank had been driven to a temporary ordnance depot in town to await rail shipment to its new home. According to a November 15 story in the *Times,* "comparatively few Gettysburg people saw this crawling fort in action during the summer though it was used every day." In early December, the tank was shipped to Camp Benning, where eventually Eisenhower and his ad hoc battalion would put it to use. On the morning of December 9, just before the Renault FT-17 was loaded on a railcar, "the Ordnance Corps detachment gave a little demonstration on Centre Square, maneuvering the tank, showing how quickly it could be turned in its own position, and various other little stunts it is capable of performing. An interested crowd watched the demonstration," stated a report in the *Times.*[38] About the same time, a detachment of African American Motor Transport Corps soldiers arrived from Camp Holabird, Maryland, to load the camp's motorcycles on trucks and then drive all of the remaining vehicles, less those needed by the Camp Colt quartermasters, to their Baltimore post. According to the *Compiler,* "During their stay in town the colored soldiers were quartered at Xavier Hall. Their conduct was above reproach and they enjoyed their stay here." The same news report mentioned that the camp commissary had "been completely cleaned out, fourteen [rail]carloads of foodstuffs being sent away."[39]

In an astounding development, a committee of renowned Gettysburg citizens was granted an audience with Secretary of War Newton Baker on January 8, 1919, for the purpose of trying to convince him of the advantages of retaining a permanent military camp in Gettysburg, with barracks to house some three thousand soldiers, adjacent to GNMP. According to the front-page story in the January 11 edition of the *Times,* "It is not the idea to use any land under control of the National Park Commission but that the Government shall purchase ground occupied by Camp Colt at the southwestern end of the town." The Gettysburg delegation stressed to the secretary and his staff that

> Gettysburg furnishes an ideal site because of its topography and natural advantages and because of the work already done there in making it a camp for the United States Regulars and for the Tank Corps. Another feature which they impressed upon the Washington officials was the fact that the lease on which more than 100 acres of the present camp ground was obtained, stipulated that this ground should be returned to the same condition in which it was found. This has since been piped for water and sewer systems, all of which would have to be removed, and the Gettysburg men declared that the land could be bought for less than this would cost. All the officials seen, seemed favorably impressed with the arguments set forth, and it is believed the town may be the site of a permanent camp.

The secretary of war embraced their proposition. The local group, according to the news article, "did not ask for a large camp . . . but Secretary of War Baker, who was almost enthusiastic over the idea, seemed to think that a considerable number of troops should be located there. . . . possibly a division. In war this would mean 30,000 men, but the peace strength would be considerably less." (If that happened, however, a portion of GNMP most certainly would have to be set aside as a permanent military installation.) Andrew Brodbeck (D), now a lame-duck congressman—who had lost his seat in the 1918 election that gave control of the nation's House of Representatives and Senate to the Republicans—promised to amend pending legislation that would have allowed the purchase of the leased land. The *Times* concluded, "The establishment of an Army post here would be in line with other National Parks in the United States, notably Chickamauga, and the stationing of troops here for twelve months out of the year would be the idea. Nothing would please Gettysburg people more than to have her own six regiments of Regulars here after the war." The editor of the *Gettysburg Compiler* also believed the proposal was a good one.[40]

A few weeks later, during the night of Friday, January 31, fire, purportedly caused by an overheated stove, destroyed three barracks used by the remaining Camp Colt soldiers, which seemed a bad omen for the locals who wanted a permanent Army post. "With the buildings there burned the personal effects of eight men, considerable Army equipment in the way of cots, bedding, and so on, and two pianos. . . . Friday was payday in the camp and a number of the men are said to have lost money in the fire," according to a story in the Saturday, February 1, edition of the *Gettysburg Times*. The barracks, which had been built close to the edge of town, were far enough away from the rest of the camp that no other government structures were threatened. Despite their proximity to the borough, the structures nonetheless were too far from the closest town fire hydrant, with the consequence that the Gettysburg Fire Department's hoses could not reach the inferno. "Had the row of barracks here been as extensive as elsewhere in the camp the loss would have been heavier for the fire stopped only when there was nothing left to burn," the reporter surmised. A "fire guard" (a barracks sentry) spotted the flames and smoke and dutifully sounded the alarm so that no personnel were hurt. The displaced occupants of the three destroyed barracks took up quarters elsewhere in the camp or in the Soldiers' Club on Middle Street.

Five days later, a board of three quartermaster officers convened to determine the cause of the fire. After interviewing the fire guard responsible for making the rounds to check on the heating stoves of the living quarters and the cooking stoves in the kitchen, the officers concluded that the fire started sometime between 8:30 P.M., when the fire guard last checked, and 9:00 P.M., when he returned from the latrine, about twenty-five yards away from the personnel quarters. Attempts to put out the blaze with available fire extinguishers proved futile. Because of a stiff breeze that evening, the flames spread rapidly, consuming the building where it began and two adjacent buildings. In the board's opinion, "the fire was caused by an overheated stove pipe, which in some manner unknown, became loose and dropped against the side of the building." The estimated damage was almost $5000, "of which amount $1950 applies to the cost of the buildings," and the rest to uniforms and equipment issued to the occupants.[41] The soldiers' private property was not included in this amount. The same day that news of the blaze made the headlines, another snippet on the front page of the *Times* publicized the departure of seven soldiers, including a lieutenant in command of the Ordnance Detachment, further decreasing the roster of remaining Camp Colt personnel.[42] Whether anyone in the town recognized the significance of their parting, it marked the beginning of the end of Camp Colt. The handwriting was on the barracks wall.

About the same time of the fire, Colonel Nicholson received notification from Congressman Brodbeck informing him that he would be submitting a bill that, if approved, would direct the secretary of war to "donate twenty cannon . . . with suitable number of shells . . . captured by the American Army from forces of the Imperial German Government . . . to be placed upon the Gettysburg National Park" at points agreed upon by the War Department and the park commission. Col. Nicholson sent a courteous but negative response to the well-meaning, lame duck congressman: "I am compelled to object to there being placed on the Field any Artillery other than that which illustrated the fight in 1863, and I am sure, with your good judgement, you will see the incongruity of placing any Artillery that fails to illustrate that epoch." Beyond that, Nicholson informed him that the law would have to be changed to allow the German guns on the park, because these artifacts "did not confine themselves to the actual conflict."[43] Luckily for later generations of visitors, Nicholson's view won the day.

When Congress adjourned on March 4, the matter of whether to make Camp Colt a permanent army post had not been decided. Congressman Brodbeck had attached the legislation to a large defense appropriation omnibus, which, thanks to a Republican filibuster, failed to pass in the House. It thus would have to wait until the next session, by which time Republicans would control both houses of Congress. Still, the editor of the *Gettysburg Times* was quixotically optimistic that the bill eventually would be passed. The legislation read, in part, "that the Secretary of War be, and is hereby authorized and directed, to acquire, by purchase, condemnation or otherwise, a suitable site for the erection of permanent buildings for a military post at Gettysburg, Pennsylvania, at a cost not exceeding $25,000." An article in the March 6 edition explained that townsfolk had different opinions on the matter: "Some take the stand that a permanent post generally lowers the moral tone of a town or city located nearby, and that a small town especially feels that influence. Others disagree with the statements about moral influences and look upon the post as a positive asset." The overall hopeful tone of the story indicated that the controlling interests of the newspaper wanted Camp Colt—or some version of it—to stay: "Whatever the general opinion may be, the fact remains that the government is making no efforts to remove any of the property it has here now, and it is likely that soldiers will be stationed at Camp Colt during the summer as before." The underlying motive behind the push to keep a permanent garrison in Gettysburg, although the article did not mention it, was based in the local economy. Soldiers not only ate in the town's restaurants and purchased goods and services from Gettysburg merchants, they also bought newspapers.

In the same vicinity of the burned camp buildings, and contrary to the desires of the Gettysburg businessmen who wanted a permanent army garrison, other plans were being laid—not for another camp, but for a long-needed civilian hospital. John M. Warner and his wife, Annie, reacting to the Spanish flu crisis, donated the land and funding for the new structures, to be named the "Annie M. Warner Hospital." Its proposed location was on land bordering the southwest edge of the town near the intersection of Washington and Franklin Streets, a twenty-acre parcel that was being leased by the U.S. government (and which figured into the plans for the permanent camp). The Warners, however, had different ideas. According to a February 8 story in the *Times*, "Mr. and Mrs. Warner, who had long thought of the gift of a hospital, were so impressed by the need of a hospital after the experience of last year that they determined to go ahead with their fine and great plans for their old home town. Both have it in their minds and hearts to push their plans through to early completion." The only barrier to breaking ground for construction was the government lease, which would end in June 1919, only a few months away. Impatient to get the process started, Warner pressed the War Department for an early release to the rental contract. By March 13, he still awaited an answer. That day, the *Times* reported that Warner was determined to build the hospital and if need be would "wait until June, when the lease runs out and he will assume possession of the property." Warner's proposal now hinged on the War Department decision concerning the establishment of a permanent garrison: "It is possible that the ground may be released as soon as the future of Camp Colt is decided," concluded the story's author. The verdict came sooner than expected.

On March 19, Camp Colt's supply officers received orders from the War Department to begin disposing federal property, such as cordwood and excess supplies. With that news, the *Times* pronounced, "CAMP COLT TO BE ABANDONED: Information Regarding the Fact Received To-Day by Quartermaster Corps." On the twenty-second, the weekly *Compiler* broadcast the same news, but its editors believed the decision was a bad one: "With the United States owning thousands of acres here, it would certainly seem that the economical thing to do would be to locate a permanent camp here on a site with a record for sanitation and health." The official orders announcing the camp's permanent closing were received at the garrison's headquarters on March 22, as part of the broad demobilization of temporary posts across the country.[44] Fortunately for future generations of Gettysburg citizens and Americans in general, GNMP would remain a place known primarily for its Civil War heritage rather than as a U.S. Army post.

With the announcement of the camp's closure, John and Annie Warner were cleared to break ground. A board of directors, recruited from upstanding citizens and physicians from across Adams County, was named to guide fund-raising efforts intended to sustain the hospital for the long run. "John Warner is giving the building and grounds," noted a *Times* reporter, "but it will depend entirely upon the people of Adams County as to whether or not funds necessary for the upkeep of the hospital are forthcoming."[45] The *Compiler* reported that the board meeting "was notable for the fact that eighteen physicians of the county were present and enthusiastic over the hospital."[46] The official ground breaking took place on March 25, 1919: "Mrs. Warner turned the first shovel of dirt Monday and now a gang of twenty men are busily engaged in digging the foundations."[47] Three months later, the hospital's cornerstone was laid.[48] After two years of fund-raising and construction, the brick, two-story Annie M. Warner Hospital and accompanying Nurses' Home opened on March 15, 1921.[49] The dark cloud that was the Spanish influenza at least ended with a silver lining for Gettysburg.

The salvage of Camp Colt property and the restoration of the landscape, both on and off GNMP, was the largest immediate problem facing the few remaining army quartermasters in Gettysburg during the winter and spring of 1919. Soon after being notified that the camp would be closed, leadership solicited competitive bids from salvage companies for the dismantlement of the garrison's structures and sale of the salvaged materials. On May 19, 1919, the War Department advised the Camp Colt chief quartermaster "to give the widest possible publicity [to salvagers] . . . so that all people who are interested may have an opportunity of bidding." Colt's chief quartermaster was well ahead of the bureaucrats in Washington. Within a week, he responded, "It will take approximately three months to salvage the camp." Concerning the return of the leased land to private owners, it was determined that there were "no tracts of land which can be immediately returned to owners and leases cancelled on account of buildings erected on same."[50] Hundreds of wood-framed structures that had been used as stables, motor pools, administrative offices, hospital facilities, mess halls, kitchens, a bakery, latrines, and sleeping quarters would have to be dismantled and their stone foundations demolished, as would forty-nine waste incinerators, two water treatment facilities, and backup power generation plants. Underground sewer lines and plumbing would need to be excavated and removed, along with company streets that had been covered with layers of cinders, gravel, and Tarvia. Utility poles suspending electrical power transmission lines and telephone cables also needed to be removed.[51] The overall task seemed daunting, but the highly unrealistic goal was to return the land to "normal" within three months of the day the demolition was to begin. It would not happen.

Official bids for the sale of Camp Colt were opened in Washington on April 27, although informal bids had been received in Gettysburg in March. The salvage contract eventually was awarded to the firm of Lewis Brothers, a wrecking company out of Rock Island, Illinois, with demolition beginning on May 24. The salvagers worked closely with the private lessors and the Gettysburg National Park Commission to ensure that damage claims were adjusted fairly. In a June 4 report to the commanding general of the U.S. Army Eastern Department, the senior quartermaster officer / Camp Colt commander, Capt. Frederick P. Desmond, elaborated on the ongoing property disposal, stating that all remaining commissary stores had been sent to a facility in New York on May 31, "completing the shipment of all Government Property in this Camp," with the exception of the remaining motor vehicles, cordwood, office supplies, and office records. The vehicles were to be sent to Camp Holabird in Baltimore, office supplies would be transported to Philadelphia, and the camp records were "being indexed and packed for shipment to Washington." The remaining personnel amounted to two officers, Desmond included, and eight enlisted men. Within three days of the report being sent, one officer and two men received their honorable discharges, leaving only Desmond and six soldiers.[52]

According to a May 31 *Harrisburg Telegraph* article about the demolition, "The work had been delayed for a week or so because the requirements of the Government made it necessary that an itemized statement of all property in the sale had to be in their hands before the tearing down was started." Local buyers had purchased some of the buildings from Lewis Brothers, and the razing of those structures was completed before the salvage firm began demolition. The article in the *Telegraph* optimistically concluded, "It will take about two months to clear the grounds of all property and put it back in condition as it was before the camp was built."[53]

At the end of the same week the camp began to come down, Gettysburg commemorated its first Memorial Day since the end of the World War, and, according to a *Times* reporter, the ceremony "had a new significance with the mingling of the veterans in blue and the boys in khaki." The writer of the article unwittingly acknowledged that although the United States allegedly fought to make the world safe for democracy, it still needed to work on its own democratic values: "The procession in Gettysburg at the usual time from the Square to the National Cemetery marked this new significance by the large squad of our sturdy boys following the Band and in turn *followed by a squad of colored Boy Scouts from York, who had assisted in the strewing of graves of the colored veterans in the morning,* members of local patriotic orders, and the veterans in blue ended the procession cared for in automobiles."[54] Fifty-four years after the end of the Civil War and passage of the Thirteenth Amendment, the graves of black Civil War veterans still were relegated to a lower commemoration status. Adherents to the Lost Cause living below the Mason-Dixon line undoubtedly would have agreed, despite a temporary waning of their grip on Civil War history, because of what David Blight has characterized as "the patriotic upheavals of World War I."[55]

The 1919 Memorial Day speaker was Justice J. Hay Brown of the Pennsylvania Supreme Court. A native of Lancaster, Pennsylvania, some fifty miles east of Gettysburg, Brown focused his remarks primarily on the Civil War and the role of Lancaster hero and Gettysburg martyr Maj. Gen. John F. Reynolds, killed on July 1, 1863. He mentioned the World War only in his closing comments, almost as an afterthought, regardless that the vestiges of Camp Colt remained across the road from the National Cemetery and the graves of some of its soldiers were only a few steps away from where he delivered his speech. Brown's encomium was well received by the crowd, apparently eager to forget the town's recent past and return to times long since enshrined in its collective memory.[56]

As the spring of 1919 gave way to the long, sultry days of summer, Camp Colt was demolished, sold off, and carted away. The War Camp Community Service activity in Gettysburg was discontinued in June, the soldiers' club it operated on West Middle Street was closed, and its recreational and office equipment put on the market. A story in the April 29 *Times* related that there was "little need for such an organization here now that Camp Colt will soon pass out of existence." By midsummer the camp salvage was wrapping up. A classified advertisement in the July 14 *Harrisburg Telegraph* gives an example of the matériel being wholesaled: "FOR SALE—At Camp Colt, Gettysburg, Pa., 2,500,000 ft. of very fine lumber; 250,000 gal. water tanks; 2 deep well pumps; 2 [two] 12-horse power gasoline engines; 150 galvanized sinks; 6 x 9 light sash; 400 doors; 150 screen doors; screen wire in 50 ft. rolls." Three weeks later, the *Times* announced the camp's closure. On August 6, a front-page headline proclaimed, "ARMY POST HERE A THING OF THE PAST." Without fanfare or sentimentality, the article mentioned the future plans of the few remaining soldiers and stated that at the end of the work week, the eleven remaining civilian workers would be discharged from their employment.

The virtual obituary of the camp appeared in the August 9 edition of the *Gettysburg Complier* under the title, "Camp Colt Gone":

> Camp Colt is a memory, a few piles of boards to tell where it had once been. Lewis Bros., of Rock Island, Ill., the wrecking company, have been on the job the past two or three months taking up pipe and pulling down buildings. About 375 buildings were in the camp and over 50,000 feet of piping of various size, and there was an enormous quantity of material to be disposed of. . . . The greater part of the wrecked material has been sold and has been taken away, much of it going by railroad cars to various destinations. A lot of the material has been purchased by our home people. A large quantity of the 4400 cords of wood have not been disposed of. J. Herman Bream became the purchaser of this wood and sold 600 cords at public sale last Saturday.

Officially, Camp Colt was no more, but GNMP would bear its scars for years to come.

While Gettysburg and the rest of the nation adjusted slowly to the postwar changes in American life, President Woodrow Wilson sailed to Europe in an effort to change the world community through implementation of the Fourteen Points. On Saturday, December 21, Wilson's Gettysburg mouthpiece, the weekly *Compiler*, announced to its readers, "PRESIDENT IS IN FRANCE: HE PLEASES ALL ALLIES WITH HIS FIRST SPEECH." After two separate trips to Europe to attend the peace negotiations, Wilson and the Allied nations eventually hammered out a series of treaties, the most important being the Treaty of Versailles. It included a provision for collective security, the League of Nations. Wilson, however, could not sell the treaty to the Republican-controlled Senate. Specifically, the upper house took issue with Article 10 of the League of Nations Covenant, which obligated the United States to go to the defense of other members of the League who might be faced with foreign aggression. A stance such as this would fly in the face of the nation's longstanding diplomatic principle of "no entangling alliances" and took away from Congress its prerogative to declare war. The *Compiler* stood behind its president, and in a headline on the front page of its August 29 edition proclaimed: "RATIFY TREATY OF PEACE. THE COUNTRY NEEDS AN END OF WAR CONDITIONS. People and Business Suffer While Senators Talk—Let the Talk End and Treaty Be Adopted." Unfortunately for the *Compiler's* editor, both of Pennsylvania's senators were members of the Republican Party. Wilson would not back down, and neither would the Senate. Thus, the United States never ratified the Treaty of Versailles, nor did it become a League member.[57] The Treaty of Versailles's harsh terms would ensure that the Germans would pay for the costs of the war, to the point of bankruptcy and starvation. When an Austrian-born corporal who had served in the German army and was wounded and gassed in Flanders began to give speeches, disgruntled German citizens listened. Within twenty years, that corporal had risen to supreme leader of the Third Reich, and the World War, part 2, would begin. But no one would have believed such a prophecy in 1919.

Remarkably, a Gettysburg sailor was a crew member of the vessel that carried President Wilson to and from Europe on his two voyages to attend the peace negotiations. The chief executive traveled on a former German liner that had been seized by the then-neutral U.S. government early in the world conflict. The vessel, whose German builders had, ironically, named it the *George Washington,* was pressed into service as a U.S. Navy ship when the United States declared war.[58] Quartermaster's Mate Thomas M. Turner enlisted in the navy on November 11, 1917, exactly one year before the armistice. According to a short blurb in the *Harrisburg Telegraph* that appeared on August 9, 1919, "the young seaman has been in the service for about two years, most of that time as a member of the crew of the George Washington, and was on that boat when President Wilson made both of his trips to France. He has crossed the ocean fourteen times."[59] Turner was home on thirty days' furlough in August, allowing him, coincidentally, to participate in Gettysburg's official salute to its World War veterans.

Soon after Camp Colt closed, Gettysburg and the rest of Adams County formally welcomed their sons and daughters home from the war, on Monday, September 1. Preparations for the celebration had begun two months earlier, when a special meeting of representatives from several Adams County camps of the Patriotic Order of the Sons of America met to begin the initial planning for the event. Those in attendance wanted to make this a countywide event, with representation on the planning committees not limited only to the organization's members.[60] A few days later, members of the new American Legion post convinced the organizers to limit the celebration to a grand, one-day affair.

Several months after the armistice, a group of socially and politically connected officers and enlisted men met in Paris on March 15–17, 1919, to form a patriotic and service organization that soon became known as the American

Military display and local veterans on the southeast corner of the Gettysburg square, September 1, 1919 (Adams County Historical Society)

Legion.[61] A few months later, Gettysburg World War veterans organized their own post which eventually would bear the numerical designation of Post 202. The July 25 *Times* reported that the first meeting had been held the night before. According to its front-page story, "An organization which bids fair to become a great power in this community was enthusiastically formed. . . . [A]nd after the adjournment of the meeting the thirty-seven men signed their names to the roll and paid both a regular fee of fifty cents and a voluntary contribution of any amount they chose." A temporary slate of officers was elected, and those present decided that the new post would enthusiastically support the welcome-home celebration, but that it should be limited to only one day. "Regret was expressed that none of the colored boys who fought with the Buffalo Division [Ninety-Second] and other outfits were present as they will be welcomed into the American Legion." Considering that Gettysburg had segregated social organizations and schools, this statement was quite remarkable. Later that year, the members of the new post voted to name it the Albert J. Lentz Post, in memory of the first Gettysburg man killed in action.[62] Before 1919 came to a close, veterans had organized two more American Legion posts, in New Oxford and Arendtsville.[63]

Finally, the big day of celebration and remembrance arrived. On September 1, the *Times* sported a banner across its front page declaring, "ADAMS COUNTY

WELCOMES HER HEROES." The *Compiler*'s headline for its September 6 edition proclaimed September 1 the "Greatest Day Locally When Adams County World War Heroes Were Honored." (This was a bit of an exaggeration, considering that Gettysburg witnessed one of the most important speeches in all of American history and only six years earlier had welcomed Union and Confederate veterans to the Peace Jubilee.) Along with nine marching bands, veterans from the Civil War, Spanish-American War and the World War marched or rode in automobiles, to the thrill of hundreds of spectators lining the streets of the county seat. The keynote speaker on September 1 was Congressman J. Hampton Moore (R) of Philadelphia, who declared, "Gettysburg and Adams County are used to big events and the manner in which you are to-day paying tribute to your returned heroes is highly creditable. You are paying tribute not only to those who made the supreme sacrifice but to those who returned."

Then, Moore reflected on the great fiftieth anniversary of the Battle of Gettysburg, when "we witnessed a reunion of hearts that had been taught to hate, and of hands that had been taught to fight." His remarks mirrored Wilson's 1913 Gettysburg speech, emphasizing reconciliation rather than actual history. However, the rest of Moore's oration was anti-Wilsonian and focused on the postwar economic problems facing Americans, particularly the high cost of living: "You come home to find you must contribute in taxes and in meeting the highest cost of living known to civilized man. . . . Our common aim should be to hold to our nation's traditions and get down to a peace basis speedily in order that you who fought our battles may have a square deal in readjustment." It was a page out of the Republican Party's playbook. Despite Moore's partisan speech, the day was considered a terrific success.

The summer of 1919 also was the first tourist season in Gettysburg since the armistice. On August 20, the *Harrisburg Telegraph* announced, "This summer, now almost gone, has been the poorest that Gettysburg, as a tourist center, has had for a number of years." Merchants believed that "while a large number of tourists have visited the town and battlefield, most of them . . . take only an hour or two to visit the places of historic interest . . . and then rush off to some other locality." The businessmen hoped that the following year would bring better times, especially since improvements to the Lincoln Highway would be completed. The decline in the tourist trade, however, was tied to several short-term problems rooted in the postwar economy, not to mention that remnants of Camp Colt still were scattered across the park.

Following the conflict, the United States changed significantly as it adapted from its wartime state, which included witnessing the greatest levels of economic deflation in U.S. history, lasting from the end of the war through 1920. The people of Adams County and the rest of the United States already had experienced other postwar changes, including the lifting of food and fuel restrictions, but Liberty bonds and war stamps continued to be sold in the county through mid-1919. With the tremendous flood of returning doughboys, with 1.6 million veterans joining the labor force, unemployment spiked.[64] In Adams County, however, with its economy based in agriculture and tourism, employment for the returning veterans was not a major problem, especially if tourism picked up. Even those who had been disabled during service were given opportunities for vocational rehabilitation at the expense of the federal government. A vocational advisor named Ulysses Simpson Grant Scull came to Gettysburg on April 30, 1919, to discuss the benefits of the government program. The Gettysburg Chapter of the Red Cross hosted the meeting and urged "every disabled soldier, sailor and marine in the county . . . to meet Mr. Scull . . . as he will be able to give them complete information on the subject."[65]

Another major postwar change, though only tangentially related to the conflict, was the national prohibition of the sale, importation, domestic production, and transportation of alcoholic beverages, effective with the ratification of the Eighteenth Amendment on January 6, 1919, and enforced by the Volstead Act (passed over Wilson's veto) beginning January 7, 1920.[66] With the amendment's enactment, church bells rang all across Adams County to celebrate the news, but hotel operators and saloon owners obviously were not happy.[67] While the state legislatures were arguing the ratification process in 1918, Congress passed the Wartime Prohibition Act on November 18, despite that the war had ended seven days earlier. This legislation banned the sale of alcoholic beverages having an alcohol content greater than 2.75 percent. In the summer of 1919, Sgt. 1st Class Edgar P. Hamilton, a Gettysburg resident stationed on another national military park–turned–military post, Fort Oglethorpe, Georgia, on the Chickamauga Battlefield, wrote a long, rambling yet scathing letter to the *Gettysburg Times,* in which he criticized the ladies of the Adams County Anti-Saloon League and Women's Christian Temperance Union for their support of the prohibition: "What is the meaning of wartime prohibition now that peace has been signed? . . . It was the young American manhood who faced . . . the German army that has made this nation a fit place to live in and entitled to a voice in its affairs, not the Anti-Saloon League." His rant continued for two long newspaper columns, but he correctly predicted that legal prohibition would not stop people from attaining and consuming alcohol.[68] Nonetheless, doughboys coming home from the war would have to celebrate their return to civilian life without *legally* downing a few cold beers.

As Gettysburg and Adams County slowly returned to normal, sans beer and liquor, the time also had come to return GNMP to its ante-war state, to persuade tourists to visit this important American shrine. In its 1919 annual report, the Gettysburg National Park Commission explained that "many small parts of the gun carriages were unscrewed and carried away and have to be constantly renewed. . . . [and] chipping from the granite markers and memorials has been reported." Though not pointing a finger directly at the soldiers who occupied the park from 1917–18, it is fairly obvious that the doughboys were the culprits, undoubtedly wanting to bring home souvenirs of the famous battlefield. The soldiers also damaged some of the concrete work in the park, mostly from reckless driving. The Emmitsburg Road bisecting the camp had been "destroyed by the heavy United States trucks." While Camp Colt still was in use, Eisenhower had agreed to work with the commission to rebuild about a mile of the road, of which its reconstruction "went on until the armistice was signed." With the departure of most of the camp's soldiers in November 1918, the commission "was obliged to hire trucks and employ labor to finish the work. . . . [for] a total cost of $7,372.57 that had to be paid . . . to rebuild the 1 mile of piking."[69]

By the time the next annual report was filed, in July 1920, much work still was required to return the battlefield to its pre-1917 state. The park commissioners explained, "All of the [military] equipment has been removed, but we regret to report nothing has been done along the line of restoration of this most interesting part of the field [between Seminary and Cemetery Ridges]. A large area remains covered with the debris of the camp; several miles of tarvia-covered roads and deep drains running in all directions mar the different areas of the battlefield."[70] The report did not even mention that the effects of the road grading and site preparation, as well as the landscape restoration, undoubtedly would change the topography of the battlefield, especially the area over which Pickett's Charge had occurred. The concrete swimming pool that had been built near the High Water Mark also required demolition, removal, and site restoration.[71] Colonel Emmor Cope's notes to the annual report indicated that an enormous amount of labor still was necessary to return the landscape to its prewar condition. According to his estimates, at least 1,428 cubic yards of refuse needed "to be removed to clear the [camp site's] areas from waste and make fills," while an additional 3,979 cubic yards of earth had to be moved to level drains, ditches and culverts, as well as the razing of temporary roads that crisscrossed the area. He made special mention that "there are about 200 ft. of paved road on . . . [one of the tracts] that must be plowed up / stone removed and leveled, [as] no estimate can be correctly made before the surface covering of tarvia and cinders is removed."

On the historic Trostle Farm, which the heroic stand of the 9th Massachusetts Battery on July 2, 1863, made famous, Cope calculated that 1,103 cubic yards of fill ground would be needed "to restore land used for Trenches, Machine-Gun Pits, and Antiseptic Tanks for the disposal of Sewage from the U.S. Army Camp from July 1, 1917 to October 31, 1919." On the Codori Farm, where George Pickett on July 3, 1863, watched from its homestead his division's immortal charge, Cope believed that nearly $1,400 worth of post-and-rail fencing, gates, walls, concrete culvert, and wire fencing had been destroyed and needed replacement. In addition to this damage, "much waste material such as wire, broken boards, wooden foundation blocks, etc., is scattered promiscuously over the different areas; this cannot be correctly estimated but must be removed." Cope determined that even when all of the restoration work was completed, "the physical conditions of the different areas will be generally restored, but the mechanical conditions of the soil will require years of careful cultivation."[72]

In early April, about the time that the 1920 annual report was being prepared, Mr. Robert Parker, an emissary from the War Department, met with Colonel Cope, as Colonel Nicholson was not in town. On inspecting the park and returning to Washington, he wrote to Nicholson to express his disappointment in not being able to meet with him. Then Parker broached the matter of the park's ongoing restoration. "I was shown the camp sites and damage done by the occupation. After seeing the destruction by the military at Chickamauga, your damages appear to be very slight," he explained. Nonetheless, it was his belief that using these parks for military purposes "is all wrong as these great national memorials should be preserved. . . . My position in this matter is a bit difficult as the military interests run counter to the interests of the Park." Despite his objections and his recommendations for fixing the problem to prevent further damage during any future wars, Parker asked Nicholson to "not involve me in any way . . . while my convictions in this matter are pronounced, there enters into my action a consideration of loyalty [to the War Department]. I should not like to be put in the position of violating that loyalty."[73] As it turned out, GNMP would see very limited military activity in the next war. Chickamauga, however, would not be so lucky.[74]

Not long after the 1920 annual report was submitted to the War Department, the Nineteenth Amendment finally was ratified by a two-thirds' majority, giving women across the country the right to vote. The *Gettysburg Compiler*, a longtime advocate for women's suffrage, proclaimed in a front-page headline in its August 21 edition, "AMERICAN WOMEN WIN THE RIGHT OF SUFFRAGE IN THIS DEMOCRACY." The article spelled out the text of the amendment and then listed the thirty-six states in the order they ratified it. (Pennsylvania was the seventh.) Then the story's writer boasted, "The Compiler has always stood for equal suffrage and it did not take any vision to see that it was bound to come. . . . County officials will leave nothing undone to have the women qualify so they can vote in the upcoming election this fall." The *Times* reported the news in far less dramatic fashion and in its August 19 edition even expressed the opinion that "in view of the short time until the November election, this is a gigantic task and will be difficult to perform." If the *Compiler*'s Democratic editors believed women's suffrage would give their candidates an edge in the 1920 elections, they would be sorely disappointed.

By that time, Woodrow Wilson was an invalid, run down by ill health and heartbreak over the United States' failure to ratify the Treaty of Versailles and thus giving up its seat in the League of Nations. Simply put, Americans were tired of Wilson and his party. The Democratic candidate and his running mate, Governor James Cox of Ohio and Assistant Secretary of the Navy Franklin D. Roosevelt, were doomed from the start. Presidential historian William E. Leuchtenburg has written that "the 1920 election was a national disavowal of the ideas for which Wilson had stood, and Cox lost in the process." Leuchtenburg believed that Cox's opponent, Republican Warren G. Harding, "capitalized on an immense feeling of nostalgia for the years before the war." During the campaign, Harding proclaimed to a Boston crowd that the country yearned for a return to *normalcy,* "thereby coining a word and defining a mood. The country, bemused by Wilsonian rhetoric, wanted to return to a reality which was concrete, which had the hardness and durability of matter."[75]

Harding won the national election by a landslide, garnering 404 electoral votes to Cox's 127. In Adams County, all of the GOP candidates scored major victories with wide margins, from Harding to Congressman Edward S. Brooks to the Republican candidates for the state legislature and senate. The *Compiler*'s editors shrugged off the Republicans' victory by surmising that the "total vote in Adams County shows that a very large number did not go to the polls." As for female voters, the *Compiler* guessed that only about a third of them—some 2,220 out of 6,000 registered—actually voted. What was not known was how many of those women who voted cast their ballots for Republicans. Of the 9,173 registered voters who went to the polls, only 3,852 voted for Cox; obviously, more women voted for Harding than the *Compiler*'s editors wanted to believe.[76]

As 1921 began, the people of Gettysburg and the surrounding towns were optimistic for better times ahead. In its New Year's Day edition, the *Times* described the previous night's celebrations as it had done in years past, and concluded, "Among the businessmen there seemed to be little sorrow as 1920 passed, for the closing months brought with them marked degrees of depressions and unsettled financial conditions. The average wage earner looked forward to 1921 with hopes for better times and a continuation of the downward trend of the high cost of living."

The new year also saw the burial of the Unknown Soldier in Arlington National Cemetery. On November 11, 1921, his remains were laid to rest amid great ceremony rivaling any funeral for a president, general, or war hero. The procession to the tomb included Harding, his cabinet, members of the Supreme Court and Congress, foreign representatives, official mourners invited as guests of the War Department, as well as former president Woodrow Wilson and members of his administration.[77] The pall bearers included Medal of Honor winners Maj. Charles Whittlesey, commander of the Lost Battalion; Sgt. Alvin York, the pacifist turned German killer; and Capt. Samuel Woodfill, the hero of Cunel, who four years earlier had trained on GNMP. When Gen. John J. Pershing, who had overall responsibility for the ceremony, was given a list of the proposed military pall bearers, he came across Woodfill's name and exclaimed, "Why, I've already selected that man as the outstanding soldier of the A.E.F."[78] Harding had called for a national observance of two minutes of silence on November 11, and Gettysburg honored it with a gathering of citizens and veterans in the town square beginning at 11:45 A.M. The *Times* described the gravity of the ceremony, one that undoubtedly echoed the somberness of November 19, 1863:

> A silent and solemn assembly in the town Centre Square bowed their heads today as the clock in the courthouse tower tolled twelve, a simple token of the homage they would pay to America's unknown dead in the World War. . . . A few short minutes after the conclusion of the prayer, during which time the church bells of the town pealed forth in solemn measure a dirge indicative of a funeral service, the town clock boomed forth the hour of high noon. At the first stroke every hat was removed and every head bowed for [the] two minutes nation-wide pause.

Standing closest to the flagpole that marked the center of the circular, grassy plot in the middle of the town square "were many members of the Albert Lentz post of the American Legion." Arrayed behind the legionnaires were the town's school students, followed by ordinary citizens, as if forming layers of a concentric circle, "who wished to pay a lasting tribute to the unknown soldier." Not surprisingly in a town whose past seemed more important than its present or future, the American Legion was not the custodian of the ceremony. Instead, the Daniel Skelly Post of the Grand Army of the Republic took center stage, and its Civil War–veteran commander was the presiding officer.

For the GNMP commissioners and the businessmen and -women who profited from heritage tourism—as well as the average wage earners who worked for them—the return to "normalcy" in 1921 was dependent on the park's ongoing restoration to its prewar condition. When the commission released its 1921 report, the environmental impact of the two military camps still had not been mitigated: "No action as yet has been taken on the detailed estimate of damage done and work needed to restore this land to its former condition. . . . No restoration work was done by the purchasers of the camp equipment after its removal." The tenant farmers who rented government land nonetheless were taking matters into their own hands. "The work needed on the Codori Farm has been taken up by the tenant and a large part of this is again under cultivation and planted in the usual farm crops. This was done voluntarily by the tenant, but it will take years to restore it to its original condition, or as it was when taken over for a United States camp."[79] The exact number of years of farming, active restoration, natural erosion, and routine park maintenance actually required to return GNMP to its prewar state probably will never be known, since the annual reports for the years 1922 through 1926 have not been found.[80] The 1927 annual report and those that followed make no mention of any further restoration of the landscape, indicating that it had been returned to some semblance of its pre-1917 state. However, in 1922, more military occupation came to GNMP, this time for only a few weeks, when 5,500 marines from the Quantico, Virginia, Marine Corps Base hiked there for maneuvers, training, and military demonstrations. The event was a minor ecological setback for the old battlefield, but it proved to be a windfall to the local economy.

Led by the legendary leatherneck Maj. Gen. Smedley Butler—who had been awarded two Medals of Honor for separate military actions—the marines spent ten days in the park, with their cantonment dubbed "Camp Harding," in honor of their commander in chief. The president had agreed to come up to Gettysburg with his wife to watch the military demonstrations, which included a reenactment of Pickett's Charge as well as a modern (1922) version of the same event, this time using machine guns, tanks, indirect artillery fire, combat aircraft, observation balloons, antiaircraft artillery, and searchlights, as well as modern communication systems, including wireless radios. The Marine Corps encampment, straddling the eastern slope of Seminary Ridge in front of the Virginia Memorial, included a small airfield, two large bath/latrine facilities (with three hundred showers apiece) and field kitchens. Temporary water and sewer lines were connected to the town's public systems. Photographs of the camp indicate that canvas-enclosed urination soakage pits were dug at the end of company streets. Likewise, lines for electricity and telephones were run from the town to the camp.[81] The marines' brief occupation of the battlefield likely did not cause too many environmental complications; the encampment and maneuvers, however, were not without their own problems.

Advance parties began arriving in late June to set up the camp and airfield. Tragedy struck on June 26 when a DH-4 biplane piloted by Capt. George W. Hamilton went into a tailspin as it was trying to land on the temporary airfield and nosedived into the ground near Steinwehr Avenue. Hamilton was killed instantly, and his mechanic, Gunnery Sergeant George Martin, flying in the rear seat, died at Warner Hospital. The *Times* recognized Hamilton's wartime service; he won the Distinguished Service Cross for heroism as an infantry officer at Belleau Wood as well as several awards for gallantry in other 1918 campaigns. He and Martin were flying with two other Marine Corps aircraft that had landed safely on the designated airfield, but a short time later another plane developed mechanical problems and was forced to ditch on the famous "Wheatfield."[82] Luckily, the aircraft missed colliding with the monuments and markers placed upon the once-bloody meadow.

To the joy of area merchants, restauranteurs and hotelkeepers, thousands of visitors descended on Gettysburg to watch the Marine Corps maneuvers. And Gettysburg's new American Legion Post 202 likewise was poised to benefit from the throngs of tourists and marines, since, by happenstance, it was sponsoring a carnival on Steinwehr Avenue, close to the boundary of GNMP and the marine camp. The legion post made sure that a provision was included in the carnival company's contract that gave "the Legion the authority to close any objectionable show and stop all gambling devices."[83]

A unique aspect of Camp Harding was the erection, near the North Carolina Memorial, of an elaborate tent complex, dubbed the Gettysburg White House, for President and Mrs. Harding and some of their entourage. It was replete with wooden floors, separate offices and living areas, electric lighting, hot and cold water, and flush toilets. The Hardings spent Saturday night, July 1, in the canvas White House, having watched earlier in the day, from the steel observation tower on Cemetery Hill, the marines' historical reenactment of Pickett's Charge. The First Couple was joined atop the tower by General Pershing; the governors of Pennsylvania and Virginia; and other dignitaries, including Acting Secretary of the Navy Theodore Roosevelt Jr., son of the twenty-sixth president and himself a World War veteran and one of the founders of the American Legion. According to the July 3 lead story in the *Times*, "Under smiling skies and with a pleasant breeze after a thunderous storm and oppressive heat earlier in the afternoon, Pickett's charge was reenacted by the Fifth and Sixth regiments of the United States Marine Corps on Saturday afternoon before the

General Smedley Butler, President Harding, General Pershing, and General John Lejeune at the 1922 USMC encampment and reenactment (Library of Congress)

distinguished visitors at Camp Harding." The heavy rains caused no problems for President Harding and the First Lady during their overnight stay in the opulent canvas quarters, but this was not the case for the marines. "Many of the tents were deluged," noted a *Times* reporter, "forcing many of the men to spend the 'night out' while others were made quite uncomfortable by the water that flowed through their tents and soaked their blankets and clothing."

On Tuesday, July 4, the marines staged their 1922 version of Pickett's Charge, using modern weapons technology and updated tactics, to the thrill of "the largest automobile crowd that ever gathered on the battlefield of Gettysburg." A *Times* writer speculated that "the immense throng which lined the avenues and fields from the National Cemetery to the Round Tops was estimated by some as 50,000 coming here in 15,000 automobiles," making the size of the battlefield assembly second only to the 1913 Peace Jubilee. One civilian became a casualty during the demonstration, when he foolishly picked up a military flare near Camp Harding and lit it with a match. Before he could throw it, the incendiary device exploded, causing severe burns to his left hand and face. The careless thrill seeker was rushed to Warner Hospital for treatment.[84] An interesting sidebar to the Marine Corps' occupation of GNMP is that the same social problems that had arisen between the soldiers and the townsfolk in 1917–18 manifested again in the summer of 1922: bootlegging, prostitution, and ill feelings between the local citizens and the servicemen. The State Police arrested three local bootleggers, two white and one black, for selling "moonshine liquor," as the *Times* reported it. The authorities locked the three men in jail, but the white culprits soon were set free on $1,000 bail, while the black suspect, unable to post that amount of money, remained incarcerated. The state troopers admitted that the wrongdoers merely were low-level agents for a larger bootlegging operation and that the police really "were seeking the men higher up." In addition to tracking down violators of the Volstead Act, the lawmen also shut down several rigged games of chance at the carnival and arrested five employees of the so-called Hawaiian Show. According to a story in the July 4 *Times:* "The indecent remarks of the girls connected with the show while performing for the crowd outside their tent, caused the police to place the 'Hawaiians' under ban. Inside, the show was declared not fit for women and children to attend. . . . All [of those taken into custody] protested but were committed to the county jail without right of Habeas Corpus, under the Pennsylvania State Health Act, to await the outcome of blood tests, which will be sent to Baltimore for analysis." None of the arrested parties actually were Hawaiian. The women soon were released, after their blood tests proved negative for venereal disease, but the male carnival worker "was found suffering from a virulent venereal disease and will be sent to a State hospital until his condition improves." By the same token, two prostitutes were arrested on July 4 for soliciting marines in the town square. "State Police are continuing their drive against alleged immoral women, who have followed the marines to their encampment here," reported the *Times.* The unfortunate ladies, both from Washington, D.C., likewise were imprisoned in the Adams County jail, and blood samples drawn to determine if they were carriers of venereal disease.[85]

The bad relations between the marines and Adams County residents also were reminiscent of the social discord between the soldiers and locals during the war, most especially with the tankers in 1918. A scathing letter to the *Gettysburg Times* by an anonymous, self-appointed Marine Corps spokesman eviscerated Gettysburgians on a number of counts of "snobbishness, over charging and petty trickery." The full content of the long, acrimonious epistle, published in the July 7 *Times* in its entirety, was fraught with bitterness toward the civilians and echoed the complaints of Camp Colt's soldiers four years earlier. "The Marines have left Gettysburg with an impression of the town that can best be described as a black eye to the battlefield city. Most of them said they would never return and a great many, in their letters to their folks, frankly stated what they thought of Gettysburg," wrote the disgruntled leatherneck. He cited specific examples of the town's collective slights toward his fellow marines, despite that the U.S. Marine Corps brought the town tens of thousands of spectators (with their tourist dollars) and national notoriety, the biggest one-shot boost to the economy since 1913. In return, the letter writer concluded, "it allowed itself to get in wrong with the Marines for the sake of a few pennies and an inexcusable snobbishness. . . . and unless a remedy is found, it shall live as long as the monuments dot the battlefield." The marines thus departed southcentral Pennsylvania with a figurative bad taste in their mouths, but they unintentionally left behind a national shrine with more scars to the landscape.

Constant downpours during the marines' encampment and maneuvers, coupled with the treading of thousands of men, horses, wheeled vehicles and tanks churned the pastoral fields between Seminary and Cemetery Ridges into a mucky quagmire. "The sea of mud and water which covered the campsite, has been changed by the hot rays to a thick, sticky mass which made it difficult to move the trucks, trailers and artillery from the camp to the hard roadbed of West Confederate avenue," a *Times* reporter observed. Tracked vehicles that had been employed to tow the artillery were put to work as recovery vehicles to extricate heavy trucks and trailers that "sank to their axles in the mud and were unable to move under their own power." Some of the trucks had become so mired that it took two tractors to pull one wheeled vehicle from the brown goop. Marine detachments remained in Gettysburg for several days to collect trash, and "fires were started in all sections of the camp site, where the refuse left behind was burned." The journalist noted that "thick smoke enveloped that section of the battlefield."[86] Once the electrical and telephone lines and the temporary water and sewer lines were removed, Mother Nature, normal farming practices, and routine park maintenance eventually erased the vestiges of Camp Harding, just as they slowly had returned Camp Colt to a semblance of its prewar appearance.

On March 8, a few months before Major General Butler and his men arrived in Gettysburg, Colonel Nicholson, the first and *only* chairman of the Gettysburg National Park Commission, passed away, at the age of seventy-nine.[87] His death marked the end of the commission's management of GNMP. Emmor B. Cope, age eighty, the original and still serving park engineer, replaced Nicholson and assumed a new title, that of superintendent. In 1925, at the request of the War Department, the eighty-three-year-old Cope prepared a study to outline the condition of GNMP. He mentioned nothing about any lingering environmental problems resulting from the two U.S. Army camps or the USMC maneuvers (although aerial photos taken in 1924 showed some subtle scars to the land, probably visible only from the air). He did note that tourism was booming, estimating that in 1925 alone the park welcomed more than 1 million visitors, who arrived either by the two passenger railroads servicing Gettysburg or by automobile.

Cope died on May 27, 1927, while still serving as the park superintendent. The official administrative history of GNMP states that "the death of Cope meant that park administration passed from last survivor of the generation of early War Department appointees who had dedicated their lives to the preservation and development of the battlefield." His passing also signaled the end of an era, portending the conclusion of the army's administration of the park. In fact, within six years of Cope's demise, the War Department no longer would be responsible for the management of any of its national parks. In 1933, those sites, GNMP included, would come under the aegis of the National Park Service.[88]

Between the end of the World War and 1933, Gettysburg and the rest of the nation had experienced many changes, including prohibition, universal suffrage, a stock market crash, the ensuing depression, and then, with the Twenty-First Amendment, a repeal of prohibition. During that same timeframe, some of the local soldiers who had perished during the war and whose remains had lain in foreign fields were brought home at the requests of their next of kin. Albert Lentz, the first Gettysburg man killed in action, was one of several who were exhumed, shipped home at government expense, and buried either in a private or national cemetery. (Lentz lies in Gettysburg National Cemetery, section 8, plot 3.) Others, whose families had decided not to repatriate their loved ones' remains, were reburied in one of eight American cemeteries laid out and administered by the new American Battle Monuments Commission, headed by none other than John J. Pershing himself. Of the 116,516 Americans who lost their lives during the war, 30,922 are interred in overseas American military cemeteries, and 4,452 are remembered on the Tablets of the Missing, either as missing in action or buried at sea.[89] The majority of the dead—about 70 percent—were brought back to the United States.

On several occasions during the Roaring Twenties, when an unchecked American economy raced toward self-destruction, legislation was introduced in Congress to authorize pilgrimages to American cemeteries in Europe for mothers and widows of fallen soldiers. In early 1929, the law finally passed, and President Calvin Coolidge signed it just before he left office. In the early 1930s, despite the Great Depression's ravages to the U.S. Treasury, both Herbert Hoover and Franklin Roosevelt authorized the pilgrimages for the Gold Star mothers and widows.[90]

The first Adams County Gold Star mother to make the go pilgrimage was Mrs. Ida F. Taylor of Bendersville, whose son Harry was killed near Montfaucon during the Argonne fight. She sailed on the SS *Republic* on July 26, 1930, to visit her boy's grave in the Meuse-Argonne American Cemetery, Romagne, France, where he rests in plot H, row 9, grave 32. A few days later, on July 30, the wife and mother of Chaplain Capt. Albert D. Bell departed for France aboard the SS

America. Their trip would take them to the Saint-Mihiel American Cemetery, Thiaucourt, France. Bell, who had died from the Spanish flu in a base hospital in the city of Toul, is buried in plot D, row 27, grave 13.[91] Mrs. Mary A. Leese of New Oxford, whose son, Gunner's Mate First Class Royal Leese, was the first Adams County man to perish in the line of duty, also made the voyage. Although Leese was lost at sea, his name was inscribed on the Tablets of the Missing in the Brookwood American Cemetery, near London, England.[92]

Mrs. Grace Rider of East Berlin likewise made the trip to see the grave of her son, Francis, who was buried near the village of Fère-en-Tardenois, France, in Oise-Aisne American Cemetery, plot B, row 9, grave 13. Afterward, she wrote a descriptive memoir of her journey, which was published in the *Gettysburg Times.* Surprisingly, she said little about the visit to her son's final resting place, noting only that she placed a wreath, supplied by the Veterans of Foreign Wars, on the grave. Her vivid description of the battle areas that she and her group then visited apparently made quite a somber impact, even though fourteen years had passed since the last guns had fired:

> The country still bears the evidence of the terrific fighting that took place here; small villages and houses being entirely shot to pieces, great holes in the ground made by the shells, devastated fields and woodlands, all remaining as mute history of war and courage, the like of which history does not record. We were watched most carefully by our guides in the traversing of the ground, being allowed to follow only paths, and here and there a beaten road, for fear that we should set off . . . [unexploded ordnance] known to still remain which if disturbed would spread death and destruction for quite a distance around it. The reason that the country and land has been left as it was after the war, we were told, was the fear of the unexploded . . . [ordnance] known to exist throughout the section. We were in cemeteries and saw battlefields from Tuesday to Saturday. We observed guns, bayonets, sabers, and war material galore. One gruesome exhibition was a German helmet in which still was wedged the skull or decomposed head of the German soldier who wore it. Not pleasant to look upon, but evidently prized by the French, who are wasting no sympathies on their old enemies, the Germans.

What went through her mind—and those of the other mothers and widows in her group, as they traveled through what the French called "La Zone Rouge"—is not known, but they undoubtedly shuddered when they realized that their own sons or husbands had perished in such a hellish scenario. Although Mrs. Rider enjoyed her month-long excursion, the reality of the trip hit home as her entourage sailed from France. At that moment, she realized that she was leaving behind the son she "had seen grown to manhood, who had lost his life in that ruthless war." Concluding, she wrote, "Many were the tears, and many a heart wrenched. More than one mother gave a longing look backward as she departed. But inexorable fate had ruled it so, and there was nothing to do but to mourn. After all, the greatest sufferers of war are the mothers who bear their burden and hide their grief as best as they can."[93] Grace Rider and her fellow mourners came back to an entire country of sufferers as Americans grappled with the problems brought on by the Great Depression—and Gettysburg suffered along with the rest of the commonwealth and the nation.

Veterans of the World War were suffering, too. In the early 1920s, the American Legion had successfully lobbied Congress to draft legislation for what officially was called the World War Adjusted Compensation Act, or Bonus Bill, as it popularly was known. Passed despite President Coolidge's veto, the new law created a veterans' benefit plan as additional compensation for their military service, which many veterans perceived as part of the compact between them and the federal government when they enlisted or were drafted. It credited veterans with adjusted service certificates—which the veterans called "bonuses"—since they were viewed as supplements to the meager pay the soldiers, sailors, and marines had received during their wartime service. The certificates earned interest and were payable in 1945. At the beginning of the Great Depression, veterans began clamoring for immediate cash payments of their bonuses, to help offset their living expenses. When traditional methods of petitioning and lobbying failed, thousands of disgruntled veterans traveled to the nation's capital in the summer of 1932 in what became known as the Bonus March.[94]

The *Gettysburg Times* printed photographs of the protestors on the first page of the May 31 and June 1 editions, but no stories about the Bonus March. A week later, the *Times* ran a story under the headline, "Local Legionnaires Do Not Favor Bonus Payment." The article explained that "the Lentz post members are opposed to a cash settlement of bonus claims which some members in Washington are now demanding." It also noted that "the post itself has refused to give any assistance to their former comrades-in-arms" and turned away two bonus marchers who stopped at its Baltimore Street post headquarters to ask for food.[95] The next day, the *Times* was forced to make a correction. In a statement from William Eckenrode, the Gettysburg post commander, the post's official position was clarified: "The Albert J. Lentz Post is in favor of a cash settlement of the bonus certificates, but is unalterably opposed to the manner in which some veterans are attempting to force their demands on congress. . . . The local post will help any legion buddies in the 'bonus army' now in Washington, but others will receive scant attention from the Albert J. Lentz post."[96] In essence, the collective stance of the post's members was that they agreed with the "ends" of the protestors, but not their "means."

Ninety miles south of Gettysburg, some seventeen thousand veterans, as well as family members and other supporters (totaling approximately forty-three thousand people), all members of the "Bonus Expeditionary Forces," or "BEF," were camped in a shantytown that they called "Hooverville," a slap at the thirty-first president, who believed that the misery of the Depression could be cured with little government intervention and a large dose of voluntarism. When their lobbying and peaceful protesting failed to move Congress to pass legislation that would give them what they wanted, authorities in Washington expected veterans to admit defeat and return home. When they did not, police intervened and all hell broke loose. Finally, Army Chief of Staff Douglas MacArthur, one of the wartime heroes of the Forty-Second Division, ordered the army to disperse the protesters and raze Hooverville.[97] MacArthur's military secretary at that time was the former Camp Colt commander, Maj. Dwight Eisenhower. Ike futilely advised his boss not to lead the military force that would disband the protestors. Decades later, he candidly told historian Stephen Ambrose, one of his early biographers, "I told that dumb son-of-a-bitch that he had no business going down there. I told him it was no place for the Chief of Staff." Nonetheless, MacArthur led his troops forward, Hooverville was burned to the ground, and the veterans were dispersed. The Bonus March had come to an inglorious end, and Hoover and MacArthur had become two of the most despised men in America.[98]

On their way home from Washington, a group from the defeated BEF trudged into Gettysburg on the last day of July and set up a headquarters and campsite. According to the *Times*, "One-hundred and fifteen members of the defeated bonus army, evicted from Washington, D.C., this week, marched into Gettysburg shortly after noon today and set up a make-shift camp in the National Park camp grounds on the Taneytown Road, at the National cemetery. They hiked here from the Mason-Dixon line, and leaders told local members of the state police that they might camp here overnight before proceeding to Lancaster." To ensure that the group remained orderly, troopers from other areas augmented the local state police force.[99]

What had been envisioned as an overnight stopover turned into a stay of more than a month and a half. The camp itself comprised tourist cabins and a latrine facility. With more than a hundred marchers present, some slept with only blankets on the ground. Father Mark Stock of St. Francis Xavier Church offered Xavier Hall for temporary lodging, and a hundred men took him up on his kind gesture. By August 4, more than two hundred bonus marchers were in town.[100] As more veterans arrived, town officials became concerned about sanitary conditions in the camp, so the State Department of Health ordered the Adams County health officer to begin inspecting it on a daily basis. Because the disciplined veterans self-regulated the appearance and cleanliness of the camp, on his first visit the doctor found "everything in first rate condition."[101]

The camp's elected leadership had decided to stay in Gettysburg until Congress reconvened in December, and they authorized the purchase of tents to accommodate more veterans. By August 10, approximately 225 men, women and children occupied the camp.[102] A week later and with no end of the occupation in sight, the Gettysburg Chamber of Commerce petitioned the town council with a unanimously approved resolution to shut down the camp and evict its occupants, "for the protection of the health, morals and safety of this community." According to a *Times* report, the chamber's directors "explained that they have received a number of complaints many of which were that a number of men had been begging at various homes. They further stated that sufficient charity work will have to be done for Gettysburg families this winter without being burdened with additional hundreds of outsiders."[103] Although the BEF had the sympathy of most of the community, with donations of food and articles of clothing coming into the camp, the August heat and dwindling food supplies caused veterans and their families to slowly depart by their own volition. In one case, a family of five left, on August 17, because the youngest child was underfed and malnourished.[104]

On August 23, the camp commander, Eldon J. Munce, appealed to Governor Gifford Pinchot for enough trucks to transport veterans and families who desired to go home, but he received no answer.[105] The request portended the coming of the end of the camp. Then, tragedy struck when a group of drunken veterans were involved in a car accident, killing one of their number, George Bowers of Lemoyne, Pennsylvania. The *Times* reported that the "fatality occurred while Bowers and several companions were returning from a Sunday afternoon picnic, which culminated in a 'drinking orgy,' according to state police, at the picnic grounds." The state troopers arrested a dozen men in the BEF camp, threw them in jail, and interrogated them, wanting to know who was driving and who had supplied the prohibited liquor. All involved were indicted for being drunk and disorderly, and the car's driver also was charged with involuntary manslaughter and driving under the influence. At the same time, the state troopers were investigating the robbery of a local service station, believing that some of the men involved in the accident also might have robbed the station, using the stolen money to purchase the alcohol.[106] The BEF was wearing out its welcome.

On August 31, the *Times* prematurely broadcasted, "COMPLETE BREAKUP OF B.E.F. CAMP UNDERWAY; TWENTY-TWO LEAVE FOR MARYLAND TODAY." In reality, the camp population slowly was diminishing, but it would be mid-September before the last of the veterans vamoosed. On September 17, the *Times* announced "BONUS CAMP TO DISBAND TODAY." A week later, the camp's commander and last to depart, Eldon Munce, likewise left town for his Oregon home on September 25, thus ending the short, mostly uneventful, and totally fruitless occupation of Gettysburg by the Bonus Expeditionary Forces.[107] But the veterans' movement to seek their World War bonus was not a total lost cause. Four years later, Congress passed, over President Franklin Roosevelt's veto, the Adjusted Compensation Payment Act, which authorized the immediate payment of the war bonuses. In the long term, it was the efforts of the World War veterans, through the lobbying of the American Legion, that the 1944 Servicemen's Readjustment Act—the GI Bill—was made law, ensuring that the next generation of war veterans was fairly rewarded for its hard-fought service.[108]

With the departure of the bonus marchers, life once again returned to normal, which in 1932 meant more hard times. In an overwhelming electoral victory that fall, Franklin Delano Roosevelt and his Democratic Party swept the November elections. Pennsylvania was one of only six states to support Herbert Hoover, but Adams County did not join the majority of the commonwealth's counties. "Riding on the high tide of the greatest national democratic landslide in 40 years," reported the *Times*, "Adams county voters swung into the democratic column. . . . Only the state remained steadfastly republicans."[109] When he took office in March, Roosevelt had the luxury of working with a House and Senate controlled by his own party, and he immediately set in motion a number of economic and social policies and laws collectively called the New Deal. The 1930s' weakened national economy triggered a drastic reduction in the number of visitors to Gettysburg, causing a severe impact to the local economy, but federal recovery programs actually benefitted GNMP. A New Deal initiative brought the Civilian Conservation Corps (CCC) to the park in the summer of 1933 to make improvements to its infrastructure and landscape, and the Public Works Administration provided funds for conservation and historic preservation projects. Eventually, two CCC camps, staffed primarily by African Americans, were located near the battlefield. One camp was disbanded in 1937, but the other, Camp No. 2 in McMillan Woods, off of Confederate Avenue on Seminary Ridge, remained in operation until 1942.[110] About the same time, the Round Top Spur of the Gettysburg & Harrisburg Railroad was abandoned, and soon thereafter the tracks were removed and the landscape restored.[111] By then, the United States was embroiled in another global conflict, and once again the old battlefield would feel the presence of the U.S. Army. But a year before the Nazi invasion of Poland began World War II in Europe, the army would return to Gettysburg to support the last reunion of the Blue and Gray, for the battle's seventy-fifth anniversary.

Since the Park Service had taken over the administration of GNMP five years earlier, the army's responsibility during the 1938 commemoration was far less complicated than it had been in 1913. In fact, the presence of the soldiers was more theatrical than practical. According to the official report, "a large, active United States Army representation . . . would do much to indelibly impress upon the minds of all that Americanism is the only form of 'ism' patriotically sanctioned in this country."[112] During an era wracked by fears of Communism, Nazism, and Fascism, with the country still in the grips of the worst depression in its history, more than anything else, the presence of the U.S. Army at the anniversary of the battle was symbolic of a strong central government.

Infantry, artillery, cavalry, armor, and coast artillery conducted maneuvers, manned displays, and marched in the parade, to the delight of the aged veterans and hundreds of thousands of spectators. In addition, the U.S. Army Air Corps staged a flyover.[113] Construction and administration of the veterans' camp was the responsibility of the Twenty-Eighth Division, Pennsylvania National Guard. But this time, unlike the Blue and Gray reunion twenty-five years earlier, there were only a few Civil War veterans. Eighteen hundred attended, with an average age of ninety-one.[114] The torch was being passed to a newer generation of warriors.

After the United States entered World War II, in December 1941, Gettysburg was not heard from much, and it nearly slipped from public notice. Few people had time or gasoline to visit, and the army had better things about which to worry than teaching officers the problems of Lee and Meade. The Eternal Light Peace Memorial, which President Roosevelt dedicated and lighted during the 1938 anniversary, had to be extinguished during evening hours, lest it be seen by an enemy aircraft. More realistically, the natural gas it consumed needed to be conserved for the war effort.[115]

About a year and a half after the remaining CCC camp was abandoned, the army selected that site to become a subpost of Fort Ritchie, Maryland, a military-intelligence training center about a thirty-minute drive southwest of Gettysburg on the Pennsylvania-Maryland border. There, on Seminary Ridge, in Camp George H. Sharpe—named in memory of the Army of the Potomac's chief of intelligence—a group of unique soldiers would train on the old battlefield beginning in November 1943. A few would learn how to gather intelligence behind German lines, but the majority, about eight hundred men, would receive instruction in psychological warfare as well as in how to create and disseminate propaganda. Unlike the young men who had flooded Gettysburg in 1917 and '18, these soldiers were a bit older, and many were accomplished writers, journalists, radio personalities, professors, illustrators, historians, and civil servants. Some were first- or second-generation immigrants from Germany, Russia, Hungary, Austria,

Poland, Italy and the like. They were fluent in at least two languages, a few still spoke with thick foreign accents, and a good number were Jews who only a few years earlier had escaped Nazi oppression. Eventually, they would comprise four mobile radio-broadcasting companies that would deploy to Europe once the second front was opened, in the summer of 1944.[116]

The *Gettysburg Times* first acknowledged Camp Sharpe's existence in its November 11, 1943 edition—coincidentally, the twenty-fifth anniversary of Armistice Day. "The abandoned CCC camp No. 2 on the Battlefield has been converted into a small army camp. . . . Because of the restrictions of censorship and in the interest of military secrecy details of the new set-up cannot be divulged." The newspaper did, however, reveal the camp's new name.

As a result of Camp Sharpe's relatively small population of soldiers and its demographic makeup, the problems that had emerged in 1918–19 (and again in 1922) did not occur in its short year of secret military activity. Also, there was limited fraternization between the soldiers and locals—especially with the young ladies—since the troops were sworn to secrecy about the nature of their training and could not divulge any information. To ensure that liquor would not "loosen lips," only the camp's officers were allowed to patronize the local bars. Enlisted men found other off-duty pursuits, including visits to the movie theaters, the USO, the town library, restaurants, and soda fountains. Some even toured the battlefield. Sweethearts or wives who lived close enough to travel to Gettysburg usually stayed at the Gettysburg Hotel, on the town square. When June 6, 1944, arrived, the mobile radio units prepared to ship out.[117] On July 8, the *Times* predicted that the camp would be closed within a month: "Major John T. Jarecki, commander of Camp Sharpe, said that he cannot confirm or deny the statement that the army camp will be discontinued by the end of this month." Regardless, by midsummer Camp Sharpe was no more. And while another batch of soldiers had already arrived, their contact with the public would be even more limited.

On June 12, 1944, fifty German prisoners of war (POWs) arrived in Gettysburg from Fort Meade, Maryland—where so many Adams County soldiers had trained in the previous war—to begin work on a POW camp along the Emmitsburg Road at GNMP. Their new stockade was on part of the old Camp Colt and the same ground occupied by the Regulars during the seventy-fifth anniversary of the battle six years earlier.[118] While the POW stockade was being prepared for habitation, its German prisoner-builders were held in the Pennsylvania National Guard armory building, just south of the intersection of the Fairfield Road and Confederate Avenue on Seminary Ridge, while their U.S. Army guards were quartered in Gettysburg High School. (The armory was completed as a New

Deal program during the same year as the anniversary commemoration and was funded through the Public Works Administration.[119]) On the first day of summer—fifteen days after the Allies assaulted the Normandy beaches—the *Times* ran a story detailing the prison pen's progress, declaring, "The stockade surrounding the camp is nearly completed and installation of sanitary facilities is all that remains before the tents go up completing the camp."

Besides the obvious fact that the U.S. government was responsible for the land under the POW camp, the main reason for putting the prisoner stockade in Gettysburg was that Adams County was in the center of an important agricultural region, and the German prisoners were an inexpensive source of labor for its fruit- and vegetable-processing plants. Despite that it was the Adams County Canners association which had successfully petitioned the federal government to bring the POWs to Gettysburg, the local representative of the U.S. Employment Service told the *Gettysburg Times* that "at such times as men are available, due to a slack period in the canneries, they are available for farm or orchard work if certain [administrative and security] requirements can be met."[120] The half-acre tent camp sat on the southwest corner of the Emmitsburg Road and Long Lane, across the lane from the Home Sweet Home Motel, a tourist accommodation. At its peak strength, the tent camp held four hundred POWs between July and November 1944. Their guards likewise were quartered under canvas adjacent to the south side of the barbed-wire enclosed camp. (All tents, for both prisoners and guards, had wood-plank flooring that allowed the interiors to remain dry during wet weather.) Guard towers were located at each of the prison pen's four corners. In addition, latrines were built and a sewage treatment facility was constructed, which was connected to the town sewer system. The U.S. Army contingent comprised sixty enlisted men and five officers, including the camp commander, the latter billeted along with his family in the Home Sweet Home. During the winter, the prisoners and guards were quartered in the buildings of the abandoned Camp Sharpe.[121]

During the camp's existence, four different escape attempts involving seven POWs occurred; only one, however, happened while the United States and Germany still were at war. The first and only wartime escape was attempted during the night of July 3–4, 1944, when prisoners Thomas Kostaniak, aged twenty-seven, and Axel Ostermaier, twenty-two, both Wehrmacht infantry sergeants, slithered through a drainage culvert in their camp that ran under the west and east sides of the Emmitsburg Road.[122] Their escape triggered a dragnet across southcentral Pennsylvania and northcentral Maryland, with the FBI, Pennsylvania and Maryland State Police, and local police and sheriff departments involved in the manhunt. The two fugitives finally were captured on the morning of July 11, twenty-five miles to the east in York County. Neither was wearing his blue-denim prison uniform (with "PW" stenciled in white paint on the back of the shirt). Both appeared in good spirits. A local farmer who offered them food enticed them to surrender, and the Pennsylvania State Police apprehended them without incident.[123]

Three more escapes were attempted, but all took place after Germany had unconditionally surrendered; the camp had remained open after the war so the canning plant operators and area farmers and fruit growers could use the prisoner labor until the U.S. Armed Forces demobilized. The escapes were short-lived, and the prisoners were returned to the stockade. The camp finally closed when the last German prisoners departed in early April 1946. The stockade was razed and the area returned to farm land. As no semipermanent structures had been built, it did not take long for the camp's footprint to disappear.[124] By then, most of Adams County's servicemen and -women had been discharged and were coming home to resume their civilian lives, and the veterans' organizations that had been formed after World War I increased their memberships as the younger veterans joined their ranks.

And now, with memories of the Great Depression and World War II behind them, tourists returned to Gettysburg and its national military park, and they brought along the money they had saved during the war as well as their pent-up demand for goods and services. Cultural historian Jim Weeks aptly observes, "By the post–World War II era television, films, magazines, and advertising in its various mediums washed the nation in a flood of colorful images. . . . [of a] popular if distorted past honed out of Westerns, Disney films and Disney Land, neocolonial housing and furniture. . . . In a nation reinvigorated by abundance, what better way to celebrate America than visually consume the past? Americans were urged to 'see the U.S.A. in your Chevrolet.'" Indeed, with no more passenger trains servicing Gettysburg, automobile and tour bus travel were the only ways to get to, and then tour the battlefield, which meant a need for additional restaurants, service stations, and motels, as well as more museums and other tourist attractions, some located with blatant disregard to the historic view-shed.[125] Once again, the local population and its bevy of entrepreneurs could look to a brighter future while still clinging to—and capitalizing on—the events of 1863, while the wars of the twentieth century could be swept conveniently under the rug.

EPILOGUE

1954

Reunion Summer

Forty-one years after the 1913 Peace Jubilee and thirty-six years after the armistice, veterans from at least three conflicts gathered on August 23, 1954, along the Emmitsburg Road in Cumberland Township just outside the Gettysburg town limits. On an unseasonably cool yet pleasant late-summer day, graying World War I Tank Corps veterans were joined by their younger armor and armored-cavalry comrades from World War II and the Korean War, along with approximately three thousand onlookers, to dedicate a pine tree and bronze plaque in memory of Camp Colt and in honor of its commander.[1] In the short span between 1918 and 1954, the United States of America had gone from being an active participant in world diplomacy, to withdrawing from affairs outside of its own hemisphere, to gradually moving back onto the world stage, to fighting in another devastating global conflict, to ascending to postwar leadership of the free world, and, finally, to assuming the mantle of Cold War police and nuclear power.

During the same time period, Dwight David Eisenhower rose steadily through the officer ranks to become, during World War II, the Supreme Commander of the Allied Expeditionary Forces (AEF) in Europe with the rank of General of the Army. After the conflict, the five-star general was appointed army chief of staff under President Harry S Truman. Upon leaving the service in 1948, Eisenhower was named president of Columbia University, before Truman recalled him to active duty in December 1949 to take the helm of the North Atlantic Treaty Organization (NATO). Then, in 1952, the former Camp Colt commander was nominated the Republican candidate for president of the United States and went on to win a landslide victory over Adlai Stevenson. In the summer of 1954,

President and Mrs. Eisenhower had occupied the Executive Mansion for little more than a year and a half.

Four years earlier, while Ike was at Columbia, the Eisenhowers bought a retirement home in Gettysburg, purchasing a 189-acre farm adjacent to GNMP and about a mile from the site of Camp Colt. About the acquisition of their farmstead, President Eisenhower later wrote, "Gettysburg had been significant in the early years of our married life and our sentimental attachments to it were reinforced by its significance in American, as well as our personal, history. . . . Of all the properties we saw the most appealing was a farm not quite 190 acres. . . . The buildings had seen better days. So had the soil. It would take work and money to modernize it. But the view of the mountains to the west was good." At the time of the Tank Corps reunion, the First Couple still was in the process of rebuilding the farm house and outbuildings; the following year, "Mr. and Mrs. Ike" would begin spending retreats at the farm, making it their weekend White House.[2] Unable to attend the reunion due to his hectic presidential schedule, the president sent a message to his former comrades, which his representative to the reunion, Lt. Gen. Floyd L. Parks, read: "Please extend my warmest greetings to everyone attending the Homecoming Reunion of the World Wars Tank Corps Association. As you review the experience gained while in the active service of your country, you can take added satisfaction from the fact that your Fellow Citizens understand and appreciate the importance of your contributions to the security of our nation. I wish you a most successful and enjoyable reunion." Parks, the commanding general of the Second Army, headquartered at Fort Meade, Maryland, was a fitting surrogate for the thirty-fourth president: as a young officer, he had commanded Company A, 333d Tank Battalion at Camp Colt.[3]

Also attending the ceremony and reunion was Brig. Gen. John Franklin, who had fought in France with the 301st Tank Battalion. Prior to and after World War II, Franklin was president of United States Lines, an ocean shipping company. During the second global conflict, he was recalled to active duty to oversee waterborne shipping as the War Department's assistant chief of transportation. He was a great-nephew of Union army general William B. Franklin.[4] Two other flag officers who saw service in both world wars also were present that day: Brig. Gen. Harry Semmes, U.S. Army Reserve, and Maj. Gen. L. C. Gaynes, retired. Semmes, who had served with the segregated 92d Infantry Division in World War II, was awarded two Distinguished Service Crosses for bravery during World War I and a third during World War II. He was a confidant and biographer of the late George S. Patton Jr., having served under him in World War I.[5] His kinfolk included the Confederate admiral Raphael Semmes, and Brig. Gen. Paul Semmes of the Army of Northern Virginia, mortally wounded at Gettysburg less than a mile south of the ceremony site.[6] Gaynes was a seasoned businessman and president of the National Trailways Bus System.[7]

The memorial tree, a stout yellow pine, was planted in soil from all forty-eight states and the territories of Alaska and Hawaii, which veterans brought with them. In most cases, the soil was taken from significant historic sites. For example, Texas sent earth from the Alamo; North Dakota provided soil from Fort Lincoln, the post from which Custer and his command departed on their way to the Little Big Horn; Louisiana gave earth from the Chalmette Battlefield, where Andrew Jackson defeated the British in 1815, and so on. A veteran from South Carolina brought soil from the Kings Mountain battlefield, where in 1780 American militia beat their Loyalist opponents. John MacDonald, the old soldier who brought it north, told a *Times* reporter that dirt from that site "would be better than some from Ft. Sumter, where some South Carolinians gleefully shot h—— out of some 'damyankees' to start the War Between the States."[8] When MacDonald deposited the soil around the tree during its dedication, he gave a hearty "rebel yell." Then, the national commander of the World Wars Tank Corps Association presented the bronze plaque to General Parks. It bore a simple inscription:

UNITED STATES ARMY TANK CORPS

This spot marks the site of Camp Colt, the birthplace of the Tank Corps of the United States Army in the spring of 1918. Behind this marker stands a tree planted in soil from each of the 48 States and dedicated in honor of THE COMMANDING OFFICER CAPTAIN DWIGHT D. EISENHOWER who on January 2, 1953 was inaugurated The 34th President of the United States of America

---

This living testament is a tribute of the affection and high esteem of his 1918 Tank Corps comrades
DEDICATED AUGUST 23, 1954 WORLD WARS TANK CORPS ASSOCIATION

The plague also included the organization's insignia, a British Mark V tank encircled by a wreath. In his address, Parks remarked, "Here at Gettysburg National Military Park we are in the very heart of American military traditions. I can think of no more appropriate spot in America to plant this pine tree which will commemorate the birthplace of the Tank Corps . . . and which will be a testimonial to the esteem held by the Tank Corps veterans for their former commander, President Eisenhower." Parks also mentioned that the living memorial

The Camp Colt Memorial Tree in 2016 (Photo by author)

was on the site of the camp headquarters. (Actually, it was not. The headquarters complex for both World War I camps was about a block closer to town, and on the other [west] side of the Emmitsburg Road. And, unfortunately, the date of Eisenhower's inauguration was wrong on the plaque—he took office on January *20,* 1953.) The reunion came to a close that night with a banquet at the Hotel Gettysburg.[9]

In a twist of fate, a much younger Ike Eisenhower had been instrumental in shaping the American memory of the AEF. Although he had not made it to the Western Front in 1918, by 1929 he probably knew more about the organization, campaigns, and logistical operations of the AEF than any trained historian in the country. A year earlier, then Major Eisenhower had been assigned by order of General Pershing to the Historical Section of the American Battle Monuments Commission (ABMC), at the recommendation of Brig. Gen. Fox Conner, Ike's former commanding officer. Connor and Eisenhower shared a love of military history, so Conner thought his protégé was a good choice for the job. For seventeen months in 1928–29, Ike assumed overall responsibility for the research, writing, and production of a 547-page guidebook that, on its eventual publication, in 1938, was titled *American Armies and Battlefields in Europe.* About this episode of Eisenhower's long and distinguished military and subsequent political career, Steven Trout writes, "The future supreme commander of Allied Forces in Western Europe became immersed not only in the history of

American participation in the First World War, a subject he came to know inside out, but also in the process of remembrance. . . . By the time of his generalship in World War II, he would understand how modern wars are memorialized, and more importantly, he would understand the urgencies that drive military commemoration."[10] This understanding would take on new meaning when as president, Ike, with his executive agency, the ABMC, would face a whole new set of "urgencies" with the design and development of cemeteries and memorials made necessary by American participation in the Second World War.

The assignment, beginning the summer of 1928, took Ike, Mamie and young son John (little Dowd Dwight—Icky—had died of scarlet fever in 1921 at the age of three) to France for one year, where Ike would become an expert on the American battlefields of a war in which he so desperately had wanted to be a combatant commander. During his many battlefield jaunts to the French countryside, Eisenhower sometimes was accompanied by Mamie and John. On one trip to Verdun, John was observed kicking a rusty object, which turned out to be an unexploded hand grenade. Luckily, the six-year-old was stopped short by his parents before the unthinkable happened.[11] (More than seven decades later, John wrote, "I know that accompanying him on his many tours around the country made a lasting impression on me." It made such an enduring imprint on John S. D. Eisenhower—a 1944 graduate of West Point, retired Army Reserve brigadier general and former ambassador to Belgium—that he wrote his own book about the U.S. contribution to the war, *Yanks: The Epic Story of the American Army in World War I.*[12]) Upon the Eisenhower family's return to the United States in 1929, Ike went back to the ABMC offices in Washington to wrap up his work before his reassignment to the War Department General Staff.[13] Twenty-one years later, Ike and Mamie would buy their Gettysburg home, with John and his own family joining them there in 1961, after *President* Eisenhower had left office.[14] By then, the ranks of the aging veterans of Ike's old Camp Colt command were beginning to thin.

The 1954 tribute to Eisenhower and his tankers was not the first World War I memorial dedicated in Adams County. On Armistice Day 1920, another bronze plaque had been unveiled in front of a capacity crowd in the courtroom of the Adams County Courthouse on Baltimore Street. Two months earlier, the county commissioners had approved the design and wording on the tablet and released the necessary funds to pay for it. The *Times* described the memorial in a front-page headline in its September 11 edition: "The tablet which will cost $323 is of bronze two feet, three inches wide, and is three feet, ten inches long. It will be erected on the Court House plot." The memorial would be dedicated to the "boys" of Adams County who gave their lives; the members of the Lentz

Post suggested that this particular noun replace the word "men" on the tablet, and the commissioners concurred.

The day of the dedication ceremony finally arrived, but the bronze tablet did not. Finally, at 10:45 A.M., the dedication committee received word that the crated tablet had been delivered to Harrisburg by train from Cleveland and was awaiting shipment on the evening run to Gettysburg. Rather than postpone the ceremony, the county treasurer volunteered to pick it up with his own truck and haul it back to Gettysburg in time for the 4:00 P.M. dedication.[15] He made it in the nick of time, and the ceremony proceeded as scheduled. Present were forty-five uniformed veterans and representatives from all three Adams County legion posts. The courtroom was packed with townsfolk waiting to hear presentations by a local minister and the county solicitor. The young son of Chaplain Albert Bell, who had died from complications of the Spanish flu while serving with the Seventy-Ninth Division in France, unveiled the tablet. Then, according to the *Times* report, "an acceptance address of surpassing excellence was delivered by Percy Eichelberger, commander of the Albert Lentz post on behalf of all of Adams County's legion members." Eichelberger had served in the Third Division as an infantryman and fought in most of the AEF's major campaigns. His speech was long and lofty, but one paragraph captured the meaning of sacrifice, which the fifty-three "boys" whose names were cast in bronze on the tablet fulfilled to the utmost:

> In the first place this tablet represents sacrifices—sacrifices so great they cannot be computed—sacrifices so great that they lay beyond the domain of mathematics. It is easy to understand in the mad launch over the top one may encounter and despise danger or even death with its terrors, but in the stillness of the night, lying in a mud walled, water filled shell hole, to contemplate the giving up of home, friends, kindred and life itself with all its joys and hopes and aspirations, and yet in honor's name resolve to go on until the supreme sacrifice is made, is something that few can understand.

Fittingly, the dedication ceremony came to a close with a rendition of the Civil War anthem, "Battle Hymn of the Republic." Now that the sacrifices of the Great War had been acknowledged and sanctified, the citizens of Gettysburg and the rest of Adams County could again look to an earlier war, one that put their little town on the world map, for solace and reflection.

It is surprising that a town so steeped in history and surrounded by a national park abounding with thousands of monuments and markers—and many more yet to come—that the World War veterans chose such a plain, commemorative

Memorial plaque in its current location on the exterior wall of the Adams County Courthouse (photo by author)

tablet to memorialize their dead comrades in arms. Yet, by affixing it to a wall of an existing public building—the Adams County Courthouse—the local community turned the entire structure into a beneficial living memorial rather than another static, somewhat useless (in a utilitarian sense) bronze or stone soldier-statue of the type that occupied thousands of northern and southern town commons after the Civil War.[16] But only a short drive from Gettysburg, the towns of Emmitsburg, Maryland, and Chambersburg, Pennsylvania, did just that, when to honor their war dead, each municipality erected a mass-produced statue of an American soldier, E. M. Viquesney's *Spirit of the American Doughboy*. Steven Trout recently observed, "Viquesney's sculpture is modern in its details [an authentic uniform and accoutrements] but essentially Victorian in its aesthetic, like an updated Civil War statue of the triumphant variety that stand atop Grand Army of the Republic monuments."[17] In a county dominated by a national park already inundated with statues dedicated to the memory of Union and Confederate military organizations, generals, and even common soldiers, the simple courthouse tablet was an expression of the Progressive spirit of Gettysburg, a place that would always be associated with an earlier epoch of its citizens' common heritage.

Percy Eichelberger, from Gardners, in the far-northern edge of the county, and his cousin Paul Foulk, a Littlestown native, were veterans who did more to preserve the local memory of the World War than any other Adams County resident.[18] Eichelberger the infantryman and Foulk the sailor took on a project to record the sacrifices and wartime endeavors of all county residents, but primarily those who served in uniform. Although Eichelberger was a combat-hardened doughboy who had sustained a battle wound, Foulk enlisted too late to participate in any wartime naval actions, making only one postwar cruise on the cargo ship *Edenton* to deliver flour to war-torn countries along the Aegean Sea for Herbert Hoover's Food Administration.[19] Both men were attending Gettysburg College when the United States declared war, both were inducted into their respective services, and both "returned to Gettysburg College to complete their college education in preparation for [their] desired professional life, disrupted by war," wrote a middle-aged Foulk in November 1941, only a few weeks shy of America's entry into another world conflict. Soon after their discharge, the cousins decided to chronicle their home county's role in the Great War, as Foulk told members of the Adams County Historical Society, "for the sake of prosperity . . . to preserve in tangible form a record of these noble deeds of the military activity, and the home work." Their efforts resulted in publication of *Adams County in the World War* in 1921.[20]

The process of researching the book, compiling the information, and then writing the narrative proved difficult and took longer than expected. "My co-editor did most of the editing work, while I scoured the county for the information we so much wanted and needed," explained Foulk. Their research methodology would impress even a trained modern-day sociologist. First, they prepared questionnaires and mailed them to every veteran; but this process was problematic. "To get a list of the servicemen was a most difficult task," Foulk recalled. "Some towns and communities had partial lists; none were complete. Day after day I spent in every section of the county gathering the names of service men [and women]. Many long hours were spent in checking the lists and adding additional names." The completed questionnaires included a wealth of military and demographic information that, whether Eichelberger and Foulk realized it at the time, would be critically important to later students of history. According to Foulk,

> We sought the man's full name, the name of his father and mother, her maiden name, his address, when he entered service, and in what camps he trained, what ranks he held, when he was promoted, on what ship he sailed overseas, from what

> ship he sailed overseas, from what port he sailed to what port, his moves in foreign service, when he sailed for home, from what port, on what ship to what port, then to what camp he was sent, and when he was discharged. We also included what wounds he had, what decorations he received.

Of course, not every veteran cooperated, and undoubtedly the cousins unintentionally missed a few names—they admitted as much in the book's foreword. Twenty years later, Foulk confessed that what he and Eichelberger had aspired to do "was a large order, but we were young, bold and unafraid," and then concluded: "How well we succeeded the record will testify."[21]

Their finished product also encompassed historical summaries of the work of various Adams County war committees, the Red Cross, the draft board, the Liberty Loan campaigns, and the sale of war savings stamps. In addition, the book included short memoirs of the wartime services of a few of the county's soldiers and sailors, even Eichelberger's own account of Château-Thierry. Most importantly, the section dedicated to the Adams County fallen was the most essential part of their book. Titled "In Memoriam," it annotates the service of the county's war dead and the nature of each serviceman's demise. When possible, photos of the deceased and/or images of their individual graves were included. Eichelberger wrote the preface to that chapter, and his leadership role in Gettysburg's American Legion post is quite evident when he warns readers "to note the work of the demagogue. . . . Fear, uncertainty and distress are everywhere in the world."[22] Echoing the national Legion's role in helping to crush radicalism, as evinced by its members' conservative reactions to the Red Scare and labor strikes, Eichelberger opined, "The demagogue is abroad in the world. He is not dressed in red alone." The will of the people was expressed by the ballot and not by anarchy or dictators, he asserted, "in a government by the people. . . . Our honored dead have fought and bled to have it so for us." But two decades later, coeditor Foulk admitted, seemingly in defeat, that "in the light of world events we now know that the Armistice was nothing more than the name implied; a cessation of open hostility. For once again the flames of war rage unchecked in many parts of the world."[23] Foulk knew that it was only a matter of time until the Unites States would be totally involved in another world war. On November 10, 1941, he did not realize just how soon an American declaration of war would come.

Of all the people associated with Gettysburg during the era of the First World War, none would have a greater role in the Second World War and its aftermath than Dwight David Eisenhower. Others made their own, smaller marks on the history of that conflict. Gettysburg College alumnus Keller Rockey was a career marine who continued to rise through the officer ranks in a variety of important

Major General Keller E. Rockey (with telephone), commanding Fifth Marine Division on Iwo Jima (Marine Corps University)

command and staff assignments. When the United Stated entered World War II, he was a full colonel and chief of staff of the Second Marine Division. Promoted to brigadier general in 1942, he served first as the director of the Marine Corps' division of war plans and policies and then as the assistant commandant of the Marine Corps. After promotion to major general, he was assigned to command the Fifth Marine Division in 1944, and he led his troops ashore the next year on the island of Iwo Jima. Six of his men became the iconic symbol of the American war effort when they raised a flag on Mount Suribachi on February 23, 1945. Rockey retired from the Marine Corps in 1950 with the rank of lieutenant general. He died in 1970 and is buried in Arlington National Cemetery.[24]

Young Ernest Wrentmore ("Henry Monroe") survived his wounds and went on to live a long life. In 1939 he was recommended for the Medal of Honor, but at that time, nominations after the fact had to be made within ten years of the incident, and the recommendation was denied. Wrentmore was recalled to active duty during World War II and served as an officer in the U.S. Army Air Forces and after the conflict served in the U.S. Air Force Reserve. He was recalled to active duty for the Korean conflict.[25] Wrentmore married several times and had a number of children, some who never knew him, all across the country. He died in 1983 and is buried in Arlington. His son, Ernest Wrentmore III, knew a little about his dad's World War I experience, but he was reintroduced to it when he read an article about the Meuse-Argonne campaign that appeared in a 2010 issue of *American Heritage* magazine. The son explained,

> That encounter sent me off on a remarkable odyssey. I had never known my father; he was 63 years old when I was born, and my parents divorced soon thereafter. I knew some of my father's story from his autobiography, *In Spite of Hell,* which my mother gave me in 1988, five years after he died. Over the years, I have tried many times to learn about him. All to no avail. It's been the largest hole in my life. My renewed interest led me on a journey that included a phone call with a newfound stepsister who still owned many of my father's belongings, including his medals, photographs signed by generals and presidents, and a family scrapbook, which was loaded with photographs and stories. A fuller, more colorful picture of him soon emerged. He was a man's man, excellent at everything from business and music to dog breeding and, of course, soldiering.[26]

Ernest Wrentmore III has tried, since learning of his father's exploits, to see that his dad finally receives the nation's highest honor.[27] As of 2017, he had not succeeded.[28]

The suffragist Lavinia Dock seemed to reach her zenith during World War I, especially when she was propelled to the national headlines for being jailed—for protesting in front of the White House—in the notorious Occoquan Prison, along with her friends Alice Paul and Lucy Burns. After the war, Dock, who never married, resided with her sisters in western Adams County near Caledonia State Park. Her somewhat radical ways put her at odds with her conservative nursing colleagues, and although she wrote extensively after the war, few of her articles were published. She later stated that her most important accomplishments in life were her commitment to women's suffrage and her contributions to nursing education. Although Dock had been born before the Civil War, she lived until 1956, dying from pneumonia after breaking her hip.[29]

Norman Randolph, the officer who had commanded Ike's development battalion at Camp Colt, retired from the army at the end of World War II with the rank of brigadier general. He became the executive secretary of the Valley Forge Park Commission in 1947, a position he held until his death in 1953.[30] In his position at Valley Forge, Randolph experienced the anxiety Col. John Nicholson had felt in 1918, when approximately forty-seven thousand young men—this time boy scouts during a national jamboree—ran roughshod over *his* national shrine during a weeklong encampment in the summer of 1950.[31] One can only wonder whether Colonel Nicholson's spirit smiled smugly down on Randolph as the scouts built fires, played ball, cut firewood, urinated on trees, and otherwise innocently defaced the landscape and cultural resources associated with the crucible of American independence.

Another Gettysburg College alum, Charles A. Willoughby—formerly Adolph Weidenbach—who as a young man came to Gettysburg as a soldier in the 5th U.S. Infantry during the 1913 Peace Jubilee, made the U.S. Army his career, serving in three wars and rising to the rank of major general. He is best known as Douglas MacArthur's G-2, or chief of intelligence, during the Korean War. In October 1950, eager to tell his five-star boss what he wanted to hear, he failed to alert MacArthur that a Chinese army was massing on the Yalu River. What happened next was a near disaster for U.S. and UN forces.[32] Willoughby retired from the Army in 1951. A fervent anti-Communist, he held fascist leanings and was a friend and advisor to Spain's Francisco Franco. Willoughby died in 1972 and is buried in Arlington.[33]

Nurse Mary "Kate" Wolf moved to California sometime after World War I. Her entry in *Adams County and the World War* states, "Miss Wolfe was the first American woman to be decorated by the French Government."[34] After an exhaustive records search, the only postwar information that could be found about Kate was her 1958 obituary in the *Gettysburg Times,* which announced, "World War One Nurse Dies: Word has been received here of the death Sunday of Mary Kate Wolfe, a native of Adams County and nurse in World War I. She was aged about 84." After chronicling her wartime exploits and listing her awards, the obituary concluded, "There are no immediate survivors. . . . Services and interment are to take place at the North Hollywood mortuary."[35]

Sam Woodfill returned to the enlisted ranks after World War I. While Woodfill received the Medal of Honor and Pershing named him the ideal American soldier of the war, his family farm in Indiana kept him so much in debt that he was forced to take an extended leave from the army to gain employment on a public works project to pay the bills. When citizens of nearby Cincinnati discovered the war hero's economic plight, the city's newspapers raised $10,000 to help him pay off his obligation, allowing him to retire from the Army in 1923 after more than thirty years of service.[36] During World War II, Woodfill was recalled to active duty, commissioned a major, and placed on recruiting duty. He died in 1951 at the age of fifty-eight and is buried in Arlington National Cemetery.[37]

Henry Kolda, the tanker who married a local girl and one of the few Camp Colt soldiers actually to make it the front, never recovered from his wartime injuries. He died with his wife, Maude, by his side on December 1, 1921, at his adopted home in Fountaindale, a hamlet in southwestern Adams County. He also left behind two young children. However tragic the loss may have been, Henry's tribute in the *Compiler* contains a total fabrication of the nature of his service-connected disabilities. According to the obituary,

> He was a driver of a tank in the Argonne, and a bomb hit the tank, killing all in charge except Kolda and he [subsequently] had a remarkable series of adventures. At one time he found himself marked with a tag meaning his case was hopeless, while one [soldier] alongside of him was marked for the hospital. Discovering the neighboring body was dead he exchanged his tag and reached help. Upon his return [to the U.S.] his condition was found to be pitiful and through the efforts of the Red Cross and the Albert Lentz Post, he was helped and an examination secured which found him totally disabled and compensation so awarded him. In the blowing up of the tank he suffered internal injuries aggravated by being gassed so that he had periodic hemorrhages in which he was totally incapacitated and the least exertion brought on these attacks. He was repeatedly helped by the Red Cross and then he would be well enough to accumulate compensation and make return.[38]

Henry was *not* part of a tank crew. He was a mechanic assigned to the tank battalion's 316th Repair and Salvage Company, whose mission was to retrieve and repair disabled tanks. Even if he *had* been a FT-17 tank driver or gunner/commander, a direct hit would have taken out both crew members—the obituary states that "all in charge" had been killed except for Kolda, who allegedly was wounded, which suggests that the machine was one of the larger, Mark IV or V tanks. The problem with that reasoning is that those tanks were not used in the Argonne offensive. And the story about Henry switching medical-disposition tags is pure hogwash, too. In reality, Kolda had been gassed, but his biggest problem was a bad case of trench foot, all of which he details to his wife in a letter written from his hospital bed on December 19, 1918: "I have what is known as Trench feet, for two months at the front we wore our shoes without taking them off more than about 5 times, [and] our feet were always wet, as we were always in mud . . . I was also gassed once but not bad."[39] In the entire eleven-page letter, this was the only time he mentioned his injuries. What is certain is that he died young, and his early demise certainly was complicated by his service-related disability, whether from weakened lungs or gangrene brought on by trench foot. Perhaps his fellow legionnaires, who helped him secure compensation, thought it best to embellish the story, thus guaranteeing a government pension for him and after he died, for his wife and children.

Sergeant Henry Kolda and his wife, Maude (Courtesy of Eric Dorr)

Near the end of *Adams County in the World War,* the coeditors inserted a collage of photographs of several local women who had served as nurses, and one veteran-amputee, Monroe Feeser of Littlestown, confined to a wheelchair and missing his right leg. Feeser's wartime record, which Foulk and Eichelberger's questionnaires made possible, explained how he was wounded and the extent of his multiple injuries. At the time of the book's publication, he had been in nine different military hospitals, and was still a patient in 1921.[40] Feeser was typical of tens of thousands of nameless doughboys who suffered long after the end of a bloody struggle that later seemed worthless, as Paul Foulk had ascertained in 1941 when the United States stood on the precipice of another world war, one that came with new horrors and a death toll far eclipsing that of the earlier conflict. Unfortunately for Foulk and those like him, the public remembrance of the Second World War and its so-called greatest generation likewise would obscure America's collective memory of its first great overseas adventure.

POSTSCRIPT

Today, most of Gettysburg's Great War vestiges have been erased, with the exception of the Camp Colt Pine Tree Memorial and its accompanying plaque, the memorial tablet on the courthouse wall, the World War I section in the national cemetery, the name of the American Legion post, and the National Park Service's meager interpretive marker on Steinwehr Avenue and its two small museum displays, one in the museum of the GNMP visitors' center and the other at Eisenhower National Historic Site. A post–World War II residential development and its accompanying recreation fields, situated on that part of the World War I camp that had been constructed on leased, private land, bear the name Colt. My two sons played sports on the baseball and soccer fields of the "rec park," as they called it, and they had friends who grew up in the Colt Park development. Few of its residents doubtless have any clue that their homes sit on a major mobilization and training site from 1917–18. For that matter, most might not even realize their houses and yards occupy part of the 1863 battlefield, despite that the entire housing area sits on the edge of the national park.

Perhaps our collective historical amnesia is a good thing. I grew up in nearby York, Pennsylvania, and a portion of my formative years was spent visiting the battlefield during the Civil War centennial. I have not forgotten the numerous motels, private residences, theme parks, restaurants, souvenir stands, and private museums that were located within the legislative boundary of GNMP, some of which stood for decades until they finally were sold outright to the federal government or faced condemnation for the public good (just as the Gettysburg Electric Railway suffered the same fate in the late nineteenth century). My sons, now adults, have no idea what the battlefield looked like only a half-century ago, when it was littered with such crass, commercial development. To them, the scene of Pickett's Charge today is nearly the same (minus monuments, tour roads, and a steel tower) as it was in 1863.

In the course of researching and writing this book, I have shared my newfound knowledge of World War I–era Gettysburg with several friends, some who are lifelong residents of Adams County, while others are just plain old Civil War buffs who come from far and wide to visit the battlefield. A few are even professional historians with solid academic credentials. Most had absolutely no clue what the battlefield was used for, or looked like, in 1917 and 1918; the few who did had only limited knowledge of Camp Colt, and only then because Eisenhower had commanded that camp. None had an inkling of how the Spanish flu ravaged the Gettysburg area or how the encampment ecologically degraded the historic battlefield. Some of my friends, especially my best friend—a retired police officer, a Civil War buff, former Union reenactor, artifact collector, and someone who understands "historical mindedness"—divulged that he "kinda wished" that I had not told him about the two camps. Now, he says, he cannot stand at the High Water Mark memorial without seeing, in his mind's eye, stables, latrines, mess halls, a huge concrete swimming pool, sundry other wood-framed buildings, tar-covered company streets plied by military motorcycles, and waste incinerators—or what we have come to call "poop furnaces"—belching their smelly, acrid smoke that wafted around and settled on the monuments of stone and bronze, silent sentinels on terrain that we had once thought of, in our youthful innocence and ignorance, as hallowed ground.

But the battlefield and the monuments survived the ordeal of the Great War and the military encampments before and after the conflict. The topography might have been altered a bit, but for the most part, the changes are not discernable to the naked eye. Before World War I and since then, generations of visitors have come and gone. The commercial tourist trappings that marred the landscape, including two rail lines and various other visitor-related enterprises, have slowly disappeared, from both sight and memory. Soldiers, marines, and cadets still come to Gettysburg during historical staff rides to learn from the old battlefield, but they do so in reverence and with respect for what is, after all, an American shrine. Despite a century and a half of both unintentional and premeditated abuse, the commemorative landscape has endured, as one hopes it will for generations to come. Gettysburg, like anywhere else, is a place with layers of history. For the sake of the general public, it is wise that the National Park Service has chosen to interpret and illuminate only one of those layers—the one that made Gettysburg renowned in the first place, one that is "far above our poor power to add or detract."

Notes

PREFACE

1. Cadet George Patton to Beatrice Ayer, *The Patton Papers:* vol. 1 of 2, *1885–1940,* ed. Martin Blumenson, 2 vols. (New York: Houghton Mifflin, 1974), 191–92.

2. Edwin Kelton to Florence Hatton, May 5, 1915, Papers of Edwin C. Kelton, U.S. Military Academy Special Collections, USMA Library, West Point, New York. The steel observation tower Kelton mentions no longer exists, having been demolished in 1968 for economic reasons.

3. Graduates of the Class of 1915 served in three major conflicts (World War I, World War II, and Korea) and a number of "small wars," such as the Mexican Punitive Expedition of 1916. The class held twenty-four future brigadier generals (one star), twenty-four major generals (two stars), seven lieutenant generals (three stars), two generals (four stars), and two generals of the army (five stars). "West Point and the Making of America," Museum of American History, Smithsonian Institution Web site, accessed Oct. 13, 2014, http://americanhistory.si.edu/westpoint/history_6b.html.

4. David M. Kennedy, *Over Here: The First World War and American Society* (New York: Oxford University Press, 1980).

PROLOGUE

1. Report of the Gettysburg National Park Commission, War Department, Gettysburg, Pa., July 1, 1913, GNMP Archives.

2. 16 U.S. Code § 430g.

3. Commonwealth of Pennsylvania, *Fiftieth Anniversary of the Battle of Gettysburg: Report of the Pennsylvania Commission.* (Harrisburg, Pa.: William S. Ray, State Printer, 1914), 11–14, 60. The total amount of money allocated by the various state governments and veterans' organizations for the anniversary came to over $1,175,000 (37).

4. Ibid.

5. General Leslie J. McNair, U.S. Army, was killed by friendly fire during Operation Cobra in the summer of 1944 in Normandy. McNair, who, as a four-star general outranked Buckner, perished as a result of overstrikes by American bombers, not from enemy action.

6. Commonwealth of Pennsylvania, *Fiftieth Anniversary of the Battle of Gettysburg,* 42–45.

7. Patton to Beatrice Ayer, July 1, 1913, *The Patton Papers:* vol. 1 of 2, *1885–1940,* ed. Martin Blumenson (New York: Houghton Mifflin, 1974), 280.

8. Commonwealth of Pennsylvania, *Fiftieth Anniversary of the Battle of Gettysburg,* 40–42, 64.

9. *Gettysburg Times,* July 3, 1913.

10. Commonwealth of Pennsylvania, *Fiftieth Anniversary of the Battle of Gettysburg,* 60.

11. *Gettysburg Times,* July 3, 1913.

12. *Gettysburg Compiler,* July 2, 1913. A. Mitchell Palmer became attorney general of the United States in 1919, near the end of Wilson's second term. He primarily is remembered in American history for ordering raids on suspected anarchists during the "Red Scare" following the war. See David M. Kennedy, *Over Here: The First World War and American Society* (New York: Oxford Univ. Press, 1980, 2004), 289–91.

13. *Star and Sentinel,* July 9, 1913.

14. Ibid.

15. Report of the Gettysburg National Military Park Commission, War Department, Gettysburg, Pa., July 1, 1914.

16. Robert L. Bloom, *A History of Adams County, Pennsylvania, 1700–1990* (Gettysburg: Adams County Historical Society, 1992), 285.

17. Woodrow Wilson, Address at Gettysburg, July 4, 1913, *The American Presidency Project,* accessed Oct. 11, 2014, http://www.presidency.ucsb.edu/ws/?pid=65370.

18. In recognition of the centennial of Wilson's first inauguration, on March 4, 2013, historian William Keylor lamented: "Wilson is widely and correctly remembered—and represented in our history books—as a progressive Democrat who introduced many liberal reforms at home and fought for the extension of democratic liberties and human rights abroad. But on the issue of race his legacy was, in fact, regressive and has been largely forgotten." Keylor, "The Long-Forgotten Racial Attitudes and Policies of Woodrow Wilson," *Professor Voices: Commentary, Insight, and Analysis,* Mar. 4, 2013, http://www.bu.edu/professorvoices/2013/03/04/the-long-forgotten-racial-attitudes-and-policies-of-woodrow-wilson/.

19. Wilson, Address at Gettysburg.

20. A. Scott Berg, *Wilson* (New York: Berkley, 2013), 305.

21. *Star and Sentinel,* May 9, 1914.

22. "Balkan Wars," *Encyclopedia Britannica,* Dec. 5, 2016, http://www.britannica.com/EBchecked/topic/50300/Balkan-Wars; *Gettysburg Times,* Jan. 13, 1914.

23. "Eddie Plank," *Baseball Reference,* accessed Oct. 13, 2014, http://www.baseball-reference.com/players/p/plankedo1.shtml?redir.

24. Hillel Kuttel, "Eddie Plank: A Favorite Son of Gettysburg," *New York Times,* June 29, 2013, SP8.

25. "Eddie Plank," National Baseball Hall of Fame Web site, accessed Oct. 30, 2014, http://baseballhall.org/hof/plank-eddie.

26. Dwight D. Eisenhower, *At Ease: Stories I Tell to Friends* (Garden City, N.Y.: Doubleday, 1967), 21, 26.

27. "Lieutenant General Keller E. Rockey, USMC," Naval History and Heritage Command Web site, accessed Oct. 31, 2014, http://www.history.navy.mil/photos/pers-us/uspers-r/k-rocky.htm (page discontinued).

28. An article titled "College Boys Respond to Call" in the *Gettysburg Times* of April 24, 1914, concerning the Veracruz incident, stated, "Sergeant Weidenbach . . . was battalion sergeant major [of] Company K, 5th United States Infantry . . . was here during the Fiftieth Anniversary celebration."

29. Ernest L. Wrentmore, *In Spite of Hell: A Factual Story of Incidents That Occurred during World War I, as Experienced by the Youngest Soldier to Have Seen Combat Duty with the American Expeditionary Forces as a Member of the Famous Company I, 60th Infantry, Fifth (Red Diamond) Division* (New York: Greenwich, 1958), vii–viii.

30. Charles Emmerson, *1913: In Search of the World before the Great War* (New York: Public Affairs, 2013), 181. In this well-written and expansive look at the world's great cities in the year before World War I, Emmerson even discusses the significance of the Battle of Gettysburg's Fiftieth Anniversary Commemoration (154–56). Concerning Lavinia Dock's participation in the 1913 suffrage demonstration and parade in Washington, see Alan Taylor, "100 Years Ago: The 1913 Women's Suffrage Parade," *Atlantic*, Mar 1, 2013, http://www.theatlantic.com/photo/2013/03/100-years-ago-the-1913-womens-suffrage-parade/100465/.

31. "Ford Motor Company Chronology," The Henry Ford Museum Web site, accessed June 15, 2017, https://www.thehenryford.org/collections-and-research/digital-resources/popular-topics/ford-company-chronology. Henry Ford was born on July 30, 1863, on his parents' farm in Dearborn, Michigan.

32. Cutler, "Eddie Plank."

33. Emmerson, *1913*, 4; "The Century of Progress: Ghent, 1913–2013," accessed Nov. 9, 2014, http://1913–2013.ghent.be/en/i-will-get-my-big-brother (site discontinued).

34. For a provocative look at the relationship of modernism to both world wars—using *Le Sacre du Printemps* as a springboard for discussion—see Modris Eksteins, *The Rites of Spring: The Great War and the Birth of the Modern Age* (New York: Houghton Mifflin, 1989).

35. Ana Carden-Coyne, "Wounded Visionaries," *Guardian* (Manchester, UK), Nov. 12, 2008.

36. A recent study that covers this period of Mexican history in great detail is M. M. McAllen, *Maximilian and Carlota: Europe's Last Empire in Mexico* (San Antonio: Trinity University Press, 2014).

37. Emmerson, *1913*, 206–21.

38. *Gettysburg Times*, Jan. 1, 1914.

39. Casualty estimates for both battles vary from source to source, but the stated approximate figures are generally accepted by most authorities.

40. Total Spanish influenza deaths worldwide were more than 50 million. Total World War I deaths (military and civilian) are estimated between 15 and 18 million.

1. BETWEEN TWO WARS

1. Readers wishing a detailed, comprehensive history of Adams County and Gettysburg are urged to consult Robert L. Bloom, *A History of Adams County, Pennsylvania, 1700–1990* (Gettysburg: Adams County Historical Society, 1992) and William A. Frassanito, *Early Photography at Gettysburg* (Gettysburg: Thomas, 1995). The countless campaign and battle studies, as well as books and essays pertaining to the larger military, political, social, cultural, and even economic consequences relating to Gettysburg and its aftermath are too numerous to list here. Among the best are Stephen W. Sears, *Gettysburg* (New York: Houghton Mifflin, 2003); Edwin Coddington, *The Gettysburg Campaign: A Study in Command* (New York: Simon & Schuster, 1968); Gregory A. Coco, *A Strange and Blighted Land: Gettysburg, the Aftermath of a Battle* (Gettysburg: Thomas, 1995); Garry Wills, *Lincoln at Gettysburg: The Words That Remade America* (New York: Simon & Schuster, 1992); Gabor S. Boritt, *The Gettysburg Gospel: The Lincoln Speech That Nobody Knows* (New York: Simon & Schuster, 2006); Margaret S. Creighton, *The Colors of Courage: Gettysburg's Forgotten History: Immigrants, Women, and African Americans in the Civil War's Defining Battle* (New York: Basic Books, 2005); Jim Weeks, *Gettysburg: Memory, Market, and an American Shrine* (Princeton, N.J.: Princeton Univ. Press, 2003); and any of the Gettysburg battle studies by Harry Pfanz and Jeff Wert.

2. See Wills, *Lincoln at Gettysburg.*

3. Coco, *Strange and Blighted Land,* 361–67. The entire book describes, in prolific detail, the grisly aftermath of the battle, and the short- and mid-range effects on the local populace.

4. For the Battle of Monocacy, see B. Franklin Cooling, *Monocacy: The Battle That Saved Washington* (Shippensburg, Pa.: White Mane, 2000); on the burning of Chambersburg, *see Blue and Gray Magazine*'s special issue authored by Ted Alexander, *History and Tour Guide of the Burning of Chambersburg and McCausland's Raid* 11, no. 6 (1994).

5. Bloom, *History of Adams County,* 187–90; Frassanito, *Early Photography at Gettysburg,* 121–28.

6. Bloom, *History of Adams County,* 242–49; 267–84. The Gettysburg Electric Railroad Company operated the trolley system, which was powered by an electrical generating plant that opened in Gettysburg in 1893.

7. Weeks, *Gettysburg,* 18–22.

8. Ibid., 23–26.

9. Bloom, *History of Adams County,* 261–68.

10. Ibid., 274–75. Bloom claimed there were five separate rail lines in Adams County at that time, but he counted the eastern and western links of the Western Maryland connecting at Gettysburg as two lines and its East Berlin spur as a separate line.

11. Weeks, *Gettysburg,* 75.

12. Bloom, *History of Adams County,* 281.

13. Ibid, 284–86, 451.

14. Ibid., 299–310. Data concerning the Gettysburg Fire Department was found in John H. C. Whiting, *Philadelphia, Pennsylvania and Delaware Insurance Directory: Containing Important And Useful Information Pertaining to the Various Kinds of Insurance Practiced in This Country* (Philadelphia: J. H. C. Whiting, 1912), 215.

15. "Borough of Gettysburg: Police Department History," *Gettysburg, Pennsylvania: Historic Crossroads,* accessed Dec. 15, 2014, http://gettysburg-pa.gov/police/history.htm (site discontinued).

16. Commonwealth of Pennsylvania, *Fiftieth Anniversary of the Battle of Gettysburg: Report of the Pennsylvania Commission* (Harrisburg, Pa.: William S. Ray, State Printer, 1914), 51–52; *Star and Sentinel,* July 2, 1913.

17. Bloom, *History of Adams County,* 83, 137–38.

18. Ibid., 305–10; *Smull's Legislative Hand Book and Manual of the State of Pennsylvania, 1911* (Harrisburg, Pa.: C. E. Aughinbaugh, 1911), 863.

19. Bloom, *History of Adams County,* 339. The *Star and Sentinel* produced a short-lived daily newspaper, from 1914 to 1917.

20. Bloom, *History of Adams County,* 447–48.

21. Ibid., 328–37; David M. Kennedy, *Over Here: The First World War and American Society* (New York: Oxford Univ. Press, 1980, 2004), 47.

22. Bloom, *History of Adams County,* 337–38.

23. Ibid., 341–42.

24. "A Brief History of The Memorial Church of The Prince of Peace, Gettysburg, Pennsylvania," Memorial Church of the Prince of Peace Web site, accessed Dec. 1, 2014, http://prince-of-peace-gettysburg.diocpa.org/About%20Us/history.html.

25. Timothy B. Smith, *The Golden Age of Battlefield Preservation: The Decade of the 1890s and the Establishment of America's First Five Military Parks* (Knoxville: Univ. of Tennessee Press, 2008), 145–52.

26. Ibid., 150.

27. Ibid., 152–53. Sickles had been a New York congressman before the war. He lost his seat after murdering his wife's lover, Phillip Barton Key II (son of Francis Scott Key). Sickles's defense attorneys, including Edwin Stanton, who would become Lincoln's second secretary of war, succeeded in getting their client acquitted by using the temporary insanity defense, its first use in American history.

28. The Gettysburg National Military Park–enabling legislation, 28 Stat. 651, is found as appendix 1 in Smith, *Golden Age of Battlefield Preservation,* 229–31.

29. U.S. v. GETTYSBURG ELECTRIC R. CO. 160 U.S. 668 (Jan. 27, 1896).

30. Smith, *Golden Age of Battlefield Preservation,* 157–58; Bloom, *History of Adams County,* 267. Most of the route of the trolley line used the rights-of-way of existing public roads, such as Baltimore Street and the Emmitsburg Road.

As progressive as *U.S. v. Gettysburg Electric Railway Co.* may have seemed, on May 18, 1898, months afterward, the Supreme Court ruled, on May 18, 1896, on the *Plessy v. Ferguson* case, in favor of the constitutionality of state laws that required racial segregation in public facilities under the prevailing "separate but equal" doctrine. This decision set back the cause of civil rights for nearly six decades and paved the way for Woodrow Wilson's segregation of federal offices.

31. 29 Stat 120.

32. Smith, *Golden Age of Battlefield Preservation,* 71; Gerald J. Pierce, "Public and Private Voices: The Typhoid Fever Experience at Camp Thomas, 1898" (PhD diss., Georgia State Univ., 2007), 2.

33. Cited in Smith, *Golden Age of Battlefield Preservation,* 72. For the best overall history of Camp Thomas, see Bradley S. Keefer, *Conflicting Memories on the "River of Death": The Chickamauga Battlefield and the Spanish-American War, 1863–1933* (Kent, Ohio: Kent State Univ. Press, 2011).

34. Smith, *Golden Age of Battlefield Preservation,* 72–73.

35. Charles M. Clement, ed. *Pennsylvania in the World War,* 2 vols. (Pittsburgh: States Publication Society, 1921), 1:101.

36. Ibid., 102. This was the 12th Regiment.

37. Ibid., 104.

38. Harlan D. Unrau, *Administrative History of Gettysburg National Military Park* (Gettysburg: National Park Service, 1991), 107–8, 116.

39. Richard Rowe, "Gettysburg 'Staff Ride,'" *Assembly* 45 (Sept. 1986): 32–33, 56, 30–31.

40. Cited in ibid., 30.

2. "THE WHOLE STRUCTURE CRUMBLES"

1. "Year in Review: 1914 American League," *Baseball Almanac*, accessed July 26, 2017, www.baseball-almanac.com/yearly/yr1914a.shtml.

2. *Gettysburg Times*, Apr. 27, 1914.

3. Jerald A. Combs, *The History of American Foreign Policy* (New York: Knopf, 1986), 190–94. Villa was born Doroteo Arango; a supporter of Francisco Madero, he sought to bring down Huerta's government after Madero was killed. When Carranza rose to power, Villa rebelled against him, too. At first the Wilson administration supported Villa, but it withdrew that support when it appeared that Carranza sought democracy in Mexico.

4. Allan Churchill ed., *Pennsylvania in the World War: An Illustrated History of the Twenty-Eighth Division*, 2 vols. (Pittsburgh: States Publications Society, 1921), 1:110–13.

5. *Adams County News*, Oct. 24, 1914.

6. For a concise study of the war's myriad causes, see James Joll, *The Origins of the First World War* (New York: Longman, 1984).

7. For a look at the hold Chamberlain still possesses on Civil War buffs in general and Gettysburg aficionados in particular, see Thomas A. Desjardin, *From These Honored Dead: How the Story of Gettysburg Shaped American Memory* (Cambridge, Mass.: Da Capo, 2003), 127–52.

8. Kathy Georg Harrison, comp., *The Location of the Monuments, Markers, and Tablets on the Gettysburg Battlefield* (Gettysburg: Eastern National Park and Monument Association, 1982).

9. On the alliance system and its impact on the outbreak of the war, see Steven E. Miller, ed, *Military Strategy and the Origins of the First World War* (Princeton, N.J.: Princeton Univ. Press, 1985).

10. *New Oxford Item*, Aug. 20, 27, 1914.

11. Almost every modern history of the First World War covers the opening engagements in great detail. For a short, readable summary, see Gerard J. De Groot, *The First World War* (New York: Palgrave, 2001), 30–33. For a longer, more detailed, yet still understandable narrative, consult Martin Gilbert, *The First World War: A Complete History* (New York: Holt, 1994), 16–99. On Turkey and Tsingtao, see Thomas G. Oakes, "The Ottoman Empire," and David T Zabecki, "Qingdao (Tsingtao), Siege of (23 August–7 November 1914)," both in*The European Powers in the First World War: An Encyclopedia*, ed. Spencer C. Tucker (New York: Garland, 1996), 525–26, 579–82.

12. Paul L. Foulk and Percy S. Eichelberger, eds., *Adams County in the World War: April 6, 1917 to November 11, 1918* (Harrisburg, Pa.: Evangelical Press, 1920), 119, 182.

13. Michael J. O'Malley III, "Black History in Pennsylvania: Communities in Common," *Heritage Matters: News of the Nation's Diverse Cultural Heritage*, Fall 2010, available online at http://npshistory.com/newsletters/heritage_matters/HM19.pdf.

14. Jim Weeks, *Gettysburg: Memory, Market, and an American Shrine* (Princeton, N.J.: Princeton Univ. Press, 2003), 94–98.

15. *Gettysburg Times,* Nov. 21, 1917.

16. "1914 World Series," *Baseball Reference,* accessed Dec. 6, 2014, http://www.baseball-reference.com/postseason/1914_WS.shtml.

17. "Connie Mack," National Baseball Hall of Fame Web site, accessed Dec. 6, 2014, http://baseballhall.org/hof/mack-connie. Mack managed the A's for an unprecedented fifty consecutive years.

18. *Gettysburg Compiler,* Dec. 26, 1914.

19. This term became the title of a chapter in the celebrated study of Great War literature by Paul Fussell, *The Great War and Modern Memory* (New York: Oxford Univ. Press, 1975), 36–74.

20. *Gettysburg Compiler,* Dec. 26, 1914.

21. For this remarkable episode, see Stanley Weintraub, *Silent Night: The Story of the World War I Christmas Truce* (New York: Free Press, 2001). This incident, which occurred in Flanders, was bastardized in 1997 by Garth Brooks in his Christmas ballad, "Belleau Wood." In it, he sings about two soldiers, an American and a German, who called a truce on Christmas Eve during World War I. However, Belleau Wood was a battle fought in June 1918. No snow, no truce. The only Christmas the Americans experienced in Europe during the actual war was in December 1917, and no informal truce had occurred since 1914. American soldiers and noncombatants did celebrate Christmas in France, Belgium, and even Germany in 1918, but by then the war was over.

22. Zouaves were French colonial infantry that wore uniforms patterned after their national dress—baggy pants, short jacket, vest, sash and fez or turban, with lots of piping and trim. They were considered elite troops. During the American Civil War, several Union regiments and a few Confederate units adopted Zouave-style uniforms and light-infantry tactics.

23. *Gettysburg Compiler,* Feb. 27, 1915. Note: Eddie would not turn forty for another six months.

24. For the role of the USCG in the Great War, see Alex Larzelere, *The Coast Guard in World War I: An Untold Story* (Annapolis: U.S. Naval Institute Press, 2003).

25. John M. Cooper, *Woodrow Wilson: A Biography* (New York: Knopf, 2009), 272–73.

26. *Gettysburg Times,* May 2, 1916.

27. Gilbert, *First World War,* 132.

28. James J. Bloom, "Neuve Chapelle, Batle of (March 1915),"in Tucker, *European Powers in the First World War,* 505–6.

29. *Gettysburg Compiler,* Apr. 17, 1915, Nov. 14, 1914; *Adams County News,* Jan. 30, 1915.

30. Thomas D. Mays, "Chemical Warfare," in Tucker, *European Powers in the First World War,* 186–87.

31. *Adams County News,* Apr. 10, 1915.

32. Omar N. Bradley and Clay Blair, *A General's Life: An Autobiography by General of the Army Omar N. Bradley* (New York: Simon & Schuster, 1983), 34.

33. Jack McCallum, "*Lusitania,* sinking of," in Tucker, *European Powers in the First World War,* 449; *Gettysburg Compiler,* May 15, 1915.

34. *Gettysburg Compiler,* May 15, 1915.

35. Robert H. Ferrell, *Woodrow Wilson and World War I, 1917–1921* (New York: Harper & Row, 1985), 10.

36. *Gettysburg Compiler,* May 15, 1915.

37. Robert H. Zeigler, *America's Great War: World War I and the American Experience* (New York: Rowman & Littlefield, 2000), 22–25; Eric Dorn Brose, *A History of the Great War: World War I and the International Crisis of the Early Twentieth Century* (New York: Oxford University Press, 2010), 116.

38. *Gettysburg Compiler,* Aug. 7, 1915.

39. Jan Finkel, "Eddie Plank," Society for American Baseball Research Web site, accessed Dec. 8, 2014, http://sabr.org/bioproj/person/339eaa5c.

40. *Gettysburg Compiler,* Oct. 16, 1915.

41. *Gettysburg Compiler,* Dec. 11, 1915

42. Allan Millet and Peter Maslowski, *For the Common Defense: A Military History of the United States of America,* rev. and expanded ed. (New York: Free Press, 1994), 340–41.

43. *Adams County News,* Mar. 18, 1916

44. *Adams County News,* June 13, 1916.

45. Mitchell Yockleson, "The United States Armed Forces and the Mexican Punitive Expedition (Part 1)," *Prologue: Quarterly of the National Archives and Records Administration* 29 (Fall 1997): 256–62.

46. Ibid.

47. Foulk and Eichelberger, *Adams County in the World War.* This volume spells out the service record of every person from Adams County who served in the Great War. I scoured the records to ascertain whether the listed persons also had served along the border or the expedition into Mexico.

48. *Adams County News,* July 29, 1916.

49. John E. Stanchak, "Clem, John Lincoln, 'Johnny,'" in *Historical Times Illustrated Encyclopedia of the Civil War,* ed. Patricia Faust (New York: Harper & Row, 1986), 145.

50. Millet and Maslowski, *For the Common Defense,* 336–37.

51. *Gettysburg Compiler,* Apr. 15, 1916.

52. Millet and Maslowski, *For the Common Defense,* 341–42.

53. Zeigler, *America's Great War,* 37.

54. Stephen B. Reed, "One Hundred Years of Price Change: The Consumer Price Index and the American Inflation Experience," *Monthly Labor Review* (Apr. 2014), http://www.bls.gov/opub/mlr/2014/article/one-hundred-years-of-price-change-the-consumer-price-index-and-the-american-inflation-experience-2.htm.

55. *Gettysburg Compiler,* July 9, Aug. 2, 1916.

56. *Gettysburg Compiler,* Aug. 12, 1916.

57. David M. Kennedy, *Over Here: The First World War and American Society,* 2d ed. (New York: Oxford Univ. Press, 2004), 12.

58. *Gettysburg Compiler,* Oct. 21, 1916.

59. Kennedy, *Over Here,* 12.

60. "1916 Presidential General Election Results—Pennsylvania," *Dave Leip's Atlas of U.S. Presidential Elections,* accessed July 26, 2017, http://uselectionatlas.org/RESULTS/state.php?year=1916&fips=42&f=0&off=0&elect=0; Robert L. Bloom, *A History of Adams County, Pennsylvania, 1700–1990* (Gettysburg: Adams County Historical Society, 1992), 451.

61. *Gettysburg Compiler,* Nov. 11, 1916

62. Zeigler, *America's Great War,* 42–43.

63. *Adams County News,* Jan. 6, 1917.

64. Quoted in Ferrell, *Woodrow Wilson and World War I,* 10.

65. Zeigler, *America's Great War,* 48–49.

66. Gilbert, *First World War,* 308.

67. Transcript of Zimmermann Telegram (2017), available online at *Our Documents,* accessed July 26, 2017, http://www.ourdocuments.gov/doc.php?doc=60&page=transcript.

68. A. Scott Berg, *Wilson* (New York: Berkley, 2013), 427.

3. WAR AND "INVASION," 1917

1. Edward F. Coffman, *The War to End All Wars: The American Military Experience in World War I* (Lexington: Univ. Press of Kentucky, 1968), 39.

2. *Gettysburg Times,* May 9, 1917.

3. *Gettysburg Compiler,* May 19, 1917.

4. *Gettysburg Times,* May 10, 1917.

5. As deployed to the American Expeditionary Forces, each infantry regiment would have an authorized strength of 112 officers and 3,720 men assigned to three battalions and a machine-gun company. The battalion comprised four companies with six officers and 250 men each.

6. *Gettysburg Times,* May 23, 1917.

7. Assistant Secretary of War William Ingraham to Chairman, Gettysburg National Park Commission, May 26, 1917, General Correspondence, 1916–17, GNMP Library.

8. Bradley S. Keefer, *Conflicting Memories on the "River of Death": The Chickamauga Battlefield and the Spanish-American War, 1863–1933* (Kent, Ohio: Kent State Univ. Press, 2013), 272–73.

9. Paul L. Foulk and Percy S. Eichelberger, eds., *Adams County in the World War: April 6, 1917 to November 11, 1918* (Harrisburg, Pa.: Evangelical Press, 1920), 11–12.

10. *Gettysburg Compiler,* Apr. 14, 1917. One article of interest to the seminary's faculty and student body that appeared in the paper a week later carried the news of the battlefield death of a former guest lecturer and scholar. Dr. Caspar René Gregory, "who delivered the Holmon Lecture at Gettysburg Theological Seminary in 1912 fell in battle for the German cause April 9, 1917." Gregory was born in Philadelphia and educated in the United States but became a German citizen, having taught in that country since 1891. The *Compiler* story reported, "He had been the professor of theology in Leipsic University and went into battle at 68 and celebrated his 70th anniversary at the front last November as a sergeant major. Gregory was the oldest man to volunteer for the German army. He died one day after being struck by Allied artillery." Actually, Gregory had been immobilized in a horse accident and was in a hospital in the Picardy region of German-occupied France when he was caught in an artillery barrage. He was unable to be evacuated, was wounded in his hospital bed on April 8, and died the next day. See Robin Schäfer, "WWI—Germany's Oldest Wartime Volunteer, Caspar René Gregory, 1846–1917," *Gott mit Uns: Germany Military History 1848–1945,* Jan. 30, 2013, https://gottmituns.net/2013/01/30/ww1-germanys-oldest-wartime-volunteer-caspar-rene-gregory-1846–1917/.

11. Foulk and Eichelberger, *Adams County in the World War,* 18–27.

12. David M. Kennedy, *Over Here: The First World War and American Society,* 2d ed. (New York: Oxford Univ. Press, 2004), 144–54.

13. Foulk and Eichelberger, *Adams County in the World War,* 13–14; *Adams County News,* June 9, 1917; *Star and Sentinel,* June 16, 1917.

14. Martin Gilbert, *First World War: A Complete History* (New York: Holt, 1994), 324–29.

15. *Star and Sentinel,* Aug. 4, 1917.

16. Foulk and Eichelberger, *Adams County in the World War,* 258–61; "The Loss of the Troopship *Tuscania,*" *Islay Info,* accessed July 28, 2017, http://www.islayinfo.com/loss-troopship-tuscania-islay.html.

17. Telegram reprinted in *New Oxford Item,* Feb. 7, 1918.

18. "The School of War: U.S. Submarines in World War I," *Undersea Warfare: The Official Magazine of the U.S. Submarine Force* (Spring 2004), available online at https://archive.is/zBDf; Foulk and Eichelberger, *Adams County in the World War,* 58–59.

19. Foulk and Eichelberger, *Adams County in the World War,* 62–63, 73; *New Oxford Item,* Jan. 31, Apr. 11, 1918.

20. It could be argued that Fort McPherson, Georgia, in the city of Atlanta, also occupied part of a Civil War battlefield, as severe fighting took place in the area in July 1864.It became a U.S. Army post in 1885 and thus had been in existence as a military installation long before World War I.

21. *Gettysburg Compiler,* June 23, 1917.

22. *Gettysburg Times,* July 9, 1917; Kennedy, *Over Here,* 186. For an in-depth look at the CTCA's work at Gettysburg, see Peter Miele, "Men, Morality, and Misbehavior: A Social Study of the World War I Camps at Gettysburg and the Town That Surrounded Them, 1917–1918," in *Duty Calls at Home: Central Pennsylvania Responds to the Great War, 1914–1918,* ed. Steven Burg, et al. (Shippensburg, Pa.: Shippensburg Univ. Center for Applied History, 2014), 45–76.

23. Benedict Crowell and Robert F. Wilson, *The Road to France:* vol. 1 of 6, *The Transportation of Troops and Military Supplies, 1917–1918* (New Haven: Yale Univ. Press, 1921), 30.

24. *Gettysburg Times,* June 2, 1917.

25. *Gettysburg Compiler,* June 9, 1917.

26. "We're in the Army Now," composed by Isham Jones with lyrics by Tell Taylor and Ole Olson (New York: Tell Taylor Music Publisher, 1917).

27. *Star and Sentinel,* May 10, 1917; *Gettysburg Times,* June 2, 1917.

28. *Adams County News,* May 26, 1917.

29. Kennedy, *Over Here,* 95, 117.

30. *Gettysburg Compiler,* April 21, 1917. Martin Weaver took out the advertisement to sell real estate locate on East Middle, Hanover, York, Railroad, Water, Fourth and Fifth Streets.

31. Kennedy, *Over Here,* 242–43.

32. Ibid., 143.

33. The Kurtz Memorial Playground no longer exists. Today, the site is occupied by the Gettysburg School District educational complex. However, there still are several athletic fields on the grounds, including a football stadium, soccer/hockey fields, tennis courts, and swings and playsets for younger students When the United States entered the war, Paul Kurtz transferred to the Army Air Service and became a pilot. Lieutenant Kurtz was killed in an accident in the late spring of 1918. (*Gettysburg Compiler,* June 1, 1918.)

34. *Gettysburg Compiler,* Aug. 31, 1917.

35. *Gettysburg Compiler,* Sept. 8, 1917. Every edition of the *Times* printed the following statement on page 2: "The Gettysburg Times takes absolutely no part in politics,

being neutral on all such matters. Anything that appears in our general news columns, concerning state or national politics, is furnished by sources which are strictly nonpartisan."

36. *Gettysburg Times,* July 5, 1917.

37. *Gettysburg Times,* June 9, 1917.

38. *Adams County News,* July 21, 28, 1917.

39. *Harrisburg Telegraph,* June 30, 1917.

40. *Gettysburg Times,* May 5, 1917.

41. Foulk and Eichelberger, *Adams County in the World War,* 32–33.

42. Kennedy, *Over Here,* 61. Creel began his career as an investigative journalist, and by the time of the war he had been the owner of the *Kansas City Independent* and the editor of the *Rocky Mountain News.*

43. *Gettysburg Times,* Dec. 21, 1917.

44. George Washington Cullum and Wirt Robinson eds., *Biographical Register of the Officers and Graduates of the U.S. Military Academy* (Saginaw, Mich.: Seemann & Peters, 1920), supplement, 6-A:377–78.

45. *Adams County News,* June 16, 1917.

46. *Sixty-First Annual Report of the Association of Graduates of the United States Military Academy* (Newburgh, N.Y.: Moore Printing, 1930).

47. Cullum and Robinson, *Biographical Register,* 598–99; Adjutant General's Office, *United States Army Register* (Washington, D.C.: GPO, 1920), 515.

48. *Adams County News,* June 16, 1917.

49. Nancy Ford Gentile, *The Great War and America: Civil-Military Relations during World War I* (Westport, Conn.: Praeger Security International, 2008), 57–70.

50. *Gettysburg Times,* Feb. 14, 1918.

51. *Adams County News,* June 16, 1917.

52. *New Oxford Item,* July 19, 1917.

53. Joseph J. Stone journal, World War I Veterans Questionnaires, 59th U.S. Infantry, 4th Division, U.S. Army Heritage and Education Center, Carlisle, Pa.

54. *Harrisburg Telegraph,* Sept. 13, 1917.

55. *Gettysburg Times,* Sept. 11, 12, 1917.

56. Howard to Nicholson, July 10, 1917, General Correspondence, 1916–17, GNMP Archives. (Also in the Archives are the blueprints of every structure that the Army built on the Park in 1917.) Howard's USMA class date was found in Cullum and Robinson's *Register.*

57. J. P. Nicholson to Secretary of War, July 19, 1917, copy in Gettysburg National Park Commission Journal for 1917, GNMP Archives.

58. *Harrisburg Telegraph,* July 21, 1917; *Annual Report of the Gettysburg National Military Park* Commission, July 1, 1918.

59. *Adams County News,* June 23, 1917.

60. *Star and Sentinel,* June 16, 1917.

61. *Harrisburg Telegraph,* July 23, 1917.

62. *Gettysburg Compiler,* July 14, 1917.

63. *Gettysburg Compiler,* June 20, 1917.

64. *New Oxford Item,* June 28, 1917.

65. *Harrisburg Telegraph,* May 15, 1919. This article announced Smiley's return from France and gave the details of his service.

66. *New Oxford Item,* July 19, 1917.

67. *New Oxford Item,* Aug. 9, Oct. 4, 1917.

68. *Adams County News,* July 28, 1917.

69. Committee for Public Information, *Official U. S. Bulletin* 1 (July 12, 1917): 7.

70. Cullum and Robinson, *Biographical Register,* 353–54.

71. Brig. Gen. Chase Kennedy to Maj. Gen. Bell, Aug. 11, 1917, Record Group 407 (Adjutant General's Office), Central Decimal Files and Project Files, 1917–1924, box 117, AG 123.05–680.43, National Archives and Record Administration (NARA) II, College Park, Md. (herafter cited as RG 407).

72. *Gettysburg Complier,* Aug. 11, 1917.

73. *New Oxford Item,* Aug. 16, 1917.

74. Cullum and Robinson, *Biographical Register,* 353–54.

75. *Gettysburg Times,* Sept. 21, 1917.

76. Attorney General to the Secretary of War, Oct. 3, 1917, RG 407.

77. *Gettysburg Times,* Oct. 3, 1917. Burnett had attended West Point but was dismissed in 1878, during his senior year, and never graduated. (*Official Register of the Officers and Cadets of the U.S. Military Academy* [June 1879], 31.)

78. *Gettysburg Compiler,* Oct. 6, 1917.

79. *New Oxford Item,* Oct. 4, 1917.

80. *New Oxford Item,* Oct. 18, 1917,

81. *New Oxford Item,* July 19, 1917; *Adams County News,* Aug. 4, 1917.

82. *Adams County News,* Aug. 4, 1917.

83. *York Daily,* Sept. 17, 1917.

84. *Star and Sentinel,* Oct. 6, 1917.

85. *Carlisle Herald,* as quoted in the *Gettysburg Times,* Nov. 6, 1917.

86. Miele, "Men, Morality, and Misbehavior," 57.

87. Ibid., 52.

88. *New Oxford Item,* Sept. 27, 1917.

89. *Gettysburg Times,* Oct. 2, 1917.

90. See, for example, *York Daily,* Aug. 1, 1917: "For the soldiers from Gettysburg the use of the YMCA and the St. John's Club has already been tendered for recreation purposes. The school board has also tendered the use of the playground on Small's meadow where the baseball diamond is about ready, the back stop having been completed."

91. *New Oxford Item,* Sept. 27, Aug. 30, 1917.

92. See for example, *Gettysburg Compiler,* Sept. 22, 1917.

93. *Star and Sentinel,* July 28, 1917.

94. *New Oxford Item,* Aug. 16, 23, Oct. 18, 1917.

95. *Gettysburg Times,* Sept. 28, Oct. 6, 1917.

96. "Remedy of the Sanitary Situation, Camp of the U.S. Troops, Gettysburg, Pa.," Records of the Office of the Surgeon General (Army), 1775–1994, Correspondence, 3/1/1917–9/30/1927, file 721.1, box 12, (Camp Colt), Record Group 112, NARA.

97. Inventory of structures at Camp, U.S. Troops, Gettysburg, Nov. 16, 1917, General Correspondence, Camp Colt, RG 393; F. L. Pleadwell, "Sanitation in Camps and Hospitals on the British Front in France," *Military Surgeon* 44 (Jan. 1919): 1–29. The author was a U.S. Navy surgeon who had been an observer with the British army on the Western Front in 1917. In 1919, the park's assistant engineer noted that there were forty-nine incinerators remaining in the abandoned camp. Either more were built in 1918 or not all of the incinerators were used for human waste. (E. M. Ewitt, "Report of the Condi-

tion of the Camp Site of the Army Camp in the Gettysburg National Park, January 20, 1919," GNPC Daily Journal, 1919, GNMP Archives.) At any rate, the 1917 inventory lists twenty incinerators.

98. *Gettysburg Times,* Aug. 15, 1917.

99. *Gettysburg Times,* Aug. 17, 22, 29, 1917.

100. *Harrisburg Telegraph,* Sept. 7, 1917; *Gettysburg Compiler,* Sept. 8, 1917.

101. *Gettysburg Times,* Sept. 8, 1917.

102. *Gettysburg Compiler,* Sept. 8, 1917.

103. *Harrisburg Telegraph,* Sept. 14, 1917.

104. After the camp was abandoned in 1919, Col. Emmor Cope, the GNMP engineer, commented on the trenches and machine-gun pits on the Trostle Farm that needed to be filled and graded. See Emmor B. Cope, "Notes to the 1920 Annual Report, Gettysburg, Pa., May 12, 1920," Records of the Gettysburg National Park Commission, GNMP Archives. Don Hinks, owner of Gettysburg Electronics (a purveyor of metal detectors), excavated an artifact known as a screw picket, or "pig tail" (from the French *queue de cochon*), used to secure barbed-wire entanglements in front of trench systems, in the vicinity of modern-day Colt Park Recreational Complex, which in 1917 was part of the U.S. camp occupied by 60th Infantry troops.

105. Allen M. Brandt, *No Magic Bullet: A Social History of Venereal Disease in the United States since 1880* (New York: Oxford Univ. Press, 1987), 61–70.

106. Thomas A. Hoff, *U.S. Doughboy, 1916–19* (Oxford: Osprey, 2005), 18–21.

107. Ernest L. Wrentmore, *In Spite of Hell: A Factual Story of Incidents That Occurred during World War I, as Experienced by the Youngest Soldier to Have Seen Combat Duty with the American Expeditionary Forces as a Member of the Famous Company I, 60th Infantry, Fifth (Red Diamond) Division* (New York: Greenwich, 1958), 11, 28–29.

108. Stone journal.

109. *Gettysburg Compiler,* July 7, 1915.

110. Nancy Gentile Ford, *Americans All! Foreign-Born Soldiers in World War I* (College Station: Texas A&M Univ. Press, 2001), 3.

111. *New Oxford Item,* Sept. 13, 27, 1917.

112. *Gettysburg Times,* Sept. 29, 1917.

113. *New Oxford Item,* Oct. 11, 1917.

114. *Star and Sentinel,* Oct. 20, 1917.

115. *New Oxford Item,* Oct. 4, 1917; Hoff, *U.S. Doughboy,* 12.

116. Stone journal.

117. *Gettysburg Times,* Nov. 2, 1917 (emphasis added).

118. *Gettysburg Times,* Nov. 3, 1917.

119. Huidekoper to Nicholson, Sept. 14, 1917; Nicholson to Burnett, Nov. 6, 1917, both in General Correspondence, GNMP Commission, 1916–17, GNMP Archives.

120. Inventory of structures at Camp, U.S. Troops, Gettysburg, Nov. 16, 1917. General Correspondence, Records of United States Army Continental Commands, 1821–1920 (Camp Colt), Record Group 393, NARA. The camp's approximate acreage was determined with Planimeter, using a plan having a scale of 1" = 500' from a blueprint of the camp layout found in the same file. Thanks to Dean Shultz, of Gettysburg, for ascertaining the approximate size of the camp.

121. *Gettysburg Times,* Nov. 26, 1917.

122. Stone journal.

4. GOODBYE GETTYSBURG, HELLO FRANCE

1. *Gettysburg Times,* Nov. 9, 1917.

2. C. Francis Reisner and Benny Davis, lyricists, with music by Billy Baskette, "Goodbye Broadway, Hello France!" (New York: Leo Feist, 1917).

3. John S. D. Eisenhower, *Yanks: The Epic Story of the American Army in World War I* (New York: Free Press, 2001), 81–86. Of course, hundreds of Americans already had died fighting for the armed forces of Canada, the U.K., and France. These were the first soldiers assigned to a U.S. military organization killed on foreign soil during the Great War.

4. *Gettysburg Times,* Sept. 26, 3, 1917.

5. History Committee, Seventy-Ninth Division Association, *History of the Seventy-Ninth Division A.E.F. during the World War: 1917–1919,* 2d ed. (Lancaster, Pa.: Steinman & Steinman, 1922), 17.

6. *Gettysburg Times,* Oct. 29, 1917.

7. *Gettysburg Compiler,* July 7, 1917.

8. *Star and Sentinel,* Sept. 29, 1917; Paul L. Foulk and Percy S. Eichelberger, eds., *Adams County in the World War: April 6, 1917 to November 11, 1918* (Harrisburg, Pa.: Evangelical Press, 1920), 240.

9. *Gettysburg Times,* June 27, 1918.

10. History Committee, *History of the Seventy-Ninth Division,* 12, 20–21, 24–26.

11. Williams to Nicholson, Oct. 30, 1917, Jan 26, 1918, General Correspondence of the GNMP Commission, GNMP Library.

12. Emmett J. Scott, *Scott's Official History of the American Negro in the World War* (Chicago: Homewood, 1919), 107–8, 130.

13. *Gettysburg Times,* Feb. 26, 1919.

14. *Gettysburg Times,* Oct. 2, 1917.

15. U.S. War Department, *Manual for Noncommissioned Officers and Privates of Infantry of the United States Army* (Washington, D.C.: GPO, 1917), 9–74.

16. History Committee, *History of the Seventy-Ninth Division,* 30.

17. Ibid., 8–9, 32–43.

18. Foulk and Eichelberger, *Adams County in the World War,* 51. The editors of this book state that he was in the Thirty-Second Division, which was a mistake, since the 149th M.G. Battalion was assigned to the Forty-Second Division. Gehring was a veteran of Mexican Border service with the Pennsylvania National Guard. He later was transferred to the Forty-Second, comprising National Guardsmen from across the United States, thus earning for the division the nickname "Rainbow Division." The place of his death was extrapolated from U.S. Army Center for Military History, *Order of Battle of the United States Land Forces in the World War:* vol. 1 of 3, *Services of Supply, and Separate Forces* (Washington, D.C.: GPO, 1988), 1:276. Gehring is buried in the Meuse-Argonne American Cemetery.

19. Clifford P. Hall and John P. Lehn, eds., *York County and the World War* (York, Pa.: N.p., 1920), 51.

20. 1st Lt. John J. Halliday to Mrs. Gehring, printed in the *Gettysburg Times,* Apr. 11, 1918.

21. Foulk and Eichelberger, *Adams County in the World War,* 69; *Order of Battle of the United States Land Forces in the World War,* 1:28–29. Rupprecht is buried in Saint-Mihiel American Cemetery.

22. *Gettysburg Compiler,* May 11, 1918. After the war, Lentz's remains were repatriated to Soldiers' National Cemetery, Gettysburg.

23. Martin Gilbert, *First World War: A Complete History* (New York: Holt, 1994), 398–401, 406–10, 420–21, 426–27.

24. *Gettysburg Times,* May 30, 1918.

25. Christian A. Bach and Henry N. Hall, *The Fourth Division: Its Services and Achievements in the World War* (N.p.: Fourth Division, 1920), 42–45.

26. Foulk and Eichelberger, *Adams County in the World War,* 73; *Gettysburg Compiler,* July 11, 1918; *Order of Battle of the United States Land Forces in the World War,* 1:48–49.

27. War Department, General Orders No. 110 (1918), available online at *Military* Times' Hall of Valor database, http://valor.militarytimes.com/recipient.php?recipientid=8918.

28. *Gettysburg Times,* Nov. 27, 1918.

29. *Gettysburg Times,* July 6, June 18, 1918; Foulk and Eichelberger, *Adams County in the World War,* 95.

30. *Gettysburg Times,* July 6, 1918.

31. Foulk and Eichelberger, *Adams County in the World War,* 78–79, 199, 257.

32. Ibid., 273.

33. S. L. A. Marshall, *World War I* (New York: American Heritage, 1985), 386; Eisenhower, *Yanks,* 161.

34. Edward Coffman, *The War to End All Wars: The American Military Experience in World War I* (Lexington: Univ. Press of Kentucky, 1968), 214.

35. *Gettysburg Compiler,* Aug. 10, 1918.

36. Eisenhower, *Yanks,* 163–69.

37. Foulk and Eichelberger, *Adams County in the World War,* 152.

38. Dominic Pence, questionnaire, World War I Survey Questionnaires, Third Division, USAHEC.

39. Kermit Roosevelt, *Quentin Roosevelt: A Sketch with Letters* (New York: Scribners, 1921), 169–72; Edward Rickenbacker, *Fighting the Flying Circus* (New York: Frederick A. Stokes Co., 1919), 194–96.

40. Foulk and Eichelberger, *Adams County in the World War,* 97, 126, 128, 158, 168, 194, 232.

41. Ibid., 56, 65, 67; *Gettysburg Times,* Oct. 16, 1918. Richwine and Rider's burial locations were found by using the American Battle Monument Commission Web site's search engine, https://www.abmc.gov/.

42. Joseph J. Stone journal, World War I Veterans Questionnaires, 59th U.S. Infantry, Fourth Division, U.S. Army Heritage and Education Center, Carlisle, Pa.

43. Eisenhower, *Yanks,* 173.

44. Stone journal.

45. American Battle Monuments Commission, *American Armies and Battlefields in Europe: A History, Guide and Reference Book* (Washington, D.C.: GPO, 1938), 39.

46. Stone journal.

47. *Gettysburg Times,* Oct. 23, 1918; Foulk and Eichelberger, *Adams County in the World War,* 49.

48. *Gettysburg Times,* Oct. 16, 1918. Mamie Eisenhower had become a good friend of Dorothy Duckstad, a new mother who had given birth to a son in June. She called on Dorothy frequently while her husband was overseas. More than fifty years later,

Mrs. Eisenhower still remembered, "I would often stop and visit her before her child was born" (Quoted in Rev. David C. Burnite, "The Breidenbaugh Home, Part 2," *Gettysburg Times,* May 19, 1987). In the autumn of 1918, the future First Lady undoubtedly was one of the first people to console the young widow. After the war, Major Duckstad was disinterred from his temporary French grave and buried in the U.S. Military Academy Cemetery (Karl Stelly, "Major John Benjamin Duckstad," Find a Grave Web site, Jan. 22, 2010, http://www.findagrave.com/cgi-bin/fg.cgi?page=gr&GSsr=81&GSvcid=77145&GRid=46976742&df=p&).

49. Foulk and Eichelberger, *Adams County in the World War,* 182.

50. Ibid., 120, 151, 209, 238–39, 241–42.

51. Susan Zeiger, "Women in the American Expeditionary Force" in *The United States in the First World War: An Encyclopedia,* ed. Anne C. Venzon (New York: Routledge, 1999), 803–5.

52. *Gettysburg Compiler,* Feb. 9, 1918.

53. Jack Caddigan and James Alexander Brennan, composers, lyrics by Louis Delamarre, "The Rose of No Man's Land" (New York: Leo Feist, 1918).

54. Lyn MacDonald, *The Roses of No Man's Land* (London: Penguin, 1993), 317.

55. *Gettysburg Compiler,* Aug. 3, 1918.

56. History Committee, *History of the Seventy-Ninth Division,* 42–47.

57. Foulk and Eichelberger, *Adams County in the World War,* 71.

58. History Committee, *History of the Seventy-Ninth Division,* 53, 55–57.

59. Ernest L. Wrentmore, *In Spite of Hell: A Factual Story of Incidents That Occurred during World War I, as Experienced by the Youngest Soldier to Have Seen Combat Duty with the American Expeditionary Forces as a Member of the Famous Company I, 60th Infantry, Fifth (Red Diamond) Division* (New York: Greenwich, 1958), 95.

60. American Battle Monuments Commission, *American Armies and Battlefields in Europe,* 108.

61. Wrentmore, *In Spite of Hell,* 104.

62. Kenyon Stevenson, ed., *The Official History of the Fifth Division, U.S.A., during the Period of Its Organization and of Its Operations in the European World War, 1917–1919,* ed. Kenyon Stevenson (Washington, D.C.: Society of the Fifth Division, 1919), 349.

63. Foulk and Eichelberger, *Adams County in the World War,* 164.

64. Eisenhower, *Yanks,* 187–88.

65. *Gettysburg Times,* Oct. 5, 1918.

66. Dale E. Wilson, *Treat 'Em Rough: The Birth of American Armor, 1917–1920* (Novato, Calif.: Presidio, 1990), 25, 92, 112.

5. "TREAT 'EM ROUGH"

1. Carlo D'Este, *Eisenhower: A Soldier's Life* (New York: Holt, 2002), 82.

2. Dwight D. Eisenhower, *At Ease: Stories I Tell to Friends* (Garden City, N.Y.: Doubleday, 1967), 111–33. Mamie spelled the baby's nickname "Ikkie," but her granddaughter, Susan Eisenhower, spells it "Ikky." See Susan Eisenhower, *Mrs. Ike: Memories and Reflections on the Life of Mamie Eisenhower* (New York: Farrar, Straus & Giroux, 1996), 51, 65.

3. Eisenhower, *At Ease,* 136.

4. Ibid.; Dale E. Wilson, *Treat 'Em Rough: The Birth of American Armor, 1917–1920* (Novato, Calif.: Presidio, 1990), 74–75. The U.S. model, which never made it overseas, was dubbed the Mark VIII.

5. Eisenhower, *At Ease,* 137.

6. *Gettysburg Times,* Mar. 7, 1918.

7. *Gettysburg Times,* Apr. 15, 1918.

8. *Gettysburg Times,* Apr. 9, 1918.

9. *Gettysburg Times,* Mar. 27, 1918.

10. Christopher Capozzola, *Uncle Sam Wants You: World War I and the Making of the Modern American Citizen* (New York: Oxford Univ. Press, 2008): 19.

11. *Gettysburg Times,* Mar. 6, 1918.

12. *Gettysburg Times,* Mar. 16, 1918.

13. Gettysburg Borough Council Minute Book # 8, 1915–1921, 205. Council minutes for January 7, 1918, recorded that Charles Culp was elected chief of police by an 8–1 vote, and one "special police" officer was authorized, making a total of three on the police force.

14. General Orders No. 7, Mar. 29, 1918, and General Orders No. 3, General Correspondence, Records of United States Army Continental Commands, 1821–1920 (Camp Colt), RG 393, NARA (hereafter cited as Camp Colt, RG 393).

15. Eisenhower, *At Ease,* 137.

16. April Strength Return for Camp Colt, WWI Strength Returns, Record Group 407 (Adjutant General's Office), Records of the Adjutant General's Office, box 1066 (HQ File), RG 407, National Archives and Record Administration (NARA) II, College Park, Md. (herafter cited as RG 407). Unfortunately, Garner's personnel file was unavailable: in 1973, 80 percent of the army's personnel records from 1912–1960 were destroyed in a fire at the National Personnel Records Center, St. Louis, Missouri.

17. *Gettysburg Times,* Mar. 23, 1918.

18. Director of the Tank Corps to the Adjutant General of the Army, Apr. 18, 1918, Records of the Adjutant General's Office, RG 407.

19. Personnel Return for Camp Colt for the month of June 1918, Records of the Adjutant General's Office, WWI Strength Returns, box 1066 (HQ File), RG 407.

20. *Gettysburg Times,* Mar. 28–29, 1918.

21. Eisenhower, *At Ease,* 138.

22. Eisenhower, *Mrs. Ike,* 53–54. Today, two of their temporary Gettysburg homes are identified by historical markers. The former Alpha Tau Omega fraternity house, adjacent to the Gettysburg College campus at 157 North Washington Street, now houses the college's Eisenhower Institute. The one at 237 Springs Avenue, which has been significantly enlarged since 1918, is now a private residence.

23. Eisenhower, *At Ease,* 150.

24. Eisenhower, "Warning to the Reader," in *At Ease,* unnumbered page between dedication page and table of contents.

25. Report of Lt. Col. F. W. Weed, MC, Apr. 12, 1918, RG 112: Records of the Office of the Surgeon General (Army), 1775–1994, Correspondence, 3/1/1917–9/30/1927, file 721.1, box 12 (Camp Colt), NARA (hereafter cited as Camp Colt, RG 112).

26. The Sibley stove was a Civil War–era invention still being used by the U.S. Army during World War I.

27. *Gettysburg Times,* Apr. 9, 1918.

28. U.S. Army Center for Military History, *Order of Battle of the United States Land Forces in the World War, Zone of the Interior:* vol. 3 of 3, part 3, *Directory of Troops,* (Washington, D.C.: GPO, 1988), 1542–47; Wilson, "*Treat 'Em Rough,*" 124.

29. *Gettysburg Times,* June 11, 1918.

30. Personnel Orders No. 46, HQ, Camp Colt, Oct. 5. 1918, Camp Colt, RG 393.

31. Camp Colt, RG 393; *Gettysburg Times,* June 12, 1918.

32. World War I Veterans' Questionnaire for 2d Lt. Charles H. Phillips, Army Heritage and Education Center.

33. Photographs of "Battling Lizzie" can be found in the Pennsylvania State Archives, RG 19 (Records of the Department of Military and Veterans' Affairs War History Commission [World War I]) General File, 1915–20, 1928, (13–1311, carton 4).

34. Eisenhower, *At Ease,* 146.

35. *Gettysburg Times,* June 6, 1918; Wilson, *Treat 'em Rough,* 76.

36. Eisenhower, *At Ease,* 147; *Gettysburg Times,* Nov. 15, 1918 (emphasis added).

37. David Bocquelet, "Renault FT Light Tank, 1917," *Tanks Encyclopedia: The Online Tank Museum,* June 10, 2014, http://www.tanks-encyclopedia.com/ww1/fr/renault_ft.php.

38. Martin Gilbert, *First World War: A Complete History* (New York: Holt, 1994), 378–79.

39. Charles F. Horne, ed., *Source Records of the Great War,* vol. 5 of 10 ([New York]: National Alumni, 1923), 392.

40. Camp Colt File, GNMP Library; Stephen Pope, ed., "Colonel Frank Summers," *The First Tank Crews: The Life Stories of Those Who Crewed the First Tanks in September 1916,* 2013, accessed June 2, 2015, http://www.firsttankcrews.com/dcoyhq.htm (site discontinued).

41. Camp Colt File, GNMP Library; Bryn Hammond, *Cambrai 1917: The Myth of The First Great Tank Battle* (London: Orion, 2009), 167–69; Alexander Turner, *Cambrai 1917: The Birth of Armoured Warfare* (Oxford: Osprey, 2007), 49–50; Pope, *First Tank Crews.*"

42. Eisenhower, *At Ease,* 147.

43. John F. Votaw, "Tanks," in *The European Powers in the First World War: An Encyclopedia,* ed. Spencer C. Tucker (New York: Garland, 1996), 684.

44. Paul L. Foulk and Percy S. Eichelberger, eds., *Adams County in the World War: April 6, 1917 to November 11, 1918* (Harrisburg, Pa.: Evangelical Press, 1920), 124

45. Hammond, *Cambrai 1917,* 353–54.

46. *United States Army in the World War, 1917–1919,* vol. 1 of 17, *Organization of the American Expeditionary Forces* (Washington, D.C.: Center for Military History, 1988), 7.

47. Eisenhower, *At Ease,* 140.

48. Allen Sinsheimer, "'We Treat 'Em Rough': The Tank Corps, Aristocracy of America," *Motor Age,* July 4, 1918, 18–19.

49. John B. Kimberly to his wife, June 22, 1918, John B. Kimberly Collection (AFC/2001/001/50472), Veterans History Project, American Folklife Center, Library of Congress.

50. *The Howitzer: The Yearbook of the United States Corps of Cadets Edited by the 1st Class* (West Point, N.Y.: U.S. Corps of Cadets, 1915), 163; Eisenhower, *At Ease,* 141–42.

51. Elisha S. Lewis, "Report of Development Battalion," Oct. 21, 1918, attached to letter from Thomas Scott to the Surgeon General of the Army, Oct. 21, 1918, box 12, file 353.91, Surg. Gen.'s Office, 1917–27, Camp Colt, RG 112 (hereafter cited as Lewis report).

52. Allen M. Brandt, *No Magic Bullet: A Social History of Veneral Disease in the United States since 1880* (New York: Oxford Univ. Press, 1987), 111.

53. Supply request from commanding officer, Development Battalion to Supply Officer, Camp Colt, for 5,160 feet of barbed wire, fifty-five twelve-foot fence posts, and staples for stockade "to be used by the venereal patients who are to be isolated by the Battalion Surgeon." Camp Colt, RG 393.

54. Lewis report.

55. Brandt, *No Magic Bullet,* 78.

56. John B. Kimberly to his wife, June 24, 1918, Kimberly Collection.

57. Brandt, *No Magic Bullet,* 62–65.

58. General Orders No. 8, Headquarters, Camp Colt, Gettysburg, Pa., Apr. 12, 1918, Camp Colt, RG 393.

59. *Gettysburg Times,* June 1, 1918.

60. Brandt, *No Magic Bullet,* 72.

61. *Gettysburg Times,* May 31, June 11, 26, 1918.

62. Eisenhower, *At Ease,* 142–43, 144.

63. Ibid., 144–45.

64. Transcript of hearing in the charge of selling liquor to soldiers, *US v. George Washington,* May 18, 1918, copy in World War I File, Adams County Historical Society, Gettysburg, Pa.

65. Gettysburg newspaper accounts always indicated whether a perpetrator was "colored," and only a few individuals identified in the news articles between 1917 and 1918 fit this description. Of the seven men hauled to U.S. District Court on similar charges on June 3, 1918, five were white and two were black (including Washington).

66. *Gettysburg Times,* June 3, 1918.

67. Report of Maj. Robert Reed on the conditions at Camp Colt, July 13, 1918, Letters to the Surgeon General's Office, 1917–23, box 12, Camp Colt, RG 112. Quoted in Gary E. Adelman and Timothy H. Smith, *Devil's Den: A History and Guide* (Gettysburg: Thomas, 1997), 80–81.

68. "War Diary of George LeRoy Aldenifer," typescript copy, Pennsylvania State Archives, RG 19.

69. *Gettysburg Times,* May 29, 1918. Leavitt returned to professional wrestling after the war and eventually adopted the nickname "Mountain Man Dean." "Mountain Man Dean," in *Online World of Wrestling,* Apr. 28, 2014, http://www.onlineworldofwrestling.com/bios/m/man-mountain-dean/.

70. *Gettysburg Times,* May 31, 1918. Americus's real name was August J. Schoenlein; he was a Baltimore native and former world welterweight champion. See Anne M., "The Most Forgotten World Champion," in *Ghosts of Baltimore,* Oct. 15, 2013, http://ghostsofbaltimore.org/2013/10/15/forgotten-world-champion/.

71. *Gettysburg Times,* June 6, 1918.

72. Wilson, *"Treat 'Em Rough,"* 62–63.

73. *Gettysburg Times,* Aug. 27, 1954; "International Con*cat*enated Order of the Hoo-Hoo," International Order of Hoo-Hoo Web site, http://www.hoo-hoo.org, accessed June 26, 2015 (emphasis added).

74. John B. Kimberly to his wife, June 16, 1918, Kimberly Collection.

75. The entire editorial was printed in the *Gettysburg Times* on August 22, 1918.

76. "Roads, Walks, Driveways, Sidewalks, etc.," General Correspondence, Camp Colt, RG 393.

77. W. C. Storrick to J. P. Nicholson, Aug. 28, 1918, GNPC Daily Journal Book for 1918, GNMP Archives.

78. David M. Kennedy, *Over Here: The First World War and American Society,* 2d ed. (New York: Oxford Univ. Press, 2004), 57.

79. Charles H. Gladfelter, *A Salutary Influence: Gettysburg College, 1832–1985,* 2 vols. (Gettysburg: Gettysburg College, 1987), 2:783.

80. *Minutes of the First Convention of the United Lutheran Church of America . . . Nov. 10–12, 1918* (Philadelphia: Board of Publication of the United Lutheran Church in America, 1918), 95–96.

81. A front-page advertisement in the October 1 edition of the *Gettysburg Times* announced, "STUDENTS Army Training Corps.—Wanted: A number of capable women as helpers in the kitchen and mess halls. Good wages. Apply to Prof. C. H. Huber."

82. Eisenhower, *At Ease,* 148.

83. Timothy C. Dowling, "Abbeville Conference (1–2 May, 1918)," in Tucker, *European Powers in the First World War,* 1.

84. Eisenhower, *At Ease,* 148.

85. Chester H. Beymer memoir, circa 1998, Camp Colt file, GNMP Library.

86. Kenneth J. Hagan, *This People's Navy: The Making of American Sea Power* (New York: Free Press, 1991), 256–57.

6. INTO THE ARGONNE

1. Robert H. Ferrell, *Woodrow Wilson and World War I, 1917–1921* (New York: Harper & Row, 1985), 78–81.

2. Byron Farwell, *Over There: The United States in the Great War, 1917–1918* (New York: Norton, 1999), 218–20.

3. Edward M. Coffman, *The War to End All Wars: The American Military Experience in World War I,* 3d ed. (Lexington: Univ. Press of Kentucky, 1998), 306.

4. Paul L. Foulk and Percy S. Eichelberger, eds., *Adams County in the World War: April 6, 1917 to November 11, 1918* (Harrisburg, Pa.: Evangelical Press, 1920), 57.

5. Ibid., 204. President Grover Cleveland was the only chief executive to serve two nonconsecutive terms, 1885–89 and 1893–97.

6. Grover C. Maus, "Thirty-Two Days in the Argonne Forest," in Foulk and Eichelberger, *Adams County in the World War,* 281.

7. *Gettysburg Times,* Oct, 7, 1918.

8. *American Armies and Battlefields in Europe,* 358–59; Foulk and Eichelberger, *Adams County in the World War,* 75.

9. Jennifer Keene, *The United States and the First World War* (Harlow, UK: Pearson, 2000), 62–63; Robert Zeiger, *America's Great War: World War I in the American Experience* (New York: Rowan & Littlefield, 2001), 104–6.

10. Foulk and Eichelberger, *Adams County in the World War,* 171.

11. John S. D. Eisenhower, *Yanks: The Epic Story of the American Army in World War I* (New York: Free Press, 2001), 212–15.

12. Paul B. Mitchell III, "What Were the Causes of the Delay of the 79th Division Capturing Montfaucon during the Meuse-Argonne Offensive in World War I?" (MA thesis, U.S. Army Command and General Staff College, 2011), 74–76.

13. Eisenhower, *Yanks,* 222–23.

14. Foulk and Eichelberger, *Adams County in the World War,* 79–80.

15. Eisenhower, *Yanks,* 223.

16. Ibid., 230–31.

17. Maus, "Thirty-Two Days in the Argonne Forest," 284.

18. Eisenhower, *Yanks,* 228–236.

19. David D. Lee, *Sergeant York: An American Hero* (Lexington: Univ. Press of Kentucky, 1985), 39.

20. Clifford P. Hall and John P. Lehn, eds., *York County and the World War* (York, Pa.: N.p., 1920), 44–45.

21. Eisenhower, *Yanks,* 232–36.

22. Foulk and Eichelberger, *Adams County in the World War,* 45.

23. *Gettysburg Times,* Dec. 20, 1918.

24. Eisenhower, *Yanks,* 250–54

25. "Medal of Honor Recipients: World War I," U.S. Army Center for Military History Web site, last updated July 23, 2013, http://www.history.army.mil/html/moh/worldwari.html.

26. Ernest L. Wrentmore, *In Spite of Hell: A Factual Story of Incidents That Occurred during World War I, as Experienced by the Youngest Soldier to Have Seen Combat Duty with the American Expeditionary Forces as a Member of the Famous Company I, 60th Infantry, Fifth (Red Diamond) Division* (New York: Greenwich, 1958), 151.

27. *Gettysburg Times,* Sept. 7, 1922.

28. *Fifteenth Annual Report of the Association of Graduates of the United States Military Academy at West Point, New York, June 10th, 1919* (Saginaw, Mich.: Seemann & Peters, 1919), 118.

29. John J. Pershing, *Final Report of General John J. Pershing, Commander in Chief of the American Expeditionary Forces* (Washington, D.C.: GPO, 1919).

30. Edward G. Lengel, *To Conquer Hell: The Meuse-Argonne, 1918, The Epic Battle That Ended the First World War* (New York: Holt, 2008), 348.

31. Wrentmore, *In Spite of Hell,* 166, 168.

32. Ibid., 185–87.

33. American Battle Monuments Commission, *American Armies and Battlefields in Europe: A History, Guide, and Reference Book* (Washington, D.C.: GPO, 1938), 213.

34. These numbers were compiled by analyzing the short memorials to Adams County's fallen servicemen in Foulk and Eichelberger, *Adams County in the World War,* 39–75. Only those men who served in France between October 1 and 31 and died from combat or flu were included in the totals. In all, twenty-three men from the county died while serving with the AEF during the Meuse-Argonne offensive between September 26 and November 11.

35. Richard Hofstadter, preface to Woodrow Wilson, "Speech on the Fourteen Points," *Great Issues in American History,* vol. 3 of of 3, *From Reconstruction to the Present Day, 1864–1981,* ed. Richard and Beatrice Hofstadter (New York: Vintage, 1982), 215.

36. Henry Kolda to his wife, Nov. 2, Dec. 19, 1918, Henry Kolda Papers, Eric L. Dorr Collection, Gettysburg Museum of History.

37. Foulk and Eichelberger, *Adams County in the World War,* 71; *Gettysburg Times,* Jan. 18, 1919.

38. Foulk and Eichelberger, *Adams County in the World War,* 45, 57.

39. *Gettysburg Times,* Dec. 12, 1918.

7. "THE WHOLE CAMP HAD TO BE CONSIDERED AS EXPOSED"

1. Jeffery K. Taubenberger and David M. Morens, "1918 Influenza: The Mother of All Pandemics" *Emerging Infectious Diseases* 12 (Jan. 2006): 15–22.

2. Dwight D. Eisenhower, *At Ease: Stories I Tell to Friends* (Garden City, N.Y.: Doubleday, 1967), 148–49; Antoni Trilla, Guillem Trilla, and Carolyn Daer, "The 1918 'Spanish Flu' in Spain," *Clinical Infectious Diseases* 47, no. 5 (2008): 668–73; John M. Barry, "The Site of Origin of the 1918 Influenza Pandemic and its Public Health Implications," in *Journal of Translational Medicine* 2, no. 3 (2004): https://www.ncbi.nlm.nih.gov/pmc/articles/PMC340389/; Carol R. Byerly, *Fever of War: The Influenza Epidemic in the U.S. Army during World War I* (New York: New York Univ. Press, 2005), 6.

3. U.S. Public Health Service, "The Great Pandemic: The United States in 1918–1919," originally published on the U.S. Department of Health and Human Services Web site, as of December 13, 2017, available at the University of North Texas Libraries Web site, https://cybercemetery.unt.edu/archive/allcollections/20090305010427/http://vietnamese.pandemicflu.gov/pandemicflu/envi/24/_1918_pandemicflu_gov/index.htm. For a thorough account of how the first two waves struck domestic Army camps, see Byerly, *Fever of War,* 72–82.

4. John M. Barry, *The Great Influenza: The Epic Story of the Deadliest Plague in History* (London: Penguin, 2005), 2–4.

5. Byerly, *Fever of War,* 8.

6. Report of Col. W. P. Chamberlain, Medical Corps, Aug. 23, 1918, RG 112: Records of the Office of the Surgeon General (Army), 1775–1994, Correspondence, 3/1/1917–9/30/1927, file 721.1, box 12 (Camp Colt), NARA (hereafter cited as Camp Colt, RG 112).

7. Files of 301st Depot Company, General Correspondence, Records of United States Army Continental Commands, 1821–1920 (Camp Colt), RG 393, NARA (hereafter cited as Camp Colt, RG 393).

8. Byerly, *Fever of War,* 74.

9. September Strength Return for Camp Colt, WWI Strength Returns, Record Group 407 (Adjutant General's Office), Records of the Adjutant General's Office, box 1066 (HQ File), RG 407, National Archives and Record Administration (NARA) II, College Park, Md. (herafter cited as RG 407).

10. *Gettysburg Times,* Oct. 1, 16, 1918.

11. Eisenhower, *At Ease,* 149.

12. G. M. Gilliland to his wife, Oct. 2, 1918, J. Karl Anderson Collection, National Soldier Factory, Gettysburg.

13. This story included eight deaths that had not been reported in the October 2 edition. Actually, twenty-five men had died in a twenty-four-hour period.

14. This number was compiled from the obituaries in the *Compiler* and the *Times* for the month of October and early November. I built a database to capture the vital statistics of those who died. All other such tabulations in this chapter come from this database.

15. Paul L. Foulk and Percy S. Eichelberger, eds., *Adams County in the World War: April 6, 1917 to November 11, 1918* (Harrisburg, Pa.: Evangelical Press, 1920), 69.

16. *Gettysburg Compiler,* Oct. 19, 1918. The little village was named after a Union division commander in the XI Corps, Francis Barlow of New York. Although his division never got near the hamlet during the battle, the people of the area gave their little settlement his name.

17. *Gettysburg Times,* Oct. 17, 18, 1918
18. *Gettysburg Times,* Oct. 28, 1918.
19. *Gettysburg Compiler,* Nov. 2, 1918.
20. *Gettysburg Times,* Oct. 22, 1918.
21. *Gettysburg Times,* Dec. 11, 1918.
22. *Gettysburg Times,* Oct. 1, 1918.
23. *Gettysburg Times,* Nov. 2, 1918.
24. *Gettysburg Times,* Sept. 25, 1918.
25. *Gettysburg Times,* Oct. 31, 1918.
26. Compiled from Foulk and Eichelberger, *Adams County in the World War.*
27. Walter L. Hand to "The President of Gettysburg College," Oct. 20, 1976, copy in the Camp Colt File, Adams County Historical Society.
28. Eisenhower, *At Ease,* 150.
29. Byerly, *Fever of War,* 84.
30. Ibid., 80.
31. Ibid.
32. This was determined by a canvas of Foulk and Eichelberger, *Adams County in the World War.* Scott's memorial is on page 69.
33. "Sanitary Inspection of Camp Colt, Gettysburg, PA, made on October 6th, 1918, by Col. S. J. Morris, M.C.," file 721.1, box 12, Camp Colt, RG 112.
34. "Sanitary Inspection of Camp Colt, Gettysburg, PA."
35. See for example, Special Orders Nos. 41, 42, 48, dated Sept. 30, Oct. 1, Oct. 4, 1918, HQ Camp Colt, RG 393.
36. *Gettysburg Compiler,* Nov. 2, 1918.
37. *Gettysburg Times,* Oct. 11, 1918.
38. *Gettysburg Times,* Oct. 24, 2016.
39. October Strength Return for Camp Colt, Records of the Adjutant General's Office, WW I Strength Returns, box 1066 (HQ File), RG 407.
40. Eisenhower, *At Ease,* 149; *Gettysburg Times,* Jan. 14, 1919.
41. This percentage was derived by dividing the number of county residents (the 1920 census placed the Adams County population at approximately 35,600; the lower number of 33,000 was used to account for the hundreds of men serving in the armed forces in 1918) into the civilian flu fatalities (113).
42. Barry, *Great Influenza,* 397.
43. Carol R. Byerly, "The U.S. Military and the Influenza Pandemic of 1918–1919," Public Health Reports 125, suppl. 3 (2010): 82–91, available online Pthe National Center for Biotechnology Information Web site, http://www.ncbi.nlm.nih.gov/pmc/articles/PMC2862337/. Byerly believes this percentage is very conservative.
44. David Weaver, "Camp Colt and Spanish Influenza—1918" (MA thesis, Shippensburg Univ., 2000), 72.
45. Using the monthly Camp Colt personnel returns for September and October, the average personnel strength was 4800 on the last day of the month (5552 on September 30 and 4047 on October 31). The total number of deaths to influenza for those two months was 149. Since most of the men departed before the end of November, the monthly return for that month could not be used, nor could the nine men who died in November be factored into the equation. Nonetheless, the samples for September and October are a good foundation for the mortality rate for Camp Colt during the crisis.
46. Byerly, "U.S. Military and the Influenza Pandemic of 1918–1919."

47. "1918 Influenza Digital Archive (Camp Crane)," Univ. of Michigan Center for the History of Medicine Web site, 2012, http://chm.med.umich.edu/research/1918-influenza-escape-communities/camp-crane.

48. Various special orders, Camp Colt, RG 393.

49. Special Orders 191, Camp Colt, RG 393. The orders stipulated that the clothing items were "necessary of the proper burial of the . . . soldier, in that all clothing belonging to this man having been destroyed, in compliance with regulations regarding infectious diseases."

50. Whittingham to Schelby [*sic*], Oct. 16, 1918, Camp Colt, RG 393.

51. Whittingham to Schelby, Oct. 16, 1918.

52. Schléby to Whittingham, Oct. 18, 1918, Camp Colt, RG 393, translation assistance provided by Frederic Castier, St. Quentin, France.

53. Whittingham to Sarah Drew, Oct. 31, 1918, Camp Colt, RG 393. A copy of business card provided by Drew is part of this correspondence: "Harley-Davidson Sales Co., Distributors for Harley-Davidson Motorcycles and, Bicycles and Merkel Motor Wheel, 533–535 West 110th St. Near Broadway."

54. Whittingham to Schléby, Oct. 22, 1918, Camp Colt, RG 393.

55. In 1919, Mrs. Montguire inquired about bringing her son home to Scotland for permanent burial, but his remains still lie in Gettysburg National Cemetery, section 8, row 1, plot 4. His headstone is not the standard government-issued marker but was privately purchased, perhaps by his mother.

56. Development Battalion file, Camp Colt, RG 393.

57. *Treat 'Em Rough,* Oct. 1918, 5, copy in possession of Eric Dorr, Gettysburg Museum of History.

8. THE END OF THE WAR AND BEYOND

1. *Gettysburg Times,* Dec. 2, 1918.

2. History Committee Seventy-Ninth Division Association, *History of the Seventy-Ninth Division, A.E.F. during the World War: 1917–1919,* 2d ed. (Lancaster, Pa: Steinman & Steinman, 1922), 315, 320, 322.

3. Paul L. Foulk and Percy S. Eichelberger, eds., *Adams County in the World War: April 6, 1917 to November 11, 1918* (Harrisburg, Pa.: Evangelical Press, 1920), 45.

4. *Gettysburg Times,* Oct. 29, 1918.

5. Carlo D'Este, *Eisenhower: A Soldier's Life* (New York: Holt, 2002), 135–36.

6. Quoted in Susan Eisenhower, *Mrs. Ike: Memories and Reflections on the Life of Mamie Eisenhower* (New York: Farrar, Straus & Giroux, 1996), 56.

7. D'Este, *Eisenhower,* 143, 727n34.

8. *Gettysburg Times,* Nov. 7, 1918.

9. *New Oxford Item,* Nov. 11, 1918.

10. Emmor B. Cope to John Nicholson, Nov. 24, 1918, General Correspondence, 1916–18, Gettysburg National Park Commission.

11. David W. Blight, *Beyond the Battlefield: Race, Memory and the American Civil War* (Amherst: Univ. of Massachusetts Press, 2002), 103.

12. *Gettysburg Times,* Nov. 13, 1918.

13. Foulk and Eichelberger, *Adams County in the World War,* 16–17.

14. "Special Orders No. 237, per letters A.G.O. 370.5," from the War Department authorization of the transfer, General Correspondence, Records of United States Army Continental Commands, 1821–1920 (Camp Colt), RG 393, NARA, (hereafter cited as Camp Colt, RG 393).

15. Dwight D. Eisenhower, *At Ease: Stories I Tell to Friends* (Garden City, N.Y.: Doublewqday, 1967), 153.

16. *Gettysburg Times,* Nov. 18, 1918; Eisenhower, *At Ease,* 152–53.

17. *Gettysburg Compiler,* Jan. 4, 1919.

18. *Gettysburg Times,* Nov. 22, 1918; Special Orders No. 5, HQ, Camp Colt, Nov. 21, 1918, Camp Colt, RG 393; "History of Fort McHenry," National Park Service Web site, last updated Feb. 26, 2015, https://www.nps.gov/fomc/learn/historyculture/history-of-fort-mchenry.htm

19. Special Orders No. 11, HQ, Camp Colt, Nov. 29, 1918, Camp Colt, RG 393.

20. *Gettysburg Times,* Nov. 23, 1918.

21. Jennifer D. Keene, *World War I: The American Soldier Experience* (Lincoln: Univ. of Nebraska Press, 2011), 182.

22. Edward F. Coffman, *The War to End All Wars: The American Military Experience in World War I* (Lexington: Univ. Press of Kentucky, 1968), 359–61.

23. Ibid.

24. Foulk and Eichelberger, *Adams County in the World War,* 168; *Harrisburg Telegraph,* May 15, 1919.

25. *Gettysburg Times,* Dec. 16, 1918.

26. Compilation by Wilbur C. Wolf, Gettysburg College Class of 1925, World War I File, Adams County Historical Society, Gettysburg.

27. *Gettysburg Compiler,* May 24, 1919.

28. G. Kurt Piehler, *Remembering War the American Way* (Washington, D.C.: Smithsonian Institution Press, 1995), 108.

29. Charles H. Gladfelter, *A Salutary Influence: Gettysburg College, 1832–1985,* 2 vols. (Gettysburg: Gettysburg College, 1987), 2:657.

30. Frederick Muhlenberg, World War I service questionnaire, File 1.1, WW I Questionnaires (MS-048), Special Collections and Archives, Musselman Library, Gettysburg College.

31. John S. Fair, WW I service questionnaire, file 1.2.

32. Survey of WW I Questionnaires, of the classes of 1890–1923, files 1.1 and 1.2.

33. Gladfelter, *Salutary Influence,* 2:555; *Gettysburg Compiler,* Dec. 14, 1918, Feb. 8, 1919.

34. Allan Millet and Peter Maslowski, *For the Common Defense: A Military History of the United States of America,* rev. and expanded ed. (New York: Free Press, 1994), 386.

35. Abdel Ross Wentz, *History of the Gettysburg Theological Seminary* (Philadelphia: United Lutheran Publication House, 1926), 275.

36. Ibid. This book's extensive alumni directory details the World War I service of its alumni.

37. *Lutheran Theological Seminary Bulletin* 1, no. 4 (1921); Foulk and Eichelberger, *Adams County in the World War,* 39–40.

38. *Gettysburg Times,* Dec. 9, 1918.

39. *Gettysburg Compiler,* Dec. 12, 1918.

40. *Gettysburg Compiler,* Jan. 18, 1919.

41. Report of Board, Feb. 6, 1919, General Correspondence, Camp Colt, RG 393.

42. *Gettysburg Times,* Feb. 1, 1919.

43. John Nicholson to Andrew Brodbeck, Jan. 24, 1919, GNPC daily journal for 1919, GNMP Archives.

44. *Gettysburg Times,* Mar. 22, 1919.

45. *Gettysburg Times,* Mar. 26, 1919.

46. *Gettysburg Compiler,* Mar. 29, 1919.

47. *Gettysburg Times,* Mar. 26, 1919.

48. *Gettysburg Compiler,* June 28, 1919.

49. *Gettysburg Times,* Mar. 15, 1921.

50. Quartermaster Construction Camp Colt, General Correspondence, Camp Colt, RG 393.

51. E. M. Ewitt, Report of the Condition of the Camp Site of the Army Camp on the Gettysburg National Military Park, January 20, 1919, GNPC daily journal for 1919.

52. Commanding Officer, Camp Colt to Commanding General, Eastern Department, Governor's Island, N.Y., Closing of Camp, June 4, 1919, General Correspondence, Camp Colt, RG 393.

53. The delay was caused when Lewis Brothers complained to the army that some of the material already had been salvaged after they purchased the rights to the camp, but Desmond accounted for the missing material. To prevent any future accusations, the company was required to inventory the remaining buildings, fixtures, and material before it could begin demolition and salvage. See Chief of Construction Division to Constructing Quartermaster, Camp Colt, May 24, 1919, "Abandonments of Reservations," General Correspondence, Camp Colt, RG 393.

54. *Gettysburg Compiler,* May 31, 1919 (emphasis added).

55. David Blight, *Race and Reunion: The Civil War in American Memory* (Cambridge, Mass.: Belknap Press of Harvard Univ. Press, 2001), 258.

56. *Gettysburg Compiler,* June 7, 1919.

57. For an excellent assessment of Wilson's role at the Paris Peace Conference and the fight over the treaty in the Senate, see Robert H. Ferrell, *Woodrow Wilson and World War I, 1917–1921* (New York: Harper & Row, 1985), 135–77.

58. "George Washington II," *Naval History and Heritage Command,* last updated Oct. 10, 2016, http://www.history.navy.mil/research/histories/ship-histories/danfs/g/george-washington-ii.html

59. Foulk and Eichelberger, *Adams County and the World War,* 179; *Harrisburg Telegraph,* Aug. 9, 1919.

60. *Gettysburg Compiler,* June 28, 1919.

61. Piehler, *Remembering War the American Way,* 111.

62. *Gettysburg Compiler,* Nov. 15, 1919

63. *New Oxford Item,* Sept. 18, 1919; *Gettysburg Compiler,* Jan. 3, 1920. The Arendtsville post, named in memory of Ira Lady, later relocated to Biglerville.

64. Robert P. Murphy, "The Depression You've Never Heard Of: 1920–1921," Foundation for Economic Education Web site, Nov. 18, 2009, https://fee.org/articles/the-depression-youve-never-heard-of-1920-1921; Ferrell, *Woodrow Wilson & World War I,* 193–94.

65. *Gettysburg Compiler,* Apr. 25, 1919.

66. William E. Leuchtenberg, *The Perils of Prosperity, 1914–1932* (Chicago: Univ. of Chicago Press, 1958), 214.

67. *Gettysburg Times,* Jan. 16, 1919.

68. *Gettysburg Times,* July 24, 1919.

69. Annual Report of the Gettysburg National Military Park Commission to the Secretary of War for 1919, GNMP Archives.

70. Annual Report of the Gettysburg National Military Park Commission to the Secretary of War for 1920, GNMP Archives.

71. Chunks of concrete from the swimming pool still remain in a weed-covered pile about twenty-five yards west of the 1st Minnesota Infantry's monument, which marks its July 3, 1863, position. Groundhogs boring their dens have inadvertently excavated camp debris that was used to fill in the hole that remained after the pool's demolition. Rusty nails and hardware as well as shards of cups, plates, and bottles are scattered around the woodchucks' holes.

72. Emmor B. Cope, Notes to the 1920 Annual Report, Gettysburg, Pa., May 12, 1920, Records of the Gettysburg National Park Commission, GNMP Archives.

73. Robert E. Parker to Col. Nicholson, Apr. 10, 1920, GNPC daily journal for 1920, GNMP Archives.

74. Keefer, *Conflicting Memories on the River of Death,* 274.

75. Leuchtenberg, *Perils of Prosperity,* 88–89.

76. *Gettysburg Compiler,* Nov. 6, 1920.

77. Piehler, *Remembering War the American Way,* 118–21.

78. Lowell Thomas, *Woodfill of the Regulars: A True Story of Adventure from the Arctic to the Argonne* (Garden City, N.Y.: Doubleday, Doran & Co., 1929), 316–17.

79. Annual Report of the Gettysburg National Military Park Commission to the Secretary of War for 1921, GNMP Archives.

80. During this timeframe, the Quartermaster Department assumed responsibility of the park from the Gettysburg National Park Commission. Either the reports for those years were lost or the Quartermaster Department did not request that they be submitted.

81. *Gettysburg Times,* June 19, 20, 1922; *Compiler,* July 1, 1922; Richard D. Fulton and James L. Rada, *The Last to Fall: The 1922 March, Battles, and Deaths of U.S. Marines at Gettysburg* (Gettysburg: Legacy Publishing, 2015), 11, 63, 66, 71. (The entire booklet details the marines' march and maneuvers—in great detail but with little historical analysis—from their departure on June 19, 1922, until their return to Quantico a month later.)

82. *Gettysburg Times,* June 26, 1922.

83. *Gettysburg Times,* June 23, 1922. When Captain Hamilton's airplane crashed on June 26, it narrowly missed the carnival.

84. *Gettysburg Times,* July 5, 1922.

85. Ibid.

86. *Gettysburg Times,* July 6, 1922.

87. *Gettysburg Times,* Mar. 9, 1922.

88. Harlan Unrau, *Administrative History of Gettysburg National Military Park* (Gettysburg: National Park Service, 1991), 121–27.

89. "World War I Burials and Memorializations," American Battle Monuments Commission Web site, accessed May 16, 2016, https://www.abmc.gov/node/1273.

90. Piehler, *Remembering War the American Way,* 102. For an exhaustive and authoritative study of the establishment of the American Battle Monuments Commission, its World War I overseas cemeteries, and the Gold Star pilgrimages, see Lisa M. Budreau, *World War I and the Politics of Commemoration in America, 1919–1933* (New York: New York Univ. Press, 2010).

91. *Gettysburg Times,* July 24, 1930.

92. *Gettysburg Times,* Feb. 3, 1931. Although the newspaper stated that she would be going to France, a search of the American Battle Monuments Commission burial database indicates that he is remembered at Brookwood.

93. *Gettysburg Times,* Sept. 2, 1932.

94. Jennifer D. Keene, *Doughboys, the Great War, and the Remaking of America* (Baltimore: Johns Hopkins Univ. Press, 2001), 6–7, 177–78.

95. *Gettysburg Times,* June 8, 1932.

96. *Gettysburg Times,* June 9, 1932.

97. Keene, *Doughboys, the Great War, and the Remaking of America,* 190–95.

98. Quoted in D'Este, *Eisenhower,* 222–24.

99. *Gettysburg Times,* July 31, 1932.

100. *Gettysburg Times,* Aug. 4–5, 1932.

101. *Gettysburg Times,* Aug. 4, 1932.

102. *Gettysburg Times,* Aug. 10, 1932.

103. *Gettysburg Times,* Aug. 16, 1932.

104. *Gettysburg Times,* Aug. 17, 1932.

105. *Gettysburg Times,* Aug. 23, 1932.

106. *Gettysburg Times,* Aug. 29–30, 1932.

107. *Gettysburg Times,* Sept. 17, 24, 1932.

108. Keene, *World War I,* 189.

109. *Gettysburg Times,* Nov. 8, 1932.

110. Unrau, *Administrative History,* 121–27.

111. *Gettysburg Times,* Feb. 2, 1942.

112. Commonwealth of Pennsylvania, *Report of the Pennsylvania Commission of the Seventy-Fifth Anniversary of the Battle of Gettysburg,* 4 vols. (Gettysburg: Times & News Publishing Co., 1939), 4:341.

113. Ibid., 324, 341–42

114. Ibid., 325. On page 444 there is an excerpt from the *Milwaukee Journal* that claimed that the youngest veteran was eighty-six, the oldest ninety-nine, and the average age ninety-one.

115. *Gettysburg Times,* Dec. 26, 1941.

116. Beverly Driver Eddy, *Camp Sharpe's "Psycho Boys": From Gettysburg to Germany* (Bennington, Vt.: Merriam Press, 2014), 5–6.

117. Ibid., 32–38.

118. *Gettysburg Times,* June 12, 1944

119. *Star and Sentinel,* Aug. 13, 1938.

120. *Gettysburg Times,* June 28, 1944.

121. Elizabeth Atkins, "'The Prisoners Are Not Hard to Handle': Cultural Views of German Prisoners of War and Their Captors in Camp Sharpe, Gettysburg, Pennsylvania" (MA thesis, Bowling Green State Univ., 2008), 54, 61–62, 27–28.

122. Ibid., 49.

123. *Gettysburg Times,* July 5, 11, 1944.

124. Atkins, "'Prisoners Are Not Hard to Handle,'" 54–55.

125. Jim Weeks, *Gettysburg: Memory, Market, and an American Shrine* (Princeton, N.J.: Princeton Univ. Press, 2003), 130, 162–63.

EPILOGUE

1. *Gettysburg Times,* Aug. 30, 1954.

2. Dwight D. Eisenhower, *At Ease: Stories I Tell to Friends* (Garden City, N.Y.: Doubleday, 1967), 358–60, Susan Eisenhower, *Mrs. Ike: Memories and Reflections on the Life of Mamie Eisenhower* (New York: Farrar, Straus & Giroux, 1996), 256–57, 287; David Eisenhower, with Julie Nixon Eisenhower *Going Home to Glory: A Memoir of Life with Dwight D. Eisenhower, 1961–1969* (New York: Simon & Schuster, 2010), 19–21.

3. *Gettysburg Times,* Aug. 30, 1954.

4. Ibid.; Charles Wardlaw, *The Transportation Corps: Movements, Training, and Supply* (Washington, D.C.: U.S. Army Center for Military History, 2003), 477.

5. *Gettysburg Times,* Aug. 30, 1954; Dale E. Wilson, *Treat 'Em Rough: Thee Birth of American Armor, 1917–1920* (Novato, Calif.: Presidio, 1990), 227.

6. For the genealogy of the Semmes family, see Harry W. Newman, *The Maryland Semmes and Kindred Families: A Genealogical History* (Westminster, Md.: Heritage, 2007).

7. *Gettysburg Times,* Aug. 30, 1954.

8. *Gettysburg Times,* Aug. 27, 1954.

9. *Gettysburg Times,* Aug. 30, 1954.

10. Eisenhower, *At Ease,* 185–87, 204; Steven Trout, *On the Battlefield of Memory: The First World War and American Remembrance, 1919–1941* (Tuscaloosa: Univ. of Alabama Press, 2010), xvi–xvii.

11. Carlo D'Este, *Eisenhower: A Soldier's Life* (New York: Holt, 2002), 194–95.

12. John S. D. Eisenhower, *Yanks: The Epic Story of the American Army in World War I* (New York: Free Press, 2001), xiv.

13. D'Este, *Eisenhower,* 196.

14. Eisenhower, *Going Home to Glory,* 46.

15. *Gettysburg Times,* Nov. 11, 1920.

16. G. Curt Piehler, *Remembering War the American Way* (Washington, D.C.: Smithsonian Institution Press, 1995), 105, 108.

17. Trout, *On the Battlefield of Memory,* 120.

18. Eichelberger's April 18, 1968, *Gettysburg Times* obituary revealed that Foulk was his cousin.

19. *Adams County in the World War,* 199; "Edenton I (No. 3696)," U.S. Naval History and Heritage Command Web site, July 7, 2015, http://www.history.navy.mil/research/histories/ship-histories/danfs/e/edenton-i.html.

20. Paul L. Foulk to the Adams County Historical Society, Nov. 10, 1941, World War I file, ACHS. This letter was read as an address to the historical society, in the same courtroom where Eichelberger had addressed the crowd attending the tablet dedication twenty-three years earlier.

21. Foulk to ACHS.

22. Paul L. Foulk and Percy S. Eichelberger, eds., *Adams County in the World War: April 6, 1917 to November 11, 1918* (Harrisburg, Pa.: Evangelical Press, 1920), 37, 38. On the American Legion's role during the Red Scare, see Piehler, *Remembering War,* 113.

23. Foulk to the ACHS.

24. "Lieutenant General Keller E. Rockey, USMC," originally published on the Naval History and Heritage Command Web site, now available online at http://archive.is/6gosh.

25. Ernest Wrentmore, *In Spite of Hell, A Factual Story of Incidents That Occurred during World War I, as Experienced by the Youngest Soldier to Have Seen Combat Duty with the American Expeditionary Forces as a Member of the Famous Company I, 60th Infantry, Fifth (Red Diamond) Division* (New York: Greenwich, 1958).

26. Ernest Wrentmore III, "Finding Father: A Reader Meets His Father on the Pages of American Heritage . . . For the First Time," *American Heritage* 6 (Spring 2011).

27. "Lexington Man's Search for Father Leads Him to Arlington National Cemetery," *Lexington Herald Leader,* June 19, 2011, http://www.kentucky.com/news/local/counties/fayette-county/article44104353.html.

28. Ernest Wrentmore III, telephone conversation, Apr. 15, 2015.

29. Mary Lou Schwartz, "Lavinia Dock: Adams County Suffragette," *Adams County History* 3 (1997): 78.

30. Michael J. Kusman, ed., *Register of Graduates and Former Cadets of the United States Military Academy, 1902–1976* (West Point: Association of Graduates, 1976), 329.

31. Lorett Treese, *Valley Forge: Making and Remaking a National Symbol* (University Park: Pennsylvania State University Press, 1995), 160–61.

32. See David Halberstam, *The Coldest Winter: America and the Korean War* (New York: Hyperion, 2007).

33. Jaclyn Campbell, "Guide to the Papers of the Major General Charles A. Willoughby," Special Collections and College Archives, Musselman Library, Gettysburg College.

34. Foulk and Eichelberger, *Adams County in the World War,* 182.

35. *Gettysburg Times,* July 16, 1958.

36. Edward G. Lengel, *To Conquer Hell: The Meuse-Argonne, 1918, The Epic Battle That Ended the First World War* (New York: Holt, 2008), 432.

37. "Remembering Sam Woodfill: Letters Help Bob Woodfill Tell More of His Relative's Story," *Madison (Ind.) Courier,* Aug. 20, 2014, http://madisoncourier.com/Content/Lifestyles/Your-Story/Article/Remembering-Maj-Sam-Woodfill/182/884/85273.

38. *Gettysburg Compiler,* Dec. 3, 1921.

39. Kolda to his wife, Dec. 19, 1918, Henry Kolda Papers, Eric L. Dorr Collection Gettysburg Museum of History.

40. Foulk and Eichelberger, *Adams County in the World War,* 254, 199.

Index

Page number in italics refer to illustrations.